MARSDEN, Arthur. British diplomacy and Tunis, 1875-1902. Africana Pub., 1972. 276p map bibl 71-180671. 12.50. ISBN 0-8419-0110-4

CHOICE   SEP. '72

History, Geography & Travel

An interesting account of the era of feverish diplomatic activity centered on the Congress of Berlin and leading to the French invasion of Tunisia in 1881. The key roles played by the British consuls in Tunis, Richard Wood and Thomas Teade, and their French counterpart, Theodore Roustan, are well done. Extensive use is made of the official government documents and the memoirs and letters of the main diplomats. The book treats the Italian dilemma over Tunisia when they tried to prevent French domination but were unable to secure the necessary help of Great Britain. In addition, the difficult and impotent position of Turkey, the nominal power in North Africa, is well treated. A must for graduate studies on North Africa, but it is less essential for a general undergraduate library.

BRITISH DIPLOMACY AND TUNIS
1875-1902

Arthur Marsden was born in South Wales in 1918. After graduating with first class honours from the University College of Wales, Aberystwyth, he spent six years on military service, ending in 1946 when he was a captain on the staff of G.H.Q., India. From then until 1963 he was a staff tutor at the University of Hull teaching international relations and social history, and was elected to the David Davies memorial fellowship, held at the University of London, from which he received a Ph.D. Thereafter he has been a member of the staff of the University of Dundee (until 1967 Queen's College, University of St. Andrews), where he is a senior lecturer. A fellow of the Royal Historical Society, he has lectured over a period of years on the continent, in Germany, Italy and France, read papers at international congresses on North African studies, and is the author of *Britain and the End of the Tunis Treaties*, as well as of articles in learned publications in Britain and the U.S.A.

Sir Richard Wood

BRITISH DIPLOMACY
AND TUNIS
1875–1902

A case study in
Mediterranean policy

ARTHUR MARSDEN

AFRICANA PUBLISHING CORPORATION · NEW YORK

Published
in the United States of America 1971
by Africana Publishing Corporation
101 Fifth Avenue
New York, N.Y. 10003

© 1971 Arthur Marsden

Library of Congress catalog card no. 71 1806 71
ISBN 0 8419 0110 4

Printed in Great Britain

ACKNOWLEDGEMENTS

THERE are many debts I have to record and it is with pleasure that I acknowledge the particular kindness and helpfulness of my former mentor, Professor W. N. Medlicott, who introduced me to what I found a very absorbing subject. I owe, also, a debt of gratitude to the officers of the Scottish Academic Press, in particular to Principal J. Steven Watson, of St. Andrews University, to Professor C. Blake, of Dundee University, and, not least, to the managing director, Mr. Douglas Grant. Professor J. A. S. Grenville, of Birmingham University, made some valuable suggestions, and others who offered salutary encouragement or helped to overcome particular difficulties were Professor D. F. Macdonald, of Dundee University; Professor Jean Ganiage, of the Sorbonne; Professor A. B. Cunningham, of Simon Fraser University, British Columbia; Dr. F. V. Parsons, of Glasgow University ; Dr. J. F. A. Mason, of Christ Church, Oxford; Mr. C. H. Fone, formerly of the Foreign Office library; Mr. D. P. Dorward, of St. Andrews University, and, sometimes unwittingly, several of my colleagues at Dundee. I am grateful also to my wife for help in drawing up the maps and other sundry tasks.

The helpfulness has been appreciated of the respective staffs of the Public Record Office, the library of the Foreign Office, the Institute of Historical Research (London), the library of the British Museum, the Royal Commonwealth Society library, the library of Christ Church, Oxford, the library of the University of Paris and also the long-suffering staff of the University of Dundee. Much of the basic research, in London, Paris and elsewhere, was made possible by the award, for a year, of the fellowship of the David Davies Memorial Institute of International Studies, while the path towards publication was smoothed by generous assistance from the Carnegie Trust for the Universities of Scotland and from the court of the University of Dundee.

Transcripts of Crown copyright material in the Public Record

Office appear by permission of the Controller of H.M. Stationery Office. Extracts from documents in the French Foreign Office archives are published with the authority of the *Commission des Archives diplomatiques et de la Documentation*. By permission of the Most Hon. the Marquess of Salisbury, it has been possible to quote from the papers of his grandfather as well as from *Biographical Studies*, written by his aunt, Lady Gwendolen Cecil, and printed privately. The use of material from the papers of Sir Richard Wood was authorised by Professor A. B. Cunningham and I am grateful to the editor of the *English Historical Review*, Mr. J. M. Wallace-Hadrill, for permission to incorporate the substance of one article.

CONTENTS

ILLUSTRATIONS

ACKNOWLEDGEMENTS

Plate 1, a painting done by 'L.M.' in 1871 and presented by the
grand-daughters of Sir Richard Wood for hanging in the British
ambassador's residence at Tunis, was photographed by kind permission of H.M. ambassador (A. R. K. Mackenzie, C.B.E.) and
reproduced by permission of Gilbert van Raepenbusch, Esq. The
photograph of Roustan is reproduced by permission of Professor
Jean Ganiage and the *Presses Universitaires de France*; that of Cambon
by permission of Messrs. Berger-Levrault; those of de Courcel
and Delcassé by permission of the publishers of the *Illustrated
London News*; those of Drummond Hay, Haggard and Johnston by

ix

permission of the former British ambassador at Tunis (A. C. E. Malcolm, C.M.G.); that of Hanotaux (from the *Service International de Microfilms*) by permission of the Ministre Plenipotentiaire, Directeur des Archives Diplomatiques, Paris; and that of Crispi by permission of the publishers of the *Memoirs of Francesco Crispi*, Messrs. Hodder and Stoughton, Ltd.

INTRODUCTION

BRITAIN'S CHANGING POSITION

This book traces the part played by a small North African country in the foreign policy of a great power in the last quarter of the nineteenth century. During that time the impact of new rivalries in Africa and Asia helped to transform the international scene. The issues that determined relations between the advanced nations ceased to be narrowly European and became world-wide in scope. What was to be the future, or lack of future, of small, independent states like Morocco, Tunis, Tripoli, Egypt, Persia, Afghanistan or Siam was now a factor of importance. As the only truly world power hitherto, Britain found that her position had inevitably changed and she was now being challenged in areas where once her predominance had been unquestioned. The novel feeling of painful uncertainty engendered was heightened in the 1890's by the fact that the major continental powers were seeing fit to insure themselves with formal alliances. It need hardly be said that much of Britain's fundamental interest overseas, what she had to defend, was commercial in character. Around 1880, the British economy was 'geared to the ability to sell to the outside world the output of one worker in every five'[1] and British trade and investment was concentrated upon three areas, the Americas, Western Europe and India, along with Australia.[2] Of these areas, India was the only one in which political control was thought of as essential to trade and the subcontinent was also the arsenal of British strength, military and commercial, in the whole of the Far East—and much of the Middle East as well. A strict observance of national interest would, therefore, dictate good relations, as far as possible, with the countries of the New World, and with Germany and France in particular in Europe,

[1] R. S. Sayers, *The Vicissitudes of an Export Economy: Britain since 1880*
[2] Saul, *British Overseas Trade*, pp. 11-12; Robinson and Gallagher, *Africa and the Victorians*, pp. 6, 10.

1

while the Mediterranean as such would not be anything like as important for its own sake and tropical Africa almost insignificant.

It is noticeable that this balance of interest was reflected broadly in British policies for as long as Lord Salisbury's influence was dominant. Until the more aggressive and ill-considered policies of Joseph Chamberlain and his supporters towards the end of the century, much of the concern of the government lay in preserving Britain's existing possessions and safeguarding communications with her focus of power in the east. 'Our safe route to India', said Kimberley in 1894, 'is round the Cape and the maintenance of friendship with South Africa is a cardinal point of Imperial policy'.[3] Anxiety over the less safe but more speedy and more important route through the Mediterranean similarly involved Britain in the affairs of Morocco, Tunis, the Eastern Mediterranean, the Nile valley, East Africa and the Red Sea. Fears for the security of India likewise induced Britain to undertake a more systematic development of her influence than hitherto in Afghanistan, Baluchistan and Persia in the west, as well as Burma and Malaya in the east. It is perhaps necessary to stress in this way the importance of south Asia in British policy, if only because that importance is so often muted in the records of the Foreign Office. A separate secretary of state after all dealt with the affairs of India and its frequently none too pliable government in Delhi.[4] It is not inconceivable that the 'division of labour' in academic circles subsequently has tended until recently to perpetuate the mental curtain erected between Downing Street and the affairs of the Indian ocean.

Tunis was, of course, one of several tottering Muslim states bordering on Britain's 'corridor of power' to the east, which, in the hands of a strong rival power, might threaten the essential communications with India. As an introduction, therefore, to a study of the part played by the Tunis question in British policy, it may be considered useful to discuss briefly the prob-

---

[3] SP/-268/I/Sec/to Sanderson/20 Oct 1894.
[4] Grenville, *Lord Salisbury and Foreign Policy*, p. 296. For a good example of how the division of political power failed to work regarding policy towards Persia, see Greaves, *Persia and the Defence of India*, pp. 206-7.

lem posed in the relations of the great powers by some of these small states, enjoying titular sovereignty but only surviving because of the rivalry of the great powers. In particular, it may be asked if it was in Britain's interest to bolster up such states and whether such a course was still possible. In order to establish some of the general characteristics in Britain's approach to the problem, it is proposed to review, firstly, the policies adopted towards the group of states occupying territory between the Bosphorus and the north western frontiers of India; and secondly, the individual problem of another North African state, Morocco.

Turkey, Persia and Afghanistan[5]

'Our policy', said Salisbury in 1890, 'remains what it has been for the last forty years, to uphold the Turkish Empire for the longest period possible'.[6] Salisbury could have gone further. He could have said that British policy had been concerned, since the 1830's, to support and encourage the development of an Ottoman power which would be capable of standing up to pressure from Russia and which, in defending its own integrity, would preserve itself as a useful buffer state between areas of British and Russian influence. For Turkey, along with Persia and Afghanistan, comprised a strategic zone where the Russians could conceivably threaten the shorter sea route to India as well as the north western land approaches to the subcontinent. Continuous attempts were made, therefore, not without some success, to prod the Sultan into modernising and reforming his shaky administrative machine, in default of which the continued existence of Turkey as a viable state seemed to be in hazard. When, too, the opportunity occurred, as it did in 1838, a

---

[5] This section of the introduction is based upon secondary works, in particular, Grenville, *Lord Salisbury and Foreign Policy*; Medlicott, *Bismarck, Gladstone and the Concert of Europe*; Monger, *The End of Isolation*; Anderson, *The Eastern Question*; Ghose, *England and Afghanistan*; Fraser-Tytler, *Afghanistan*; Greaves, *Persia and the Defence of India*; Gopal, *British Policy in India*; Gopal, *The Vice-royalty of Lord Ripon*; Seton-Watson, *The Russian Empire*; Jefferson, 'Lord Salisbury and the Eastern Question, 1890–1898', *Slavonic and East European Review*, vol. xxxix (1960–1); Gillard, "Salisbury and the Indian Defence Problem, 1885–1902", in Bourne and Watt, *Studies in International History*.

[6] SP 59/to Lytton/23 Sep 1890.

commercial treaty was signed in order to do away with Turkish monopolies, benefit British trade and, it was hoped, stimulate the Turkish economy and hence Turkish defensive strength. Help was given to improve the standard of military and naval officers, though, as it happened, with little success. Similarly British distrust of Russia lay behind the desire to keep Russian influence at a distance from India's north west frontier. What complicated matters was that Persia had historical claims to Afghanistan and to much of Transcaucasia besides. Britain, understandably in favour of the *status quo*, found herself in 1837 opposing a Persian attempt, made with Russian encouragement, to seize Herat, a key town of importance to Indian security. Two years later she was making war against the Amir of Afghanistan because he, in turn, appeared too ready to welcome Russian influence. Basically the British position was defensive, while the Russians had long-term expansionist aims. Yet there was no more desire in Moscow than in London for an armed clash and the Crimean war has been described, with justice, as 'the result of miscalculations and muddle rather than of deliberate aggression by any party'.[7]

Britain faced many more difficulties in the last quarter of the century than previously. In the aftermath of the Franco Prussian war, the newly proven strength of Germany created a stalemate in western Europe that restricted the field in which the powers could safely squabble—without risking all—to the Balkans and the non-European world. The construction of the Suez canal also increased the importance for Britain of the more dangerous Mediterranean route to the east, at a time when her ability to defend it against possible enemies, especially Russia and France, had diminished and their power of offence had appreciably increased. While Russia significantly flexed her muscles with the denunciation, in 1871, of the Black Sea clauses of the Treaty of Paris, Britain's buffer state policy faced mortal danger. For Turkey, threatened internally and externally by the movement for the emancipation of subject Christian peoples, collapsed into bankruptcy in 1876 under the burden of over-ambitious reforms and eighteen years of unwise borrowing abroad. The Russo-Turkish war, therefore, marked

[7] Seton-Watson, *The Russian Empire*, p. 320.

the end of an era for the policy of Britain. Her acquisition of Cyprus in 1878, as a base from which to contain any future Russian advance at the expense of Ottoman integrity, was a tacit recognition that Turkey was by herself incapable of insulating Anglo-Russian hostility. The Turkish empire was now, in terms of power, more or less a vacuum. Only the threat of a major war stood between it and further drastic dissection. Consequently the statesmen in London, who still believed an independent Constantinople essential to imperial security, could do little more than to attempt—in their own interests— to cosset the 'sick man' for as long as possible, though gloomily expecting his demise at any moment.

As if this were not enough, the Russians, after their setback in Turkey signalised by the Treaty of Paris of 1856, had turned their attentions further east. Advancing on a broad front east and west of the Aral Sea, they reached—by the beginning of the 1880's—the often imprecisely delimited frontiers of Persia and Afghanistan. While it is true that they began to move south with some misgiving, there was from the first an awareness that the territories they were occupying could supply economic needs, especially the raw cotton their developing industries could not always obtain easily from the U.S.A. Much more ominous for British peace of mind, however, was their belief, prompted by news of the Indian mutiny in 1857, that a forward policy might be able to exploit real hostility towards Britain in that part of the world. As strategic Russian railroads penetrated into central Asia, so Russian power in the region increased to a marked degree. With all the advantage of operating on 'internal lines', Russia could now at will distract British attention from any point of friction on her long perimeter by exerting pressure at other points where interests clashed.

British policy obviously had to undergo an 'agonising reappraisal'. Hitherto, as in the case of Turkey, there had simply been a rather general desire to see strong friendly states occupying the approaches to India. Described often as the policy of 'masterly inactivity', this had made sense when, at the beginning of the 1860's, over 1500 miles of independent Turko-man territory lay between Russia and India's Persian and Afghan neighbours. Yet this very antipathy to involvement beyond the

frontiers of British India had resulted in agents being withdrawn and even requests for assistance or guarantees directed
against Russia being disregarded, so that British influence
naturally declined. Periodic discussions with the Russians
themselves, for example in 1869 and 1873, showed that there
would be no binding arrangement on spheres of influence so
long as 'masterly inactivity' was to be expected from the British
and Indian governments. Indeed, under an agreement between
Clarendon and Gortchakov in 1875, Russia was clearly free
to expand up to the 'legitimate' limits of Afghanistan itself—
wherever they were.

When, however, Salisbury became secretary of state for India
in the same year, he was convinced that the Russians were
aiming at what were thought to be the key strategic points of
Merv and Herat (in addition to their ambitions in the Balkans).
In place of inactivity, masterly or otherwise, a more vigorous
or 'forward' policy was authorised, which the viceroy, Lytton,
carried rather further than intended. This, in general, sought
to create a strong, cohesive Afghan state, dominated by Britain,
in whose hands would be the conduct of foreign relations. It
was to be a state with clearly defined boundaries. When therefore the Afghans received a Russian mission in Kabul, an Anglo-
Afghan war broke out after which, under the Treaty of Gandamak in 1879, Britain secured from the Afghans all she required.
However, the massacre of a British mission subsequently
appointed led the viceroy, wrongly, to blame and imprison the
Amir of Afghanistan, so that the country seemed on the verge of
disintegration. This situation led to another temporary change
in British policy, by which Persia rather than Afghanistan
would become the principal buffer behind which India would
be secure. In preference to occupying Herat itself, the London
cabinet proposed to place both it and the whole of Seistan under
the control of Persia, which, it was sanguinely hoped, would be
more open to pressure from the sea.[8] Logically this policy was
in line with the argument, strongly advanced by Lytton, that
a divided Afghanistan was much to be preferred to a cohesive

---

[8] Persia had been irritated by the treaty of 1857 under which Afghanistan
got Herat and also by the decision of a British commission in 1872 which had,
at the Shah's request, fixed the Persian–Afghanistan boundary in Seistan, an
area formerly subject to Herat.

state directed by a single Amir at Kabul. His suggestion had some temporary influence. For, to Salisbury, it seemed common prudence to let Persia have Herat rather than see it fall into the hands of some local leader probably incapable of resisting Russian might. As it so happened, the Shah temporised, an Amir capable of uniting the country came to power in Afghanistan, a Liberal administration came to power in London, and the new policy was overthrown. Salisbury's successor, Granville, reminded the Persians that the treaty of 1857 precluded any intervention by them in Afghanistan and said that he regarded that treaty as still being in force.

Under pressure from their new viceroy, Lord Ripon, the Liberals in fact accepted as necessary the creation of a friendly buffer state in Afghanistan, and, in 1880, they secured control over that country's foreign policy in exchange for a subsidy and a guarantee against unprovoked aggression. The terms were substantially the same as those of the treaty of Gandamak, since Ripon was able to get the instructions he had received from London reversed in favour of the 'forward' theories which he had himself adopted and which involved an advanced frontier for India. 'The present government', said the secretary of state for India (Hartington), 'have admitted as plainly as any other that the integrity and independence of Afghanistan is a matter to them of vital importance'.[9] Since the Russians were prepared to agree that Afghanistan was beyond their sphere of influence, it was obviously desirable to obtain a clear agreement as to the northern boundaries of the country as soon as possible. Before this was accomplished, however, there was to be the one major Anglo-Russian crisis of the period over central Asia.

Hitherto the British attitude had been based on somewhat mixed motives. On the one hand there was fairly general agreement that Russia was immune to attack and that her expansion into central Asia was bound to continue. Yet, though Afghanistan was considered by the 'forward' school as a dyke which, if breached, would 'let in the ocean', statesmen like Salisbury, Cranbrook and Lytton thought the chances of an actual assault by the Russians to be slight, and there were those

---

[9] Hansard, vol. cclxiv (col. 433) 1 Aug 1881, quoted Ghose, p. 141.

BDT B

who even saw the Russian conquests as no more than the triumph of civilisation over barbarism. Salisbury himself, never an alarmist, drew satisfaction from the reflection that the impecunious Russian government would hardly relish the expense of a major campaign nor welcome the problem of transporting the impedimenta necessary to fight a European-type war across such difficult terrain. From the beginning of the 1880's, however, a pervasive atmosphere of gloom and defeatism hung more and more over Whitehall as the strategic position of Russia improved, the relative ability of Britain to defend her interests decreased, and the old Palmerstonian policy of protecting the short route to India by means of strength at Constantinople came under fire. To the strategists, Russia seemed clearly able to bring much greater military pressure to bear on Persia than Britain, and Persia occupied the important central sector in the buffer zone stretching from Turkey to Afghanistan. Furthermore an increasingly estranged Commander of the Faithful at Constantinople was assumed to exert a much more pronounced influence on Muslim central Asia, and one hostile to Britain, than he actually did. The shock of the Russian occupation of Merv in 1884, therefore, served notice to London that time was running out if a satisfactory delimitation of Afghanistan's northern frontiers was to be made. What followed was a British warning to Russia that 'Herat meant war' and, the year after, the war scare over Penjdeh, in the disputed territory between the Heri Hud and Oxus rivers. That there was no war was because neither of the governments, certainly not the British, wanted one, though it took two more years and much wearisome diplomatic haggling before a working delimitation of the Afghan frontiers was finally made.[10]

The pattern of British policy was by now set. It was to bolster up the indigenous administration in Afghanistan, and Salisbury, between 1885 and 1892, can be seen pursuing a similar policy in Persia. There, too, energetic attempts were made to strengthen the Shah's government and to induce it to improve its chances of withstanding Russian encroachments by launching a pro-gramme of internal reforms. Yet little real headway was made. Salisbury's dearest wish, nourished since the days when he had

[10] The final settlement was in 1895.

been Indian secretary, was to see a network of strategic railways from India to Seistan by way of Herat and from the Persian Gulf to Teheran. His ambitions, however, were largely frustrated by disagreement on the part of some of his colleagues, by the division of responsibility between the Foreign Office on the one hand and the Indian Office and viceroy on the other, and by the opposition of the Persians themselves. It went without saying that the Russians, unable themselves to afford the development of railways in the north of Persia, made every effort to prevent the building of any in the south by British enterprise. Indeed, in November 1890 they prevailed upon the Shah to sign an agreement that he would sanction no railway construction for ten years.

None of the three states, therefore, that comprised Britain's buffer zone in the Near East and central Asia could be described as much more than a broken reed. As early as 1880, Salisbury had been anticipating an early demise of the guardian on the western flank, Turkey, and hoping that the fatality would not actually occur until a railway had been built to Kandahar or, more hopefully, until 'the revolution in Russia' had taken place. Diplomacy, it seemed in London, provided the only chance of propping up any of the three states. For there was little belief in Britain's ability to meet a military challenge by Russia at all points, especially when Russia's friendship with France developed. Diplomacy had, of course, improved Britain's position in 1887. That was when the none too precise Mediterranean agreement of February, with Italy and Austria, was extended with the express purpose of preserving the integrity of Bulgaria and Turkey, thus successfully associating the Triple Alliance powers with the defence of Constantinople and implicitly negativing Bismarck's attempt (in the 'Reinsurance' treaty) to keep on good terms with Russia.

Militarily, however, British thinking was entirely defensive and somewhat defeatist. In the event of a Russian invasion through southern Afghanistan, the 'war plan' of 1891 envisaged the occupation of Kandahar and, if Turkey were friendly, a repeat of the tactics of the Crimean war. If Turkey were not friendly, the military experts thought it would be necessary to join the Triple Alliance. Simultaneously the Admiralty was coming to the conclusion that, in the event of hostilities with both France and Russia, the Straits could not be invested in the face of Turkish antagonism. Not until 1895, however, did the cabinet—including a reluctant Salisbury—finally adopt the point of view of the naval experts. Had this not happened, the prime minister would have been prepared to continue the policy of propping up the Turkish empire and inducing it to reform itself, by force if necessary. For, though he did not himself share the belief that it was absolutely necessary to keep the Russians out of Constantinople, he did think that British prestige was involved in maintaining the traditional policy. Now, however, not only was it impossible for Britain alone to defend the Turks, but, after their massacres of the Armenians, it was more than doubtful whether public opinion in Britain would allow the government to make the attempt. Perforce Britain's main concern in the Near East switched from the defence of Constantinople to the defence of the Nile valley. Though Salisbury was over-pessimistic about the chances Turkey had of surviving for any length of time, he certainly still wished to keep the 'sick man' alive as long as possible. Britain's traditional policy in the Near East was, therefore, in the process of fading away and, after a brief intervention in Balkan affairs in support of Greece in 1897, was no more. Neither Russia singly nor the powers in concert would co-operate and there was nothing further that Salisbury could do.

Meanwhile Russia, partly under the impetus of large-scale foreign loans, had embarked on the sustained programme of investment in railways that made the 1890's notable for her. It is true that the Russian economy would have expanded more quickly had the attempt not been made to develop the whole empire at once rather than to concentrate on the most advanced regions; but emphasis on state control was pronounced and state control meant that priority, even in times of financial stringency, was given to railroads of military importance. By the end of the century, new lines bore witness to the rejection of industrial integration with western Europe. While in the far east the Trans-Siberian railway had reached Lake Baikal, in the south Russian rolling stock was moving from the shores of the Caspian Sea through Merv to Kushka, and another route from European Russia stretched out through Orenburg and Aralsk towards Tashkent. All this had its effect on British policy. Already at the beginning of the 1890's, Salisbury was clearly beginning to concentrate on saving British interests in the south of Persia only, leaving the north as a Russian sphere of influence. Indecisiveness predominated. While Persia became ever weaker, the government in London urged the construction of a railway to Seistan. The government in Calcutta disagreed. It felt that it would have no troops to spare for Persia and that Afghanistan was, in any case, the area of decisive importance.

By the end of the century, Salisbury's leadership was being seriously questioned and he was gloomily forecasting a Russian 'grab' at most of China when the Trans-Siberian railway was completed. Coupled with this move, he anticipated, would be an advance on India if Afghanistan were unprotected—to compel British acquiescence in the subjugation of China. For Russia was taking advantage of British preoccupation with the Boer war to hamstring the Persians with a second disastrous loan and to attempt, unsuccessfully as it transpired, to erode Britain's control of Afghanistan's foreign relations by request-ing direct economic links with Kabul. What helped in the end to clarify British policy was the challenging influence of yet another viceroy of the 'forward' school. Appointed in 1898, Curzon had little faith in the buffer states bordering India's frontiers. He believed that Persia should be partitioned into British and Russian spheres of influence and that it was neces-sary to curb the self-sufficiency of the strong Amir of Afghanis-tan, Abdur Rahman, whose independent attitude was made possible by subsidies and by the freedom, allowed him since 1893, to import arms without restriction. This cut little ice with Salisbury. For he felt that Russia was by now in a position to seize Persia at will and was quite capable of tearing up the agreements of 1872–73 (reaffirmed by her several times) that Afghanistan was 'outside her sphere of action'. On top of this, an obdurate chancellor of the exchequer refused to step in with government-sponsored loans to Persia where private business-men feared to tread—even to counteract the financial strangle-hold of relatively impecunious Russia. In Afghanistan, also, Salisbury felt little could be done except to appease the Amir by sending him the agreed amounts of money and arms with the hope that he would, in time, fulfil his obligations in foreign affairs.

In the cases of both Persia and Afghanistan there had been, therefore, certain long-term features discernible in British policy. There had been a reluctance to shoulder any political or territorial responsibilities or to take any step that might disturb the *status quo*. Every effort that cost no public money had been made to maintain the territorial integrity and viability of the two states, to develop their resources and to breathe life into their administrative machines. In Persia this policy had been visibly failing, but the insistence of Curzon—added to a successful Russian veto on a proposed Indian government loan—did eventually lead to a clear declaration of British policy on the part of Salisbury's successor at the Foreign Office. In 1902 Lansdowne warned the Shah that Britain could not allow any other power to acquire political predominance in Seistan and southern Persia, nor tolerate a Russian naval or military station in the gulf. This hardly veiled intimation that Britain would resist a further Russian advance with 'all means at her disposal' was, however, made with the belief that all means at her disposal were unlikely to be enough. It was this conviction that, for some years, had in fact helped to popularise the idea in Whitehall that Britain needed an ally or allies. Viewed from London the situation in the area from Constantinople to Kabul was alarming. The defence of Egypt and the Nile valley had for years replaced in importance the defence of Turkey and British weakness in the Straits had just been publicly demonstrated by the ineffectiveness of a lone protest when the Turks allowed four Russian torpedo boats to pass through into the Black Sea. Naval influence at Constantinople had in any case been written off by the Admiralty strategists. Even more disturbing perhaps was the fact that when Lansdowne had declared himself ready, if necessary, to preserve British interests in southern Persia by active intervention, the military experts asserted that they had not sufficient force at their disposal for the purpose. As for the third buffer state, Afghanistan, little more appeared possible there than to make a show of friendship and hope for the best. For the Amir, while able to call on British support in the event of hostilities with Russia, jealously preserved his independence, so that Chamberlain even suggested abdicating responsibility for Afghanistan and defending India on its own borders. The prevailing view in British and Indian government circles may have underestimated the capacity of British imperial forces on land and overestimated the capacity of the Russians for operating in force over difficult terrain; but there was no hiding the fact that conditions had changed and that the buffer states could no longer perform the task of holding Russia at arm's length. There was one really effective solution to the problem of a Russian empire that had the advantage of working on internal lines and was liable to encroach at any time not merely in the Near East or central Asia but in Tibet or China. That was to come to mutually satisfactory terms with the Russians themselves when and if possible. How that was eventually achieved forms no part of this discussion, which has been concerned to outline the part played in British policy by some of the strategically placed oriental states which posed problems that help to put into perspective those posed by Tunisia.

MOROCCO[11]

Morocco was not the subject of a major international crisis until the early years of the present century. Yet statesmen in London, from Palmerston onwards, had evolved policies towards Morocco which had much in common with policies pursued towards other strategically placed and backward states. Geography was the reason why most powers showed an interest in

[11] This section is based upon secondary works, especially Parsons, 'The "Morocco Question" in 1884: An Early Crisis', *English Historical Review*, vol. lxxvii (1962), 'The North-West African Company and the British Government, 1875–95', *Historical Journal*, vol. 1 (1958), 'The Proposed Madrid Conference on Morocco, 1887–88', *Historical Journal*, vol. 8 (1963), Review article, 'L'Allemagne et le Maroc de 1870 à 1905', *English Historical Review*, vol. lxxxiv (1969); Medlicott, *Bismarck, Gladstone and the Concert of Europe*; Flournoy, *British Policy towards Morocco in the Age of Palmerston*; Bartlett, 'Great Britain and the Spanish Change of Policy towards Morocco in June 1878', *Bulletin of the Institute of Historical Research*, vol. xxxi (1958); Grenville, op. cit.; Monger, op. cit.; Taylor, 'British Policy in Morocco, 1886-1902', *English Historical Review*, vol. lxvi (1951); Anderson, *The First Moroccan Crisis, 1904–1906*; Miège, *Le Maroc et l'Europe*; de Leone, *La colonizzazione dell'Africa del Nord*; Guillen, *L'Allemagne et le Maroc de 1870 à 1905*; Cruickshank, *Morocco at the Parting of the Ways*; Nicolson, *Lord Carnock*.

the country, and no advanced knowledge of military science is necessary to appreciate the importance of the Sherifian empire for Britain. A strong European power established there could threaten not merely to close the western entrance to the Mediterranean in time of emergency but to place in hazard the longer route to India round the Cape. To avoid such a contingency, therefore, became one of the most enduring preoccupations of British policy. What was more, enlightened self interest in the commercial field was thought likely to bolster up the independence and integrity of the sultan's possessions, if only because growing prosperity resulting from greater trade might reasonably be expected to increase the viability of the empire. The more Morocco could stand on its own feet, the less was there any chance of a Moroccan 'question' bedevilling international relations. Peace and quiet was, in fact, what successive British foreign ministers earnestly desired for the area, but conditions in the empire were not exactly conducive to the fulfilment of that desire, especially towards the end of the century.

For Morocco was hardly a state at all in west European terms. It consisted in truth largely of insubordinate tribal groups, frequently quarrelling one with another, and loosely united under the temporal sway of a not strictly hereditary religious leader who, to survive, had to play the game of 'divide and rule'. Even boundaries were ill-defined, since the empire was really one of the spirit, embracing as subjects all those who acknowledged the sultan as the one and only 'commander of the faithful'. The court perambulated round the country and the sultan's writ could be said to run chiefly in the area where he happened to be at any given time, dispensing *ad hoc* and rather arbitrary justice. He reigned, but could not really be said to head an administration. Those who wanted something done, made payments to officials, a mode of procedure regarded by most Europeans as simply bribery, and only extra-territorial rights, backed up by occasional gunboat visits, enabled the subjects of Christian powers to hold their own. Intrigue was rife, and for many foreign representatives intrigue and negotiation were synonymous procedures. Like the other once dreaded Barbary states, Morocco was therefore in no condition to stand up to attack by a major power.

Fortunately for the sultan, British policy was aimed by the 1830's at preventing other powers from dominating any part of the North African littoral. It is true that, at a moment of British preoccupation, the French did seize their opportunity to begin the long drawn out subjugation of the territories of the Deys of Algiers; but London successfully vetoed European ambitions in Tunis and Tripoli during the same period, and performed a similar favour for Morocco. For example, a promise was extracted from France in 1836 that there would be no expansion by her beyond the confines of Algeria, a promise reaffirmed several times in the succeeding decade under diplomatic pressure from London. This was not without importance, because much traditional tribal feuding had now become, in the eyes of Paris, raids into French territory in Algeria (especially after a delimitation agreement in 1845). It is not very surprising that the agent of British policy in Morocco, the redoubtable Sir John Drummond Hay, should for a period of years have exercised a predominant influence at the court of the sultan, particularly in the 1850's. He was, after all, seeking no exclusive privileges for British citizens.

There were perennial fears in London, however, that some untoward incident might lead to the collapse and partition of Morocco, so that every effort was made by Hay to smooth over international disputes in which that country was involved. All persuasion possible was also brought into play to prevail on the sultan to reform and, what seemed axiomatic in London, to thereby strengthen his ramshackle government. All possible arguments were advanced to show that the growth of foreign commerce would produce a resurgence of Moroccan power, military as well as economic. Every attempt at reform, however, came up against a blank wall of inertia and xenophobia that was not without its logic. Change, especially one involving an appreciable influx of 'infidel' Christian merchants, would probably be more dangerous to the stability of Morocco than failure to adapt to new conditions in the outside world. As it was, the right of European powers to 'protect' Moroccan nationals was already a serious handicap, since this absolved the latter from payment of taxes or submission to the processes of Moorish justice. Drummond Hay could achieve, therefore, little more than the reduction of tariffs and the abolition of monopolies, by no means an exclusive advantage favouring his compatriots. This was in accordance with Britain's normal 'open door' policy in backward countries, a policy which of course gave to the dominant industrial power great opportunities. As far as the trade of Morocco was concerned, this was certainly true until the last quarter of the century.

The Sherifian empire had two dangerous neighbours, not only France, whose Algerian frontier was constantly troubled by unruly Moroccan tribesmen, but also Spain who could on occasion exercise an ugly pressure from her strip of territory along the northern coast and who felt she had almost a prescriptive right to influence in the country. Nor could there be much doubt that Spain would have extended her sway in Morocco had the other powers been distracted by some urgent preoccupation. Between 1858 and 1860 Britain had to come out strongly in support of the Moors against Spain. It was more than fortunate that the France of Napoleon III was content to consolidate its influence in Algeria and showed but little interest in the rest of the Maghrib. After their harrowing defeat by the Prussians, the French were in no condition for most of the 1870's to worry over what was, to them, a relatively minor problem. Spain, however, took the chance to press home her grievances and, in 1870, 1875–76 and especially 1878 there were Spanish-Moroccan crises, with British influence constantly exerted in an attempt to ward off the implied threat to the integrity of Morocco. For those were years of increasing international tension, culminating in the bankruptcy of the Ottoman empire, the Russo-Turkish war, the British occupation of Cyprus and the apparent possibility of a really serious Anglo-French quarrel. Despite all this, the Spaniards were to be found within a short space of time giving active, if transient, support for Britain's efforts to maintain the *status quo*, and the reason was not far to seek.

Defeat by the Germans had left the French terrified at the very thought of complications that might bring them again face to face with the late enemy; but at the same time there was an understandable desire to restore national prestige by any means involving no risk. As too the German chancellor had been dropping hints for some time into British and French ears that partition of tottering Muslim governments would serve to avoid rather than promote a European war, and as Bismarck would in any case welcome the prospect of the irrevocably alienated French diverting their energies to the Mediterranean, it seemed quite safe for Paris to show an increased interest in Morocco. The Beaconsfield government in London might be dazzled even by the suggestion of Egypt becoming British. There was, however, small chance of it agreeing to the purchase of French acquiescence (if in fact purchasable) by blessing a French occupation of Syria in the east and of Morocco in the west, the minimum that would be asked in exchange. Morocco was still too important and the possibility of Gibraltar being neutralised by a hostile power in Tangier too awful to contemplate. So the French began to demonstrate greater interest in Morocco, as in Tunis, but not too great an interest—since political circles in the homeland were hopelessly divided on the issue of colonial ventures. However, the mere hint of gain to France in Morocco was enough to make the Spaniards discover the virtues of the *status quo* and Drummond Hay found he had acquired for himself new allies for the time being. Though Salisbury, now foreign minister, had little confidence in the ability of the Moorish government to survive, every effort was still made to strengthen it. Reform was urged, recruits trained for a new army, economic projects sponsored and the first of many attempts was initiated to conclude a commercial treaty that would help to develop the resources of the country—all to little avail. When, however, a new sultan seemed ready to take the first step towards clearing out his Augean stable by a move to abolish the scandal of foreign *protégés*, his venture was foiled. By the time an international conference had been summoned at Madrid in 1880 to deal with the question, the Gladstone administration had replaced that of Beaconsfield, and, with little understanding of the almost traditional policy towards Morocco and the other decadent Muslim states, left most decisions to the permanent officials. To them the conference seemed capable of only one result, that of making Morocco a major issue causing dissension between the powers. The British delegate was therefore something of a 'lame dog' at Madrid but what gave the

coup de grâce to this effort to cause a breakthrough in Morocco
was the attitude of a power whose positive interests in the
country were hard to discover—Italy. France, of course,
supported the *protégé* system since it enabled her to intervene
freely in Moroccan affairs, which was reason enough for Spain
to show implacable opposition. Italy, however, had little to
lose but the hope of fishing in troubled waters in the future,
and was at the very moment even engaged in a bitter struggle
with France—for ascendancy in Tunis. With the weight of
Britain and Spain balanced by that of France and Italy, the
decisive voice was that of another power with not much at stake
in Morocco at the time, Germany. Effective influence was that
of Bismarck and, probably aware of Gladstone's disinterest,
he came down confidently from the fence to settle the issue in
favour of protection.

As Anglo-French relations deteriorated in the early 1880's,
a consequence of British resentment at the way the French
occupied Tunis and virulent French resentment at the very fact
of a British occupation of Egypt, relations in Morocco reflected
the change. An active French agent used the *protégé* system.
more blatantly than ever, and, for Morocco, more dangerously.
He even encouraged a local potentate to attempt to seize the
throne and placed him and his supporters under the protection
of France, only to have an alarmed foreign minister in Paris
apply the brake to his over-ambitious policy. Indeed, signs
never seemed to be lacking to indicate that Morocco was about
to be the subject of a major international dispute; but the fact
of the matter was that, however much suspicion and however
much backbiting rivalry existed between the foreign representatives in Tangier, none of the powers desired an international
crisis over this particular question.

The objectives of the two main protagonists, Britain and
France, were not, at this stage, at variance. France was not
really interested in the coast facing Gibraltar and Britain was
not very concerned over minor rectifications of the frontier
between Algiers and Morocco. The policies of the European
governments were, however, sometimes frustrated by unsuitable
local agents or by the activities of the more unscrupulous of the
concession hunters among their nationals. Both factors played

their part in weakening the once dominant British influence over the sultan, a development evident even before the retirement of Drummond Hay in 1886. The strength of that influence had stemmed from the ostensibly disinterested advice given. One or two cases, however, such as those concerning the Eastern Telegraph Company and the North West African Company,[12] the mistaken belief of Hay's successors, Kirby Green and Euan Smith, that intimidation was the best way to deal with the Maghzen, and the inclination of both of them on occasion to present London with a *fait accompli* not in strict accord with the spirit of their instructions, all resulted in Anglo-Moroccan relations deteriorating further and to a general suspicion of Britain's motives. Though the local tools were apt to turn in Salisbury's hand during his second ministry, he pursued at a higher level a policy which, among other things, served to neutralise any French disposition to expand seriously into the Sherifian empire. He clearly needed diplomatic support against France at both ends of the Mediterranean, in Egypt as well as in Morocco, and this he got from the Italians. The effect of the agreement reached, in 1887, was reinforced by the promise to the Italians that the Germans now felt safe to give—for assistance to Italy against any French expansion into Tripoli or Morocco. The Mediterranean *status quo* was now reasonably secure for a period and Salisbury resisted all suggestions that preparations be made to seize Tangier in event of a French occupation of Morocco.

It was not, of course, that there were to be no alarms and frustrations. The persistent attempts of the British representative to secure an up-to-date commercial treaty, intended to breathe new life into the decaying empire, were frustrated by a contrary commercial agreement negotiated by the German representative. In 1891 also, the French began to lay claim to the group of oases around Tuat, having convinced themselves against all the evidence that they were in Algerian territory. By now Germany seemed ready to take any opportunity for an anti-French move in the Mediterranean, and endeavoured to stimulate joint action by Italy, Spain and Britain. The Italians,

[12] For details see Parsons, 'The North-West African Company and the British Government, 1875–95', *Historical Journal*, vol. 1, (1958).

with possible gains in Tripoli in mind, needed little prodding. But the main German ambition, to use the issue to align Britain publicly with Italy against France, was not realised, and Salisbury poured cold water on Italian requests for a joint protest. This, it will be seen, was in line with his policy of 'watering Crispi's wine' in connection with similar problems arising in the south of Tunisia. Indeed German and Italian insistence, until the volatile Crispi fell from power in 1891, seemed to make Salisbury more rather than less tolerant of French actions, though he was nevertheless determined not to lose the useful connection with the Italians and the central powers. When, after 1892, increasing German unfriendliness undermined the policy hitherto pursued, Rosebery and Salisbury made persistent efforts to secure a better relationship with France. In view, however, of the British decision not to evacuate Egypt, a real reconciliation was impossible until the eventual confrontation at Fashoda resulted in a radical reassessment of policy at Paris.

As for Morocco, Britain still aimed at letting sleeping dogs lie for as long as they would. It is not a little ironic, therefore, that it should be a belated attempt at reform, as advised by Britons of influence in the empire, that helped to create chaos and anarchy of a sort to make European intervention well nigh inevitable.[13] Rebellion spread rapidly from 1900 onwards so that within three years the sultan's authority was limited to a few of the chief towns. It is not particularly surprising that the acerbity and the element of war hysteria in Anglo-French relations immediately after Fashoda should have had its reflection in renewed rivalry in Morocco and the idea of reforms and loans sponsored by the 'English ring round the Sultan' was thought particularly obnoxious at the Quai d'Orsay. It is not surprising either that Britain, distracted by the Boer war, witnessed in the south of Morocco an intensified policy of 'peaceful penetration' on the part of France. This, of course,

---

[13] The last sultan with a pretence to real authority, Mulai Hassan, died in 1894 and a wily Grand Vizier, Ba Ahmed, dominated an increasingly weak government until his death in 1900. The young Sultan, Abd-el-Aziz was much under the influence of a British-born professional soldier, Kaid Maclean, who had friendly relations with Sir Arthur Nicolson, the British representative.

had never worried Salisbury, though he—and Lansdowne after him—went as far now as to assert a determination to occupy Tangier should there be real danger.

It would be invidious to recapitulate the well-known part that the Sherifian empire played in the development of the Anglo-French entente of 1904. To note some of the significant factors leading to the abandonment of Britain's almost traditional policy towards Morocco should perhaps suffice. Lansdowne, like Salisbury, was initially concerned to avoid any international crisis over that country, with the result that he did not take up French hints of possible partition. So complete, however, did the collapse of the sultan's authority become that, in the very nature of the case, it virtually compelled the emergence of an informal British understanding with France in defence of the *status quo*—a *status quo* seen in Paris as excluding any German ambitions and in no way hindering those of France. In the end, of course, there was a general settlement of Anglo-French differences, involving the principal bargain through which a recognition by Britain of predominant French interest in Morocco was exchanged for a like recognition by France of predominant British interest in Egypt. The decisive factors in bringing about this revolutionary change in British policy were twofold. In the first place the balance of opinion in Foreign Office circles had become increasingly convinced that the most dangerous possible enemy was Germany, with whom relations were at a low ebb. In the second place, the impending clash in the far east between Britain's ally, Japan, and France's ally, Russia, acted as a catalyst in the process of forging an entente based on a settlement of colonial disagreements. There was the understandable hope in London that such an agreement would mean that France would restrain, or at least not support, the Russians against Britain. Moreover the Quai d'Orsay was prepared to meet the fundamental British demands for the neutralisation of the Mediterranean coast of Morocco (where the Admiralty was still ready to combat French influence tooth and nail), for the absence of discrimination against British trade, and for the recognition of the legitimate rights of Spain. There was, too, some feeling that France's continual 'nibbling at the cherry' of Moroccan independence would in no great time erode Britain's ability to use rights in Morocco as a bargaining counter. This horse-trading with France is sometimes felt to be the logical consummation of the policy pursued by Salisbury, and Rosebery, after 1892. After all, it created no formal alliance engagement and Germany's 'Egyptian baton', the use of which Salisbury had resented so much, was no more. Whether Salisbury would have made such an agreement is, however, open to doubt. Certainly his successor did not fully comprehend the price which Britain would have to pay for the deliberate exclusion of Germany from the settlement in Morocco, where she had expressed determination that there should be no partition without the express approval of an international congress. When, therefore, London and Paris agreed to provide mutual diplomatic aid to protect the arrangements over Morocco and Egypt, this assured that the almost inevitable pressure from Berlin would align Britain more and more firmly on the side of France.

The British attitude towards Morocco in the last quarter of the nineteenth century reveals important facets of general policy. What predominates throughout is the concern of the Foreign Office to prevent a strategically important area, one dominating lines of communication vital to Britain, falling into the hands of a hostile power. Equally noticeable is the disposition to avoid any course of action liable to precipitate a head-on clash with other European countries. Every effort was made to bolster up the ramshackle Sherifian empire as long as humanly possible, if only because the dangers of European conflict arising from a collapse of that empire were incalculable. Partition was never an object of policy (except to a dissident member of the cabinet like Chamberlain), and vague plans for seizing Tangier were to be operative only in an emergency provoked by others. The long-standing British sponsorship of reform, as a means of increasing the ability of Morocco to remain independent and valuable as a buffer state, did not prove a very practical proposition. In the end reform was to help accelerate the very breakdown that it was designed to avoid.

From the British point of view, the Moroccan question was, to a considerable extent, a problem of Anglo-French relations. What helped the pacific policies of Salisbury and Rosebery there was the fact that essential British and French interests were not incompatible. France was not fundamentally concerned to acquire the coast opposite Gibraltar and British statesmen were not much worried by French attempts to round off their African empire by 'rectification' of the Algerian frontier. Apart therefore from periodic suspicions arising from the over-zealous activities of the respective representatives, bad relations in Morocco were often the reflection of a clash between British and French policies over a much wider field. However, even if Salisbury did call on the support of Spain and Italy to check French ambitions in the 1880's and if his successor, Lansdowne, did develop a similar policy between 1901 and 1903 based on German support, there is no mistaking the determination shown by the former in the 1890's to reduce friction between London and Paris.

A survey of British policy in the last quarter of the last century towards Morocco, the near east and central Asia, might have led an intelligent observer in 1870 to expect that policy towards Tunis would show similar characteristics. For there too was to be found a tottering Muslim state, strategically placed along the important Mediterranean corridor to the east. It might be reasonable to anticipate a British policy which sought to preserve the *status quo*, to avoid incidents likely to lead to international complications, and to bolster up the economic and military strength of the country. It might be logical to expect to find there agents of the powers exacerbating local squabbles in their efforts to further the interests of their own countrymen, and to find the British representative striving to maintain the 'open door' to trade by means of a modern commercial treaty. How far British policy towards Tunis conformed to this pattern and how far it diverged, it is one of the purposes of this study to examine. Tunis, it will be found, was something of a special case.

1

BRITAIN AND THE TUNIS OF THE BEYS, 1875–1879

BRITAIN'S TRADITIONAL POLICY

In exchange for our support, England gives us *carte blanche* in Tunisia, in agreement with Bismarck, who is delighted to find this opportunity to embroil us with Italy.[1]

The French, however, were not exactly given a free hand in the Regency of Tunis as a result of arrangements at the Congress of Berlin in 1878 as Deschanel suggests. For Britain possessed treaty rights there and successive ministries were disposed to insist on those rights long after the French occupation three years later. A matter of hardly more than secondary importance in itself, the Tunis question for more than a generation assumed a position of varying significance in European affairs: it provided a field of conflict and dissention at a time when the alliances and alignments of the great powers were in a process of radical change. Nor was it in any way remarkable that Tunis should be a diplomatic battleground of the nations. A backward country possessing a fine natural harbour in Biserta, Tunis in the hands of a strong power might, from its very strategic position opposite Sicily, 'seize the Mediterranean by the throat',[2] and no name was more capable of making the worried Italian 'catch his breath' than that of Tunis.[3] For a generation the Tunis question soured the relations of France and Italy as effectively as the Egyptian question soured the

---

[1] Deschanel, *Histoire de la politique extérieure de la France*, p. 259. The two introductory paragraphs consist of general comments based on the succeeding chapters. The earlier period covered by the first two chapters is more familiar to historians than the later, and is, therefore, dealt with in less detail than the succeeding chapters, except for the question of Britain's treaty of 1875 with Tunis, which is not so well known, and a few other important points.

[2] A phrase of Hanotaux; *La Paix latine*, p. 276.

[3] Toscano, 'Tunis', *Berliner Monatshefte*, Feb 1939, p. 119.

relations of France and England, and more permanently. For a generation the Tunis question acted as one of the lesser irritants that added perennially to the exacerbation of Anglo-French relations. As a base of operations in the scramble for North Africa, Tunis was to raise the hope of the French and the dismay of the Italians, and, in the end, it played no insignificant part in a major re-alignment of the great powers.

As for the country itself, its rulers, or Beys, had, by the end of the 1860's, borrowed heavily and unwisely from Europe, especially from France (by no means a disinterested lender), and invited intervention by their complete failure to arrest the decay of the Regency, a decay owing much to the corruption of the ministers and favourites they autocratically and capriciously chose. Not only the all-influential neighbour, France, but also England and the nascent Italy had come to play a considerable part in the affairs of the Regency and their representatives enjoyed the benefits of 'Capitulations', then so common in eastern countries. Condescendingly granted by Beys in the distant past, the rights enjoyed by foreigners were extensive. Justice for Europeans was the responsibility of the consul, who often dispensed it in person. He would maintain his special guards, his 'janissaries', as well as his own prison, and could call on the Bey for assistance in securing the execution of his sentences. His residence was a sanctuary for anyone he chose to admit and he might take under his wing as 'protected persons' even Tunisian subjects, who were thus placed in a privileged position before the law of their own country.[4] While arrangements like these were essential to secure fair play for Christian merchants and colonists in the domain of a Muslim autocrat, the attempts of the various consuls to administer a multiplicity of legal codes led inevitably to chaos and partisanship. In addition,

---

[4] 'Protected' persons of other nationalities received the same privileges. P.H.X. (d'Estournelles de Constant), *La Politique française et ses origines*, pp. 360-3; *Revue des Deux Mondes*, vol. 79, section IV; P. Cambon, *Correspondance*, vol. 1, p. 170; Ganiage, 'Les Européens en Tunisie', *Cahiers de Tunisie*, vol. 3, pp. 400-3; *Les Origines du protectorat français en Tunisie*, pp. 50-52, 54-55; Safwat, *Tunis and the Powers*, pp. 38-56; Charmes, *La Tunisie et la Tripolitaine*, quoted by Dupuy, *La Tunisie dans les lettres d'expression française*, p. 45; Lewis, *The Emergence of Modern Turkey*, pp. 448-9. Miller states that the Capitulations, dating from 1535, were 'the most practical result of the Franco-Turkish alliance'; *The Ottoman Empire*, pp. 2-3.

the direction of sanitary matters in Tunis had been confided by the Bey to the Consular Corps, which also had a considerable say in municipal affairs, while a large part of the revenues of a bankrupt Regency had been placed in 1869 under the control of a Financial Commission dominated by the representatives of France, England and Italy. Nor was this all. For, amidst the intrigue and venality that pervaded the ever weaker oriental court, each powerful foreign agent sought to advance the interests of his country and its often concession-hungry 'colony'—in the face of the rivalry of his diplomatic colleagues. 'If you live long in this atmosphere, its infectious influence may corrupt you', said a young visitor, later to be British Consul-General, and Harry Johnston, pronounced Francophile though he was, vividly portrayed the attitude of the colonists;

> To them, especially if they be French, there is nothing interesting or edifying in the spectacle of a fine people and a beautiful language and a superb architecture slowly sinking into decay. . . . They only see before them a country to be 'exploité', highly cultivated if it be possible, a fortune to be quickly made out of its riches in one way or another, and then off to Paris! Where the hardships of living and working in one of the most charming climates and interesting portions of the earth's surface are to be atoned for and forgotten amid the gaieties of the most artificial city in the world.[5]

By 1870, British policy towards the Regency and towards the inveterate rivalry of France had acquired certain well-defined features. Ever since the Sultan Selim had reconquered Tunis from the Spaniards in 1573, the Porte had laid claim to suzerainty over the country and from that date each Bey had obtained his Firman of Investiture from the Sultan, though otherwise enjoying almost absolute independence. As successive British governments had invariably considered Tunis of great importance, they had always refused to recognise the Bey in any other

---

[5] JP/MSS treatise on Tunis/Chap. 6. A similar view was expressed in an article by Gabriel Charmes, *Journal des Débats*, 13 June 1882; FO 102/140/37/Reade to Granville/21 June 1882. For general developments leading to the position in 1870, see Ganiage, op. cit., chaps. 1-7 (the most exhaustive survey); Safwat, op. cit., chaps 1 and 2; Langer, 'The European Powers and the French occupation of Tunis' (1), *American Historical Review*, vol. 31, pp. 55-78; Raymond, 'Les Tentatives anglaises de pénétration économique en Tunisie', *Revue Historique*, vol. 214, pp. 48-58.

capacity than that of a vassal of the Porte. The French, on the other hand, from the time they had established themselves in Algeria, had insisted increasingly and for obvious reasons on the 'autonomy' of the Regency. In the next half decade they twice ordered their fleet to prevent any attempt at a landing by the Turks (clumsily ambitious after their recovery of Tripoli in 1837) and by the 1860's were openly asserting that there was no political connection between the Bey and the Sultan, but merely a spiritual relationship. Indeed, they actually attempted to prevent the envoys of Constantinople reaching Tunis. British policies ran counter to those of France. There was an uneasy feeling that the possession of the Tunisian coast and anchorages would augment French power in the central Mediterranean, in addition to bringing forward all the unwelcome problems that would stem from an increased disposition in Europe for sharing out the possessions of the Porte. Britain, moreover, was the power responsible for safeguarding the interests of the Maltese, who constituted, after the Italians, the largest foreign 'colony' in the Regency.

British statesmen had, therefore, given warnings to France in 1836 and 1843 that they would not acquiesce in the conquest of Tunis by her. Later, when Mustapha Bey announced to Queen Victoria his succession in 1855, he was hurt to receive a reply not from her, as befitted an independent sovereign, but from the foreign secretary. Lord Palmerston summed up the British attitude in a terse comment:

> Our policy has always been to maintain his dependency on the Sultan, as a safeguard against his becoming a vassal of France.[6]

When Britain gave another warning, in 1864, that she could not 'admit any exclusive right of France in Tunis', the French Emperor himself disclaimed territorial designs there. In spite of this, however, the Quai d'Orsay declined a proposition from London that Britain, France and Italy should jointly declare that they had no wish or intention of interfering in the internal government of Tunis, nor with the exercise by the Bey of his just prerogative. Whatever imperial assurances were received, therefore, from Paris, it is not surprising that within two

[6] FO 102/150/Memo by Hertslet/23 Oct 1874; ibid/90/Wood to Granville/ 14 Oct 1871; D.D.F. 1/1/106.

years the Foreign Office was convinced that officialdom in
both France and Algeria was making a sustained effort to reduce
Tunis to a dependency,[7] and this view was strengthened in
1867 when a secret report was received that the French
Emperor in Council had issued a Decree which—though not
put into effect—had authorised the occupation by 8000 troopers
of the coast of the Regency.[8]

British policy in Tunis owed much to the energy and indeed
the initiative of Richard Wood, an extremely able and intelligent
man, who had been Agent and Consul-General there since
1855. Born, as it were, almost into the service of the British
Embassy at Constantinople, for his father was dragoman there,
Wood soon found his worth appreciated by Stratford Canning,
the ambassador. After schooling in Exeter, the young man was
sent to Syria in 1831, at the time of the invasion by Mehemet
Ali's armies, to learn the language and get to know the feudal
chiefs. Within four years he was on a particularly dangerous
mission, again in the same part of the world. According to him,
this was to report on the political situation, the reliability of
the Prince of the Lebanon, the strength of the Egyptian and
Turkish armies, the loyalty of the Turkish commander and the
extent of Egyptian encroachments under Ibrahim Pasha on the
left bank of the Euphrates. During this enterprise he was twice
wounded, discovered a secret plot between Egyptian and
Turkish generals, made a dramatic escape down the Tigris on
a raft of inflated skins and secured single-handed the submission
of an important Kurdish chieftain, in revolt against the sultan.
Once again in Syria in 1840, during the Egyptian invasion,
Wood supported the outnumbered Turkish forces by distribu-
ting some 83,000 muskets to the local population (from Egyptian
stores!) to carry on guerrilla warfare. On top of this he under-
took the administration of the country at the request of the
Porte for the duration of the campaign. These missions had done
much to further the policy of preventing the Mediterranean

[7] FO/102/150/Memo by Hertslet/23 Oct 1874. Lord Stanley (Derby), the
foreign secretary, was personally rather indifferent and declined to believe in
a possible French annexation. It has been argued however that, but for the
Franco-Prussian War, Tunis would have been French in 1870; Newton,
Lord Lyons, vol. 1, pp. 199-200. The Italian government certainly feared
that possibility; Gorrini, Tunisi e Biserta, p. 8 and n. 1.
[8] WP/Wood to Hammond/29 Oct 67; ibid/Memo by Wood/9 July 1870.

becoming a French lake and there was always a certain independence of mind in the way Wood interpreted his instructions,
albeit a circumspect independence. Often regarded as hostile
to France, which he denied, it is more true to say that he completely identified himself in his private as well as his official
capacity with the policy of bolstering up the independence of
the Ottoman empire and furthering the political and commercial
interests of the country he represented. This throughout his
long career brought him frequently into conflict with the
ambitions of France. In that conflict his acumen and command
of the principal Mediterranean languages, Arabic, Turkish,
Greek, French and Italian, as well as his understanding of the
oriental mind and the labyrinth of intrigue that surrounded the
oriental court, made him a formidable opponent.[9]

On his arrival in Tunis, he had found the numerous Maltese
colony living in wretched and unhealthy conditions. In 1863,
in spite of the disgust and resentment of his French and
Italian colleagues, he had secured from a reluctant beylical
government an important convention which substantially
improved conditions for the Maltese. For it gave British subjects a right which no Mohammedan government had hitherto
conceded to foreigners, the right to possess real property in the
Regency, even though suits between Europeans—and Europeans and natives—were to be heard by a Tunisian court, the
Sharâa, with the consul merely executing judgement. The
result had been much material progress and extensive urban
development.[10] In addition, it was Wood's boast that his copious

[9] WP/Memo as to the Services of Sir Richard Wood/to Salisbury, 11 Mar
1879. The best account of his early career is in A. B. Cunningham, *The
Early Correspondence of Richard Wood, 1830–41*. Wood became dragoman
at the Constantinople embassy in 1834 and consul at Damascus in 1841.
Rumours in circles hostile to Wood stated that he came from a family half
Jew and half Armenian and that 'Wood' was a translation of the Arabic
'Rattab'. It is very difficult to discover any reliable information on this; but
it may be noted that there was an equally colourful explanation of the ante-
cedents of the French representative, Roustan. The question is discussed by
Professor Ganiage, op. cit., pp. 25-26, who has since been conviced by papers
of the Raffo family—with which Wood was connected—of Wood's Jewish
ancestry and the anglicisation of his name; private letter to author, 11 Jan
1971.
[10] Ibid. See A. P., vol. lxvi, p. 1159, *Convention relative to the holding of
Real Property by British subjects*, 10 Oct 1863. The convention was adopted
by Italy in 1868 and France in 1871. The Porte had made similar concessions,
but only 'on paper'.

knowledge of Islamic law had made it possible for him to urge successfully upon the Bey a programme of reforms—promulgated in what were termed Organic Laws. He was not so keen, however, to remember that those laws had not been particularly effective.

Yet he could claim to have rendered a signal service to the beylical government at a moment when it was in desperate straits. Ministerial corruption coupled with the fact that the national exchequer had never really recovered from the loss of income following the abolition of the slave trade, had made the ruler of Tunis an easy prey for unscrupulous financiers. His indebtedness increased. Particularly notorious 'loans' were made to him in 1863, 1865 and 1867 by that evil genius of Tunis, Erlanger, the Paris banker and his associates. These transactions seemed to have given a deadly blow to the shaky finances of the government, which in fact received only a fraction of the proceeds of the loans. It was Wood who now energetically resisted a declaration of insolvency which, as the events of 1867 had showed, could easily have led to a French occupation. Instead he successfully proposed the establishment of an international financial commission.[11] France, Italy and Britain were represented on that commission which was accorded a decisive voice in the fiscal affairs of the Tunisian government.

Events in Europe rather than in Tunis now frustrated French policy. With their defeat at the hands of the Germans during the Franco-Prussian war, the prestige of the French in Tunis suffered a disastrous decline. French policy had perforce to adapt itself to this new state of affairs. Where before 1871 the

[11] WP/Memo as to the Services of Sir Richard Wood/to Salisbury, 11 Mar 1879. There was talk of a French annexation in 1868, when the French delivered an ultimatum to the Bey, declaring to the Italians that they intended not occupation but the protection of their interests; Gorrini, op. cit., p. 8. Of the 1863 'loan' of 35 million francs, the Bey actually received under 6 million and worse was to follow. When general French diplomatic support for this large-scale plundering was exhausted, Erlanger had recourse to his associate, Baron Erlanger (and Co.) of Frankfort, who, as an acquaintance of Bismarck, got strong German support for further preposterous demands; FO 102/90/78/Wood to Granville/3 Oct 1871; ibid/93/4.13.16.18.26/4 Feb, 21 May, 19 June, 15 July, 20 Aug 1872; ibid/Tel/Granville to Wood/18 July 1872. Ganiage deals at length with how the small and disreputable house of Erlanger secured such important 'business', how prominent men—even French ministers—became involved and how the Tunisian prime minister and others shared the conspiracy and the spoils; op. cit., chap. 6 and pp. 335-61.

French had attempted to overthrow the independence of the Regency, now French diplomats tried to maintain the *status quo*.[12] The Italians had very different ideas. In Rome there was a widespread feeling that, if Tunis were to fall under the sway of any European country, that country should be Italy. The existence of an Italian colony there far greater numerically than that of France, the appeal of a colonial possession as a sort of 'status symbol', and the importance of the Mediterranean enhanced by the opening of the Suez canal in 1869, all caused increasingly greedy eyes to be cast on the nearby Barbary coast. Previously, during Tunisian insurrections in 1864, the Italian cabinet had surreptitiously prepared an expedition of some 22,000 men to take possession of a portion of Tunisian territory, apparently with the connivance of France, an expedition countermanded—according to the surprisingly well-informed Wood—as a result of Turkish threats.[13] Four years later, Italy signed a convention with the Bey which consolidated her extra-territorial privileges and assured her of most-favoured-nation treatment in commercial matters.[14] Now, in 1871, the relative impotence of France seemed to stimulate the aggressiveness of Italy. Almost immediately, in the 'Gedeida farm' question, a case as trivial as it was dubious (involving the usual fantastic claim for damages) was construed as a 'violation of domicile'. This led to a demand by Italy for so extensive an increase in consular rights of jurisdiction that, in the opinion of Wood, it would have amounted to an 'abdication of the Bey's territorial sovereign rights'. Once again, England and Turkey—this time

[12] D.D.F. 1/1/8.65.106.
[13] FO 102/150/Memo by Hertslet/23 Oct 1874; ibid/99/43/Wood to Derby/15/Sep 1874; D.D.F. 1/1/119; Gorrini, op. cit., p. 6; Peteani, *La questione libica nella diplomazia europea*, pp. 13-17. Much has been made of Napoleon III's alleged 'offer' of Tunis to Italy in 1864 (e.g. Chiala, *Pagine di storia contemporanea*, vol. 2, p. 223; Cilibrizzi, *Storia parlamentare, politica e diplomatica d'Italia*, vol. 2, p. 213; Toscano, op. cit., p. 120) but positive evidence is slight and Cowley, in Paris, heard that he had simply said that 'personally he should not have the slightest objection'; 499 Conf/to Russell/28 April 1865, in FO 335/116/3/10 Conf/FO to Wood/2 May 1865. Wood attributed diminished Franco-Italian rivalry to the Emperor's readiness to see part of Tunis fall to Italy (with the River Madjerdah presumably going to France); FO 102/90/40 Sec & Conf/Wood to Granville/ 10 May 1871.
[14] 'La Question italienne en Tunisie' (preface by Delbos), *Cahiers d'Information Français*, No. 3, p. 5; Toscano, op. cit., p. 119. Concluded on 8 Sep 1868, this treaty was to be of great significance in the future.

with French aid—caused an Italian expedition to stay, chafing, in its home port.[15] The direction of affairs at the Quirinal was at this time again in the hands of the Marchese Visconti Venosta, hero of the Risorgimento, former supporter of Cavour and a man well disposed towards France. It is not surprising that he was now ready to recognise that the miserably poor Italian state could not afford 'the luxury of an Algeria', and that Tunisia had become a forbidden fruit which he would 'refuse if offered on a plate'.[16]

For Wood the road was now clear to advance the traditional British policy and his first endeavour was to 'place the Regency beyond the reach of foreign attack and aggression'[17] by the established method of maintaining the Bey's legal dependence on the Sultan. In 1864 the increasing fear in Tunis of European invasion had enabled Wood to induce the Bey to set aside his rooted but now lesser preoccupation with Ottoman ambitions and agree that the security of Tunis and its ruler depended on a 'frank and formal recognition of the Suzerainty of the Sultan'. French determination had then prevented the promulgation of a Firman which would have given that recognition publicly. It was only because the French were no longer in a position to exercise such pressure in Tunis and because the temporarily aggressive attitude of Italy had increased apprehensions in the Regency that the Bey now consented to issue the Firman advised by Wood. This meant that Britain could henceforward argue with more force that Tunis was a Turkish possession and, as such, came under the provisions of the Treaty of Paris of 1856, which bound the signatory powers to intervene and mediate in any dispute with Turkey. In practice, any real change in the relationship of Regency and Porte had been sedulously avoided. The one thing the Bey lost was the dangerous sovereign right to alter the frontiers of Tunis,[18] for the only likely alteration

---

[15] After delay, arbitration was agreed and, as the award was in favour of the Bey, there was much criticism of the Rome government in the Italian press. FO 102/90/2, 3, 17, 18, 19, 25, 28, 30, 34/Wood to Granville/14, 17 Jan, 11, 21, 21 Feb, 14, 15, 20, 28 Mar 1871; ibid/93/35, 36/28, 29 Oct 1872; ibid/95/10/12 May 1873; D.D.F. 1/1/65.

[16] FO 335/134/2/Derby to Wood/11 Jan 1875, encl.

[17] FO 102/90/40 Sec & Conf/Wood to Granville/10 May 1871.

[18] FO 102/90/57, 81, 84, 86, 88, 91/Wood to Granville/22 July, 3, 14, 21, 31 Oct, 25 Nov 1871; ibid/95/20/28 July 1873; ibid/103/437/Elliott to Granville/ 28 Dec 1871.

would be the dismemberment of his country. As for the French, after making strenuous efforts to enlist the support of Italy, Austria and Russia against the Firman, they were reduced to a simple refusal to recognise its validity. Their policy now sought to avoid anything that menaced the *status quo*, since, as the foreign minister, de Rémusat, said, they could not hope to 'modify it to their advantage'.[19]

THE CONVENTION OF 19 JULY, 1875

Wood's star was now in the ascendant and he had replaced the French representative in the affections of the Beylical government. It was clear to him, however, that there would be a challenge to meet when France recovered from her drubbing at the hands of the Germans. If only really substantial British economic interests were involved, he was sure that such a challenge would be easier to counter and support for a vigorous policy more likely to be forthcoming from London. Notwithstanding Tunisian reluctance to permit the formation of foreign companies, he now obtained important concessions for the construction of a railway and a gas works, with the object of 'introducing foreign capital and thereby developing the resources of the country and adding to its prosperity'.[20] Central to his efforts in the field was his concern to conclude a modern commercial treaty in place of antiquated arrangements dating to the days of the Corsairs, privateers and Christian slaves. When the news reached him that the French were beginning negotiations for a treaty, he took advantage of the fact that fourteen years previously the foreign secretary, Clarendon, had told him the sort of treaty Britain would like when possible. He blithely informed Lord Granville, now in office, that the time was ripe for carrying out 'Lord Clarendon's instructions', and notified the Tunisian government of his intention to revise the Anglo-Tunisian treaties. Nearly all the terms he proposed had the object of clearing away obstacles to the development of British trade and enterprise in Tunis. Restrictive monopolies,

[19] Ibid. D.D.F. 1/1/106; FO 102/103/391, 400 Conf/Elliott to Granville/ 31 Oct, 14 Nov 1871; WP/Memo by Wood/11 Mar 1879.
[20] WP/Memo by Wood/to Salisbury, 11 Mar 1878; Ganiage, op. cit., pp. 422-3; Raymond, op. cit., p. 59; Blet, *France d'Outre-Mer*, p. 73.

which successive beys had not infrequently granted, were to be virtually abolished, while clause after clause of Wood's draft was designed so to free British enterprise that he covered practically every field of activity in which a business or professional man might be interested in the future. These included the abolition of nearly all monopolies, the right to carry on coasting trade, the formation of societies, joint stock companies and banks, the establishment of factories, the free exercise of all kinds of industry, arts and professions, and the importation of agricultural machinery, cattle and steam machinery. In return, Wood thought Britain should as a *quid pro quo* agree to an increase in most import duties from three to eight per cent, and also to permit the Bey, under conditions, to prohibit the import of gunpowder, which was being extensively smuggled by Maltese. Under a Treaty of Friendship which was also proposed, the two countries would refer any serious dispute to arbitration, and this, if other powers were led to adopt it, would not only deter the impetuous severing of relations that occurred periodically, but place the Bey:

> . . . in a much more favourable position to settle the dispute or question without being constrained to yield concessions likely to engender fresh differences.[21]

The Foreign Office began a leisurely examination of the question. Wood's drafts had been modelled on The General Treaty and Convention of Commerce with Morocco of 9 December 1856, which Clarendon had sent him 'for his partial guidance' and which had been substantially amended. As usual the Consul-General's opinion was rated highly and Granville wrote to him frankly:

> Your intimate knowledge of the requirements of British interests in the Regency makes me well satisfied that the general provisions which you have proposed for their protection are well calculated to attain their object.[22]

Nevertheless, several important changes were made and some of the phraseology was altered. For the convention with

[21] FO 102/103/74/Wood to Granville/12 Sep 1871. The proposals were communicated to his 'French colleague'.
[22] Ibid. FO 102/103/5/Granville to Wood/28 May 1872; ibid/FO to Board of Trade/22 April 1872.

Morocco treated that country as an independent state, but Britain naturally insisted that any agreement should treat Tunis as being under the suzerainty of the Porte. For the same reason it was deemed advisable to discard the idea of a separate political treaty and include the essential points in the proposed commercial convention. The most important change of all was inadvertently caused by Henry Bergne, a Foreign Office Clerk, whom Granville had asked for a report. Wood, following the precedent of the Italian treaty of 1868 with Tunis (as indeed were the French in their negotiations with the Bey), had suggested that the convention should last for twenty-eight years, with provision for it to continue for another twenty-one years, if not denounced, and for modifications every seven years. Bergne objected to this because on the one hand the life of the treaty was abnormally long and on the other because it could be terminated with nothing in its place. What he preferred, and persuaded Granville to accept, was a stipulation of the Morocco Convention, in which, as he said:

> . . . the period of fixed duration is much shorter, at the end of which either Party may call for a revision, but the Convention is to remain in force until the revision shall have been finished, and a new Convention concluded.[23]

Little did he know that he was constructing for British interest in Tunis that 'fortress position' which, until the close of the century, was to cause so much irritation to the French. The former Anglo-Tunisian treaties, with the single understandable exception of the 1863 convention, were not confirmed, being regarded as antiquated and 'even undignified'.[24] The initiative, therefore, had been Wood's, and the only thing which seemed of concern to Granville directly was whether, in view especially of the recent Firman, the Bey could conclude a treaty without the concurrence of the Porte. Wood forthwith wrote to Sir Henry Elliot, the British ambassador at Constantinople, who obtained an assurance from Server Pasha, the Grand Vizier, that:

[23] Ibid. FO 102/103/Memo/20 Dec 1871; ibid./Pr/to Bergne/17 Feb 1872; ibid/Memo by H. Elliot/15 Mar 1872; ibid./FO to Board of Trade/22 April 1872.
[24] FO 102/103/5/Granville to Wood/28 May 1872.

> The Porte entertains . . . no intention of raising difficulties in
> the relations between the Bey and foreign states, or of preventing
> him from entering as heretofore into international arrangements
> of a purely and bona fide commercial character.[25]

The path to success was not to be smooth. In July 1872
Wood reported that, when he broached the matter of a new
convention, the Bey was 'highly gratified and thankful' especially for the information that no rights were required which
limited his internal authority. Nevertheless, by the following
February, apologies were going to London for the delay in
negotiating the convention, the ostensible reason for which was
that the French chargé d'affaires (as the Consul-General was
often termed) had submitted certain proposals in his draft
treaty which the Bey was unwilling to accept and which made
him hesitate to commence negotiations with Wood lest he
should 'unnecessarily wound the susceptibility' of the French
representative. According to the Tunisian Prime Minister,
objections had been raised to reconfirming the article in French
treaties from 1604 to 1830 by which the Capitulations between
France and the Porte were applied to the Regency and also to a
binding commitment to maintain the International Financial
Commission.[26]

The second was a sore point for Wood. The Financial
Commission set up by the three powers in 1869 had two sections,
an executive board and a board of control. In the latter,
though French nationals were the principal creditors, England
and Italy had triumphantly acquired equal representation,
while in the former the only European was a French Inspector
of Finances. It is not surprising that Wood, who was certainly
not inimical to the Commission as such, was soon found
complaining that the Tunisian Government—with the connivance of France—was emasculating the powers of the board
of control and refusing to permit it to 'verify and approve' the
operations of the executive board as it should do. Paris seemed
quite satisfied with the presence of a French official in the
administration of Tunisian affairs, in which sphere the execu-

[25] Ibid/437/Elliott to Granville/28 Dec 1871; ibid/74/Wood to Granville/
12 Sep 1871, min.
[26] Ibid/17/Wood to Granville/8 July 1872; ibid/3 Col/Wood to Granville/
4 Feb 1873; FO 335/128/9/1/Granville to Wood/21 Feb 1873.

tive board inevitably played an increasing role.[27] Moreover, there was an essential divergence of purpose between the Financial Commission, whose major preoccupation was to ensure that Tunisian revenues and resources were used to pay the interest on the now unified Tunisian debt promptly, and Wood's policies of stimulating English enterprise and promoting commercial stability in the Regency in order to prevent Tunis being dominated by any one foreign power.[28] At the same time the rascally and aged Prime Minister, Mustapha Kaznadar, whose greedy corruption had made possible the diastrous Erlanger loans, had come to resent the Commission's restrictions on his liberty of action, and now found a field of common interest with the English Consul-General, who— though he would not attempt to destroy the Commission— needed the Prime Minister's cooperation, both to get concessions for English nationals and to prevent the Commission from rendering those concessions nugatory. He was now pre-eminent among the foreign representatives[29] and the driving force that was Richard Wood was determined that the financial might of the city of London should make itself felt in Tunis. There can be little doubt that he was responsible for the visit to England of Si Hamida Ben Ayad, a British 'protected person' and confidential friend of the Prime Minister, a visit which resulted in an important concession to a certain Harvey

[27] WP/Wood to Hammond/9 July 1870; ibid/Memo by Wood/16 Aug 1870. In 1871, Wood fought to save the Commission; Ganiage, op. cit., pp. 401-2. See also A. P., vol. lxxv, report by Consul-General Reade, 1880 (on the financial condition of Tunis).

[28] Ibid. One example was a virtually new export, esparto grass (used for paper making) which Wood induced Messrs. Perry & Bury of Liverpool to undertake—an enterprise of great value to southern Tunis. The Financial Commission imposed a 20 per cent export tax, in spite of which esparto grass became a staple product: A.P. lxx, *Report by Sir R. Wood on the Trade and Commerce of Tunis*; Ganiage, op. cit., p. 423. The Commission also claimed to overrule concessions for public works by a duty on the imported materials; FO 335/128/9/4/Granville to Wood/15 April 1873. When the 'assigned revenues', those most easily collected, were not enough for the debt interest, as was usually the case, the Tunisian Treasury would borrow again to meet the deficit and suffering was great; Reade, op. cit.; 'La France en Tunisie', *Revue des Deux Mondes*, vol. 79, pp. 788-9 (in d'Estournelles de Constant, op. cit., part 3, chap. 2).

[29] Gorrini, op. cit., p. 45. See also note 20. *N.B.* The Title of Prime Minister (and occasionally Grand Vizier), though not existing officially, was normally used by the Consular Corps to describe the minister who had most power from the autocratic Bey.

Ranking for the establishment of a bank. When it became known that it was to be a bank of issue and 'to have the assistance of and preference on the part of the Government as much as lay in its power' (clause 3), national interest and anxiety over the 'veritable monopoly' and 'disasters easy to foresee' led to a protest from the Consular Corps as well as the Financial Commission. The Bey was prevailed upon to withdraw the concession.[30]

That the niceties of a policy framed and carried out largely by Wood were not entirely understood by Granville is clear, and the foreign secretary frankly admitted:

> I am rather puzzled by the Tunisian question. The power of the purse is undoubtedly in the hands of the (? bond) holders. The French have no objection to making use of this power, while the Italian Consul is I believe a rogue.
>
> It is a matter of degree—how far we can leave administrative power to the Bey, without risk to the revenue we are bound to collect.[31]

He was content to rely on Wood's expertise and, when any burning question reached his desk, to act on the advice of legal experts. Already in April 1873 he had inclined to the French view that the Bey had no power to make concessions for railways and public works against the wishes of the Commission and, four months later, took the same line in a question of farming revenues by auction.[32] For some months he now countered the French view that the concession to Ranking created a privileged government deposit bank, by arguing that British policy was not to interfere in the affairs of private speculators, and even went as far as to say that a 'completely different and intolerable position' was created when a foreign government brought all possible pressure to bear 'to induce the Bey of Tunis to forfeit his word to a British company'.[33] The issue was finally referred

[30] In 1871, the Commission had strenuously opposed the concession of the Mint to Ben Ayad, who was supported by Wood. FO/102/95/39/Wood to Granville/14 Oct 1873; FO/335/128/9/Projet de Décret; ibid/Consular Corps to Wood/28 May 1873.

[31] PRO 30/29/109/Granville to Lyons/25 June 1873.

[32] FO 335/128/9/4/Granville to Wood/15 April 1873; ibid/11/3 July 1873; ibid/13/1 Aug 1873, with copy of 361/Granville to Lyons/29 July 1873.

[33] PRO 30/29/109/Granville to Lytton/11 Oct 1873; FO 335/128/9/13/ to Wood/1 Aug 1873; ibid/14 Conf/15 Aug 1873; ibid/17/22 Oct 1873 (with 199/Lytton to Granville/10 Oct 1873).

to Gladstone. It has been suggested that the essential test of policy for the Liberal Prime Minister was not 'British interests' but 'civilisation and humanity'.[34] Certainly the jungle war of diplomacy in the corrupt undergrowth of Tunisian politics was quite foreign to him and there is no mistaking his distaste for a 'promise of preference' couched in the most vague terms. Yet his only hint at action was 'to suppose it well worth the while' for the parties to surrender or alter the article containing that promise.[35] The outcome was that, despite the Bey's withdrawal of the concession, Wood was to be found informing Granville's successor in March, 1874, that he had 'maintained the concession' and the bank was functioning, though prepared to surrender the rights of currency issue.[36]

In the summer of 1873, undeterred by the fact that his economic policies were beginning to come under such heavy fire, Wood had commenced the negotiations which had been authorised more than a year previously. The discussions proceeded smoothly and only one question gave rise to a serious difference of view point—consular jurisdiction in civil and criminal cases. The Prime Minister complained that a Tunisian subject could never know under which law differences arising between him and a foreigner would be settled; objections were raised to embodying in a solemn treaty the 'encroachments' on the jurisdiction of the Tunisian government, and the Bey himself inveighed against the 'humiliation' of passively assisting in a foreign criminal's trial, with no other right than 'concurring' with the Consul the degree of punishment. Wood naturally argued the obstacles in the way of a Christian obtaining justice in Mohammedan courts and was able to say that in a single treaty, that with Austria on 17 January 1856 the Bey had in fact already conceded the right of criminal jurisdiction.[37] Nine months were now to elapse and a change of government in London to occur before Wood got an answer to his proposals

[34] Seton-Watson, *Disraeli, Gladstone and the Eastern Question*, p. 566.
[35] Ramm (ed.), *The Political Correspondence of Mr Gladstone and Lord Granville, 1868–1876*, vol. 2, Nos. 912, 928.
[36] FO 335/131/17/Wood to Derby/24 Mar 1874. The determination had also been born to include a clause on the rights and claims of the Bank of Tunis in the treaty under negotiation; FO 335/128/9/17/Granville to Wood/ 22 Oct 1873; ibid/103/3 Ccl/Derby to Wood/13 May 1874.
[73] FO 102/103/22/Wood to Granville/4 Aug 1873.

BDT D

in detail, during which time the Board of Trade and the Law Officers of the Crown were consulted and the settlement of a relevant case in Morocco was awaited. A compromise had been suggested by Mustapha Kaznadar, the Prime Minister, that Tunis should concede the right of criminal jurisdiction—if England still insisted on the necessity for so humiliating a stipulation—on the understanding that another condition of the Austrian treaty on the trial of civil and criminal cases was included. Derby agreed, provided that Mixed Courts were established, at the same time insisting on 'express provision . . . for the trial of British subjects having committed crimes' and suggesting that the 'humiliation' of the Bey could be avoided by omitting reference to his 'concurrence'—a procedure that would obviously involve an increase in consular power. Suits between foreigners were to be decided solely by the foreign consuls. The only other amendment of note was a clause respecting the 'rights and claims of the Bank of Tunis' and Wood was authorised to sign the convention.[38]

That possibility, however, now no longer existed, for there had been in the meantime considerable political changes in Tunis itself entailing the fall of Mustapha Kaznadar, on whose complaisance and on whose hostility towards the Financial Commission the commercial concessions arranged by Wood so much depended, and his replacement by his rival, General Keireddin. A man of Circassian origin, with a reputation, rare in the Beylical court, 'of being thoroughly honest', the general was ambitious, practical, strong minded and rather haughty.[39] As President of the Financial Commission, his opposition to the corruption of Kaznadar, his father-in-law, as well no doubt as personal interest, had led him to concert with the now determined French the campaign against the Prime Minister, which succeeded largely through influencing the increasingly senile Bey by making judicious use of his disreputable young favourite. Keirredin in power meant to Wood that his whole policy was in

[38] Ibid/Memoranda/28 Jan, 2 May 1874; ibid/FO to Board of Trade/ 20 Aug 1873; ibid/1459/Board of Trade to FO/14 Nov 1873; ibid/3 Ccl/ Derby to Wood/13 May 1874.
[39] Wood had 'never' heard him accused of corruption in any single instance. WP/Wood to Layard/22 Oct 1878; WP/Layard to Wood/3 Oct 1878. The 'sons' of the Bey, Greek and Circassian slaves he had brought up, occupied the highest posts.

jeopardy and that no new concession would be granted to Englishmen 'without a previous reference to Paris', which, in view of the 'systematic hostility of his French colleagues, would be futile.[40] All that was left was for Wood to try—and fail—to obtain British 'protection' for the fallen minister who was disgraced and ruined, since it could not be seen in London what the government had to do 'with these Tunisian intrigues and speculations'.[41]

French activities in Tunis now resulted in a rumour that the Bey was about to repudiate the Firman and place Tunis under the suzerainty of France, a rumour which led to concern in Constantinople, Rome, Berlin and London, which was categorically repudiated in Paris and which led to a restatement of British policy towards Tunis. Lord Lyons, the ambassador in Paris, told the French that the affairs of the Regency were 'particularly interesting and important to Her Majesty's Government', especially in view of the neighbourhood of Malta, and Granville, in a conversation with the German ambassador, Münster, said that Britain had always felt a strong objection to the 'rectification' of the Tunis-Algeria boundary:

> . . . as it would not only give the French a commanding position
> in the Mediterranean but would put Tunis entirely at the mercy
> of France . . .[42]

The resilience of Wood, as his influence at the Bardo collapsed, was remarkable. Instead of writing off Keirredin as incorrigibly a 'creature of France', the way his less percipient Italian colleague did,[43] he set himself the hard task of winning the confidence of a minister with whom he had crossed swords so frequently. He had, moreover, that patience so essential to the successful diplomat. For a period he confined his activities to consular routine, even taking a long leave of absence, in the

---

[40] FO 102/95/29 Conf/Wood to Granville/8 Sep 1873.

[41] Ibid/39, 40 Conf/Wood to Granville/14, 14 Oct 1873; ibid/20/Granville to Wood/29 Nov 1873. Luckily for him, Ben Ayad, who negotiated with Ranking, already enjoyed protected status.

[42] FO 335/131/3/Granville to Wood/7 Jan 74; ibid/4 Conf/Granville to Wood/14 Jan 1874. encl/1091/Lyons to Granville/28 Dec 1873; ibid/8/ Granville to Russell/13 Jan 1874; ibid/363/Paget to Granville/17 Dec 1873; FO 102/95/Tel/Granville to Wood/29 Dec 1873; ibid/99/1, 4/Wood to Granville/2, 20 Jan 1874.

[43] Gorrini, op. cit., p. 46, n.1.

confidence that this would be taken by Keirredin as indifference to Tunisian affairs, and that other foreign agents would not be able to resist the opportunity to intrigue or bring pressure to bear on the government—thus enlightening the new Prime Minister as to the realities of the situation. So indeed it transpired. Décazes, in Paris, soon had to admit that the interference of the French representative (de Vallat) in Tunisian internal affairs had 'given rise to disquiet and difficulty, without advancing French interests', and de Vallat's inept successor (de Billing) gave serious offence. At the same time the Italian representative did nothing to conceal the fact that Keirredin's premiership was 'specially distasteful' to him.[44] On the other hand, as the man who had negotiated the Firman at Constantinople, who desired the confidence of the consular body and who was basically pro-Tunisian rather than pro-French, Keirredin soon came to resent the interference of his erstwhile colleague, the French Vice-President of the Financial Commission, as much as his predecessor had done, to castigate it as 'unbearable' and to make representations until he was recalled.[45]

By the autumn of 1874, therefore, Wood's position had quite changed. The contradictory policies of individual French representatives and the colonial ambitions of Italy (as well as the 'dubious' policies of Germany) were attacked by Keirredin, who confided to the English Agent that he had resolved to depend on English support and would:

> . . . encourage all English enterprises and undertakings, the execution of which was in any way practicable.[46]

A minister whose natural sympathies inclined him towards France had come to agree that the best chance of Tunisian independence lay in the policies of Wood. Another important factor which may have helped to change the affiliation of the Tunisian minister was the attitude of Bismarck. When rumours of impending French suzerainty became current, the German Chancellor had taken an unexpectedly strong line and said that he would not tolerate any such development, even sending a

[44] FO 102/99/7 Conf/FO to Wood/12 Feb 1874; ibid/43, 51, 62, 64/ Wood to Derby/15 Sep 27, Oct, 22, 23 Dec 1874.
[45] FO 102/99/13/Wood to Derby/25 Feb 1874.
[46] As note 44.

naval force to impress the point upon the Bey.[47] Wood had many private confidants and, for a junior diplomat, often showed himself incredibly well informed on matters of high politics. In August 1874 Derby was told, on the authority of 'an authentic and confidential source', that Bismarck had suggested to the French President, Marshall MacMahon, that:

> ... instead of meditating the reconquest of Alsace and Lorraine, which would plunge the two nations into a fresh and disastrous war, France should seek a compensation for her lost provinces in the annexation of the Regency of Tunis and even that of Tripoli if necessary, and that he (the Prince) would undertake to keep quiet Great Britain and Italy in the event they should attempt to interfere with her.[48]

If Wood used this information to influence Keirredin, as he had done the news of the earlier German intervention, it would undoubtedly have carried some weight with the man who later became sincerely attached to the Anglo-Turkish alliance as 'the sole means' of saving the Ottoman Empire.[49] The British Consul-General was quite competent to develop the theme that the power which had, only a few years previously, helped the Russians to remove one of the conventional safeguards— for Turkey—of the Paris Treaty of 1856, the neutralisation of the Black Sea, would without compunction contemplate the disintegration of Turkey and its Empire, in order to prevent another Franco-German war.[50]

Whatever the truth of the matter, the door to English concessions was now certainly not closed and, while some concern was being shown in London over what seemed ominous French designs—to build a railway from Algeria to Biserta, to excavate the port of Carthage and cut a canal from Gabès to create an inland sea—Wood was accomplishing what, to one

---

[47] FO 102/99/11, 12/Wood to Granville/9, 16 Feb 1874; Newton, op. cit., vol. 2, pp. 55, 60.

[48] FO 102/99/38 Sec & Conf/Wood to Derby/11 Aug 1874. This tallies absolutely with Bismarck's well-known intimation to Hohenlohe of his impending change of policy towards France, *five months later*; G. P. 1/194. Ironically, on the same day the French consul was declaiming against 'the notorious support he (Bismarck) is according to Italian pretensions' and the numerous German visitors to the interior 'with an object easy to appreciate'; AAE/Tunis/42/3/Roustan to Décazes/5 Jan 1875.

[49] WP/Wood to Layard/22 Oct 1878.

[50] See note 48.

Frenchman at least, was his 'crowning achievement'. This was
the 'barrier between Algiers and Tunis' erected by new English
railway concessions.[51] Not that Keirredin wished to have only
an English string to his bow. For he was endeavouring to heal
the breach with the French and, with perhaps a little oriental
exaggeration and language similar to that he had used to Wood,
he informed the new French Consul-General, the energetic
Roustan, of his 'firm intention to procede in harmony with him
and no-one else', describing Wood's policy as personal rather
than official.[52] The negotiations for the Anglo-Tunisian treaty,
however, were now continuing. When in January 1875 they
were nearly completed, Keirredin passed on the information
to Roustan, who took the opportunity to argue that the unrestricted Maltese importation of gunpowder could be serious
to France in the event of an Algerian insurrection. Wood, of
course, unknown to him had already proposed to rectify this
and when Keirredin extended his confidence by showing
Roustan the 'voluminous document' of the draft treaty in March,
the French agent was of course highly gratified. What seemed
quite inexplicable to him was 'how the English government
could have consented to so notable a derogation of its rights' as
to defer to the Bey and his representatives the judgement of
civil and commercial cases. This 'surrender' would place Tunis
in a more favourable position than Turkey or Egypt and was
something he would not even dare to propose to Paris for
adoption.[53] However, after some further delay caused by an
argument with the Financial Commission, Wood was able to
report the acceptance of the draft treaty with only minor
modifications to four of its forty-two articles. The controversial
Bank of Tunis clause was dropped, but, as it was to the bank

[51] D.D.F. 1/2/49. 193; FO 102/150/Memo by Hertslet/23 Oct 1874.
Tunisian public opinion was opposed to the Inland Sea; AAE/Tunis
Ccl/60/17/Roustan to Décazes/16 Mar 1875. The Italians were attempting
to make common cause with England against French attempts at economic
penetration; Bloch, Les Relations entre la France et la Grande-Bretagne, p. 91.
[52] AAE/Tunis/42/2/Roustan to Décazes/5 Jan 1875. Décazes rejoiced
that Keirredin was not opposed to the independence of the country or 'our
legitimate influence', and that he tried to give a 'character of confidence'
from the first in his relations with Roustan; ibid/2/to Roustan/12 Feb 1875.
[53] Ibid/6, 12, 13/Roustan to Décazes/26 Jan, 15, 15 Mar 1875; AAE/
Tunis/Ccl/60/15/Roustan to Décazes/15 Mar 1875. The Italian Consul,
Pinna, felt the same about Wood's concessions in jurisdiction.

that the important Concession of Inland Railways had been granted by the government, its establishment might be considered to have been tacitly recognised as an accomplished fact. To the satisfaction also of the Foreign Office, the Bey accepted the article on criminal jurisdiction to which he had taken so great an exception, including the words, 'in concurrence with H.H. the Bey'. Wood was authorised to sign the convention, which he did on 19 July 1875.[54]

The signature of the treaty represented a considerable triumph for the policies of Wood, though it was in some important respects to be a Pyrrhic victory. The Tunisian garden could now be unrestrictedly fertilised by English capital and enriched by English skills. There were now guarantees for the position of the Consul and his staff; the maximum freedom for trade; rights to import with taxes not exceeding eight per cent *ad valorem* and no further internal imposts; freedom to develop coastal trade; the abolition of all but a few restrictive trade monopolies; the right (under conditions) to establish commercial, industrial and banking companies and to practise any art, profession or industry; and, of course, the new jurisdictional arrangements. Two clauses only, against slavery and piracy, served as a reminder of the 'bad old days'. While provision was, of course, made for revision of the agreement after seven years, a point of great importance for the future was that the convention was to remain in force until such revision had been agreed.[55] Wood had turned on the tap for the flow of English trade and capital that was intended to bolster Tunisian independence and counter undue economic domination by any one power. The Regency too, under the wiser administration of Keirredin was more prosperous and stable than it had been for years.[56] Unfortunately for him, turning the tap was not enough, for there was no pressure in the pipeline. Though Britain occupied the place of pre-eminence in the field of

[54] FO 102/103/14, 14 Ccl/Wood to Derby/6 April, 27 Sep 1875; ibid/ 5 Ccl/Derby to Wood/31 May 1875. The text is in A.P., vol. lxxxiv, pp. 123 seq., *General Convention between the Governments of Great Britain and Tunis.*
[55] Ibid. Some contemporary writers disregard the treaty. Bloch says, 'It remained a dead letter', op. cit., p. 91; Ganiage apparently does not mention it, op. cit.
[56] FO 102/101/23/Wood to Derby/18 June 1875.

international trade, and in 1870 had exported more than France, Germany and Italy together, an international industrial and commercial crisis, following upon a financial crisis, became general in 1876 and English industry bore the brunt of it for three years.[57] Not only were there no new enterprises launched in Tunis but many of those for whom concessions had been obtained failed.[58] What is more they were falling into the hands of the French, who, as they recovered from the German war, developed an economic offensive of their own, with ultimate aims far different from those of Wood.

In October 1875 Décazes himself was deploring any further expansion of British interests in Tunis, which would 'little by little put the principal industrial resources of the country in the hands of English subjects', and hoping that 'equilibrium should be maintained as much as possible between the rival English and Italian claims'.[59] An acid note was even sent to Roustan to push him to greater activity, after the chargé d'affaires had emphasised the difficulties facing a French engineer in obtaining substantially the railway concession just awarded to the English company. Décazes wrote:

> All projects tending to increase the frequency of commercial relations between Algeria and the Regency have claims on our sympathy. . . . The efforts many of your colleagues make under your eyes to assure the development of the industrial interests of their nationals in Tunisia are for us a motive for not losing sight of the economic advantages which, more than anyone, we have the right to claim by virtue of geographic necessity.[60]

Roustan was far from being a man who needed 'pushing'. From the moment he arrived in Tunis he had seen Wood only as a hated and dangerous adversary, with whom he was prepared to cooperate after a fashion for a year or two to curb the ambitions of Italy.[61] By May 1876, indeed, the prized Tunis–Beja railway concession had been transferred, 'precipitately' as Wood said,

[57] Ensor, *England*, pp. 104-11.
[58] For details see Ganiage, op. cit., pp. 463-4, 566. Raymond, op. cit., pp. 64-5.
[59] AAE/Tunis/42/16/Décazes to Roustan/21 Oct 1875.
[60] Ibid/15/Décazes to Roustan 20/Oct 1875.
[61] Ibid/2/Roustan to Décazes/5 Jan 1875.

to a French company by Keirredin, who told Roustan that the 'whole commercial and even political future of Tunis' was in French hands, as there could be no longer any serious question of English or Italian influence. As the company received the unusual benefit of a guaranteed profit from the Republic, the chances of failure were obviously negligible.[62] Roustan was in fact more and more to receive the support of the kind which made success possible. The understandable hesitation of the Bey to place the whole of a railway to Algeria under one French direction was overcome by intrigue and sheer chicanery. Provision was made that the final link to the frontier should be conceded to a new company, a company which existed only long enough to hand over its concession to the existing Bône-Guelma company. The means by which Roustan came to exercise what Waddington in 1878 was to describe as the 'protectorate in fact' were—as he reported himself—by 'promises and menaces' to the vain and corrupt Ben Ismail, handsome favourite of the Bey, who was awarded the Legion of Honour for his 'services' on the recommendation of Roustan.[63] The fact that Wood got the Bey to recongise his obligation to help Turkey in her war with Russia was hardly a consolation[64] and his long protracted efforts were to receive their *coup de grâce* in the continuing Near Eastern crisis which had become serious in 1876.

In that year Turkey had collapsed into bankruptcy under the incubus of a financial and administrative reform programme it had been unable to sustain and this was a blow to the Mediterranean policy pursued by Britain virtually since the 1830's. For the fear on both sides of the channel of Russian expansion into the Eastern Mediterranean and elsewhere, had been a fear great

[62] FO 102/104/24, 32/Wood to Derby/29 June 12 Aug 1876; D.D.F. 1/2/49.193. A year later, by a little sharp practice, the company got a concession which made a link with Algeria possible; FO 102/108/38/Wood to Derby/28 Aug 1877.

[63] AAE/Tunis/46/Roustan to MFA/22 Jan 1878; ibid/4, Tel 2, 6/25, 28, 29 Jan 1878; ibid/61 Ccl/7/12 Feb 1878; FO 102/108/38/Wood to Derby/28 Aug 1877; ibid/111/to Salisbury/21 May 1878; D.D.F. 1/2/193.234.300; JP/MSS chap. 7/1880; H. Johnston, *The Story of My Life*, p. 68; A. Johnston, *Life and Letters of Sir Harry Johnston*, p. 31. Chosen for his 'good looks', Ismail was 'nervous about the advance of age'.

[64] FO 102/108/44, 45, 48 Conf/to Derby/15 Oct, 5, 5 Nov 1877; D.D.F. 1/2/213.216.220.221.

enough by now to cement Anglo-French rivalry in Constantinople and Cairo into a convenient and effective, though
guarded, cooperation. Britain's main concern was to protect the
more direct route to India (of enhanced importance after the
opening of the Suez canal in 1869), and the land forces of a
revitalised stable and reformed Turkey were to have comple-
mented the British navy in holding the Russians in check by
defending the Straits and Asia Minor. The Turkish failure
meant that this strategy was no longer adequate. The Russians
too—apart from racial and religious feeling towards many
Turkish subjects—had for a long time been hoping for the
opportunity to overthrow the arrangements made by the Treaty
of Paris in 1856 and recover the mouth of the Danube. Their intervention in force(1877-78) and the drastic terms they imposed
upon Turkey led to the assumption in London that the risk of
war was preferable to English acquiescence, so that, in the
circumstances, it was almost inevitable that the Congress of
Berlin should have been held to circumscribe Russian ambitions.[65]

Both the prime minister, Beaconsfield, and Salisbury
had come to the conclusion that only a British occupation of a
place d'armes in the Eastern Mediterranean could hope to
prevent the 'Asiatic Empire' of Turkey disintegrating and
falling into the clutches of the Russians, since it would have
been 'ridiculous', in the view of Salisbury, to attempt to exercise such a 'protective office' from Malta.[66] For France, too, had
made it quite clear that she was 'paralysed by the fear of an
attack from Germany', and that it was unsafe for Britain to rely
on her assistance in the case of Russian aggression in the east.[67]

[65] Robinson, Gallagher and Denny, *Africa and the Victorians*, pp. 76-
82; Sumner, *Russia and the Balkans*; Medlicott, *The Congress of Berlin
and After*, chap. 1; *Bismarck, Gladstone and the Concert of Europe*,
chap. 1; Seton-Watson, *Disraeli, Gladstone and the Eastern Question*, chaps.
1-9.
[66] Lee, *Great Britain and the Cyprus Convention Policy*, p. 32; Cecil, *Life
of Salisbury*, vol. 2, pp. 83, 85-6, 129-30, 213-14; Kennedy, *Salisbury*,
p. 373. If the Russian expansion could be checked, Salisbury thought that the
Turks had a 'fair chance' of holding Constantinople 'for a considerable
period'.
[67] FO 27/2304/2, 16 Conf, 38/Lyons to Derby/1, 5, 15 Jan 1878; ibid/
2305/145 Sec/12 Feb 1878. Austria was also unhelpful; Buckle, op. cit.,
p. 248;Langer, *European Alliances and Alignments*. p. 137.

An attempt by Beaconsfield to include her in a Mediterranean League along with Austria, Italy and Greece proved abortive,[68] with the result that Britain was left to face 'the consequences of Russian encroachment' in Asia alone, in spite of the military action France was pledged to take under the tripartite treaty of 1856. Yet Salisbury had no idea of acquiring Turkish territory for its own sake or of courting the serious breach with France that a monopoly of influence in the Nile valley would have entailed.[69] Indeed, making the observation that 'logic is no use' in negotiating with the French, he is soon found casting round for a 'sweetener' to enable them to wipe away the crocodile tears that would flow when the news of the *place d'armes* chosen (Cyprus) was broken to them. This was so even though the necessity for such a base, to 'mount guard over the en-dangered (Turkish) territory', was, in his eyes, caused by the desertion of 'the Ally who should have made things easy' for Britain.[70]

Obviously no concession to France was possible in Egypt without endangering the route to the east and the same con-sideration precluded abandoning the traditional policy of supporting the none too secure independence of Morocco.[71] In Tunis, however, Salisbury claimed to have no fear of French expansion[72] and it is not surprising that he should consider some form of compensation there as a means of avoiding the expected French recriminations and jealousies over Cyprus. Yet the acquisition of Tunis would have been surely far more than adequate compensation for possible French susceptibili-ties. The impoverished little island of Cyprus, half the size of

[68] FO 363/5/Memo by Tenterden and drafts/9 Mar 1878; FO 45/337/175, 237, 239/Paget to Derby/1, 28, 29 Mar 1878; Buckle, op. cit., pp. 253-5; Crispi, *Memoirs*, vol. 2, pp. 95-7; Peteani, op. cit., pp. 22-3. The Italians refused to participate.

[69] Cecil, op. cit., p. 332; FO 27/2305/130 Sec/Lyons to Derby/8 Feb 1878; Newton, op. cit., p. 123; SP/26/Salisbury to Lyons/22 May 1878. There was no intention of taking Egypt, while France took Tunis, as suggested by the Germans; Buckle, op. cit., 58, 342, 353.

[70] Ibid. The secret agreement of 4 June 1878, under which the Turks conditionally ceded Cyprus, had been preceded, on 30 May 1878, by an-other secret agreement under which the Russians agreed to alter the terms imposed on the Turks; Buckle, op. cit., pp. 283-93; Newton, op. cit., pp. 142-3.

[71] Medlicott, op. cit., pp. 123-5.

[72] SP/26/to Lyons/11 May 1878.

Wales and lacking a deep-water harbour, was hardly the equivalent of the larger and far more populous Tunisia, with its
vaunted anchorage at Biserta.[73] As no-one was more conscious
of what constituted a fair bargain than Salisbury, what he
promised the French at Berlin obviously needs careful consideration.

SALISBURY'S 'OFFER' OF TUNIS

He (Salisbury) lacks honesty, and believes in Prevarication. . . .
He is the man who suggested to the French to take Carthage,
and then denied that he advised them to take Tunis.[74]

This gibe is a blunt contemporary version of what has been
often asserted ever since, that Salisbury made promises at
Berlin which he had no intention of keeping. This view is on
longer tenable. Before the Congress met, Salisbury wrote to
Lord Lyons, the ambassador at Paris, that the idea of a French
acquisition of Tunis was 'an extension of French territory and
influence of which they should not have the slightest jealousy
or fear'.[75] In saying this he made it clear that he was not assuming that Turkey would wish to give up Tunis. He was quite
aware that Lyons believed the French would strongly object to
the Cyprus Convention when they got to hear about it, but
Salisbury hoped that the power of the British battleship fleet
assembled at Portsmouth would limit French action to the
coining of 'epigrams'.[76] The convention was, in fact, kept from
the French until nearly the end of the Congress, presumably
because they might otherwise not have participated.[77]
Waddington was informed, therefore, only on 6 July, 1878, by a
long private letter from Salisbury, in which insistence was laid on
the 'provisional character' of the convention and Britain's

[73] R.I.I.A. Memorandum, *Cyprus* (1955), Appendix 2; Lee, op. cit.,
pp. 165, 189; Roberts, *History of French Colonial Policy*, vol. 1, pp. 263, 269,
270; *Encyclopédie Mensuelle d'Outre-Mer*, 'Tunisia' (1952), p. 25.
[74] Letterpress by 'Jehu Junior' on a *Vanity Fair* cartoon, reproduced in
Kennedy, *Salisbury*, pp. 376-8.
[75] SP/26/to Lyons/11 May 1878.
[76] SP/26/Salisbury to Lyons/5 June 1878; SP/7/Lyons to Salisbury/7
June 1878.
[77] Ibid; FO 27/2310/Lyons to Salisbury/5 June 1878. The questions of
Egypt, Syria and the Holy Places were specifically excluded.

inability without it to defend Asiatic Turkey.[78]It was two days before the French minister telegraphed thenews to Paris, saying that, in spite of Salisbury's assurances, he was 'very disturbed' and promising a full report on the discussions the following day. It may or may not be of significance that no trace of the promised report can be found in the Quaid' Orsay.[79] Salisbury in the meantime had telegraphed that, 'Waddington . . . offers little objection'; he described the reactions of the powers more fully on 10 July:

> Italy I think is rather angry—and Russia of course. But the French have shown no sign of discontent.

His observation two days later that there had been 'no unpleasant feeling to speak of' was accompanied by the information that 'fortunately—very fortunately—Waddington had been squared' five days before.[80]

Beaconsfield and Salisbury were soon made aware that their optimism was not justified. In Paris there was a 'veritable explosion of wrath and indignation',[81] Lyons telegraphed. The *République Française*, Gambetta's influential journal, fulminated against English hypocrisy and referred to the Cyprus Convention as a diplomatic pistol shot. It was even rumoured in Paris that Waddington would receive instructions to walk out of the Congress. There were to be no dramatic gestures. Waddington's signature was already on the Berlin Act and he explained that:

[78] SP/A22/Salisbury to Waddington/6 July 1878 (also FO 363/4); Newton, op. cit., pp. 149-50; Fo 146/2037/426A/Tenterden to Lyons/7 July 1878. See also Lee, op. cit., p. 100, n. 35 and D.D.F. 1/2/p. 352 n. 1.

[79] Ibid.: D.D.F. 1/2/325. Hanotaux later claimed to be told by Florian, secretary at the French Embassy, regarding Salisbury's idea of compensation in Tunis, that he had taken himself a 'plan elaborated by Waddington' to President MacMahon; Hanotaux Papers (Box 6), quoted by Serra, 'L'accordo italo-francese del 1896 sulla Tunisia', *Rivista Storica Italiana*, vol. 73 (3), p. 2 n (1961). This is the 'well attested' incident referred to by Hanotaux in *Contemporary France*, vol. 4, pp. 384-5.

[80] SP(also FO 363)/A22/Salisbury to the Queen and Cross/7 July 1878; SP/Tel 3 Sec/Salisbury to Lyons/10 July 1878; Cecil, op. cit., vol. 2, pp. 294-5. Waddington had signed all the Congress protocols, which were almost finished.

[81] FO 27/2311/548, 549, 556, 559/Lyons to Salisbury/10, 10, 11, 13 July 1878; FO 363/2/Pr & Most Conf/Lyons to Salisbury/10 July 1878; SP/7/Lyons to Salisbury/12, 16 July 1875; FO 146/2061/617 Sec/Lyons to Salisbury/6 Aug 1878; Newton, op. cit., pp. 151-4.

. . . we have obtained the explanations and assurances of which I have immediately apprised you and it cannot be proper to take our observations before the Congress. We are waiting for the opportunity (nous nous sommes réservé) to follow up with the London Cabinet the conversations which admit of the terms it has come to. . . .[82]

The evidence for what had actually passed between Salisbury and Waddington is thus very scanty. The French minister was informed of the existence of the Cyprus Convention on 6 July. A day later he had been 'squared' according to Salisbury. Yet only twenty-four hours after Salisbury thought that Waddington had acquiesced, the Frenchman was reporting that he was 'very disturbed'—in spite of his conviction that the British statesmen had made an agreement with him. Salisbury himself still detected 'no sign of discontent'.

It has been said that 'diplomacy is not the art of conversation; it is the art of negotiating agreements in precise and ratifiable form'.[83] Unfortunately, so far as the Tunis question was concerned, conversation at Berlin would seem to have triumphed at the expense of precision. Salisbury himself supported the convention that no minutes should be made of cabinet meetings, so that the 'flow of suggestions' could attain the 'freedom and fullness' of private conversation, even though he had himself been involved in some of the serious misunderstandings that ensued.[84] Salisbury extended the practice of making no official record of cabinet discussions to not recording every conversation with foreign diplomats, especially when dealing with matters of an exploratory or inconclusive nature. Over the many years he conducted British policy his omissions in this respect led at worst to confusion and at best to gaps in the record of British diplomacy. Salisbury made no note of his conversations with Waddington at Berlin, regarding them as of a 'private character', nor did he send any summary to Lyons in Paris, as

[82] D.D.F. 1/2/327. The French text reads, '. . . nous avions obtenu les explications et les assurances dont je vous ai immédiatement instruit et il ne pouvait entrer dans nos convenances de porter nos observations devant le Congrès. Nous nous sommes réservé de suivre avec le Cabinet de Londres les entretiens que comportent les arrangements qu'il a pris . . .'.
[83] Nicolson, *Diplomacy*, p. 101.
[84] Hankey, *Diplomacy by Conference*, pp. 75, 62-66.

would have been normal after a diplomatic conversation in the Foreign Office.[85]

When Waddington returned to Paris, it would have been somewhat unnatural if the excitement over Cyprus had had no effect on him as he began to disclose his version of the conversations. Within a few days he telegraphed to Roustan that France 'might be led in a short time' to assert her protectorate over Tunis with the consent of Britain and Germany. Speaking to Lyons, he claimed that the Cyprus question would have led to war 'or something very like war' had the chambers been in session. He now asked through the ambassador that the British government should publish Salisbury's explanations and assurances in a 'written, official and so to speak binding shape'. This was 'essential to his own position' and would also help to reconcile the French people. The annexation of Tunis, he added, would not necessarily serve French interests best; what he hoped for was a 'virtual alliance' between the two countries.[86] The fact that Waddington intended to send a despatch to commit him formally made Salisbury a 'little anxious', particularly as he thought that the Frenchman had got his facts wrong.[87] After his recent experiences with the secret Anglo-Russian and Anglo-Turkish conventions, he could not be expected to relish another formal commitment which would hardly please the English public, the Turks or the Italians. The promises were 'difficult to make the subject of binding assurances', he explained to Lyons in a private letter; he would not object if France occupied Tunis, but publicly to encourage her to do so, he added with a touch of irony, 'would be a little difficult', as he could not presume to 'give away other people's property'. The

[85] FO 27/2300/Salisbury to Lyons/7 Aug 78. See also Marsden, *Britain and the End of the Tunis Treaties*, p. 69, n.3.
[86] FO 27/2311/572/Lyons to Salisbury/19 July 1878.
[87] PRO 30/29/143/Salisbury to Granville/14 May 1881. Why Salisbury did not immediately deny Waddington's account, as he considered it inaccurate, he explained three years later, when, incidentally, he had the strongest reasons not to appear responsible for 'offering' Tunis to France. The despatch contained, he said, 'wild proposals for an alliance against Germany for the defence of Holland and Belgium: and threats that unless such an alliance is accepted France will side with Russia'. Consequently he had thought it better not to instruct Lyons to answer such a conversation but to deal with the Tunis question separately in answer to Waddington's own despatches. Gambetta also seems to have spoken strongly to the Prince of Wales in favour of an alliance; Newton, op. cit., p. 157.

Italians would also expect to have some say in what happened
to Tunis. What he suggested, therefore, was a despatch from
Paris in which Waddington would avoid peremptory language
and describe in very general terms 'the territorial points on the
African coast in which France takes an interest'. Salisbury
would then, in as cordial a way as possible, give the assurances
he thought proper.[88]

Salisbury's apprehensions were fully justified. When the
French despatch arrived, he found that Waddington had recorded in it all he remembered of the various discussions at Berlin
as if a single formal conversation had taken place during which
Salisbury had offered him 'annexation pure and simple'.
Statements were attributed to Salisbury that were, in the
future, to be quoted a thousand times and more. 'Take Tunis
if you wish, . . . England will not oppose you there and will
respect your decisions', he was alleged to have said, and, in more
dramatic vein, 'You cannot leave Carthage in the hands of the
barbarians'. In a covering letter Waddington instructed the
ambassador, d'Harcourt, to insist on a categorical answer pledging the English government to give France *carte blanche* in
Tunis, as well as complete and public satisfaction to French
wishes regarding the status of Egypt and Syria (discussed in a
second despatch).[89]

Salisbury reacted vigorously. By quoting single phrases and
vividness in translation, Waddington had, he complained:

> . . . rather given the aspect of positive proposals to observations
> made in the course of a *private and somewhat speculative dis-
> cussion* upon the possible tenour of events under certain possible
> contingencies.

The French minister, he said, made him appear to be giving
away what was not England's to give and, even though he
conceded that Waddington had 'remembered with entire
accuracy the general drift' of his remarks at Berlin, he denied
any offer of annexation. All that he had said was that England
looked with pleasure upon 'any *legitimate* extension of the

[88] SP/26/Salisbury to Lyons/20 July 1878; Newton, op. cit., pp. 154-5;
SP/7/Lyons to Salisbury/21 July 1878.
[89] D.D.F. 1/2/330.331.332; FO 146/2037/426a/Salisbury to Lyons/24
July 1878.

civilising influences of France'. Waddington had ignored his important qualifying references to the rights and claims of other powers, Turkey and Italy in particular, he wrote acidly in a private note to Lyons.[90] For some reason d'Harcourt did not report to Paris these very specific objections on Salisbury's part. On the contrary, according to him Salisbury had agreed there would be no British opposition to exclusive French domination over Tunis and had objected only to the familiarity of the language attributed to him. He was reported as saying:

> I do not deny having spoken those words; but they are in the form of familiar conversation which at first sight I would prefer not to see reproduced textually in a despatch, and I would like to see my opinion rendered in a more diplomatic form.

D'Harcourt, however, did make the observation that Salisbury seemed less inclined to fall in with French wishes than he had been.[91] Waddington's satisfaction when this report reached Paris was clearly not justified[92] and, indeed, the third participant in the talks at Berlin agreed, not with his version of them, but with Salisbury's. For Beaconsfield, too, would not accept the views regarding Tunis attributed to Salisbury and himself, though he did agree that there was 'no jealousy of France's influence in that part of the Mediterranean'.[93]

By a further mischance the diplomatic bag containing Salisbury's remarks did not arrive before Lyons discussed the two French despatches with Waddington, who read out extracts

[90] FO 146/2037/459 Sec/Salisbury to Lyons/24 July 1878. The italics are mine. Salisbury claimed that Waddington had 'accurately recollected the substance of a portion of one conversation'; but there was, however, an absence of pretension on Britain's part.

[91] D.D.F. 1/2/334. Salisbury's version is borne out by a private letter to Lyons, 'The general tenour is quite accurate, but his vivacious French by no means renders the tone of my communication—and what is of more importance *he omits my qualifying references* to the rights and claims of other powers—Turkey and Italy especially'; SP/24 July 1878. The important phrase in italics is missing in Newton's biography (op. cit., p. 158)—considerably weakening Salisbury's complaint. Yet Newton has been extensively quoted; e.g. Ganiage, op. cit., p. 518; Bardoux, *Quand Bismarck dominait l'Europe*, p. 161.

[92] D.D.F. 1/2/335; SP/7/Lyons to Salisbury/26 July 1878. Waddington thought Salisbury had 'recognised the perfect exactitude with which he had reproduced his words'.

[93] SP/20/Salisbury to the Queen/25 July 1878.

BDT E

from d'Harcourt's report. The British ambassador, therefore, misled by this as to Salisbury's real wishes, simply suggested to the French minister that he should rewrite his despatch about Tunis or write a completely new despatch 'in more diplomatic language', which, though unwilling, the latter agreed to do.[94] When Waddington's new despatch arrived, it was no less explicit than its precedessor and roundly asserted that Salisbury had said:

> Do at Tunis what you think proper. . . . England will not oppose you there and will respect your decisions.

In addition to this Waddington expressed a wish for his original despatch to be kept in London as a *procès-verbal* of the 'intimate and cordial but perfectly official conversations'.[95] D'Harcourt describes Salisbury's reaction to this in a private letter. Salisbury, he said, continued to 'make some difficulties' and was still protesting that the words he had spoken had 'no official character', for which reason no British record had been kept of them. 'They were not, according to him', wrote the ambassador, 'an incitement for us to get possession of Tunis, but a conjecture (prévision) that we will do it in the event of the Ottoman Empire breaking up more and more'. In spite of this, Beaconsfield and Salisbury were, he said, prepared to put on paper that the French would be able to make of Tunis 'what suited them'.[96]

The draft of Britain's official reply to Waddington was put before the cabinet. Just before it was sent, a message from Lyons described the irritation in France over the Cyprus Convention, the insinuations that the French might retaliate, the widespread attacks on Waddington and how that minister was relying on the 'explanations and assurances' received at Berlin to defend himself.[97] The London despatch was most

[94] SP/7/Lyons to Salisbury/26 July 1878. When he received Salisbury's despatch, Lyons seems to have failed to notice the discrepancy between the two accounts.

[95] D.D.F. 1/2/336 and n. France, according to Waddington, was to regulate at will 'the nature and extent of her relations with the Bey' and Britain had accepted in advance 'all the consequences' possibly implied in this as to the 'ultimate destiny' of Tunis.

[96] Waddington Papers/d'Harcourt to Waddington/27 July 1878, D.D.F. 1/3/Appendix 2.

[97] FO 27/2312/617 Sec/Lyons to Salisbury/6 Aug 1878.

carefully worded and Salisbury emphasised that it was to be 'quite private and confidential' since, if published, 'in a defiant manner by the French' it might compromise relations with Italy.[98] Once again the private character of the Berlin conversations, the inability to confirm actual words used, and the 'general justice' of Waddington's recollections, were reiterated, but it is clear that any idea of an 'offer' which France could immediately accept was studiously eschewed. The position of France in North Africa was bound to enable her to 'press with decisive force' on Tunis, a result Britain had 'long recognised as inevitable' and accepted 'without reluctance'; the British statement continued:

> England has no special interests in this region which could possibly lead her to view with apprehension and distrust the legitimate and expanding influence of France.

Waddington must have misconceived him, said Salisbury, in understanding that he 'forboded an early fall of the existing government of Tunis' and Britain had not 'arrived at any opinion' upon the position Italy might assume.[99] This was undoubtedly far from the colourful recollections of Waddington, yet he and MacMahon regarded it as 'perfectly satisfactory', and, as if to emphasise the difference, a blunt but hardly frank message was on its way at that moment to Tunis, in answer to enquiries from a Wood made anxious by rumours of an English offer of annexation. Salisbury had written:

> Reply that no offer of the annexation of Tunis to France has ever been made by Her Majesty's Government to the French Government.[100]

The frequently accepted picture of Salisbury 'offering' Tunis to France in a most flamboyant manner at Berlin and afterwards confirming his promises with the utmost reluctance[101] is hardly adequate. It is clear that Salisbury intended to allay French

[98] SP/26/Salisbury to Lyons/10 Aug 1878.
[99] FO 27/2300/493/Salisbury to Lyons/7 Aug 1878.
[100] FO 27/2312/638/Lyons to Salisbury/14 Aug 1878; FO 102/111/42/ Wood to Salisbury/23 July 1878; A.P., vol. xcix, *Affairs of Tunis I*, to Wood/ 7 Aug 1878.
[101] Two recent works, for example, are, Bloch, op. cit., p. 244, and Raymond, op. cit., pp. 119, 126.

irritation over the Cyprus Convention by means of assurances which included the renunciation, possibly unofficial, of any British opposition to the development of French influence in the Regency. Even if the statements attributed to him by Waddington are not questioned, it makes a great deal of difference if the context of those statements was a 'private and somewhat speculative discussion' on the future or lack of future of the Ottoman Empire. That there was a genuine misunderstanding between Salisbury and Waddington seems more than probable and, if the experienced d'Harcourt could misunderstand Salisbury's position, so obviously could the French minister. Salisbury's case was inadequately argued at the time, owing to a series of accidents, and accounts based mainly on the published French documents may explain Waddington's policy but certainly not Salisbury's. There was a remarkable consistency between the views privately expressed by Salisbury before the Congress began and his account of the conversations three months later. He consistently declared Britain's 'disinterestedness' in Tunis but asserted that this could not affect the rights of other interested powers. It is reasonable to infer that he intended to give Paris an anonymous and unofficial bond which would slowly mature rather than a publicly signed cheque to be cashed immediately—an informal assurance of 'neutrality' in Tunis, which would remove the only effective obstacle to eventual French domination rather than a guarantee of support for annexation. What had not been anticipated was the extreme violence of the French reaction over Cyprus, the desperation of Waddington—who had not even mentioned an exchange of notes at Berlin—to get the 'assurances' on paper, and the hints of an alliance with Russia as an alternative. If as much reliance is put on Salisbury's account of the Berlin conversations as on Waddington's, then there was now a reluctant British agreement to put those assurances in a cautiously worded despatch, an agreement which involved an appreciable but not complete surrender to the French point of view. Beaconsfield, it will be remembered, had corroborated Salisbury's not Waddington's version of the conversations, and his experience of negotiating with the French minister led him to say to Salisbury in September, 1878:

I think Waddington, though he may not always intend it, a somewhat dangerous animal to deal with. I have not the slightest confidence in Waddington; he is feeble and sly, which feeble men often are.[102]

It may be noted that Salisbury compared his own action during the months of March to July 1878 to the 'desperate struggles which a man makes in clambering back to the safe foothold from which he ought never to have departed'.[103]

SALISBURY, CORTI AND RICHARD WOOD

Italy was the one country with decided interests in Tunis which had been virtually ignored by Salisbury at Berlin. Waddington asserted that Salisbury, when offering him Tunis, had 'suggested that the Italians could take Tripoli', a proposition to which he had expressed no strong objection.[104] Well known indeed is the monumental antipathy of the Italian delegate at Berlin towards 'compensations' as such. The fact is that the Cairoli government itself was not interested in compensation in Mediterranean Africa but in the unlikely possibility of Austrian concessions in the north.[105] On the question of Cyprus, the Italians were said to have been 'more sore than the French', so much so that Corti, rightly, expected it to lead to his downfall on his return to Italy with 'clean but empty hands'.[106] When the second Italian delegate, de Launay, complained to Salisbury that they had not even heard of the Anglo-Turkish convention before publication, the English minister—he said—allowed him in discussion:

> . . . to infer from his veiled utterances that Italy might dream of expansion in the direction of Tripoli or Tunis.

According to the Italian record, Salisbury then observed that there was on that coast 'room enough' for France and Italy to satisfy themselves and de Launay concluded that he was

---

[102] Buckle, op. cit., p. 373.   [103] Cecil, *Biographical Studies*, p. 31.
[104] D.D.F. 1/2/330. 332; FO 27/2311/572/Lyons to Salisbury/19 July 1878; A careful search later revealed no other F.O. record on this 'offer'; PRO 30/29/182/min. by E.B./4 June 1883.
[105] Langer, op. cit., p. 220.
[106] FO 363/1/Bertie to Tenterden/14 July 1878; SP/A11/MacDonald to Currie/13 Aug 1878.

thinking of Tunis for France and Tripoli for Italy, a consideration pressed on him by Odo Russell, the English ambassador
at Berlin, because 'the idea of occupation or a protectorate over
Tunisia had now made so much progress in France'.[107] There
is therefore room for believing that there was at Berlin a little
'speculative' discussion by way of comfort for the Italians, in
which Tripoli was mentioned. But much obviously depended
on the testimony of Corti, which unfortunately was not to be
relied upon, and he was not interested anyway in the question
of 'compensations'.[108] Later, in 1883, he approached Granville,
then in office, regarding a statement in 1881 by Dilke, who had
not given a positive denial to a parliamentary question as to
whether a record existed of a conversation with Salisbury
involving compensation for Italy in Tripoli. He 'totally denied'
being present at such a conversation but, according to Dilke,
virtually contradicted himself by telling him that:

> ... 'it was quite possible that Lord Salisbury had said why don't
> you take Tripoli', but that he (Corti) 'disapproved profoundly of
> those conversations'.[109]

As for the important Anglo-French conversations, the Italians
had little reliable information. For some reason, their ambassador at London, Menabrea, understood Salisbury was to say
on 13 August 1878 that he had spoken during the Conference
about 'Tunisia and the French aspirations' only to find Waddington averse to such discussion. Rome was told that the French
minister wished to return from the Congress with clean hands
and not to consider annexation.[110]

---

[107] Gorrini, op. cit., pp. 20-21; Crispi, op. cit., p. 118; Chiala, *Pagine di
storia contemporanea*, vol. 2, p. 94. De Launay did not pursue his discussion
with Salisbury 'as he was not authorised' to discuss Italian expansion.

[108] The vexed question as to whether the Germans 'offered' Tunis to
Italy as well as France depends largely on conversations half remembered by
him; Gorrini, op. cit., p. 19. Two viewpoints on the inconclusive evidence
are seen in the detailed note by Ganiage (op. cit., pp. 515-16) and that of
Peteani (op. cit., p. 28). Corti admitted himself that his short experience as a
minister 'proved to him how unfitted he was for the duties allotted to him';
Corti Memo/10 Aug 1878, copy in SP/All/MacDonald to Currie/13 Aug 1878.

[109] PRO 30/29/182/Memo with minutes/31 May 1883. Corti denied the
conversations in 1881 and Dilke had told the Italian Ambassador, Menabrea,
that 'proofs' existed in the F.O.; Crispi, op. cit., pp. 114-16; Gwynn and
Tuckwell, *Life of Sir Charles Dilke*, vol. 1, p. 382; FO 403/21/222 Conf/
Granville to Paget/27 May 1881. See note 104.

[110] Gorrini, op. cit., pp. 24, 106-7.

Back in Paris Waddington, in considering what advantage to derive from the 'assurances' of Salisbury, obviously had to tread carefully. In one sense it would clearly help to dispel some of the criticism of his own part at Berlin if he could show that, after Cyprus, his own hands were not quite so clean or empty. Yet the 'age of imperialism' had not exactly arrived for France, and, even though the first edition of Leroy-Beaulieu's famous *De la colonisation chez les peuples modernes*, had been published in 1874, it was virtually a scientific study for a rather indifferent French public and lacked the propagandist embellishments of later editions.[111] Moreover, if Waddington had replaced the Russian orientation of his predecessor's policy by an English orientation, he had always to be personally on guard against the accusations, however unjustified, that 'the Englishman Waddington' was showing undue complaisance towards Britain.[112] French policy also was moving into the phase defined by Hanotaux as 'a perpetual transaction between the policy of revenge and the policy of abdication', and the very fact that Bismarck might underwrite an advance into Tunis would in itself cause suspicion. The powerful Gambetta was himself hostile to the idea.[113]

'MacMahon and his military party' (Salisbury's description) were, however, in favour of acquiring Tunis and Waddington, having intimated to Roustan on 19 July 1878 the possibility of an early protectorate, began to work out the practical details, together with a draft treaty for the Bey's signature which included the strategic points to be occupied. By 1 September, however, Waddington had realised that, in view of the obstacles in the way, it would be some time before any plans could go ahead. The chief of these, as he had recognised from the beginning, would be Italy, and the second—it seemed from the reports of Roustan—the 'action of Mr. Wood'.[114] Both led him

[111] Moon, *Imperialism and World Politics*, p. 45. Algeria was not regarded as a 'happy experience', Betts, 'L'Influence des méthodes hollandaises et anglaises sur la doctrine coloniale française a la fin du XIXᵉ siècle', *Cahiers d'Histoire*, vol. 3, p. 35.
[112] De Freycinet, *Souvenirs*, p. 87; SP/7/Lyons to Salisbury/22 Nov 1878. Men in his own office accused him of being 'in the tow of England'.
[113] Deschanel, op. cit., p. 260; Hanotaux, op. cit., p. 384-5; Roberts, *History of French Colonial Policy*, p. 260.
[114] Gorrini, op. cit., pp. 28, 107; D.D.F. 1/2/328.329.330.337.339.340.

to London. Salisbury's warnings about Italian susceptibilities had evidently been taken to heart, for, on 17 August, Waddington had sounded Lyons on the subject and on the possibility of the acquisition of Tripoli reconciling Italy to a French Tunisia. The answer he got was obsolutely in line with Salisbury's policy at and after Berlin. The ambassador advised against any 'brilliant stroke' in Tunis, which would embitter the Italians, and thought it best:

> ... to allow the inevitable advance of French preponderance to take its natural course; and to promote it by improving means of communication between the Regency and Algeria and civilising measures of a similar kind.[115]

This was the policy of the slowly maturing bond involving no more than benevolent inactivity by Britain towards Tunisian political affairs, and it became even clearer in a direct interview with Salisbury. Waddington showed himself gratifyingly opposed to the advance of Slav influence in Europe and Asia, but, when he now suggested that England should 'divert the Italians' by obtaining from the Porte the cession of Tripoli to them, Salisbury 'declined to give any kind of encouragement to the idea'.[116] By October d'Harcourt had conceived the mistaken idea that Salisbury and Beaconsfield had become 'colder' since the Congress under the influence in the administration of the 'old antagonism towards France' and that, as public enthusiasm for Cyprus waned, unwillingness to pay the very substantial 'compensation' to France in Egypt and Tunis increased.[117] Salisbury's assurances on Egypt, however, were also precisely restricted to a simple engagement not to occupy the country or to place the French through violence in a subordinate position. Nevertheless he 'had faith in English influence in Egypt drawing ahead', a faith based on the 'natural superiority which a good Englishman in such a position was pretty sure to show'. In the Egyptian question also, Italian cooperation could be useful, another reason for not offending Italy by open encourage-

---

[115] FO 146/2061/651 Very Conf/Lyons to Salisbury/17 Aug 1878.
[116] SP/20/Salisbury to the Queen/7 Sep 1878; FO 27/2356/Salisbury to Adams/10 Sep 1878. He did say he had 'not the slightest desire to favour' an Italian protectorate.
[117] D.D.F. 1/2/350.

ment for an immediate French protectorate in Tunis. It is not without significance, therefore, that de Launay reported having been advised by Salisbury, while still at Berlin, to 'stand on the alert in those parts'. In August the 'offer' of Tunis by Britain was denied.[118] The retention of Wood in the Regency, especially a Wood still working for the maintenance of the *status quo*, along with the natural anxieties of Italy for the future of its numerous colony, might indeed seem a reasonable guarantee against the precipitous development of unrestricted French influence there.

In Tunis, the information available to Wood was as good as ever, except that from London, from whence he had received only Salisbury's brief 'no offer of annexation' message in July. He reported rumours accurately describing Roustan's visit to Paris in August to receive instructions regarding Britain's alleged proposition 'that France should either take possession or establish her Protectorate' as well as other evidence. Then he said that he had published in Arabic a Beaconsfield assurance supporting the integrity of the Ottoman Dominions. All this drew from Salisbury only a laconic, 'Report has been already contradicted'. When Wood had 'set the Bey's mind at rest', a despatch followed, drafted and heavily amended by Salisbury himself, designed to induce the Bey:

> . . . to dismiss from his thoughts any apprehension of sinister intentions on the part of either France or Italy; it is in his interest to live at peace with them, and to avoid giving to either power any legitimate cause for complaint.

No neighbouring powers would then 'form wishes inconsistent with his security'.[119] There was some chance indeed that the now precarious independence of Tunis might have been preserved for a considerable time balanced between a hesitant France and the pressure of Italian interests. Two factors served to shake the balance almost immediately. The Italians were not merely 'on the alert' but, unaware of the extent of their danger

---

[118] SP/26/Salisbury to Lyons/10 Aug 1878; Cecil, *Life of Salisbury*, vol. 2, pp. 331-5; Giaccardi, *La conquista di Tunisi*, pp. 65-66; FO 45/340/402 Conf/MacDonnell to Salisbury/26 Aug 1878.

[119] FO 102/111/46, 47, 61/Wood to Salisbury/12, 20 Aug, 8 Oct 1878; ibid/17, 18, 25/Salisbury to Wood/4, 6 Sep, 9 Oct 1878.

and of Britain's change of policy, actively beginning to challenge the French advance from a position of relative military weakness.[120] At the same time the fact that the sagacious Wood, presumably in the interests of secrecy, had not been taken into Salisbury's confidence, meant he had no chance to adapt himself to the new situation. All he was told was that war would 'almost certainly result from the acquisition of territory or special privileges in Tunis by Italy', a warning the French themselves conveyed to Rome.[121]

Wood, however, was a marked man. The virulent hatred which (as has been seen) Roustan, from the moment of his arrival had nourished for him, saw its opportunity and came into the open. In September 1878 Wood was moved to 'deeply regret' that his 'French colleagues, with a few rare exceptions' should persistently try to prove their zeal by accusing him of 'imaginary intrigues'.[122] At the same time Roustan, feeling entitled to an acquiescence that Wood did not even know was expected of him, was complaining to Paris of his 'particularly hostile attitude'. According to Waddington, Salisbury—who was passing through Paris—agreed that Wood was 'too old an offender to mend his ways' and would have to be recalled.[123] The crisis came over a concession granted to a predatory but well connected and officially supported French adventurer, Sancy, against whom the Bey finally dared to act. Bismarck intimated that the 'pear was ripe' and the international situation seemed favourable for the establishment of a protectorate, so that the feeble case was vigorously taken up by France and an ultimatum sent. To French dismay, however, the Bey finally yielded, after having ascertained from Wood that England would not guarantee Tunisian territory from violation.[124] In their disappointment

---

[120] Gorrini, op. cit., p. 28. A deputy, Mussi, sent 'on mission', proposed 'arrangements' with Italy at Biserta, supported 'preposterous claims' by a 'notorious' adventurer and intervened against another supported by Roustan. Then an old enemy of Roustan, Maccio, was appointed Consul-General; FO 102/111/51, 52, 58, 62/Wood to Salisbury/26, 27 Aug, 24 Sep, 8 Oct 1878.

[121] FO 102/111/20 Conf/Salisbury to Wood/18 Sep 1878; D.D.F. 1/2/352.

[122] FO 102/111/56/Wood to Salisbury/5 Sep 1878.

[123] SP/A8/Waddington to Salisbury/13 Jan 1879; FO 27/2302/Salisbury to Lyons/22 Oct 1878; D.D.F. 1/2/340.342; SP/7/Lyons to Salisbury/15 Oct 1878.

[124] Roustan's unpleasant story is summarised in AAE/Tunis/47/39/to MFA/29 Mar 1879. FO 102/111/70, 71/Wood to Salisbury/28, 31 Dec 1878; ibid/124/7 Conf/16 Jan 1879; FO 27/2361/—, 26 Tel/Lyons to Salisbury/3,

Thomas F. Reade

Théodore Roustan

Paul Cambon

de Courcel

Roustan and Waddington took up a diplomatic vendetta almost
without parallel against Wood who, with the new Italian representative, Maccio, was felt to have prompted the Bey's initial
defiance. According to Lyons, it was 'no use to argue with
Waddington or any Frenchman about him' and Waddington
wrote personally to Salisbury, even though he had been
unofficially informed that, under a retirement rule, Wood
was within weeks be a victim in a 'general massacre of aged
Innocents'. The evidence against Wood seems almost entirely
presumptive and consists of Roustan's usual diatribes against
'intolerable pressures suggested by influences', his 'attitude'
and wish for 'not only preponderant but exclusive influence',
so that even Waddington 'did not suppose that Sir Richard
deliberately disobeyed' his instructions to be strictly neutral.[125]
Even now Salisbury considered keeping Wood at Tunis 'till he
be removed by superannuation' to show displeasure at French
denunciation of commercial treaties with England, a policy
opposed by the suffering Lyons as Tunis was the place about
which the French were then 'most susceptible'.[126] Wood, who
had robustly endeavoured to reduce his official age, was therefore suddenly and summarily dismissed on the transparent
pretext of a reorganisation of the consular service. The Foreign
Office tried to mitigate Wood's 'mental distress' by generous
compensation, a pension equal to his 'salary and emoluments'
and inclusion in the honours list, so that his 'retreat' was made
'very honourable'.[127] So incredible was the French phobia

---

9 Jan 1879; SP/A8/7 Jan 1879; D.D.F. 1/2/364.366.367.368.369.372.374;
G.P. 3/655; Ganiage, op. cit., pp. 533-545. Those who put honesty before
national policy were censured; a French Official was recalled and the Austrian
Consul disavowed by his government.
[125] SP/A8/Lyons to Salisbury/10 Jan 1879; ibid/Waddington to Salisbury/
13 Jan 1879; ibid/Salisbury to Waddington/22 Jan 1879; FO 27/2361/28/
Lyons to Salisbury/10 Jan 1879; SP/26/Salisbury to Lyons/4 Jan 1879;
AAE/Tunis/47/9, 39/Roustan to MFA/14 Jan, 29 Mar 1879; D.D.F. 1/2/375.
[126] SP/26/Tel. Sec/Salisbury to Lyons/13 Jan 1879; SP/A8/Lyons to
Salisbury/14 Jan 1879.
[127] SP/26/Conf/Salisbury to Lyons/6 Mar 1879; SP/8/Lyons to Salisbury/
14 Mar 1879; FO 102/124/Wood to Salisbury/8, 10/29 Jan, 12 Feb 1879;
ibid/to Wood/8 Jan 1879; ibid/125/Tel; Conslr. 4, 6, 7, Nil, Nil/to Wood/24,
26 Feb, 5, 15 Mar, 6, 25 June 1879; ibid/Lister to Surrie/22 Feb 1879; ibid/
Separate, 12 Conslr/Wood to Salisbury/26 Feb 10 Mar 1879; WP/Lister to
Wood/4 Mar, 6 June 1879; WP/Pauncefote to Wood/25 June 1879; WP/
Kennedy to Wood/1 Aug 1879; WP/to Lister/27 June 1879; WP/to Paunce-
fote/22 July 1879; WP/to Salisbury/24 Aug 1879.

against Wood that there arose a fear of his leaving his 'sting' behind at the Consulate, by securing an appointment there for a close associate, and a prime minister of France actually sent his 'very particular thanks' for sight of a reassuring list of the consular employees in Tunis.[128]

Lest Wood be written off as merely hostile to France, it should be recorded that the Italians—through eyes perhaps as unfriendly as those of Roustan—saw him as 'in the end' hostile to Italy, 'generally indifferent, but rather benevolent towards France', and blamed him for the British government's lack of interest in Tunis.[129] Salisbury, of course, continued to refuse the numerous Italian requests to pull their Tunisian chestnuts out of the French fire, though 'far from wishing to discourage the Italians' in the attempt and asserted his 'absolute impartiality' between Italian and French claims and the 'absence of political interest' on Britain's part.[130] He hoped that posterity would not judge him by his 1878 policies which only consisted of 'picking up the china that Derby had broken'.[131] As for Tunis, Wood had gone, and with him half a century of British policy; but his self-perpetuating treaty remained and the lesser man who took his place was to become bitterly hostile to French influence.

[128] SP/8/Lyons to Salisbury/1, 15, 24 April 1879; SP/20/Salisbury to Lyons/24 April 1879.
[129] Gorrini, op. cit., pp. 18, 46-47.
[130] SP/28/Salisbury to Paget/14 Feb, 25 July 1879.
[131] Cecil, *Biographical Studies*, p. 31.

2

BRITAIN AND
THE FRENCH PROTECTORATE, 1880–1888

GRANVILLE, THE ENFIDA CASE AND THE OCCUPATION

If Cyprus and the Transaaal were as valuable as they are valueless, I would repudiate them because they are obtained by means
dishonourable to the character of the country.[1]

L iberal criticisms of the Beaconsfield Government's policies
as well as the policies themselves, left Gladstone and Granville many embarrassing legacies when they came to power in
1880, and attempted to translate 'civilisation and humanity'
into diplomatic action. True, Gladstone's hopes in self rule for
the nascent nationalities under the Ottoman yoke and Granville's expectation of the imminent collapse of Turkey were not
so far from Salisbury's belief that Turkey would inevitably
decay. The difference between them lay in the importance
attached by Salisbury to propping up the Turkish government
yet awhile in the interests of the route to India. Moreover, the
Porte's evasiveness towards the stipulations of the Berlin
agreement had increased as the Russian threat diminished, and
the new British cabinet endeavoured to get the powers to concert in employing coercion over the Montenegrin and Greek
frontier issues, the first of which questions was settled, primarily
because of British pressure, in October 1880. Hopes, however,
that French support would be forthcoming to compose the

---

[1] Morley, *Life of Gladstone*, vol. 2, pp. 267-8. For the place of Tunis in
international politics, 1880-81, see Medlicott, *Bismarck, Gladstone and the
Concert of Europe*, passim., *Congress of Berlin and After*, chaps. 9 and 10;
Langer, *American History Review*, vol. 31, pp. 252-65, *Alliances and Alignments*, chap. 7. Studies on Tunis itself are Ganiage, *Les Origines du protectorat français en Tunisie*, chap. 11-13; Raymond, 'Les Libéraux anglais et la
question tunisienne', *Cahiers de Tunisie*, vol. 3, pp. 422-65; Safwat, *Tunis
and the Great Powers*, chaps. 4-5.

Greek question had waned by the beginning of 1881.[2] French eyes were elsewhere.

It would be invidious to recapitulate the story of Franco-Italian rivalry in Tunis, now being fanned to a blaze by Roustan and Maccio, which Cairoli, a man with an infinite capacity for ignoring the relative weakness of Italy, did nothing to check.[3] Official circles in an ever stronger France were at this time far from united in desiring a forward colonial policy.[4] It was, however, in the circumstances, not unnatural that the hesitant Freycinet, after prudently confirming that the German attitude was unchanged, should seek an equal confirmation that Salisbury's promises remained valid. This seemed especially desirable as an unofficial approach to the Bey to establish a protectorate had met with stolid resistance in May 1880.[5] After having vainly considered the abrogation of the hated Anglo-Turkish convention by purchasing the 'fee simple of Cyprus',[6] the Liberals were even more angry over the compensation promised. A month of French insistence only got from Granville that Britain had 'no jealousy' of French influence, wished simply to maintain her 'commercial and maritime rights', and adhered to the reservations of Salisbury regarding Italy and Turkey. Such an answer caused dismay in Paris where 'something more' in the form of 'sympathetic support' had been anticipated.[7] This

[2] PRO 30/29/202/Granville to Lyons/1 May 1880; Lee, *Great Britain and the Cyprus Convention Policy of 1878*, pp. 38, 159-61; Knaplund, *Letters from the Berlin Embassy*, pp. 136-7, 183; Seton-Watson, *Disraeli, Gladstone and the Eastern Question*, p. 565; Medlicott, *Bismarck, Gladstone and The Concert of Europe*, chaps. 6, 8, pp. 138, 163, 196-7, 237. There was much dissention in the cabinet between the Gladstonian Radicals and the Whigs; Robinson, Gallagher and Denny, *Africa and the Victorians*, p. 92.

[3] The state-supported purchase of the Tunis–Goletta railway (ostensibly already sold to a French company), and demands for cable rights by the Italians caused bitter feeling; D.D.F. 1/3/171.184.191.193.196.204.209; Ganiage, op. cit., pp. 564-88; Safwat. op. cit., pp. 268-274. Later the Italians said ignorance of the Berlin promises was responsible; Gorrini, *Tunisi e Biserta*, p. 28.

[4] Medlicott, op. cit., pp. 114-51.

[5] D.D.F. 1/3/109.110.142.150.

[6] Ramm, *Political Correspondence of Mr Gladstone and Lord Granville, 1876-1886*, vol. I, pp. 129 n. 3, 130, 134 n. 1; Medlicott, 'The Gladstone Government and the Cyprus Convention, 1880-85'. *Journal of Modern History*, pp. 190-93.

[7] FO 27/2421/698/Granville to Lyons/17 June 1880; ibid/2422/846, 928/6, 15 July 1880; ibid/2432/Tel 579/Lyons to Granville/6, 8 July 1880; D.D.F. 1/3/209. France complained of the 'lukewarmness' of the new cabinet; FO 27/2435/921 Most Conf/Adams to Granville/28 Sep 1880.

was virtually, however, unwillingly Salisbury's policy, plus the first hint of determination to preserve Britain's trading privileges. In the same way, therefore, that the cabinet had come to accept the necessity for implementing the Berlin Treaty, if possible 'by the Concert of Europe', it had taken a step towards implementing the Berlin promises. This was in spite of Gladstone's opinion (disclosed in 1882) that, of all the 'outrages' committed by Salisbury 'including the *fibs*' his 'three secret treaties' were the worst.[8] Nor was there any greater disposition to intervene in Franco-Italian disputes and, though Granville attempted to soothe the excited protagonists, Paget in Rome turned the 'deafest possible ear' to any hint of support in Italy in Tunis.[9]

Ironically enough, however, the fate of the Regency was decided during a dispute between the London cabinet and the new French ministry of Ferry, who personally was 'in no haste to act'. True the single-minded Roustan and his unscrupulous agents—including the flamboyant Colonel Allegro—were openly preparing the way for occupation, with the support now of Barthélemy-Saint-Hilaire, foreign minister, and de Courcel, director of political affairs. What still dictated a conciliatory policy was the attitude of the president and, more decisive for Ferry, the influential Gambetta. In the new year, a mission was despatched to the Italians.[10] The Anglo-French dispute hinged on the practice under Moslem law of Shoofà, or pre-emption, whereby possession of an estate could be obtained against the will of a purchaser. Tunisia was a country where not only was uncertainty over title deeds notorious, but there were two sectarian courts, the Hanefi, which permitted owners of contiguous property to claim the right of Shoofà, and the Maleki, which permitted only co-proprietors to do so. The Enfida, a vast estate comprising some of the richest land in

[8] Q.V.L. series 2, vol. 3, p. 141; Ramm, op. cit., pp. 413-14.
[9] PRO 3029/182/Paget to Granville/22 June 1880; FO 45/400/10 July 1880; FO 27/2422/928, 936/Granville to Lyons/15, 17 July 1880; D.D.F. 1/3/225; Giaccardi, *La conquista di Tunisi*, pp. 167-69.
[10] JP/Diary/21 Mar, 8-21 April 1880; JP/MSS 'The Tunisian Question'/ no date; D.D.F. 1/3/358 n.; H. Johnston, *Story of My Life*, pp. 65-66; A. Johnston, *Life and Letters of Sir Harry Johnston*, pp. 32-3; Giaccardi, op. cit., pp. 220-28; Julien, 'Jules Ferry', *Les Politiques d'expansion Impérialiste* pp. 24-26. Freycinet made the doubtful assertion later that he had been about to land marines; *Souvenirs*, p. 168.

Tunis, was sold to the Société Marseillaise by the former prime minister, Keirredin, and though the precaution against Shoofà had been taken of not selling a strip of land encircling the estate, a neighbouring British landowner, Levy, claimed to own plots inside the Enfida. Levy formally took possession of the estate, but had his servants later ejected by French consular and company officials. They in turn soon found themselves opposed by Tunisian officialdom and the local inhabitants. The main reason for this was that the local courts and the Bey's objections to the alienation of an estate originally given by him as illegal, had been both disregarded—on Saint-Hilaire's instructions.[11] Honestly to establish the 'rights' of such a case, as the Liberals now attempted to do, was probably impossible. The case involved after all the avaricious claims of private individuals, powerful political interests and imprecise law administered by a weak and corrupt government. Moreover, information available was coloured (like so many subsequent histories) by the partisan reports of the local representatives of the powers. Cases like Sancy's had shown that Roustan's drive for control would not be troubled by legal scruples. Further-more, Wood's pedestrian successor, Reade, son and former secretary of a previous dynamic agent there, dreamed of 'maintaining and increasing the English influence already fostered by Sir Richard Wood'.[12] Palpably ignorant of the Berlin promises, he was the one person (apart possibly from his masters) apparently incapable of seeing that a French protectorate was probably imminent.[13] 'Deservedly esteemed and appreciated' hitherto by both French and Italians, he was stirred into a bitter and active antagonism by the high-handed and wounding action of Roustan in the Enfida.[14] He was ably abetted by Broadley, a Freemason of orthodox religious beliefs. An extremely clever lawyer and writer, now Levy's counsel, Broadley had previously absconded from Bengal—where he had

[11] FO 102/143/34, 3, 4/Reade to Granville/6 Dec 1880, 17, 17 Jan 1881; Macnaghten, *On the Principles of Mahommedan Law*, p. 47, in FO 102/146/ Santillana to Granville/1 Oct 1881; *Annual Register, 1881*, pp. 221-2; D.D.F. 1/3/324.
[12] A. L. Reade, *The Reades of Blackwood Hill*, pp. 60-64.
[13] H. Johnston, op. cit., p. 58.
[14] JP/MSS treatise on Tunis/chap. 6; JP/MSS 'The Tunisian Question'/ no date.

been Assistant Magistrate—seemingly to avoid prosecution on serious criminal charges.[15] To Roustan and the Quai d'Orsay, Levy was naturally a 'man of straw', the agent of interests hostile to France and the 'legitimate' expansion of her influence. Reade argued that he was simply seeking to exercise an established right, while Broadley secured from Wood a testimonial that Levy had, over twenty years, 'maintained the character for honesty, which British merchants have so justly acquired in the Levant'.[16] On their side, the stiff-necked Levy and his associates could combine self interest with the righteous glow of defenders of Tunisian independence.[17] The problem was too much for Granville and his irritation with the unwanted squabble was shared by Lyons, who thought Tunis not worth even coolness with France.[18] They tended henceforth to vent their annoyance on the head of the unfortunate Reade for his part in raising the question.

As the French had got their word in at an early date in London and Reade's presentation of the awkward and unfamiliar case left much to be desired, Foreign Office opinion at first tended to accept the French view. Granville therefore simply authorised support of Levy's right to a legal hearing, provided his action was not 'simply vexatious'.[19] It is not surprising that he readily acquiesced in a French suggestion to immobilise the factious consuls and do nothing to exacerbate the matter until the discussions in London could be resumed with fuller information.[20] Saint-Hilaire, however, was simultaneously urging intervention in force upon his ministerial council, but succeeded in obtaining sanction for the despatch of one ship only, the 'Friedland'.[21] With almost incredible fatuity, he proceeded to inform Lyons—and 'on his word of honour' the

[15] FO 335/128/9/3, 6/to Wood/5 April, 8 May 1873; ibid/131/Broadley to Wood/17, 19 Feb 1873; *Who Was Who, 1916-1918*. Reade was very close to the passionately Francophobe Broadley; JP/Diary/passim.; H. Johnston, op. cit., pp. 62-63.

[16] See note 11. FO 102/143/Guest to Granville/1 Feb 1881, encl.; ibid/144/102 Most Conf/Paget to Gran/16 Mar 1881.

[17] FO 102/144/Tels/Levy to Khaireddin/12 Nov. 22 Dec 1880, and letter of Levy's brother, with Dilke Memo/7 April 1881.

[18] PRO 30/29/171/Lyons to Granville/18 Jan 1881.

[19] FO 102/143/31/Granville to Reade/29 Dec 1880.

[20] Ibid/Bertie Memo/5 Feb 1881; FO 102/143/Tel/Granville to Reade/4 Feb 1881.

[21] Ganiage, op. cit., pp. 618-19; D.D.F. 1/3/358 n.1.

BDT F

Italian ambassador, Cialdini—that this action was intended simply to obtain satisfaction over the Enfida.[22] Naturally, the reverse happened. This 'foolish escapade of the French', as Gladstone called it, resulted in a government, which had serious doubts as to the soundness of Levy's position and feared he might be another Don Pacifico, sending the 'Thunderer' to checkmate the 'Friedland' until the latter was withdrawn shortly after.[23] The French now denied that its presence had had anything to do with the Enfida.[24] Granville wanted 'fair play' for Levy, and felt he was risking war to secure it.[25] Unfortunately he could not make up his mind what the fair play was that he desired. While the French hinted at arbitration and categorically declined to submit to a decision by Tunisian courts, it was clearly impossible to compel Levy to forgo his legal rights. The Law Officers in London, constantly consulted and obviously unhappy, took until early March to decide that the dispute should be settled in either the British or French consular court—something on which there was sure to be no agreement. Reade was forbidden to do anything and his presence in Tunis was deplored by Granville—even, unofficially, to the French ambassador.[26]

The 'Thunderer' incident and the subsequent indecision gave the impression to Reade and the Bey that the 'traditional policy' was operative.[27] It also probably played its part, along with Italian activities and excited French opinion, in enabling de Courcel to persuade Gambetta, and consequently Ferry,

[22] PRO 30/29/171/Lyons to Granville/4 Feb 1881; A.P., vol. xcix/4/16; Gorrini, op. cit., p. 114. Fantastic rumours of a Turkish 'threat' had some influence, and the already menacing Roustan was instructed to again demand a Treaty of Protectorate from the Bey; D.D.F. 1/3/353.355.

[23] PRO 30/29/202/Granville to Lyons/2 Feb 1881; ibid/137/to Northbrook/3 Feb 1881; ibid/124/to Gladstone/4 Feb 1881; ibid/Gladstone to Granville/4 Feb 1881; ibid/143/Granville cabinet memo/5 Feb 1881; Ramm, op. cit., vol. 1, p. 241. Selbourne, Lord Chancellor, felt antipathy towards the idea of Shoofà (as did Tenterden and Pauncefote) and the 'chess game' over the Enfida; FO 102/143/Granville Memoranda, Pauncefote to Tenterden, Selbourne memo/9, —, 11 Feb 1881.

[24] D.D.F. 1/3/363; FO 102/144/113 Most Conf/Paget to Granville/25 Mar 1881, encls.

[25] PRO 30/29/202/Granville to Lyons/9, 10 Feb 1881; ibid/177/to Northbrook/14 Mar 1881; The fleet was ready; ibid/from Northbrook/14 Mar 1881.

[26] FO 102/144/Law Officers to Granville/3 Mar 1881; ibid/Dallas Memo/24 Mar 1881; ibid/14 Tel/Granville to Reade/19 Mar 1881; PRO 30/29/202/Granville to Lyons/16 Mar 1881; D.D.F. 1/3/421.

[27] FO 102/143/19/Reade to Granville 14 Feb 1881.

that armed intervention was now imperative.[28] How an 'oppor-
tune' raid of Kroumir tribesmen was used as a pretext for
invasion, as long anticipated by Roustan, and how 'chastising'
tribesmen was used as the pretext for general occupation needs
no recapitulation.[29] Granville was as perplexed as ever. At first
the French had intimated that there would be no interference
with the rights of foreigners and no annexation of Tunis,
though saying soon after that the Bey would have to make a
'proper' treaty with France. The Italians—not concerned in the
Enfida affair—demanded vigorous cooperation from Britain.[30]
Personally indisposed to seeing an unilateral seizure of Tunis
unchallenged, Granville told Lyons to look 'mysterious' while
the government made up its mind. That task was, however,
anything but facilitated by a French 'leak' to *The Times* of the
despatch with Salisbury's promises and by Admiral Spratt
drawing official attention to the eulogistic report he had drawn
up in 1864 on the naval possibilities of Biserta.[31] Granville was
impressed. He felt the risk of war was 'appalling', but France
would 'think twice' before facing England, Italy and the Arabs.
Gladstone, however, was averse to combination with the
Italians and felt that the acquisition of Cyprus, as well as
Salisbury's promises, made no more than 'friendly remonstrance'
possible.[32] The First Lord, Northbrook, agreed, and Granville
was immobilised, saying:

> I suppose our best policy is to do nothing to irritate the
> French unnecessarily and at the same time nothing to reassure
> them as to possible results.[33]

[28] Apparently 23 Mar 1881. Ganiage, op. cit., pp. 635-40; Julien, op. cit.
p. 26; PRO 30/29/171 Lyons to Granville/18 Mar 1881. The lull in Franco-
Italian animosity since Nov had ended; Gorrini, op. cit., pp. 112, 114, 116.
[29] FO 27/2491/305.310.313.323 Very Conf, 327.336/Lyons to Granville/
3, 5, 6, 8, 9, 12 April 1881; Ganiage, op. cit., pp. 661-7; Freycinet, *Souvenirs*,
p. 169.
[30] A.P./xcix/Tunis 2/7/Granville to Menabrea/6 April 1881; ibid/29/
Lyons to Granville/11 April 1881; ibid/47/Granville to Paget/20 April 1881;
Gorrini, op. cit., pp. 41, 112-13, 118.
[31] PRO 30/29/202/Granville to Lyons/6, 22 April 1881; ibid/171/Lyons
to Granville/12 April 1881; ibid/137/Northbrook to Granville/19 April 1881,
encl./Spratt to Paget/28 July 1864; D.D.F. 1/3/432.
[32] PRO 30/29/124/Granville to Gladstone/21, 25 April 1881; ibid/202/
Granville to Lyons/22 April 1881; ibid/Tel, Pr, Tel/124/Gladstone to Gran-
ville/22, 22, 26 April 1881; Ramm, op. cit., pp. 262-3, 267, n. 4.
[33] PRO 30/29/Granville to Gladstone/27 April 1881; Ramm, op. cit.,
p. 268.

Moreover, Britain was beholden to Bismarck for aid in the Greek question, about to be concluded,[34] and Bismarck was a constant supporter of French action in Tunis. That support would not waver at a time when his planned reconstruction of the Dreikaiserbund had been possibly placed in jeopardy by the Tsar's assassination in March, after which France went ahead.[35] Granville could 'bark but not bite', which the French quickly sensed; for the 'humbugging' declarations of Saint-Hilaire were seen for what they were when Biserta and Tabarca fort were occupied and the march on Tunis began. This was accompanied by further assurances, even that the occupation would cease when satisfactory arrangements with the Bey had been made, arrangements which would, however, 'resemble protection'.[36] When offers of cooperation against France had come from Italy and Russia, Granville's impractical idea of rousing the Concert of Europe by including Germany and Austria was again scotched by his colleagues. Consequently the Treaty of Bardo, so like a protectorate that Lyons could see no difference, was forced on the Bey by the French on 12 May 1881.[37]

The disgruntled Granville—who had no wish to see France get an 'overwhelming preponderance in the Mediterranean'—determined to salvage as much as possible. Saint-Hilaire was therefore informed, before he presented his terms to the Bey, that the British government could not 'acquiesce tacitly in any arrangements being entered into contrary to their established interests'.[38] An exchange of correspondence followed. To 'prevent any occasion of future misapprehension', Granville made it clear (in a despatch approved by the cabinet) that the English treaty of 19 July 1875, which secured to British sub-

---

[34] Ramm, op. cit., pp. 257-8; Fitzmaurice, *Lord Granville*, vol. 2, p. 231; Knaplund, op. cit., pp. 183-4.

[35] Medlicott, *Bismarck, Gladstone and the Concert of Europe*, pp. 282-304, 308-9; D.D.F. 1/3/418.422.458.478.489.495.513. He rejoiced that France was in his 'Tunis trap'; Knaplund, op. cit., p. 220.

[36] PRO 30/29/171/Lyons to Granville/3 May 1881; FO 27/2492/380, 432, 450/Lyons to Granville/25 April 1881, 5, 10 May 1881; FO 403/21/39 Tel/27 April 1881; AP./xcix/2/99/Granville to Lyons/2 May 1881.

[37] A.P./xcix/2/108/Granville to Paget/4 May 1881; ibid/110/to Wyndham/ 4 May 1881; Gwyn and Tuckwell, *Dilke*, vol. 1, p. 380; de Card, *Traités de protectorat*, pp. 159-61; D.D.F. 1/3/495.509.523.526.531. The Russian offer was then disavowed; FO 403/21/406/Goschen to Granville/21 May 1881.

[38] A.P./xcix/2/121/Granville to Lyons/7 May 1881; D.D.F. 1/3/515; Ramm, op. cit., p. 265.

jects any privileges granted to subjects of 'any other nation whatever', remained in force. He went on to observe that the creditors should 'express their views' if changes in the Financial Commission were proposed. Noting French assurances that no port would be annexed and that 'at the present time' no project for a military port at Biserta existed, he asserted that British ships would have the right to use any future commercial port there on the same terms as French or Tunisian vessels.[39] Granville felt 'a more vigorous line' to have been impossible, but, as there was 'a great deal of soreness about Tunis' in Britain, the cabinet decided on measures to 'make a Tory attack impossible'. This they decided to do by publishing the despatches on Salisbury's promises of 1878, which, they felt, had 'cut the ground' from under their feet. As Salisbury objected that the despatches 'did not bear the full explanation on the face of them' and castigated Waddington's 'inaccurate recollections', the most damaging of them was omitted.[40]

The Enfida problem, however, remained. Granville, fortified by legal opinion, had readily decided in April to declare that Britain was 'not called on to interfere'. Lyons, however, had 'not seen his way' to acting on the instruction, as the French might 'soon have the Tunisian Tribunals under their thumb'. He told them therefore that the case should be decided under Tunisian law and the European treaties.[41] Lyons' apprehensions were justified. Reports of unsuccessful pressure on the Hanefi court were followed by a Beylical decree transferring

[39] The capitulations and the 8 per cent maximum tariff were also specifically mentioned. A.P./xcix/6/54/Granville to Challemel-Lacour/20 May 1881; ibid/3/2/to Lyons/13 May 1881; FO 27/2493/474, 480/Lyons to Granville/14, 16 May 1881; Gladstone Papers/44642/cabinet min/20 May 1881. Gladstone wrote, 'As to notice about not fortifying Biserta, *prendre acte* (take note)'; ibid/cabinet min/3 May 1881. A report of 26 May, however, said Biserta 'was not of the importance' Wood placed on it; FO 403/21/Sir G. Balfour to Dilke.

[40] PRO 30/29/143/Granville to Cabinet Colleagues/14 May 1881; ibid/ Salisbury to Granville/14 May 1881; ibid/137/Northbrook to Granville/ 13 May 1881; ibid/202/Granville to Lyons/13, 16, 18 May, 15 June 1881; Ramm, op. cit., pp. 274-5; Gladstone P./44642/cabinet min/-May 1881. Salisbury had even written (irregularly?) to Lyons in April in case Saint-Hilaire published them; Newton, *Lord Lyons*, vol. 2, p. 242. They were not; PRO 30/29/171/Lyons to Granville/8 May 1881.

[41] FO 102/144/Law Officers to Granville/8 April 1881; ibid/Granville to Reade/19 April 1881; ibid/379/to Lyons/21 April (amended); ibid/Conf/ Lyons to Tenterden/29 April 1881; ibid/426/Lyons to Granville/4 May 1881; Q.V.L./2 vol. 3, pp. 209-210.

the case to the Maleki court, tantamount to deciding the case against Levy, who was immediately dispossessed, unheard, in 'preliminary proceedings'. In the long drawn-out argument that followed, the French claimed that the Bey had acted 'in the plenitude of his sovereign authority' and that they couldn't intervene with a 'normal' judicial decision. The same Foreign Office voices that doubted Levy's case were now raised against this 'mockery of justice'. Granville sent stinging despatches to Paris, and it was only in May 1882 that the dispute ended by the French company buying Levy's land at a grossly inflated price.[42] Whether the company was 'softened' by the Rochefort case it is impossible to say. For Roustan had allowed himself to be unwisely provoked into a libel action by allegations of corruption motivating the occupation—and lost his case.[43]

Apart from the Enfida, Granville was hoping to let the Tunis question 'settle down', and the cabinet quietly accepted the appointment of Roustan as 'intermediary' or foreign minister of the Bey, though urging Saint-Hilaire to avoid such 'unpalatable surprises' without warning. Simultaneously Granville was advising Italian moderation in the face of the fear developing in Rome of a perpetual French occupation and of an 'intolerable' menace from Biserta.[44] A British warning was sent, however, against any French 'interference' in Tripoli[45] and diminished Anglo-French cordiality after the occupation of Tunis had its effect on the increasingly serious situation in Egypt.[46]

[42] FO 363/1/Adams to Tenterden/26 July 1881; ibid/2/Lyons to Tenterden/2 Dec 1881; PRO 30/29/171/Lyons to Granville/2 Dec 1881; ibid/Granville to Lyons/4 April 1882; FO 102/144/59 Tel, 67 Tel/Reade to Gran/10, 25 June 1881; ibid/146/Law Officers to FO/27 Oct 1881; ibid/1124, 1180, 399/Granville to Lyons/17 Nov, 2 Dec 1881, 12 April 1882; ibid/90 Tel, 1073, 1130/Lyons to Granville/19 Nov, 1, 16 Dec 1881; ibid/33/Reade to Granville/27 May 1881.

[43] FO 102/146/119 Tel/Reade to Granville/22 Dec 1881; PRO 30/29/171/Lyons to Granville/16, 30 Dec 1881; Broadley, The Last Punic War, pp. 247-293; Ganiage, op. cit., pp. 640-661, 685-693.

[44] FO 403/21/61 Tel/Reade to Granville/15 June 1881; ibid/594 Conf/Granville to Lyons/22 June 1881; ibid/23/56 Conf/Paget to Granville/23 Feb 1882; Gladstone P./44642/Cabinet Min/13, 15 June 1881; PRO 30/29/171/Lyons to Granville/21 June 1881.

[45] FO 27/2495/639 Conf, 688/Lyons to Granville/1, 17 July 1881; PRO 30/29/143/Draft and notes/July 1881; ibid/209/Granville to Menabrea/26 July 1881; Ramm, op. cit., pp. 284-5.

[46] Giaccardi, op. cit., pp. 324-5, 344-5; Knaplund, Gladstone's Foreign Policy, pp. 167-9; Ramm, op. cit., p. 374.

READE'S BATTLE WITH CAMBON

In the years after the occupation there was a major deterioration in Anglo-French relations. No comment is necessary on the well-known developments in Egypt that were responsible for this, how the fall of events led to non-participation by the French in the British occupation and bitter resentment after, nor how the system gratuitously established there by Gladstone enabled France and the powers to hamstring the British authorities at will. Gladstone's European Concert had ceased to be practical politics and it may be argued that, as a consequence, his policy was now hesitant and showed reluctance to partake in or to encourage Europe's expansion overseas.[47] In Tunis, there was a period of adjustment to the new state of affairs, marked by a series of probably inevitable disputations, the treatment of which in London seemed to depend on the merits of the disputes themselves and the personalities involved more than on considered policy. Reade's father had assisted Sir Hudson Lowe when Napoleon was at St. Helena and later as Consul-General at Tunis had resisted French designs there. His son had always dreamed of gaining 'the same power and good name as his father possessed before him' and, one of the family of almost 'hereditary' Mediterranean consuls bred in the tradition of fatherly protection of British subjects, was generally esteemed.[48] Yet being 'such an Arab himself', as Iddesleigh remarked, he was almost fanatically resolved to preserve time-hallowed rights,[49] but his well meaning mediocrity denied him Wood's grasp of high policy and was to permit him only a blind resistance to French encroachments without the ability to carry the home government with him. The architect of French Tunisia was Roustan's successor, Paul Cambon, the energetic ex-prefect of Lille, who was determined to secure effective

---

[47] Medlicott, op. cit., pp. 305-15, 319; Newton, op. cit., chaps. 15-16. Robinson, Gallacher and Denny give a detailed account of the Egyptian crisis; op. cit., pp. 100-155.

[48] See notes 12-14 and the memorial of the Anglo-Maltese colony; FO 102/164/Mansfield to Granville/10 Jan 1885. See also Serra, 'L'accordo italo-francese del 1896 sulla Tunisia', Rivista Storica Italiana, vol. 73, p. 2, n. He was 'very ordinary' to Cambon; Correspondance, vol. 1, p. 183.

[49] Lang, Life, Letters and Diaries of Sir Stafford Northcote, p. 242; AAE/Tunis/75/192/d'Estournelles to Challemel-Lacour/4 Aug 1883.

control of Tunis through a proper treaty of protectorate and the abolition both of the Financial Commission and the capitulatory powers of what he called the 'ridiculous' foreign consuls, whom he simply saw as obstacles to good administration.[50] In the inevitable clash between the two men, each blamed the other for the fact that minor issues were increasingly referred to London and Paris,[51] but the cards were heavily stacked against Reade. There was a feeling in the Foreign Office that he had misinformed it in the Enfida case and that things were not as they should be in the Consulate-General.[52] In addition, Cambon's able assistant, d'Estournelles de Constant, came straight from the London Embassy, was thought 'a really charming fellow, pleasant and attractive in society, . . . and very free from the usual French prejudice' against Britain—and was the acknowledged friend of Dilke to boot.[53]

When Reade, therefore, reacted in June 1882 to inspired articles attacking the 'state within a state' of consular power and developing Cambon's ideas, Dilke cryptically observed:

> . . . Reade ought to know of my private correspondence with Baron d'Estournelles on lines suggested by Pauncefote and agreed by Granville.[54]

In fact Reade's attempt to avoid unsympathetic French officials by dealing with the Tunisian prime minister rather than with Cambon, in his capacity as the foreign minister of the Bey, was ended through this unofficial French influence.[55] In default of instructions from the cautiously equivocal Freycinet, Cambon himself began the erosion of consular privileges, for example, by claiming to try by court martial Italian and Maltese civilians involved in disputes with military personnel.[56] When Granville

[50] P. Cambon, op. cit., vol. 1, pp. 161, 170, 174; *Dictionnaire de Biographie Française*, vol. 7, p. 964. An account of Cambon's work in Tunisia is found in Eubank, *Paul Cambon*, pp. 16-33.

[51] AAE/Tunis/77/293/Cambon to Ferry/29 Dec 1883; FO 102/140/22 May 1882.

[52] FO 102/152/Lister, Tenterden Memoranda/18, 21 Oct 1881.

[53] FO 335/154/Pr/Sanderson to Reade/5 April 1882; Gwyn and Tuckwell, op. cit., vol. 1, p. 545, vol. 2, p. 234.

[54] FO 102/140/37/Reade to Granville/21 June 1882.

[55] Ibid/38, 43, 44/Reade to Granville/3 July, 16, 23 Aug 1882; ibid/9.14/ Granville to Reade/23 June, 5 Aug 1882.

[56] FO 102/140/46, 47, 27 Tel. 53, 56, 59/Reade to Granville/5, 7, 25 Sep, 3, 4, 19 Oct 1882; Cambon, op. cit., pp. 172-3, 179-80.

received a demand for the abolition of the Capitulations as soon as French courts were established, he told the French ambassador—but not Reade—that he 'recognised the justice' of the French claim and would give 'the most friendly consideration' to any proposition. Of his own policy he said:

> We had from the commencement made our recognition of the position acquired by France dependent upon the maintenance of all commercial rights and privileges secured to us by Convention with the Regency, and our consent to any modification of the Capitulations would be made subject to that reservation.[57]

What Granville objected to was not the French salving the Egyptian wound to their vanity with 'spirited' colonial expansion but the establishing of 'differential privileges in favour of their own subjects'.[58] On 8 June 1883 Cambon got the treaty he wanted, by which the Bey pledged himself to the 'administrative, judicial and financial reforms' France thought useful[59] and as French courts were now established, urgent requests were made for the renunciation of Britain's Capitulations.[60] Granville replied that, subject to reserves and explanations, he was disposed to waive those rights that prevented the new French courts exercising civil and criminal jurisdiction.[61] At this moment occurred a particularly unpleasant incident in which a French officer used his sword on a Maltese, Mangano, whom the military then arrested. The argument about jurisdiction thus reopened between London and Paris, fanned criticism of French justice by an ever more emotionally involved Reade, whose associates kept the London press informed.[62] Though such disputes increased, Granville informed Waddington on

[57] FO 102/159/1170/Granville to Plunkett/17 Oct 1882; ibid/327/to Fraser/18 Oct 1882; FO 27/2569/1012 Conf/Plunkett to Granville/15 Sep 1882; ibid/2570/1059 Conf, 1060, 1103/2, 3, 19 Oct 1882. Dilke spoke publicly; de Card, op. cit., p. 27 n.
[58] PRO 30/29/203/to Lyons/2 May 1883; FO 27/2618/65 Sec/Lyons to Granville/23 Jan 1883.   [59] De Card, op. cit., p. 161.
[60] FO 102/159/21, 23/Reade to Granville/21, 26 April 1883; ibid/d'Aunay note/10 May 1883; ibid/569, 584/Granville to Lyons/4, 12 June 1883; FO 27/2616/584/12 June 1883. D.D.F. 1/5/30.
[61] FO 102/159/Granville to Tissot/20 June 1883; ibid/160/Parliamentary Question/24 July 1883; D.D.F. 1/5/48. Pauncefote ignored a suggestion to inform Reade, 'to prepare him in some measure for the inevitable'; FO 102/149/Reade to Granville/14 Nov 1883, min.
[62] AAE/Tunis/75/War Minister to MFA/12 July 1883; ibid/167/Robin to MFA/14 July 1882; ibid/Tel, Tel, 173, 192, 193/d'Estournelles to MFA/

16 November that consular jurisdiction would be abandoned on five conditions, only one of which caused the French to demur. Suggested originally by Reade, this required the immediate settlement of outstanding British claims against the Tunisian governments.[63] Cambon immediately pointed out to the Quai d'Orsay that one particularly large debt to a wealthy Tunisian, Ben Ayad, could not be admitted, as it would 'prepare a new bankruptcy of the Tunisian Government'.[64]

The parochially minded Tunis-bred consul was no match for the astute Cambon, who confessed himself now obliged to 'defend himself by all means'.[65] While Reade struggled to compile a list of unsettled 'cases',[66] d'Estournelles was surreptitiously and irregularly despatched to London, to blacken Reade's reputation there. While the latter was counted on to bore everyone with detail, d'Estournelles would 'talk big', act as if Reade were a 'worthy man but a little cracked' and 'do business wholesale with Pauncefote'—without details. Ferry was even told that Reade was motivated by bribery.[67] The plan seems to have worked well. Before Reade joined the discussion in London, the envoy, having had about a fortnight unhampered, reported all the Foreign Office 'roused against the unfortunate' and, nine days later, was able to telegraph, 'Reade and Broadley squashed'.[68] British consular jurisdiction was suppressed on 1 January 1884, even before the settlement of the claims, the arbitration of which was arranged on innocuous terms virtually drafted by Cambon.[69] The other interested

16, 18, 19 July, 4, 9 Aug 1883; FO 102/148/33, 34, 41/Reade to Granville/11, 11 July, 7 Aug 1883; FO 27/2621/441, 452/Lyons to Granville/14, 19 July 1883; ibid/2624/723/22 Oct 1883; ibid/2616/704/Granville to Lyons/19 July 1883; ibid/2617/1093/16 Nov 1883.

[63] FO 102/160/Granville to Waddington/16 Nov 1883; ibid/Tel 12/Reade to Granville/3 July 1883; FO 27/2617/1111/Granville to Lyons/21 Nov 1883; D.D.F. 1/5/136.

[64] AAE/Tunis/77/251/Cambon to MFA/3 Nov 1883; Cambon, op. cit., p. 202.

[65] Cambon, op. cit., p. 198. This included the seemingly normal interception of correspondence; ibid.

[66] FO 102/150/Tel 8/Granville to Reade/24 Nov 1883; ibid/32/Reade to Granville/9 Dec 1883.   [67] Cambon, op. cit., pp. 196-213.

[68] Ibid. FO 102/150/Tel 31/Reade to Granville/2 Dec 1883; ibid/149/65/19 Dec 1883; ibid/Tel 11/Granville to Reade/10 Dec 1883; D.D.F. 1/5/154.

[69] Cambon, op. cit., pp. 211-12; FO 102/160/Waddington to Granville 29, 31 Dec 1883; ibid/151/Tel 13/to Arpa/28 Dec 1883; ibid/Pauncefote to Catalani/5 Jan 1884; D.D.F. 1/5/179.

nations followed suit, including Italy which, as privately intimated to Granville, made a point of only suspending her capitulatory rights. Hitherto even Germany had hesitated.[70]

As a crowning blow to Reade, the principal cases submitted to arbitration were lost. Ben Ayad had years previously rescued the Bey in a financial crisis and neither Wood nor his successor had achieved a financial settlement. Indeed Cambon, in January, 1884, offered to compound the debt for a handsome sum (800,000 francs). However, at the arbitration, ancient beylical claims were suddenly produced. As balancing claims on the government before 1870 were considered obliterated by the decree of 1869 (reaffirmed in Cambon's 'terms'), this resulted in Ben Ayad being declared substantially in debt to the government.[71] As a pronounced Francophobe, involved in Wood's ambitions and the Enfida question, he was the *bête noire* of the French at a time when there was a marked tendency to reward those who had supported the occupation. He was sure of an unsympathetic hearing in official quarters, was 'fair game' to his enemies and, being unfortunately of litigious disposition, set his family on the path from great wealth to the near destitution it suffered by the end of the century.[72] The other important case occupying Reade's attention concerned the export of esparto grass for paper making, a trade almost entirely in British hands. After a Frenchman had been granted a monopoly of the most important esparto areas in 1881, an English firm, impressed by the favours he received, bought the concession, only to find that Cambon now insisted on onerous conditions. Upon this the company claimed extravagant damages and, though the conditions were withdrawn, persisted, only to have the claim rejected.[73]

[70] FO 102/160/25 Conf/Lumley to Granville/1 Feb 1884; ibid/from Ampthill/19 Jan 1884; ibid/from Rumbold/3 Jan 1884; D.D.F. 1/5/120.227. 262.

[71] FO 102/170/30, Tel 22/Reade to Granville/11 June, 20 Oct 1883; ibid/171/'Tel 15, 21/5, 9 May 1884; ibid/16/23 April 1884; ibid/Pr/Dingli to Reade/20 May 1884; D.D.F. 1/5/259. Cambon had opposed arbitration to the last; ibid/155/Tel 3/Reade to Granville/27 Feb 1884.

[72] FO 102/170/31, 32/Reade to Granville/16, 19 June 1883; ibid/171/11/22 Mar 1884; FO 27/3547/Berkeley to Lansdowne/24 Sep 1901; Ganiage, op. cit., pp. 559, 591-603; A. Johnston, op. cit., p. 32.

[73] FO 102/158/Paper Makers' Association to Granville/16 Nov 1881; ibid/12, 28/Reade to Granville/22 Mar 1882, 17 June 1884; ibid/167/10/ Sandwith to Rosebery/12 Mar 1886.

In achieving his second main objective, Cambon's difficulties came from Paris rather than Rome. The Treaty of Marsa of 8 June 1883 envisaged a French guarantee of a Beylical loan for the conversion or paying off of the Tunisian debt and the abolition of the Financial Commission;[74] but it was only in April, 1884, that the French Chambers passed the necessary vote. Granville had not encouraged earlier Italian hints for opposition or the demanding of concessions, provided the creditors were paid in full. Now, with Anglophobia at its height, Ferry seemed inclined to ignore England. Nevertheless, when the French conditions were finally made known, neither London nor Rome were disposed to object, as the creditors seemed content. Granville, it is true—still mindful of treaty rights—was 'not prepared to learn' of a definitive agreement without previous consultation. In October, the Commission ceased to exist[75] and the departure of Reade in the new year seemed to set the seal on the establishment of French Tunisia. His world had been destroyed and he died almost immediately, in Johnston's opinion, of a broken heart.[76]

BRITISH REPRESENTATIVES IN TUNIS

In English practice an 'agent and consul-general' was regarded as 'a diplomatic agent in the ordinary sense of the term' and the title was increasingly applied to the representative in Tunis after 1683. It was synonymous with the minor diplomatic ranks of 'commissioner' or 'chargé d'affaires', by which the French and Spanish representatives, for example, were known, and it was the normal form of British representation in the nine-teenth century in vassal-states like Egypt.[77] Unlike the ordinary

[74] As note 59. Cambon, op. cit., pp. 216-20, 224-6; H. Cambon, *Histoire de la régence de Tunis*, pp. 174-6, 180. D'Estournelles describes financial policy, *La Politique française en Tunisie*, chap. 2; *Revue des Deux Mondes*, vol. 79, pp. 787-791.

[75] FO 102/162/Plunkett to Granville/18 Sep 1883; ibid/Nigra to Granville/17 Sep 1883, 10 July 1884; ibid/89, 192, 314/Lyons to Granville/19 Feb, 4 April, 29 May 1884; ibid/236/Granville to Lyons/17 April 1884; ibid/Waddington to Granville/2 July 1884; ibid/126/Lumley to Granville/9 Aug 1884/ibid/Granville to Waddington/21 Aug 1884; FO 335/160/Granville to Reade/23 Aug 1884. Eubank, op. cit., pp. 21-23.

[76] H. Johnston, op. cit., p. 58.

[77] Satow, *Guide to Diplomatic Practice*, vol. 1, pp. 232, 237-8; PRO note (Tunis catalogue); Ganiage, 'Les Européens en Tunisie', *Cahiers de Tunisie*, vol. 3, pp. 397-9.

British consul in the Ottoman dominions, the agent at Tunis corresponded directly with the Foreign Office,[78] though a man like Wood also wrote at will to the Constantinople embassy. When sacrificing him in 1879, Salisbury originally intended to suppress the Consulate-General leaving 'a man on reduced salary—a Consul or Agent.' In the event only the reduced salary was effected (£1600 to £900), as Reade was entitled to the rank of Consul-General, and even that economy was counter-acted by Wood's generous pension (£1848). The saving effected through replacement of the two paid Vice-Consuls by two trading Vice-Consuls was similarly negatived because the appointment of a Consular judge became necessary. The authority for this was rushed through during the Enfida case.[79]

Much light is thrown on the workings of the Consulate-General in this period by an official enquiry resulting from investigation of allegations indicating 'great carelessness and laxity' as well as corruption, received in London. Another revealing factor was the mutual hostility which soon sprang up between Reade and the excitable new judge, Dr. Arpa—if only because the latter reported adversely on Levy's Enfida claim. The lengthy report (127 pp.) of Sir Adrian Dingli, judge at Malta and, incidentally, former 'patron and supporter' of Dr. Arpa, shows the effect of 'the jealousies so rampant in, and the suspicions inherent to, a small trading community in Barbary'. What was established was Reade's close relationship with Broadley, Levy (the Enfida claimant) and Ben Ayad. It was clear that both Wood and especially Reade had been glad to

[78] Safwat, op. cit., p. 61.
[79] SP/26/Salisbury to Lyons/6 Mar 1879; WP/Lister to Wood/6 June 1879; FO 102/141/13 Conslr/Reade to Granville/7 Oct 1882, mins; ibid/144/Pr/Tenterden to Lyons/3 May 1881; ibid/154/FO to Reilly/28 Mar, 5 April 1881. There were also Vice-Consuls and Consular Agents in important centres, usually unpaid and 'trading'. Reade had two and seven respectively, all trading, on 1 Jan 1885; ibid/163/1 Conslr/to Granville. Playfair thought them admirably selected; FO 27/2745/74/to Salisbury/16 Nov 1885. Wood's two Vice-Consuls, in Tunis and Susa, were, however, paid (FO 102/125/4 Conslr/to Salisbury/7 Jan 1879), and reduction of both to unpaid status unwisely left his overworked successors with no reliable deputy (see note 82). In 1893, Drummond Hay, having only 'two Maltese clerks, indifferently acquainted with the English Language', and having to leave his post under his Italian colleague during absence, successfully demanded a paid Vice-Consul ('who should be an English gentleman'); FO 27/3139/Nil Conslr, Tel/Drummond Hay to Rosebery/7 Oct, 28 Nov 1893; ibid/Pr/to Currie/7 Oct 1893; FO 27/3190/5 Consl/FO to Drummond Hay/3 Feb 1894.

make use of Broadley's legal expertise, when available, and that, though 'no magistrate or Judge in Europe gave greater attention to the cases brought before him' than Reade did, advocates felt that Broadley's influence was too great when legal, technical questions, in which Reade was inexperienced, were involved. Levy too had acted on occasion as Reade's interpreter in dealings with the local authorities. There was also the question of 'carelessness and laxity' in administration. It was found that the bitter, former chief clerk, himself responsible for the more serious accusations, was seen to have been retained at his post for six years, in spite of known dishonesty. On the other hand, an accusing Consular Agent, dismissed by Reade, was described as 'in a state of mental debility' and unfit for reinstatement. Dingli felt that the suspicions of Consulate partisanship would disappear now that a consular judge had been appointed. He recommended also that Consular staff should be brought 'to a level with its duties' and afforded a 'decent subsistence' to reduce the incentive to dishonesty. The Foreign Office concluded that the allegations of corruption were 'all moonshine', but also that, in dealing justice:

> ... the state of things existing under the old system, as appears from this Report, was a reproach to British administration.[80]

Reade's administrative difficulties were not, however, over, for the recommendations on staff were virtually ignored. What was worse, his Pro-Consul, a banker and trader doing increasing business with French notables, ceased to attend at the Consulate after the occupation and finally, as Reade put it, 'threw in his lot with the invaders and occupiers of the Regency' by heading a petition calling for the abolition of Consular jurisdiction.[81] Not surprisingly, with no-one to deputise for him, with his post 'ruinously expensive', with the Ben Ayad fiasco making him 'the laughing stock of the place', with his health failing, and with the French continuing to act in what he considered an 'arbitrary and shameful manner', Reade felt his presence in

[80] FO 102/153/Dingli to Granville/13 May, mins., -July 1882; ibid/152/ Conslr Nos. 24, 30, 31/Reade to Granville/20 Sep, 5, 5 Oct 1881; ibid/Lister Memo/18 Oct 1881.
[81] FO 102/160/41/Reade to Granville/7 Aug 1883.

Tunis 'scarcely possible'.[82] Granville was content to retire him and Arpa, as 'for political reasons' it was desired to reduce the post to a simple Consulate. When this was done in April, 1885, the new consul, Sandwith, was placed under the orders of the Consul-General in Algiers, the Francophile Colonel Playfair.[83]

The French appreciated that Reade's departure marked the end of the campaign by 'some English subject' against their protectorate.[84] Yet there was always something unreal in the new arrangement, which seemed almost like an invitation to a French annexation. It must, after all, be remembered that Algiers and Tunis had little connection and their affairs were, in fact dealt with by different ministries in Paris. Inevitably Sandwith came to correspond with London, even though his despatches might be sent 'under flying seal' via Playfair, or sometimes—especially at first—as a 'copy' of one sent to Playfair. The practical difficulties of Playfair making representation in Algiers and of his subordinate being so nearly equal in position, obviously meant that the change made would become one of outward form rather than substance. For some years Tunisian questions were of lesser importance, with the French building on the foundations laid by Cambon and the Gladstone and Salisbury governments guarding against too great an encroachment on British conventional rights. Yet even minor disputes showed a latent capacity for raising principles of importance and causing trouble. A French determination in 1886 to send to Algiers for trial a now respectable Maltese, sentenced to death there for manslaughter twenty years before, led to British protests in Algiers, Tunis and Paris, and Salisbury, even when the prosecution was suspended by the French 'reserving all rights', continued to protest that the claim was 'totally inadmissable'. He quoted Granville's reservations when surrendering consular jurisdiction and complained that:

[82] FO 102/155/Reade/Memo/15 Jan 1884; ibid/Pr/to Staveley/10 May, 6, 24 June 1884; ibid/21 Conslr/to Granville/8 Dec 1884.

[83] The original intention was to suppress the Agency only, but there were Treasury difficulties. Ibid/Tel 15/FO to Reade/18 July 1884; ibid/157/FO to Treasury/16 Oct, 13 Dec 1884; ibid/Treasury to FO/25 Nov 1884; PRO 30/29/208/Granville to Nigra/9 Jan 1885; FO 102/163/to Sandwith/20 Mar, 21 April 1885. The salary was reduced (£1000 to £700) and Playfair's increased (£800 to £900). In France, what was taken as Granville's 'act of kindness' was remembered; Le Soir, 3 Nov 1889, FO 27/2958/25 Conslr/ from Lytton/3 Nov 1889.   [84] D.D.F. 1/5/529.

... the French Government seem to think that Her Majesty's Government have consented to surrender the rights which have been secured to this country under the Treaties and Capitulations.[85]

Similarly, questions like the 'practical monopoly' of the Esparto concession continued to cause friction.[86]

It would have been far from easy to preserve good relations with French officialdom in normal circumstances, but, with the prevailing Anglophobia, both Playfair and Sandwith felt it was 'as if instructions had been sent to thwart them on every possible occasion'.[87] The want of cordiality between Sandwith's successor, Ricketts, a man prone to legal argumentation, and the French was more marked, and he incurred the same censure as Reade, for not communicating freely with the French Resident-General. At a time when Tunisian questions were again reappearing on the international stage, Salisbury, in 1889, restrained the ardour of his consul, telling him that treaty rights 'should not be converted into instruments for embarrassing the ordinary functions of the local administration'. He felt that Ricketts wilfully misunderstood those instructions 'because he did not like them'.[88] Nevertheless a debate about the vexed and highly complicated question of a Real Property decree became so involved that some of the voluminous and heartbreaking papers seem to have been conveniently 'lost' in the Foreign Office, to re-emerge two years later when any protest was no longer possible.[89]

On the appointment of the competent Robert Drummond Hay in 1889, the Tunis Consulate became again independent of Algiers and, as the new consul 'felt acutely the inferiority of his

[85] FO 102/167/56/Sandwith to Rosebery/3, 4 Mar 1886; ibid/Tels/FO to Sandwith/1, 29 Nov 1886; FO 27/2802/Conslr-51, 54/to Lyons/2, 19 Nov 1886; ibid/2860/Conslr-6, 8, 17, 20, 39/18, 26 Jan, 22 Feb, 11 Mar, 17 May 1887; ibid/61 Conslr/to Egerton/24 Aug 1887.

[86] FO 102/167/10, 15, 17/Sandwith to Rosebery/12, 27 Mar, 5 April 1886; FO 27/2803/25 Col/FO to Lyons/30 Mar 1886; ibid/2812/80 Conslr/Playfair to Iddesleigh/21 Dec 1886.

[87] FO 27/2812/71/Playfair to Rosebery/23 Oct 1886.

[88] FO 27/2953/118/Lytton to Salisbury/4 Mar 1889; ibid/2950/204a/ Salisbury to Lytton/30 Mar 1889; ibid/2970/Tel, 36, 40/to Ricketts/16, 18 May, 14 June 1889; ibid/2971/45/Ricketts to Salisbury/22 June 1889. French FO officials were also provocative; ibid/2997/Lytton to Salisbury/22 Jan 1890.

[89] FO 27/2951/319/Salisbury to Lytton/25 July 1889, encls; ibid/3052/42/ Drummond Hay to Salisbury/7 Sep 1891, min.

R. H. Drummond Hay

W. H. D. Haggard

H. H. Johnston

René Millet

position' as a 'mere consul' he was created Consul-General in
1891. His salary still remained vastly inferior to that of colleagues with far smaller responsibilities. When he had demonstrated the impossibility of delegating trust to a pro-consul
trading from the Consulate itself, a salaried Vice-Consul was at
last appointed.[90] His successor, Haggard, appointed in 1894,
ranked as a minister, but failed in an attempt to get the Tunis
consulate restored to the dignity of an Agency, though there
were, according to him, 'few Diplomatic posts that had anything
like as much to do'. There were, however, Foreign Office doubts
whether all the assiduous and loquacious despatch-writing of
the brother of Rider-Haggard, the novelist, was strictly necessary.[91] What is surely ironic is that the most Francophile of all,
Harry Johnston, a former Commissioner, should have held
office during the unpleasantness of the Fashoda crisis.[92] That
was at a time when the endemic and ludicrous French suspicion
of lady missionaries from Britain was even leading to their
prosecution for handing out bibles and religious tracts—under a
law against scurrilous literature.[93]

[90] FO 27/2958/46 Conslr/Salisbury to Lytton/11 Dec 1889; ibid/3052/
22, Nil/Drummond Hay to Salisbury/17 June, 17 Nov 1891; ibid/3139/21
Conslr, Nil/to Rosebery/24 Aug, 7 Oct 1893; ibid/3094/3/Salisbury to
Drummond Hay/20 Jan 1892; ibid/3190/5 Conslr/3 Feb 1894.
[91] FO 27/3237/13/Haggard to FO/4 Feb 1895; ibid/3239/Separate/to
Salisbury/4 Oct 1895; ibid/3345/8/23 Jan 1897.
[92] Oliver, *Sir Harry Johnston and the Scramble for Africa*, pp. 278-284.
[93] FO 27/3528/passim.

3

BRITISH POLICY AND TUNIS, 1888–1892

MASSOWAH AND THE ITALIAN SCHOOLS

A good deal has been going on at Rome which has been both disquieting and puzzling.[1]

As an epitaph to the diplomatic activity of the years 1887 to 1891, these words of Salisbury are perhaps not inappropriate. For, in the prevailing circumstances, Italy, and also Tunis by virtue of the Italian interest in it, played a central role in affairs. This Salisbury certainly had to take into account. Though English rivalry with Russia at Constantinople (and elsewhere) had played its part in inducing Britain to enter into the second Mediterranean Agreement with Austria and Italy, Salisbury was already aware that, in the Bosphorus, Britain's interests were less vital then those of her partners and increasingly aware of the corollary, that the situation forbade an evacuation of Egypt. To him, the danger was that Russia might fortify her ambitions by a close association with France, or that the Germans, to avoid a development equally unpleasant for them, might buy off the Muscovite by a promise of support unwelcome to London. Moreover, the English minister could not avoid these pitfalls by resurrecting the liberal *entente* with France, so long as resentment over the occupation of Egypt burned in the French heart and was exacerbated by lesser irritations in other parts of Africa, the Far East and even Newfoundland. Surely the logic of the situation indicated that the maintenance of close relations with Italy, and through her with the Central Powers was essential if Britain were to ward off the possible recreation of the *Dreikaiserbund*.[2] Not until the Franco-

[1] SP/68/Salisbury to Dufferin/28 Dec 1888.
[2] Cecil, *Life of Salisbury*, vol. 4, pp. 50-1, 69-71, 78-9; Newton, *Lord Lyons*, vol. 2, p. 409; *Cambridge History of the British Empire*, vol. 3, p. 260; Langer, *European Alliances*, p. 430.

Russian Alliance was an accomplished fact could Italy's friendship be regarded as expendable.

As long as this commanding, if temporary, position occupied by Italy was dominated by the volatile and excitable Crispi, who returned to power in August 1887, it was to be expected that much that was 'disquieting and puzzling' would afflict the international scene. It may be that Franco-Italian antagonism was inevitable in view of the depth of Italian feeling over Tunis and the growth of protectionism in both countries, but it was Italy which, though destined to suffer most from a commercial war, had denounced the existing commercial arrangements in December 1886.[3] Though ostensibly seeking better trade relations with France, Crispi made a rupture almost certain by arrogant talk of 'bringing the French to their knees' and especially by his attitude over an incident concerning the position of Tunisians in Italy, when French consular archives in Florence were violated. In a number of ways the French showed that they, too, could be childishly unpleasant and plainly intimated that no agreement was possible while Italy retained her adherence to the Triple Alliance.[4] Impulsive and headstrong, Crispi, who might be said perhaps to have had a defective sense of diplomatic realities, was determined to extract the maximum of advantage from the closer relations with Germany and England arising from the agreements of 1887.[5] What encouraged Crispi, however, naturally dismayed the French. As a result of indications that England was co-operating with the Triple Alliance and as a result of further broad hints in a Bismarck speech in February they became apprehensive. Their alarm increased as a result of innocuous parliamentary statements by Salisbury and Fergusson, as a result of rumours that Italy had been promised Tunis by Germany after a successful war and as a result of a British fleet visit to Italy during the Franco-Italian commercial

[3] *Memoirs of Crispi*, vol. 2, chap. 7, passim; D.D.F. 1/7/324; D.D.F. 8/183; Langer, *European Alliances*, pp. 474-75; *Franco-Russian Alliances*, p. 117.
[4] FO 27/2904/Lytton to Salisbury/17 Jan 1888; FO 45/601/16 Conf., 41 Conf., 44 Sec/Kennedy to Salisbury/31 Jan, 21, 24 Feb 1888; Crispi, op. cit., pp. 254, 274-75.
[5] Ibid.; Crispi, op. cit., p. 462; FO 45/601/49/Kennedy to Salisbury/25 Feb 1888; Peteani, *La questione libica nella diplomazia europea*, pp. 65-74. The agreements were the treaty with Germany, concluded after the renewal of the Triple Alliance on 20 Feb, and the Mediterranean Agreements of March and Dec, with Britain.

crisis. France therefore made great efforts to discover England's precise commitments. The feeling of isolation in Paris even produced a suggestion that:

> . . . the best guarantee of the *status quo* in the Mediterranean would be some direct understanding between France, England and Italy on a basis of general disinterestedness . . .

Another dove of peace was loosed in August, but seems never to have got further than Berlin.[6]

It is not surprising, in the circumstances, that a series of crises and incidents should occur nor that Tunis should feature large in them. In May trouble arose over Massowah, which had been occupied in (1885 according to the Italian record) in accordance with 'a plan concerted with France to intervene in the Soudan'. The object had been to establish a triple *condominium* with England, a plan rendered nugatory by the fall of Khartoum.[7] The reason for the quarrel that now arose was that the Italians claimed to exercise full sovereignty in Massowah as a result of the occupation while the French contended that they were entitled to rights under the Capitulations. For France also had its Crispi in Goblet, equally excitable and hot-tempered, equally prone to act in an impulsive and offensive manner and to recoil in fright at the possible consequences of his own offensiveness. The new French minister proposed to sell France's assumed rights at Massowah in exchange for a formal renunciation of the Italian Capitulatory rights in Tunis. Crispi seems to have passed through an apprehensive phase, during which he declared that if France recognized Italy's sovereign rights in Massowah, he was ready for the complete abrogation of Italian rights to jurisdiction in Tunis, which had been only suspended in 1884. No doubt he was influenced by the opinion of Bismarck, which was that the situation in France was 'decidedly dangerous' and that the government in Paris might risk a war with Italy in order to 'prevent the triumph of Caesarism' at home. The Germans, however, had no wish to see the concept of a Mediterranean Entente upset by a Franco-

---

[6] FO 27/2904/84 Sec, 114 Sec/Lytton to Salisbury/9, 21 Feb 1888; FO 45/601/27 Very Conf/Kennedy to Salisbury/9 Feb 1888; D.D.F. 1/7/41. 60.89.193.294.478.504.507, Peteani, op. cit., pp. 79-82.

[7] FO 45/716/32 Conf/Clare Ford to Rosebery/31 Jan 1894 (encl.)

Italian reconciliation in the Tunis question and intimated to the French that 'should serious trouble arise, Germany would be obliged to place herself on the side of Italy'. As a consequence, Crispi felt emboldened to hold out for a better bargain and declare that he would answer no further communications on the subject from Goblet.[8]

This was the sort of situation that was to face Salisbury more than once while Crispi remained in power. There was no inclination at Hatfield to give the Italians support similar to that accorded by the Germans. Indeed, far from increasing his obligations beyond those undertaken in the previous year, Salisbury was concerned not to increase his dependence on Germany and to avoid conflict with the French if possible, a wise decision if only because of Britain's relatively weakened naval position in the Mediterranean.[9] Initially Salisbury had not regarded the dispute as having any great importance; nor did there seem to be a real danger of hostilities. Lytton, in spite of the background militarism of Boulanger and occasionally absurd and menacing statements from the Floquet ministry, consistently reported that an unstable and isolated France would not dare go to war, even with the irritating Italy, in case the new friends of the latter (especially England) would join her on the battlefield.[10] Italy was no more likely to move against France without the assurance of English help, which was very far from assured. It is true that Crispi had endeavoured to assume in the spring that he could call on English support and vaingloriously claimed that a visit of the channel squadron had forestalled a French attack;[11] but a chilling answer to a

---

[8] Crispi, op. cit., pp. 307-338; FO 27/2905/215/Lytton to Salisbury/ 5 April 1888; ibid/2906/290 Conf/Lytton to Salisbury/18 May 1888; D.D.F. 1/7/179.183.187.189.191.192.195.216. In July, Goblet said that, in the absence of a friendly agreement with Italy over Tunis he would 'probably be obliged to act with authority'.

[9] Cecil, op. cit., vol. 4, pp. 70-71, 95, 106; Marder, *British Naval Policy*, pp. 129-132.

[10] FO 27/2906/290 Conf. 305 Conf/Lytton to Salisbury/18, 24 May 1888; ibid/2907/399 Conf/19 July 1888.

[11] FO 45/601/27 Very Conf. 44 Sec 55 Sec/Kennedy to Salisbury/9, 24 Feb, 5 Mar 1888; Marder, op. cit., pp. 128-9; Langer, *European Alliances*, pp. 465-7, 475-6. Brin, Minister of Marine, in Dec commented on the 'immense impression' made in Italy and the consequent general belief that 'England would protect the coasts of Italy from attack'; FO 45/603/326 Conf/Kennedy to Salisbury/12 Dec 1888.

parliamentary question in London stated that there was 'no agreement, binding the country to material action', no military commitment.[12] Again in July, the febrile imagination of the Italian affected to see in the illness of the Bey of Tunis a French opportunity to plot the annexation of the Regency. He announced that the departure of a 'considerable French squadron' was imminent and claimed that the time had arrived for the two countries to despatch a force to Tunisian waters. To all of this Salisbury returned cold, discouraging answers. He did not see 'any danger of adventurous policy' on the part of France in the then strained condition of Europe and:

> . . . any naval movement would have a provocative effect especially as, if France did intend to annex Tunis, she would do it by a movement of troops from Algeria and not by any naval action.[13]

At this time he was pursuing a strictly 'legal' policy towards the internal affairs of the Regency, and was restraining Ricketts, the Consul-General, from actions irritating to the French Residency. Indeed, his estimate of the slight importance to be accorded to the Massowah question must have been strengthened early in August by a conversation with Robilant, the new Italian ambassador, who did not as much as mention the dispute, leaving the impression that:

> . . . too much importance was attached to trivial questions in diplomatic communications and especially in those which came from Italy.[14]

A day later, however, he had the information that, if war arose, 'Germany would be forced to take the Italian side', and that changed everything for Salisbury. Hitherto he had told Waddington that Germany was 'for nothing' in the dispute, which was 'not to be looked upon as entering in the field of her policy'. Pressed now to advise the French to drop their contentions against Italy, he realised that the affair no longer had 'the narrow local significance' he had attached to it.[15] On their side,

---

[12] G.P. 4/941.

[13] FO 45/600/146a Sec 149 Sec 150 Sec/Salisbury to Kennedy/20, 23, 23 July 1888.

[14] FO 45/600/162/Salisbury to Kennedy/6 Aug 1888.

[15] FO 27/2903/393 Sec/Salisbury to Lytton/7 Aug 1888; D.D.F. 1/7/189. 192.201. Also note 10.

the Italians made a great effort to commit Salisbury. All he had been asked for before was his opinion on Capitulations in countries like Massowah, formerly under Mussulman administration, and had answered that 'in territory administered by a Christian and civilised power, the existence of Capitulations could not be justified'.[16] The emphasis now, however, was on Tunis. To prevent their own argument being turned against them there, the Italians were anxious to point out that 'the government was still Mussulman'. though much under French guidance. Far from leaping to champion the Italian cause, Salisbury expressed no view as to the legal position, save to suggest that there might be grounds for a compromise, and asserted that it was hardly worth struggling for the 'scanty remnant' of the Capitulations which Italy had not already surrendered. Moreover he bluntly remarked that it was a matter not considered of 'capital importance' or one which could interest Britain and commented sardonically that:

> . . . it was hardly in the interests of Italy to insist on the importance of Tunis being entirely Christian. It could only become so by the annexation of Tunis to France.

Cross examined on the question of annexation, he said he understood that France had no such intention, but, if it took place he would object strongly, especially on account of Biserta. He would then join other powers in a protest, but refused to be drawn as to what 'ulterior action' he would take, since such action was dependent on public opinion. On the question of Italian suspicions of French intentions in Tripoli, he dryly observed that 'the French were apt to entertain similar suspicions' of Italy, though he would regard the passing of the territory into other hands 'as very grave indeed', in view of the effect on the Suez Canal and Egypt. In other words the Italians got nothing tangible and, far from urging the French to cease their opposition to Italy, Salisbury simply gave Waddington the gist of the arguments he had used against the Italian policy on Capitulations in Tunis.[17] It is not to be wondered at that Crispi

16 Crispi, op. cit., pp. 317-18; FO 403/112/2/412a/Salisbury to Egerton/18 Aug 1888.
17 Ibid.; FO 45/600/172 Conf/Salisbury to Kennedy/17 Aug 1888; D.D.F. 1/7/201 n.1.

complained that the attitude of Salisbury and 'press organs reflecting the views of Her Majesty's Government' had been less friendly since the beginning of August. On hearing this the British minister simply made the impatient observation that he had not even seen the Italian Ambassador recently and that the papers attacked his government more frequently than the Italian.[18] In fact, no trouble was taken to hide from the French British irritation with the conduct and methods of a country which, as Pauncefote put it, 'was playing the frog which wanted to become bigger than the ox'.[19]

Faced by Germany and Italy, however, France seemed to resign herself to a defeat over Massowah.[20] Yet Goblet was really determined to make gains in Tunis at the expense of the Italians; but, instead of quietly and prudently 'slicing the salami' and eroding the Italian position there gradually, he foolishly took the risk of a head-on collision on a question over which the Italians were at their most sensitive. For the preservation of national identity by the large Italian colony in Tunis naturally depended on the freedom of their schools and associations, and these were directly affected by two Beylical decrees issued on 15 September. The first subjected all schools to inspection by the Director of Public Instruction in the Regency and the second prohibited the formation of any society without the permission of the authorities.[21] Throughout the peninsula there was no doubt that these measures were in retaliation for the recent Massowah incident,[22] and the sympathetic Ricketts concluded that the effect of the schools decree would be:

> . . . to force the language of a very insignificant minority on the masses, giving the French authorities at the same time a right to interfere in the establishments and depriving the Italians and

---

[18] FO 45/603/239 Conf/Kennedy to Salisbury/15 Sep 1888. The *Morning Post* and *Standard* were the papers. Salisbury denied communicating with any.
[19] D.D.F. 1/7/231.232.237.247. By July, Salisbury had concluded the fault was mainly Italy's; Cecil, op. cit., p. 103.
[20] D.D.F. 1/7/214 n.2. Goblet 'did not wish to continue the discussion'.
[21] FO 27/2924/16/Ricketts to Salisbury/25 Sep 1888; ibid/2907/492/ Egerton to Salisbury/27 Sep 1888; FO 403/112/9/Robilant to Salisbury/ 24 Sep 1888; Crispi, op. cit., pp. 349-51.
[22] FO 45/603/248/Kennedy to Salisbury/25 Sep 1888; Crispi, op. cit., p. 351 n.1.

others of that freedom of action which has been enjoyed by them in the management of their own schools.[23]

The Italians in fact considered their schools as public schools and they were established and financed by the Italian State. To the perennial outrage of French ideas on assimilation, it was possible then, as much later, 'for an Italian to live in Tunisia his whole civil life from birth to death in an exclusively Italian environment'.[24] Having thrown down the gage, however, Goblet was soon forced to retreat, and references to the 'sovereign rights' of the Bey in issuing the decrees were quickly followed by assurances. He now said that 'none of the rights reposing on previous engagements would be affected' and that the 'greatest prudence and conciliation' would be used in applying the laws to Italians, if indeed they were applied at all.[25]

Crispi soon showed that he was only too glad to take up the French challenge by declaring that he intended to resist the decree on the inspection of schools[26] and it was clear that, as in the Massowah incident, he had German support. From Berlin Salisbury learned that the French had been told that Germany was 'not prepared to acquiesce' in the application of the decree and Holstein confidentially informed Malet that this was to prevent a bipartite controversy between Crispi and Goblet.

By becoming a party to it, the German Government hoped to restrain the vigour of Crispi, and to modify M. Goblet's attitude by the consideration that Italy was not alone in disapproving the law.[27]

---

[23] As note 20. There were 5 Italian, 6 French and 2 British (missionary) schools and the population was said to comprise 1,300,000 Arabs, 45,000 foreigners (mainly Italians and Maltese) and 4,000 French. Unreliable French figures, according to S. H. Roberts, gave 10,000 French, 11,000 Italians and 11,700 Maltese; *History of French Colonial Policy*, p. 286. Crispi claimed 28,000 Italians in Tunis; op. cit., p. 352.

[24] Rood Balek, *L'Afrique française* (1921), p. 73, quoted Roberts, op. cit., p. 288. FO 27/2924/17/Ricketts to Salisbury/29 Sep 1888. In 1935, Monchicourt indignantly made the same point in *Le Statut des Italiens en Tunisie*, quoted extensively by Delbos in *La Question italienne en Tunisie*, especially p. 10.

[25] FO 403/112/499/Egerton to Salisbury/30 Sep 1888. Crispi, op. cit., pp. 351-3.

[26] FO 45/603/256/Kennedy to Salisbury/7 Oct 1888; ibid/604/Tel 38/7 Oct 1888; FO 27/2908/506/Egerton to Salisbury/4 Oct 1888.

[27] FO 403/112/19/302 Conf/Malet to Salisbury/6 Oct 1888; Crispi, op. cit., p. 355.

Now, as in the previous quarrel, the Italians endeavoured to involve Salisbury and with much the same result. Crispi urged Britain to join his resistance to the decree, as 'a very important British School' and the interests of the large Maltese population were involved, but Salisbury had already referred the legal issues to the Law Officers of the Crown and the question was 'under consideration'.[28] All Crispi's efforts at this time to make a common front with the London Government against the French in less urgent disputes involving Tunis, were equally unsuccessful. In sour arguments over the 'violation of treaties' in the matter of Real Property, the new municipal taxes and French jurisdiction, all the exhortations from Rome to 'joint action' or to 'concerted measures' were met with further temporisation.[29]

By the middle of October Salisbury was unburdening himself, in his private correspondence with Lytton, of the irritation he felt towards both the French and the Italians. On the Tunisian decrees he wrote, 'We really are very little interested in the matter', and when a breach seemed imminent he made excuses for expressing no opinion to the Italians on the legality of the decrees. He found difficulties in formulating an opinion and there was the awkward fact that the British colony in the Regency had made no protest. He even told the Italians that they were concerning themselves with 'a matter of little importance' and that they were 'foolish to stir'.[30] Towards the French he was critical but, significantly, less scathing than towards the Italians. The decrees were stigmatised as 'unnecessary and inopportune' but the worried French ambassador, Jusserand, was comforted with the opinion that it was 'not in the least likely' that the Italians (or their Germans friends) nourished warlike designs against France. He was very doubtful also whether they would take the grave step of rescinding the proto-

[28] FO 45/603/262 Conf/Kennedy to Salisbury/9 Oct 1888; FO 403/112/20/ Robilant to Salisbury/8 Oct 1888; ibid/Salisbury to Robilant/16 Oct 1888. Crispi's memoirs are very misleading on this point, dating the Law Officers' opinion (favourable to the Italian view) as 21 Oct instead of 21 Nov; op. cit., p. 358, contradicted on p. 361. Compare FO 403/112/L.O.'s to Salisbury/21 Nov. 1888.

[29] FO 403/112/4/Robilant to Salisbury/27 Aug 1888; ibid/105/Salisbury to Kennedy/14 Sep; ibid/to Robilant/17 Sep 1888; ibid/169/Ccl/Kennedy to Salisbury/18 Oct 1888.

[30] SP/59/Salisbury to Lytton/25 Oct 1888; Cecil, op. cit., p. 104.

col relating to their rights under the Capitulations.[31] Yet he saw clearly that Crispi would not have found 'opportunities to quarrel' but for Goblet:

> It seems as if Crispi was bent on getting up a quarrel: and that Goblet, or rather I suppose Charmes, out of sheer irritability and 'cussedness' would give them every opportunity for it. The Massowah Capitulations, the Tripolitan boundary, the Tunis schools and now the occupation of Harrar and the future fate of Morocco—such a collection of small affairs in so short a space of time can not be entirely accidental.

Salisbury was equally aware that the impetuous Crispi could go no further than pleased the Germans, whose influence on him was 'unbounded', and he was convinced that the Germans did not want war at that moment. For he knew that Goblet had appealed to Berlin for counsel of moderation to Crispi and had agreed that, though unable to cancel his decree, he would make 'all reasonable concessions'. In obedience to 'his master's voice' Crispi had affected indifference to the decree, provided it were not to be applied to Italian schools and the matter seemed virtually settled.[32]

Bismarck was in fact restraining his impetuous Italian friend and German policies in Europe were dictating closer relations with England.[33] It is true that the French had been told that their decree was illegal and pressure had been exerted to get them to make 'every possible concession'. On the other hand Münster, the German Ambassador in Paris, claimed the credit for getting his Italian colleague to emasculate a Crispi ultimatum which demanded the revocation of the decree in a specified period.[34] Now, therefore, as a result of German intervention, Goblet was ready to give a written declaration that his decree would not apply to Italian schools, but it is clear that success simply made Crispi feel that he could get even more. 'Dis-

---

[31] Ibid.; FO 27/2903/482/Salisbury to Lytton/15 Oct 1888; D.D.F. 1/7/247.
[32] Ibid.; FO 403/112/324 Conf/Beauclerk to Salisbury/19 Oct 1888.
[33] Owing partly to closer Franco-Russian cooperation and the succession of William II in July 1888; Langer, op. cit., p. 493. *History of the Times*, vol. 3, pp. 142-3.
[34] FO 27/2908/534 Conf/Lytton to Salisbury/25 Oct 1888; Crispi, op. cit., p. 356. (N.B. A time limit implies an ultimatum; H. Nicolson, *Diplomacy*, p. 249) D.D.F. 1/7/252.257.

quieting and puzzling' events began to occur. Possibly as a crude Italian effort to induce Britain to declare her support, it was asserted by Menabrea, the Italian Ambassador, that Goblet was claiming English recognition of the validity of the decree. All this did was to draw from Salisbury a statement that he had not expressed an opinion and had reserved all British rights.[35]

To the surprise of their allies, the Italians now announced that they would resist the proposed French declaration 'with all means in their power' unless not only existing schools were exempted from it, but also all that might be established in the future. Menabrea claimed to have told Goblet:

> Do what you please about your Beylical Decree. We shall continue to treat it as *non avenu* (void) . . . France must judge for herself as to the expediency of prolonging the theoretical assertion of an irritating and illegitimate pretention of which the practical application will be strenuously resisted by Italy if ever it is attempted in reference to Italian subjects or interests.[36]

This 'conciliatory ultimatum', as Menabrea termed it, was castigated even by Münster as 'unreasonable and aggressive', but when Goblet rejected it after a fierce quarrel, the Italian ambassador declared that 'his last word . . . had been spoken'. In the stalemate that ensued Lytton was of the opinion that only a French attempt to enforce the 'obnoxious decree' on existing Italian schools could afford a pretext for Italian action. As for Goblet, he anticipated no complications unless the Italians deliberately opened new schools without notice. The French minister in fact was now trusting to the 'healing influences of time' and to the excellent personal relations between Berio, the Italian Consul General at Tunis, and Massicault, the French Resident General, to prevent further complications.[37]

The situation which now developed was not without its humour. Incredible complications ensued, during which Crispi's consummate facility for disregarding the consequences of his own policies found expression in a assertion that relations

[35] FO 27/2908/534 Conf/Lytton to Salisbury/25 Oct 1888; FO 27/2908/535 Conf/Lytton to Salisbury/25 Oct 1888; ibid/2903/502/Salisbury to Lytton/30 Oct 1888; Crispi, op. cit., p. 361.

[36] FO 27/2908/534 Conf/Lytton to Salisbury/25 Oct 1888. Also FO 403/112/336/Beauclerk to Salisbury/27 Oct 1888; FO 27/2952/2 Conf/Lytton to Salisbury/2 Jan 1889.   [37] Ibid.; Crispi, op. cit., pp. 358-361.

with France were again 'not only friendly but cordial'.[38] The ubiquitous Cardinal Lavigerie intervened privately with a promise to try to obtain Tripoli for the Italians and so end the quarrel.[39] According to Crispi's published account, in which there are obvious *lacunae*, the whole question was to have been dealt with exclusively at Paris and Berio disobeyed his instructions by having discussions in Tunis with Massicault.[40] Goblet on his side seemed to think that his suggestion for a practical local solution in Tunis had been approved, but Menabrea, questioned later (by Lytton) on 'the Italian demands' made at Tunis was completely in the dark. Berio, in fact, was reported as having claimed that Italy was 'supported by the German and English governments but more especially by the latter' in demanding the establishment of Italian Government public schools with exemption from inspection and the exclusion from Tunisian law of Italian associations. This drew another statement from Salisbury which was reassuring only to the French:

> Her Majesty's Government have not taken any action in support of the Italian demands on which they are not at present prepared to offer an opinion.[41]

Obviously Crispi had not endeared himself the more to Salisbury by his latest move, which was calculated to bring relations with France again to boiling point. For his intention to establish new public schools in Tunis had just become known in London and, while Berio was engaged in the purchase of sites, the director of government schools in Rome arrived with a body of official teachers. Then, while Berio 'under instructions' refused to discuss the preparations with Massicault, Goblet could only extract from Menabrea that the matter was in the hands of Berio and that Rome was not even in communication with him on the

[38] FO 45/603/323/Kennedy to Salisbury/12 Dec 1888.
[39] The letter was to the physician of H. H. Tayib Bey; FO 27/2924/26 Conf/Ricketts to Salisbury/27 Nov 1888. As Lavigerie was personally detested by Goblet and Crispi, his proposition was even more fantastic; FO 27/2908/628 Conf/Lytton to Salisbury/28 Dec 1888.
[40] Crispi, op. cit., pp. 364-66. According to Ricketts there was an exchange of abortive legalistic notes in Oct., FO 27/2924/19/to Salisbury/25 Oct 1888.
[41] FO 27/2908/Tel 612, 613, 622/Lytton to Salisbury/20, 20, 22 Dec 1888; ibid/2903/Tel 562/Salisbury to Lytton/21 Dec 1888; ibid/2952/2 Conf/Lytton to Salisbury/2 Jan 1889. Holstein, however, had earlier remarked on the 'favourable change' in the British attitude; Crispi, op. cit., p. 360.

subject. Berio's demands had, in fact, been made in reply to an attempt by Massicault to get an understanding on draft regulations for the schools. When Salisbury got a full report of the circumstances he made an even more emphatic statement to the effect that he had no knowledge of the demands and therefore 'could not have supported them even if they were considered to be well founded'.[42] Berio was now blamed by Crispi for exceeding his instructions and was 'to his surprise and mortification' forbidden to hold any further communication with Massicault on the subject. Goblet had, therefore, failed to negotiate with both Menabrea in Paris and Berio in Tunis. When he now instructed Mariani in Rome to request explanations from Crispi himself, he was told that:

> . . . the government of Italy owes no account to the French government of any arrangements it may see fit to make in reference to the requirements of its own subjects in Tunis.[43]

It seemed by now in Paris that the object of Italian policy was to destroy the French Protectorate, and, as passive submission was rejected, it was feared that 'a collision might occur at any moment'. The French government regretted that it 'would be compelled, however reluctantly', to arrest all persons concerned in opening unauthorised schools and to suppress the schools by force. Goblet himself said he had been assured by both the German and the Austrian ambassadors that if Italy provoked a quarrel, 'she would do so at her own risk and peril'. He feared, nevertheless, that Crispi might be calculating that, whatever the cause of conflict, 'Germany and Austria certainly, and England probably, would be obliged to come to her rescue'.[44] That his apprehensions had some justification was soon to be demonstrated by Austria. For six months Kalnoky had not hidden his disapproval of his Italian ally's provocative behaviour from Goblet nor hesitated to counsel moderation at Rome and he

[42] FO 27/2952/2 Conf/Lytton to Salisbury/2 Jan 1889; FO 403/112/567/ Salisbury to Lytton/27 Dec 1888; D.D.F. 1/7/290.291.292. On 3 Dec Mariani was told that, if commercial negotiations were mentioned, they would be declined until the Tunis question was settled to France's satisfaction.

[43] Ibid.; see especially FO 27/2952/2 Conf/Lytton to Salisbury/2 Jan 1889.

[44] FO 27/2908/623 Conf/Lytton to Salisbury/27 Dec 1888. Austria had long counselled moderation and was not really interested; FO 403/112/ 348 Conf/Paget to Salisbury/13 Nov 1888; Crispi, op. cit., pp. 358, 361.

considered the move to open new schools as 'untimely and unjustifiable'. However, rumours that Austrian relations with Germany and Italy had changed as well as the pressure of events were soon to compel him to tell the French frankly that, if a Franco-Italian war developed over Tunis, it would be impossible to localise it. 'Whatever the origin', Austria would not side with France.[45]

The voice which counted the more in the ear of Crispi was, however, that which came from Friedrichsruh rather than Vienna and of Bismarck's influence Salisbury was well aware. For the benefit of Dufferin, the new British Ambassador at Rome, he now wrote privately a perspicacious appreciation of the situation. As he saw it, Germany had been 'ceaselessly building up diplomatic breakwaters' against France and Russia and had forced Austria to join her in an Alliance with Italy, which latter country was showing in its demeanour the consequence of admission 'to the honour of fighting for two ancient dynasties'. The outcome of Crispi's attempts (in 1888) to reap the maximum profit from his investment in powerful allies seemed to the British Minister to be two-fold. In the first place there had been his 'grabs' in East Africa at Zeila, Harrar, Suakin and Kismayo on the Zanzibar Coast. All this seemed to Salisbury of no general importance though it had resulted in a 'slightly lower temperature' in relations between London and Rome; but the second consequence appeared 'much more dangerous'. As Herbert Bismarck had told him, if there was to be a war, it was in Italy's interest that it should take place as soon as possible.[46] For the 'armed peace' was leading that country rapidly to financial ruin, whereas a conflict could give rise to hopes of 'Albania certainly, Nice possibly and perhaps Tunis and Tripoli'. As for the consequence:

> The consequence is that Crispi has been perpetually getting up little quarrels with the French—Massowah, Suez Canal

[45] The French were told, however, that this was 'only a formal expression of the general relationship in which Austria stands to Italy'. FO 27/2952/21/ Lytton to Salisbury/16 Jan 1889; ibid/2908/613/20 Dec 1888; FO 403/112/1 Tel/Paget to Salisbury/7 Jan 1889; D.D.F. 1/7/260.298.300; Crispi, op. cit., pp. 358, 361-2.
[46] SP/68/Salisbury to Dufferin/28 Dec 1888. The hot-headed Damiani, Italian Under-Secretary, and the impetuous Blanc, at Constantinople, had been heard to argue in favour of war.

Convention, Tunis Schools, Tripolitan boundary, Treaty of Commerce, Morocco boundary, etc. etc. etc. France has kept her temper pretty well but the danger arising out of the Tunis schools quarrel is not over yet.

From the German point of view it was no doubt convenient 'to have on hand someone content to take upon himself in case of need the role of *provocateur*';[47] but Crispi was obviously too enthusiastic and ebullient a performer in the part. Salisbury saw Berlin as 'bothered and anxious' and with a desire to avoid war enhanced by the failure of the new German rifle.[48]
As far as the German Chancellor was concerned Salisbury could not have been far off the mark. It is still perhaps impossible to say what motive was uppermost in Bismarck's mind. It may be that he felt that the key to the situation lay in the hand of Salisbury or that he wanted Salisbury to take his Mediterranean chestnuts out of the fire for him. During the alarms in the spring of 1888, Herbert Bismarck had intimated confidentially:

> It is an absolute fact that England has the power to prevent the outbreak of a Franco-Italian war, which we also have pressing reasons for avoiding. . . . If now England makes it clear in Paris that a declaration of war by her would follow a French attack on Italy, I consider that it would be the most certain way to frustrate it.[49]

It may be argued that, when Crispi had seemed disposed to a sensible bargain with the French during August, the Germans had thrown fat on the dying fire of Italian provocation with their promise of help 'should serious trouble arise'. At the same time, however, they had been urging Britain to become strong 'not merely pacific'[50] and their ostensibly aggressive action in Rome may have been partly due to a determination not to see the emasculation of the Franco-Italian quarrel over Tunis, which had done so much to impel Italy towards the Triple Alliance in the first place. This would indeed explain the apparently contradictory German attempts to control the evil spirit which they had unleashed and to avert hostilities. After all,

---

[47] SP/68/Salisbury to Dufferin/28 Dec 1888; D.D.F. 1/7/247/
[48] Ibid.   [49] G.P. 6/1281.   [50] G.P. 4/942.

as Holstein pointed out in October, if they really had wanted war, they wouldn't have minded the 'fountains of bitterness' between Italy and France.[51] Moreover, if the Germans were anxious to keep the alliance of Italy, they were also seeking rather than commanding better relations with Britain. The proposal for an Anglo-German alliance in January 1889, therefore, is a question of some relevance, since it throws light on Italy's precarious position, which turned so much on the situation in the Mediterranean. As is well known, the possibility of 'blackmailing' England in Egypt and Bulgaria, so recently so successful, had diminished. In addition, the danger seemed real to Berlin of French Boulangism—or its aftermath—leading to a war of revenge, supported on Germany's other flank by Russia. Bismarck, perhaps believed that such a contingency could best be forestalled by an alliance with a rearmed England, and proposed a one-, two- or three-year alliance against France. As this was to be openly sanctioned by Parliament, it could serve to preserve the peace for the time being, 'perhaps for a long time'. He was concerned, like the German General Staff, to see Britain become 'as strong as she potentially should be' and to increase further the apparent intimacy which had been signalised by a far-reaching exchange of naval information. His immediate cause for alarm may have been the persistent French pressure on Italy. Certainly Bismarck showed no signs by now of any willingness to allow conflicting Anglo-German hopes of empire to imperil the interests of German security in Europe. As early as October 1888, he had even dropped an oblique hint that he would have 'willingly accepted any risk of displeasing Russia' if he had a real defensive alliance with England. The ageing and increasingly rancorous Chancellor must have been particularly sanguine if he really expected Salisbury to fall at last into his net. For though the English statesman was also concerned over Boulangism in France, he distrusted the 'uncertain staff' of German friendliness as well as the 'uncertain humours' of Bismarck himself. The last thing he wanted was a war with France, and he noted that Bismarck's offer did not mention Russia. It may be reasonably inferred that he preferred to rely on an increase in British naval strength, which expert enquiry

[51] FO 403/112/19/302 Conf/Malet to Salisbury/6 Oct 1888.

BDT H

had just shown to be inadequate, rather than risk an open alliance, which would be almost inevitably unpopular in England, and which all Bismarck's arguments could hardly show to be necessary for that country. This was a time, indeed, when the Court of St. James was still cool towards Germany as a result of earlier indiscretions by William II. Furthermore the hostility of the Russian press and signs of Franco-Russian cooperation suggested that the danger of real intimacy between Germany and Russia was no more in the offing than that other development which might dismay England—a reconciliation between France and Germany. When 'the hateful Herbert' brought up the subject again in March 1889, urging that an alliance 'especially the appearance of it' would strengthen Crispi and the steadfastness of Italy, it is not surprising that Salisbury, in spite of a great show of cordiality, left the alliance proposition 'on the table'. Cordiality was the most he required and it may be said that his real answer was to Bismarck the 'two power standard', a navy equal to any two European navies combined, which it was the intention of the Naval Defence Act of the same month to create. The German solicitude to bolster up Crispi, 'the only man strong enough to keep Italy on the right way', and to ward off the danger of a conquered Italy becoming a 'mere vassal of France' was tacitly ignored.[52]

The importance of Italy in the policy of Germany therefore, as well as in that of England, had had the consequence of enabling Crispi to call on reluctant German support almost to the point of rupture with France. There had ensued what

---

[52] G.P. 4/942-945; Cecil, *Life of Salisbury*, vol. 4, pp. 71, 100-121; Q.V.L., series 3, p. 484; Langer, *European Alliances*, pp. 488-494, 510, *Franco-Russian Alliance*, pp. 32-4; Tunstall, 'Imperial Defence', *Cambridge History of the British Empire*, vol. 3, pp. 243-4; Brandenburg, *From Bismarck to the World War*, p. 9; *Berliner Monatshefte*, vol. 13, pp. 24-31. Because of the scanty record of the discussions, there have been various controverting interpretations of the significance of the alliance offer. Möller, (*Historische Vierteljahrschrift*, vol. 31, pp. 507-527, and *Historische Zeitschrift*, vol. 163, pp. 100-113) argues that Bismarck's main object was to cure the young Kaiser of Anglophilia, but Schüssler disagrees and Kluke, more convincingly, asserts that Bismarck was making a clumsy and misconceived but nevertheless genuine attempt at an English alliance. Francis Joseph was told in August, 1889, that this had been the object for ten years; ibid., vol. 163, pp. 547-554; vol 175, pp. 285-306. It may be noted that Italy was not mentioned in the original alliance offer, and Bismarck, possibly searching for the basis of an agreement, made much of the awkwardness for England of French hostility in the event of an Anglo-American war.

Pauncefote termed 'a very serious complication' in which the Italians seemed in the wrong. Salisbury, however, would not consider trying to influence Crispi directly, since the Italian appeared to be trailing his coat for 'reasons too good [to him] to be overcome by any motives we have to offer', and his attitude was summed up in the words:

> Germany and Austria are in a difficult position . . . But I mistrust the line Germany is taking.[53]

What Salisbury actually did was to broach the matter with the Germans and Austrians. Vienna was told that 'the affair threatened a disturbance' and that, though the French had been originally at fault, they had now made every concession and it appeared that 'Crispi was deliberately provoking a rupture'. Asked on 7 January 1889 whether he was taking any action, an obviously reluctant Kalnoky 'had no confirmation' that the question was threatening.[54] Salisbury seems to have left no record of the conversation he then intended to have with Hatzfeldt but it is at least logical to suppose that the Germans, in the five days before they were to propose to Britain an alliance that was to be 'the surest way to obtain peace', would be already paying heed to the British Minister's views.[55] The sequence of events that followed is instructive. By 8 January Goblet had received assurances from the Central Powers that they were exercising a moderating influence at Rome, though in French eyes these assurances seemed contradicted by the behaviour of Crispi,[56] and it was on 9 January that Austria made her declaration as to where she would stand in a Franco-Italian war. On 12 January indeed Berio was purchasing premises in Tunis for a new school and two days later Münster and Lytton in Paris agreed that Menabrea 'seemed to have mounted his high horse' on the question. Tension was acute. Yet the risk of an immediate explosion had quite passed and Crispi had given Paris an assurance that he did not intend to open any new schools at Tunis 'for the moment'.[57] Nevertheless, he would give no pledge

---

[53] FO 27/2952/2 Conf/Lytton to Salisbury/2 Jan 1889, mins.
[54] FO 403/112/1 Tel/Salisbury to Paget/6 Jan 1889; ibid/Tel/Paget to Salisbury/7 Jan 1889.
[55] See note 51. [56] D.D.F. 1/7/296.
[57] FO 27/2952/21/Lytton to Salisbury/16 Jan 1889; SP/58/14 Jan 1889.

regarding the future, in spite of French efforts. This was evidently, as Dufferin said, 'with a view to keeping open the Tunis question, and having at hand a means of appealing to the passions of the Italian people'. It was only left for the almost equally fatuous Goblet, who had recovered his nerve now that the danger had receded, to use 'some very threatening language to the Austrian Ambassador at Paris in reference to Crispi's perversity and aggressive methods'; but the Italian, though refusing to close the schools question, remained quiet, at all events as far as Tunis was concerned.[58] It is perhaps fairly safe to assume that it was Bismarck's influence with Crispi that had wrought the change. As a German diplomat observed:

> Bismarck had sufficient authority to prevent Crispi starting a war by a rash act.[59]

As for Kalnoky, he had given a somewhat apologetic warning to France, as he presumably could have done no less if he wished to preserve the alliance with Italy at a time when he was pressing moderation upon an unwilling Crispi. His distaste for and lack of interest in the whole business was shown in a curious way during the heated exchanges of January when, with obvious untruth, he denied any knowledge of French complaints over the opening of new Italian schools in Tunis.[60] The question at issue had indeed not been settled but a position of stalemate had been created, with France making no attempt to enforce her decree on old Italian schools and Italy making no attempt to open new ones.[61]

Crispi had barely managed to preserve his position in Tunis and there never had been any chance of improving it without a willingness by his allies or England to risk war on his behalf. As Pauncefote remarked at this time over another Tunisian problem:

[58] SP/66/Dufferin to Salisbury/24 Jan, 7 Feb 1889. The French demands had been reduced to (a) notification of new schools and (b) liability of schools for inspection 'to a reasonable degree' for hygienic purposes. The German and Austrian ambassadors said they had suppressed Crispi's 'exuberances'.
[59] Ibid. It need hardly be said that Crispi's memoirs contain no reference to the pressure of his allies; op. cit., pp. 365-6. Information from Vienna suggested that Crispi's resolution had already weakened when Salisbury acted; FO 403/112/5/Paget to Salisbury/7 Jan 1889.
[60] Lytton to Salisbury/SP/58/14 Jan 1889; FO 27/2952/28/18 Jan 1889.
[61] Ibid. The question was re-argued in the following autumn, with similar results; Crispi, op. cit., pp. 366-7.

They [the French] will carry on their aim by degrees and kill
M. Crispi *à coup d'épingles*.[62]

Moreover, a vital interest of Italy, the restoration of commercial
relations with France, was now hopelessly compromised and the
French were quite determined that a complete agreement over
Tunis was an essential prerequisite.[63] Seven years later indeed
they were to carry their point. As for the French themselves, it
is hard to disagree with Lytton's description of the Floquet
Government record as 'brief and evil'. For corrupt practices
and policies calculated to stimulate 'Boulangism' at home had
been paralleled by the sort of political ineptitude abroad which
gave Crispi his chance to make trouble. A position hastily
assumed in the Massowah question had been as readily abandoned and the ill-timed schools decree had led to a serious clash
with Italy, with no perceptible advantage to France.[64] In the
'Ruritanian' atmosphere created by Crispi and Goblet, Bismarck
had had the difficult task of giving the volatile Italian enough
support to keep him firmly in the alliance, without giving him
enough to provoke the war by which alone Crispi could have
triumphed. Kalnoky, uninterested and disapproving, had only
wanted a speedy end to the whole affair.

Salisbury had received in November 1888 the considered
opinion of the Law Officers of the Crown that Britain was
entitled to contest the legality of the schools decree. If he had
wished to support Italy against France, he could therefore have
advanced the best of reasons.[65] Yet he did not do so. He appreciated the reasons for the apparent 'zig zag' in German policy, at
one time bullying France to please Italy and at another 'trying
to keep Crispi quiet'. He understood the Germans' anxiety to
keep in power an Italian minister who suited them better than
any other, and their anxiety to avoid a war in which there was
nothing to gain and much to risk. In spite, however, of the
discouragement he had given to Italy, and the comfort he had
accorded, at times, to France, he still could argue that British
policy had 'altered a little—not much':

[62] FO 27/2971/3/Ricketts to Salisbury/8 Jan 1889, min.
[63] D.D.F. 1/7/310.316.324.346.
[64] FO 27/2908/544 Conf, 547 Conf/Lytton to Salisbury/30, 31 Oct 1888.
[65] FO 403/112/L.O.'s to Salisbury/21 Nov 1888. Salisbury could have
taken a pro-Italian line also in the numerous local disputes in Tunis.

At first we were very cordial with Italy, which is our normal policy. But as Crispi's character developed we came to the conclusion that it was better to give him a wider berth. We have therefore declined to pronounce ourselves in his quarrel with France; or to give him any definite assurances as to the future, beyond the expression of a strong desire to maintain the *status quo* in the Mediterranean.

England, he concluded, would be inclined to go to the assistance of an Italy 'gratuitously' attacked by France, but not back a war arising out of 'one of Crispi's trumpery quarrels'.[66]

SALISBURY AND THE CRISPI PROBLEM

The barometer is at calm . . . M. Crispi has had to put some water in his wine.

In uttering these reassuring words to Waddington in February 1889, Salisbury plainly intimated that this desirable consummation was the result of his care not to encourage Italian claims in Tunis and of support for this line from 'the two German Empires'.[67] Watering Crispi's wine, however, was to prove only a temporary expedient. For, in spite of the check to his ambitions in the matter of the Italian schools in Tunis, Crispi managed to keep up the fight from a distance. Soon, in spite of the condition of Italian finances, he was busy developing state schools abroad to serve as a means of curbing the spread of the French language and influence in the east and of restoring Italian to its former position as the *lingua franca* of the Levant.[68] However calm the barometer had been in February, it was not long before Crispi, sweltering in the heat of July in Rome, was again raising storms and trying to bring into play on his behalf the might of his powerful friends. He soon declared his intention of denouncing the Protocol by which, five years before, Italy had suspended her capitulatory rights to jurisdiction in Tunis.[69] This dangerous procedure met with immediate discouragement from Kalnoky, who had since the spring been

[66] SP/68/Salisbury to Dufferin/28 Dec 1888; Cecil, op. cit., p. 105.
[67] D.D.F. 1/7/321.
[68] FO 45/623/66 Conf/Dufferin to Salisbury/16 Mar 1889; ibid/624/140/ Dering to Salisbury/22 June 1889; ibid/625/211/Dering to Salisbury/10 Oct 1889; ibid/646/10/Dufferin to Salisbury/9 Jan 1890.
[69] FO 403/112/117 Conf/Salisbury to Maude/2 July 1889.

rejecting repeated Italian proposals for a naval and military agreement, on the grounds that Austria was interested in the East rather than the West of the Mediterranean. He now asked the Italian Cabinet to consider the possible consequences and (as if echoing Bismarck) urged it to make sure beforehand of the support of Britain 'in all Mediterranean questions which might bring it into conflict with France'.[70] When Salisbury and Bismarck showed themselves equally cool, Crispi presumably realised that his wine was still being watered, as no more was heard of his proposal, and it is significant that Waddington was informed confidentially in London of what had happened.[71]

At the same time the endemic antagonism between the Italian Government and the Vatican had reached a pitch of new intensity. As a result of 'information' received, Crispi concluded that an exasperated France had intervened to induce the Pope to leave Rome so as to provide 'a pretext for a quarrel with Italy', and the pendulum of his emotions swung violently from aggressiveness to what would appear to have been genuine panic.[72] If his information had been correct the situation would indeed have been alarming. He saw the Russians, whose influence in the Balkans Austria had foolishly allowed to increase, massing 'on the Austrian frontier'.[73] He saw the French, 'full of illusions' as to their strength, out to provoke a war with Germany and Italy, and urgent preparations at home bore witness to his concern.[74] A deputy was sent to confer with Bismarck on the 'threatening danger', but his most frenzied appeal for help went to Salisbury. Crispi let the English minister know that:

> ... France would most certainly send her fleet into the Mediterranean, in order to strike Italy a 'coup foudroyant', and that Russia would at the same time send a powerful army into the Balkan States. . . . His main trust lay upon England, according to the secret Agreement of 1887; his only fear was that English help might arrive too late.

[70] Ibid.; Langer, *European Alliances*, pp. 479-80.
[71] FO 403/112/Salisbury to Deym/4 July 1889; ibid/202/Paget to Salisbury/10 July 1889; D.D.F. 1/7/419.
[72] FO 45/624/159 Most Conf/Dering to Salisbury/23 July 1889; ibid/622/163 Sec/Salisbury to Dering/24 July 1889; Langer, op. cit., pp. 472-3; Crispi, *Memoirs*, vol. 2, pp. 393, 400-6.
[73] FO 45/624/158 Very Conf/Dering to Salisbury/22 July 1889.
[74] Ibid/160 Sec/Dering to Salisbury/23 July 1889; Crispi, op. cit., pp. 394-5.

What Crispi wanted was that an excuse should be found to send a 'powerful British fleet' to the Mediterranean and he humbly promised to avoid any provocation to France, especially over Tunis. The question of consular jurisdiction had been 'laid aside for the present'.[75]

Salisbury showed as little inclination as ever to give Crispi any definite assurances. His information was that the Pope had resolved not to leave Rome and he replied that he 'did not at all share Signor Crispi's apprehensions,' believing the probability of a French attack to be small. On the subject of 'English help', Salisbury was brutally frank:

> Some phrases in the communication [from Catalani] caused me, further, to add that there were no engagements between this country and Italy, *pledging either to material action* and that I must not be understood as making any.

Crispi was allowed one crumb of comfort. This was to know that the British Mediterranean fleet was to be strengthened after the autumn manœuvres 'in view of the present aspect of Mediterranean politics'.[76] As for the Germans, they were equally incredulous concerning the possibility of a French attack, but considerably more cordial and reassuring towards the worried Italian, confidently asserting that England would help, provided France were the aggressor.[77] Rumours of an English engagement to defend the Italian coasts did in fact gain currency, but Salisbury denied any pledge to the Triple Alliance when Waddington took up the question later in the year. Salisbury reminded him how he had consistently refused to associate himself with 'the efforts of M. Crispi to reopen the Tunis question' and of the many occasions on which the French Ambassador had thanked him for it.[78] In spite of this, King Humbert was reputed to have told Prince Napoleon in January 1890 that his coasts were safe as he had a 'formal promise', from the Court of St. James's, of naval help in time of

[75] FO 45/622/162 Sec/Salisbury to Dering/24 July 1889; Crispi, op. cit., p. 396.
[76] Ibid.; FO 45/622/163 Sec/Salisbury to Dering/24 July 1889. The phrase in italics was added to the draft by Salisbury.
[77] Crispi, op. cit., pp. 407-16. They had heard that Admiral Hoskins had orders to resist a French attack on Italy unless outnumbered; Langer, op. cit., p. 481. Crispi had heard something similar in 1888; op. cit., p. 349.
[78] D.D.F. 1/7/456.504.

need so that he could 'mobilise his army in security'. It is difficult to say in this case whether it was a question of the wish being father to the thought, a genuine inability to understand Salisbury's categorical denial of an engagement involving material action, or of knowing dishonesty by Crispi to preserve his reputation at home.[79] A somewhat more accurate picture of Salisbury's role in the Tunisian imbroglio of 1889 is found in articles, violently hostile to Crispi, by Deloncle, the 'intimate friend and adviser of Spuller', the French foreign minister:

> . . . the attitude of England in these circumstances has been most correct; from the time she inclined before the *fait accompli* of our protectorate in Tunis, she has loyally refrained from causing us any embarrassment.[80]

England would, in all probability, still have succoured an Italy 'gratuitously' attacked by France but the tergiversations of Crispi, from whom the British representative had not been able to extract 'any one fact' upon which his July fears had been based,[81] had not been without their effect. It seemed evident to Salisbury that the Germans were anxious about Crispi's activities and that confidence between the members of the Triple Alliance had been replaced by suspicion:

> Italy suspects Austria — Austria suspects Germany — and Germany thinks both her humble allies exceedingly insubordinate.[82]

Salisbury's own attitude had been made clear earlier and it had not changed. His disapproval of Crispi could only be increased by incessant hostile squabbles between the latter and the Porte,

---

[79] *Figaro*, 3 June 1891; FO 27/3039/Lytton to Salisbury/3 June 1891; Langer, *Franco-Prussian Alliance*, p. 167. Crispi said publicly in October, 'No-one would now attack Italy because she was strong and had powerful allies'; FO 45/625/217/Dering to Salisbury/15 Oct 1889. He still continued to dominate parliament though facing more criticism than formerly; FO 45/623/42a/Dufferin to Salisbury/16 Feb 1889; ibid/52 Conf/Dering to Salisbury/1 Mar 1889; ibid/646/24 Conf/Dufferin to Salisbury/8 Feb 1890.

[80] FO 27/2956/489, 494, 497A Conf/Lytton to Salisbury/4, 7, 9 Nov 1889. Obviously 'inspired', the articles referred incidentally to the information Salisbury had given on Crispi's attempts to get support in London and Berlin for restoring the capitulations.

[81] FO 45/625/165/Dering to Salisbury/1 Aug 1889.

[82] SP/68/Salisbury to Dufferin/15 Nov 1889; SnP/-268/I/Salisbury to Sanderson/9 Oct 1889.

for these threatened to drive the Turk into the arms of Russia.[83] As for Crispi himself, for whose problems there was to be no solution yet in a war fought by his allies, he was again forced into a conciliatory attitude towards the hated France. Relations suddenly became 'excellent' and, to loose a dove of peace, he even abolished the differential tariff against that country.[84]

THE ANGLO-FRENCH NEGOTIATIONS

It is ironic that, at the moment that Crispi's exuberant effervescence had been effectively, if temporarily, subdued, a combination of factors served to advance the problems of Tunis, and other similar questions, to the forefront of Great Power politics. By 1889 Salisbury had decided against any early evacuation of Egypt[85] and, indeed, much of his diplomacy in the following three years was devoted to consolidating and extending British strategic control over the Nile Valley and the route to the Far East. As little financial support seemed possible for political reasons, expansion had to be left to chartered companies,[86] but this in itself involved the veritable certainty of conflicts between the nationals of interested European countries, in regions where rights were still ill-defined. The possibility of such conflicts was increased because Salisbury had perforce to delay the intended reconquest of the Nile Valley and watershed until Egypt could shoulder a substantial part of the cost.[87] In addition to possible Belgian or French threats from the Congo, the irritating Crispi had in mind expansion from Massowah and claimed that the Italian protectorate of Abys-

---

[83] FO 45/622/94 Conf, 185 Conf/Salisbury to Dufferin, to Dering/ 8 May, 10 Aug 1889; FO 45/624/102 Conf, 109 Conf, 114 Conf, 133 Conf/to Salisbury/2, 12, 15 May, 11 June 1889; ibid/625/180, 204 Very Conf/16 Aug, 1 Oct 1889; ibid/626/47 Tel, 48 Tel/to Dering/2, 2 Oct 1889; ibid/28 Tel/ to Salisbury/7 Aug 1889.

[84] Langer, Franco-Russian Alliance, pp. 117-18; Albertini, Origins of the War of 1914, vol. 1, p. 68.

[85] Cecil, Life of Salisbury, vol. 4, pp. 139-40, 252. For the commercial importance of the Suez Canal route to Britain see Cambridge History of the British Empire, vol. 3, pp. 200-3.

[86] Cecil, op. cit., pp. 139-40, 280-1, 309-11; Q.V.L., series 3, vol. 1, p. 459; Langer, Diplomacy of Imperialism, p. 108. A good example of the relation between the government, the companies and private finance is found in Oliver, Sir Harry Johnston, chap. 5, especially pp. 151-5.

[87] Ibid.; Cecil, op. cit., pp. 326-8; G.P. 8/1778.

sinia, established—as he said—by the Treaty of Ucciali in 1889, extended to Kassala and the Nile. In March assurances were given that there was 'nothing further from the wishes of the Italian Government' than to interfere in the African regions under Anglo-Egyptian influence.[88] By the end of the year, however, Salisbury was expressing regret at Crispi policies calculated 'to injure Italy', and grumbling that, after Kassala, a new justification 'would not be wanting' for the occupation even of Khartoum by Italy.[89]

Far more serious was the possibility that the squabbles between English and German companies in East Africa, which by the spring of 1890 were arousing disproportionate public animosity in the metropolitan countries, would adversely affect the good relations now existing between the governments in London and Berlin.[90] British aspirations in the Nile Valley were directly challenged when the redoubtable Dr. Karl Peters declared a German protectorate over Uganda in March.[91] As Salisbury concluded three months later:

> . . . any indefinite postponement of a settlement in Africa would render it very difficult to maintain terms of amity with Germany, and would force us to change our system of alliances in Europe . . .

—and the cost of a French alliance was the evacuation of Egypt.[92] Luckily for him, the principal interest of Bismarck and his successor was in Europe not Africa, and it was possible to strike a bargain with Germany as Britain possessed the island of Heligoland, strategically important to the owners of the new Kiel canal. The Germans' East African interests 'merely came forward as matters for concession' and they agreed to a partial surrender of those interests in exchange for Heligoland.[93]

There were, however, two capitals in which the resulting

[88] FO 45/648/Tel 18a/Dufferin to Salisbury/3 Mar 1890.
[89] Ibid/Tel 48, Tel 56/Salisbury to Dufferin/29 Aug, 12 Nov 1890. A compromise was worked out in February, 1891.
[90] Langer, op. cit., p. 6; G.P. 8/1688.
[91] Langer, op. cit., pp. 112-16; Kennedy, *Salisbury*, pp. 216-17; Cecil, op. cit., pp. 278-80.
[92] Q.V.L., series 3, vol. 1, pp. 613-14.
[93] G.P. 8/1681; Cecil, op. cit., pp. 294-300; Kennedy, op. cit., pp. 217-21. Caprivi also criticised Italy's policy in Abyssinia as forgetful that her general Mediterranean interests depended on British goodwill; G.P. 8/1973.

Anglo-German satisfaction was as gall and wormwood, and where was immediately conjured up the spectre of England moving into a Quadruple Alliance. In St. Petersburg the Russians had a particular excuse for peevishness because of the refusal of the Germans at this very moment to renew Bismarck's Reinsurance Treaty.[94] In Paris the news of the agreement was received with an explosion of indignation. For the smouldering resentment over Egypt had recently been exacerbated by a 'violent development' in the Newfoundland Fisheries Dispute,[95] and a France, which had overcome Boulangism, rebuilt its military and naval strength and developed increasingly important economic ties with Moscow, was a Phoenix with which to reckon.[96] Moreover, the permanent officials at the Quai d'Orsay under Charmes and the colonial ministry under the 'practical and energetic' Étienne echoed the spirit of the new *Comité de l'Afrique français* which nourished the idea of a French empire stretching from coast to coast across the north of Africa.[97] Already, since the beginning of April when the Porte had reopened negotiations for an evacuation of Egypt, there had been some verbal fencing between Waddington and Salisbury who, though still paying lip service to eventual evacuation, was thinking of reconquering the Sudan.[98] Privately and publicly Ribot had declared that France would 'never consent without protest' to English possession of the Nile and Suez Canal.[99] In the midst of so much acrimony, it is not surprising that the French should have reacted sharply when they heard that, in the new agreement, Germany had consented to an English protectorate over Zanzibar. Not that France had much in the way of material interest to defend there, but she had been a

[94] Langer, op. cit., pp. 7-9; *Franco-Russian Alliance*, pp. 79-81. Stanley's famous comment was, '. . . a new pair of trousers for a suspender button' (ibid. p. 78) and Salisbury told Lansdowne that he ought to like the agreement and that 'it was likely to be carried through without serious hindrance'; LP/277/29/27 June 1890.

[95] Cecil, op. cit., p. 317. Irritation towards England was greater than towards Germany; G.P. 8/1691.

[96] Lytton described the French as 'profuse in demonstrations of anticipatory gratitude' towards the Russians; FO 27/2956/566 Conf/to Salisbury/ 24 Dec 1889; Langer, op. cit., pp. 118-19.

[97] FO 27/2997/19 Sec/Lytton to Salisbury/22 Jan 1890; Hanotaux, *Fachoda*, p. 60; Langer, *Diplomacy of Imperialism*, pp. 125-6.

[98] G.P. 8/1775-80; D.D.F. 1/8/19.20.45.63.

[99] FO 27/2998/138 Conf, 223/Lytton to Salisbury/1 April, 11 June 1890.

signatory to the convention of 1862. She now claimed to have suffered 'moral damage' and expected compensation for her legal rights.[100]

In a remarkable conversation on Egypt with Waddington, Salisbury gave a broad hint as to what he considered a fair settlement to be. After discussing, in allegorical vein, well worn English argument why France should not oppose financial reforms or attempt to 'dismiss the gardener because the flowers were good' and equally well worn French arguments for a speedy end to the occupation, Salisbury suddenly, and obviously with premeditation, produced a copy of the occupation convention between France and the Bey of Tunis. From this he read an extract ending with the words:

> This occupation will cease when the French and Tunisian military authorities recognise by common agreement that the local administration is in a condition to guarantee the maintenance of order.

He then told Waddington, according to an account in his own writing, that he looked upon the French interpretation of this stipulation 'as one that should guide them in the application of a similar undertaking in Egypt'.[101] The Foreign Office record of the conversations that followed is obviously incomplete,[102] and Waddington too was obviously an ambassador with influence above the ordinary on the now insecure government at home. After an apparently reluctant Salisbury (who said he had 'forgotten' to consult France about the Zanzibar protectorate) had been induced to ask for the consent of the French, they were not long in making known the price they put on their assumed legal rights.[103] Ribot was pulled two ways. On the one hand he seemed 'really alarmed at the increasing isolation of France' and inclined to share the general suspicion that the Heligoland Treaty was more than a friendly settlement of

[100] D.D.F. 1/8/83.86.87.90; Cecil, op. cit., p. 318. Ribot 'could scarcely contain his anger'; G.P. 8/1690.

[101] FO 27/2995/226/Salisbury to Lytton/21 June 1890. The extract was article 2 of the treaty of 12 May 1881; in Rouard de Card, Traités de protectorat conclus par la France en Afrique, pp. 159-61.

[102] FO 27/3384/Memo. by Streatfield/20 Oct 1894. Salisbury became more secretive after the use of the 1878 records by Granville and Gladstone in 1881; Temperley, 'British Secret Diplomacy', Cambridge Historical Journal, vol. 6, p. 14. See note 116.   [103] D.D.F. 1/8/91.96.

lesser difficulties; all of which would suggest that caution and prudence were necessary. On the other hand there was the need to obtain what he called 'some substantial benefit for France' in order to disarm the criticism of his chauvinist political opponents. At this moment therefore he was professing conciliatory intentions, saying he would be glad to find a way to drop discussion of Egypt so as 'not to have upon his hands at the same time and in an acutely critical condition, three such questions as Newfoundland, Zanzibar and Egypt'. Yet, at the same time, he began pressing for 'compensation' and, though he professed to think impossible any British encouragement for a German attack on France, he said grimly to Lytton:

> ... we have now a powerful army, and if we are compelled to use it in self defence we shall do so without fear of the result.[104]

Ribot, however, merely mentioned the possibility of compensation for France in Madagascar *or* Tunis, and it was Waddington who formulated a list of stiff demands and carried the minister with him. It was 'of first importance', he declared, to get England's treaty with Tunis modified so that it expired at the same time as the Italian treaty (in 1896 or sooner)—with a guarantee to Britain of most favoured nation treatment. To this were added demands for a formal recognition of the French Protectorate in Madagascar, for the exclusion of any protectorate at Muscat and for commissioners to delimit spheres of influence in the region of the Niger and Southern Africa. It was over Tunis that Waddington correctly anticipated opposition from Salisbury and wanted acceptance of his demand to be made *sine qua non* for agreement.[105]

There were special reasons why in 1890 the French should want a change in Tunis. In the first place the Regency had been passing through an economic crisis and this gave added urgency to the long-standing endeavours of agricultural and mercantile interests in Tunis to secure the free entry of Tunisian produce

---

[104] FO 27/2998/242, 245, 246 Conf/Lytton to Salisbury/26, 28, 28 June 1890. Ribot was not a first-class minister, was disliked by the Embassies and Legations and his personality hindered the détente with Russia; FO 27/3221/37 Conf/Dufferin to Kimberley/31 Jan 1895.
[105] D.D.F. 1/8/97.99.

into France.[106] For such was the 'logic' of French protectionism that a Tunis which could grant no special tariff privileges to French merchandise had its own produce subjected to the prohibitive general tariff. Tunis in fact paid not only more duty than colonies like Algeria but more duty than other countries whose produce came under the conventional tariff.[107] In March a bill was laid before the French Parliament, and, when Salisbury was informed that it established special tariffs for Tunisian goods entering France and reciprocity for French goods entering Tunis, he made immediate representations to Ribot. He reasserted English treaty rights and the inability of the French to establish for themselves special economic privileges not enjoyed by British subjects. The offensive clause on French produce entering Tunis, which had been published in the French papers, was, however, absent from the official text which Ribot showed Lytton, and the incipient protest died on Salisbury's lips.[108] In June, however, the French Commission on the Tariff, by a narrow majority, called on the government to establish differential treatment in favour of France. Ribot managed, with some difficulty, to get the awkward resolution, which Salisbury thought a 'direct violation' of England's 1875 treaty, shelved and the bill was passed unaltered.[109] Lytton's opinion some time previously had been that protectionist feeling was so strong that no favour would be politically possible for Tunisian produce without equivalent 'compensation' for French

[106] FO 27/3015/3 Ccl/Drummond Hay to Salisbury; ibid/3014/4/18 Jan 1890; ibid/3924/3 Ccl/Ricketts to Salisbury/18 Feb 1888.

[107] FO 27/3004/77 Ccl, 101 Ccl/Lytton to Salisbury/16 Mar, 7 April 1890. Roberts, in a questionable passage based on partisan sources, wrongly asserts that six countries, including England and Italy, paid less than the French rate of 8 per cent; *History of French Colonial Policy*, p. 283. Under article 7 of the Convention of 19 July 1875 between Britain and Tunis, British produce was also liable to 8 per cent duty; *Accounts and Papers* vol. lxxxiv. Sir Joseph Crowe gives details of the discrimination against Tunisian produce and said that France could not put the new tariff into force 'at *home* or in Tunis' without protest from foreign powers; FO 27/3004/77 Ccl/Lytton to Salisbury/16 Mar 1890, encl. Herslet, however, still felt France 'probably' entitled to admit Tunisian produce as in memo. with FO 27/2924/3 Ccl/Ricketts to Salisbury/18 Feb 1888.

[108] Ibid.; FO 27/3003/44 Ccl/Salisbury to Lytton/26 Mar 1890; ibid/58 Ccl/to Egerton/24 April 1890; ibid/3004/101 Ccl/Lytton to Salisbury/7 April 1890.

[109] FO 27/3005/168 Ccl, 185 Ccl/Lytton to Salisbury/13, 24 June 1890; ibid/3006/194 Ccl/5 July 1890; ibid/3003/82 Ccl/Salisbury to Lytton/21 June 1890.

produce, it is perhaps a fair comment that the free admission
now of much Tunisian merchandise resulted from the indignant
chauvinism aroused by the Zanzibar question and what Lytton
called the 'unanimity of feeling displayed in favour of treating
Tunis as a French colony'.[110] It is not surprising to find the
British colony there in July submitting a long memorial complaining of 'the determination which the French authorities
have shown of favouring their own citizens in Tunis'.[111]

Salisbury was in no easy position. Not only had he to consider
the intensity of French feeling, but Crispi had conceived a
mighty fear that England, to secure French acquiescence in the
Heligoland Treaty, might be surrendering her rights in Tunis
and permitting the French to annex it. He got the Germans to
urge Salisbury that any compensation to France should be in
Madagascar not Tunis and Salisbury had assured Hatzfeldt, the
ambassador, that there was no talk of Tunis in the negotiations
with France.[112] Confronted now with Waddington's determined
demand for a surrender over Tunis, the English minister had
little room for manœuvre. Failure to reach a settlement with
France was something he felt he had to avoid, if only to escape
placing weapons in the hands of the Francophile opposition at
home, at a time when the Heligoland bill had not been passed.[113]
To yield in Tunis, however, would lead obviously to the
estrangement of Italy,[114] with possibly dire consequences to the
Mediterranean Entente and the Triple Alliance. At the same
time Britain's position in the Mediterranean would be weakened.
The only parallel to Tunis, as Salisbury had obliquely hinted
to Waddington, was Egypt. Only a French surrender over
Egypt, a remote contingency, could have compensated England

[110] FO 27/3004/101 Ccl/Lytton to Salisbury/7 April 1890; ibid/2999/254,
255/4.5 July 1890; ibid/3006/237 Ccl, 285 Ccl/22 Aug, 18 Oct 1890. Roberts
says the law was passed 'to harm English trade elsewhere'; op. cit., p. 283.
Leroy-Beaulieu says that, in the next three years, the external trade of Tunis
increased by about half; L'Économiste Française, 10 Aug 1895.
[111] FO 27/3014/33 Conf/Drummond Hay to Salisbury/29 July 1890.
[112] FO 27/2998/248 Conf/Lytton to Salisbury/29 June 1890; ibid/3001/
Tel 50 Sec/27 June 1890; G.P. 8/1865.1867. note p. 27. As will be seen,
Crispi was soon fulminating against a French 'treaty of annexation' with the
Bey's heirs.
[113] G.P. 8/1700.1699; Q.V.L., series 3, vol. 3, p. 621. On the second reading, said Waddington on 26 July, all supported compensation for France;
D.D.F. 1/8/132.
[114] Langer, Franco-Russian Alliance, p. 123.

in the Mediterranean in such circumstances. The ingredients of an Anglo-French reconciliation were certainly not present and much sterile haggling therefore took place. The French tried to show that English trade in Tunis was small so that the concessions demanded there were trifling. Tunis, they said, would be England's only real concession, as recognising Madagascar was simply to regularise existing conditions. Ribot refused to dissociate Egyptian finance from the Zanzibar question and argued that English expansion in Africa in disregard of France might lead to his fall and replacement by someone who was compelled by an exasperated public opinion to arbitrarily annex Tunis. Salisbury says that the French told him bluntly that:

> . . . their consent to the solution desired by Egypt would be largely dependent on the willingness of this country to accept a change in its conventional relations towards Tunis.[115]

For his part, Salisbury maintained that the protectorate over Zanzibar, like that over Tunis, did not 'violate' the sovereignty of the ruler and therefore did not require the sanction of France under the 1862 convention. He was apparently surprised that France should have taken up the 'delicate' question of Tunis. Of course he appreciated the fact that he could not decline to enter upon revision of the 1875 treaty (under article 40), though he could not be compelled to assent to any particular change. The French were told that what they asked was 'very serious' and he foresaw objections because it would offend Italy and because it would obviously lead to protectionism in Tunis. The question involved 'many grounds for consideration' and, until the convention had been 'thoroughly examined', clause by clause, he could not say what Britain could accept in place of it.[116] At this juncture Salisbury received what he called 'rather an

---

[115] FO 27/2999/257 Conf/Lytton to Salisbury/6 July 1890; ibid/2996/260. 260A/Salisbury to Lytton/11 July 1890; D.D.F. 1/8/101.104.109. England wished to apply part of the economies resulting from the conversion of the Egyptian debt to the abolition of the *corvée*.

[116] Ibid.; Cecil, op. cit., pp. 318-19; G.P. 8/1691. An FO search in 1894 failed to find anything addressed to Waddington on the subject or 'any further correspondence either in the Commercial [sections] of Western and Eastern Department Indexes for 1891–92 or in the Tunis Confidential Print for 1891–1893'; FO 27/3384/Memo. Streatfield/20 Oct 1894. Important correspondence however was, for some reason, missed.

BDT I

excited letter' from Waddington. The government in Paris was being urged by the Radicals (under Floquet, Lacroix and Clemenceau) to challenge England by annexing Tunis, and the normally cautious Ribot had even felt compelled to hint at the possibility in public. He was clearly anxious to be able to report a diplomatic success.[117] Waddington's letter intimated that, if an immediate settlement were not reached, 'the present cabinet would be overturned and replaced by an Anti-English Ministry'. This would involve his resignation.[118]

Salisbury was presumably still disposed to be as conciliatory to France as the circumstances permitted. For on the following day, instead of a 'thorough' and inevitably leisurely examination of the 1875 treaty, he gave his answer to Waddington's proposal. He agreed freely to a commission at Paris to determine boundaries in the region of Lake Tchad and to the 'mutual regularisation' of their positions at Madagascar and Zanzibar. He even, with a request for secrecy, agreed in principle that the 1875 treaty should be abrogated at the same time as the Italian treaty—if France would make concessions over Egypt:

> I require as a condition that he shall give the Egyptian Government a free hand over all the economies resulting from conversion.[119]

Nevertheless Salisbury's evaluation of British commercial interests in Tunis had been based on information from the Board of Trade, whose statistics were now found to be incorrect. Just how incorrect was the picture London had of Tunisian trade and how misleading were the official French trade figures in Tunis, was not to be discovered until 1895. The Chambers of Commerce in Manchester and elsewhere were protesting vigorously and Salisbury was soon confessing to Waddington that British trade with Tunis was 'much more important than he had thought'. It may be noted, however, that he had made

[117] G.P. 8/1691. Lytton was advising strongly against reliance on French gratitude; FO 27/257 Conf/6 July 1890.
[118] SP/59/Waddington to Salisbury/13 July 1890; ibid/Tel/Salisbury to Lytton/13 July 1890. Salisbury's suggestion for compensatory 'small advantages' in Algerian tariffs (D.D.F. 1/8/109) was turned down flat. Much of the letter is published, in translation, in D.D.F. 1/8/p. 154, note 1. There is some discrepancy between this and Salisbury's copy, which does not include the phrase, '. . . I have no doubt that you will accept our prppositions'.
[119] FO 27/3001/Tel 18/Salisbury to Lytton/14 July 1890; D.D.F. 1/8/113.

his request for secrecy, according to Waddington, in order to 'present the abrogation of the treaty as a *fait accompli*' to the M.P.'s representing the cotton industry. Within twenty-four hours, indeed, of the offer to Waddington, Lytton was cautioned by private telegram to take no action and Salisbury soon made significant amendments to his terms:

> In view of the unfortunate mistake made by the Board of Trade as to Tunis statistics, I have now restricted my offer to accept most favoured nation treatment for all goods except cotton goods; but those to be subject to a maximum duty of 10 per cent which is the new Egyptian and Turkish rate and also the new African rate agreed upon at Brussels.[120]

Salisbury need not have hurried himself. His original offer was one which Ribot was unwilling and unable to accept. The Egyptian economies were not to be bargained against the Tunis Treaty nor could he 'appear to yield to pressure'.[121] The climax came on 18 July. Waddington, 'asking much to obtain a little', proposed that Britain should agree to French demands over Madagascar, the area of Lake Tchad and the Tunis Treaty in exchange for recognition of the Zanzibar Protectorate. Salisbury's keen sense of what constituted an equal transaction was absolutely affronted. He heatedly pointed out that, whether French consent was necessary or not in Zanzibar, it had 'rather a technical than a practical value' and went on with some bitterness, to tell the French that they gave him cause to regret his 'good behaviour' and refusal to support Italian intrigue in Tunis. He firmly rejected any idea of compensation in Tunis for the recognition of Zanzibar and any revision of the Tunis treaty which did not protect English cotton goods for all time. The French told him that it was the perpetuity of the English treaty that they wanted to get rid of; but Salisbury expressed doubt of ever obtaining the consent of the Chambers of Commerce to placing what he now called 'the large cotton trade between England and Tunis' at the mercy of French Customs legislation.[122]

---

[120] FO 27/3003/Tel 1 Ccl/Salisbury to Lytton/16 July 1890; SP/59/ Salisbury to Lytton/15 July 1890; SP/58/Lytton to Salisbury/16 July 1890; D.D.F. 1/8/113.123. See also next chapter, notes 54 and 56.
[121] FO 27/3001/Tel 55/Lytton to Salisbury/16 July 1890; D.D.F. 1/8/116.
[122] FO 27/3001/Tel 19/Salisbury to Lytton/18 July 1890; D.D.F. 1/8/121.

In spite of this, Ribot—referred again to the promise in principle of abrogation and declared that, after all the publicity, it was 'impossible not to insist on satisfaction'. Almost naïvely he suggested that Salisbury might make the desired concession as if to facilitate future good relations, without mention of Zanzibar,[123] seeming not to realise, as Waddington did, that the French demands were exorbitant. Salisbury, however, was in no mind to make a present of Tunis for the *beaux yeux* of France, when Waddington appeared with two new proposals on 21 July. Britain was asked to recognise the Madagascar protectorate together with French influence south of Algeria and to emasculate her Tunis treaty by excepting France from its most-favoured-nation clause. Salisbury's heels, however, were now well dug in and he not only 'emphatically' declined to associate the questions of Tunis and Zanzibar, but refused to admit, in a forthcoming Parliamentary statement, that France had a veto on the protectorate over Zanzibar.[124] There were signs, however, that French resolve was weakening. After all, even if the Tunisian pear was not entirely theirs, they had made a good bargain without it. As Waddington observed, and cynically, in view of the warmth of his arguments with Salisbury:

> Madagascar and the Empire of the Soudan are well worth the trivial position we occupy at Zanzibar between England and Germany and where moreover our interests will be protected as in the past.

Lytton wrote privately to 'his dear chief' with the comment that 'Ribot could make a very good show with these results'.[125]

Agreement was in fact achieved on this basis, though Waddington urged Ribot in vain to make a large concession in Egypt to obtain the abrogation of the Tunis Treaty.[126] In addition to Madagascar, Britain had by the convention recognised the sphere of influence of France to the south of her Mediterranean possessions up to a line from Say, on the Niger, to Barruwa, on Lake Tchad. Ribot might have made a mistake

---

[123] D.D.F. 1/8/124.
[124] FO 27/3001/Tel 21/Salisbury to Lytton/21 July 1890; D.D.F. 1/8/127.
[125] Ibid.; SP/58/Lytton to Salisbury/24 July 1890.
[126] D.D.F. 1/8/132.133.136. The text is also available in Hanotaux, *Fachoda*, pp. 273-5.

at the outset by 'talking big' in the Chamber about the importance of French interests in Zanzibar and might now have to
admit that France had no interests there;[127] but Waddington was
surely right when he said that they had got 'great compensations
for trivial sacrifice'.[128] Salisbury, in defending British policy,
might irritate him by gibing reference to the 'light land' of the
Sahara, but in a few years the British minister was to find that
he had given more than he realised and was describing the
French interpretation of the agreement as 'monstrous'.[129] One
other stipulation of importance for the future was made by an
exchange of notes, referring to the hinterland of Algeria, Tunis
and Tripoli. Because Salisbury was reluctant to admit that a
protectorate could have a hinterland, Tunis was not mentioned,
but the French got round his objection by saying that it was of
no importance 'as Algeria circled Tunisia and extended as far
as Ghadames'. The formula agreed also deliberately left the
rights of the Sultan vague. As Salisbury said:

> In signing today's arrangement, I wish to record that it does
> not affect the rights the Sultan may have on the southern
> frontiers of the Tripolitan provinces.[130]

The French were to make much of this in the future.

Unlike the crises over Massowah and the Tunis schools,
when Bismarck had been in power, one of the significant
features in the Anglo-French negotiations had been the relatively insignificant part played by the Germans. Apart from the
friendly intervention on behalf of Italy, they took almost no part
in the negotiations, and, even when the French protested to
them against the Heligoland Treaty, it was felt at the Wilhelm-
strasse that England wanted to deal with the matter alone or
would have asked for support. Whether London should even
hear of the protest was left to Hatzfeldt's discretion. Nevertheless the backing of Germany in the question was there when

---

[127] Ibid.; SP/58/to Salisbury/29 July 1890.
[128] Ibid. It is ironic to find a man who was to be Resident describing the
convention later as 'a monument to French simplicity'; Millet, *Notre
Politique extérieure*, p. 157.
[129] FO 27/3277/Tel 5 Af/Dufferin to Salisbury/17 Feb 1896; ibid/3273/56
Af/Salisbury to Dufferin/21 Feb 1896; SP/59/Waddington to Salisbury/
13 Aug 1890; Cecil, op. cit., pp. 322-4; Kennedy, op. cit., pp. 223-5.
[130] Ibid.; D.D.F. 1/8/141. See note 148.

wanted and Salisbury was anxious, for domestic reasons, not to appear to provoke France until the Heligoland bill was safely on the statute book. When that was done, he felt he could safely refuse to consider any convention with Turkey fixing a date for the evacuation of Egypt. For, in his mind, Tunis was now a 'card that had to be in England's hand on account of Egypt', and, of course, on account of Italy.[131] Salisbury therefore was obviously continuing his policy of cordial but informal relations with Germany. The threat to those relations in Africa had been successfully averted, but by an agreement which had exacerbated the existing animosity of France to the point of near explosion. The anger of France, which emphasised the dependency of Salisbury on the Germans, had been partly assuaged by substantial concessions, which were, however, in turn to whip up to a fury all the fears and suspicions of Crispi as to Italy's position in the Mediterranean.

TUNIS AND THE POWERS

Even the French were aware of the extent to which Salisbury had kept the Italians in ignorance during his negotiations with France,[132] and in Rome that ignorance bred apprehension. For a short time there had been an improvement in Franco-Italian relations resulting in abortive discussions on possible compensation in Tripoli for Italy's rights in Tunis.[133] This period of calm now came to an end. Crispi's alarm in June at the possibility that Britain might be bargaining away her position in the Regency has been noted,[134] and soon he found an excellent excuse for a display of his ambitious pyrotechnics. A report was received that France had concluded a secret treaty with the two heirs of the Bey, who had renounced the succession in return for a pension.[135] Crispi immediately affected to assume the

[131] G.P. 8/1692-1703, 1787.
[132] D.D.F. 1/8/118.123. Some information was received through Kalnoky; Crispi, op. cit., p. 461.
[133] Langer, European Alliances, p. 11; Franco-Russian Alliance, p. 122.
[134] See note 112.
[135] FO 27/3014/Tel/Drummond Hay to Salisbury/14 July 1890; Crispi, op. cit., pp. 440, 443-4; D.D.F. 1/8/115. Crispi's suspicion of the Anglo-French negotiations was strengthened because Salisbury, who knew, said nothing about this; G.P. 8/1870.1881.

worst and called for the assistance of his allies. Italy, he said, 'could never stand' such an agreement, which would 'render the French masters of the Mediterranean' and, in such a contingency, Germany would be bound to come to her assistance under the terms of the alliance. In all his talk, however, of not wanting to 'push matters to extremities', he gave his game away by his hints at 'guarantees' and 'compensations'.[136]

Caprivi, the new German Chancellor, was less anxious, if anything, than Bismarck to fight Crispi's battles. To him it was questionable whether any annexation of Tunis involved the *casus foederis*. Doubtful also whether the Italian alliance was worth a particularly inconvenient war with France, he felt it was England who should be asked if she would fight for Mediterranean interests.[137] Nevertheless the Germans were extremely loth to needlessly lose an ally and:

> ... through the summer Hatzfeldt was almost feverishly anxious about Crispi's state of mind; evidently fearing that the growing difficulties in his position internally might induce him to change camps, if he were adequately paid for the evolution. . . .[138]

Salisbury, in the middle of a difficult phase in his negotiations with France, was not pleased, since he guessed that Crispi's objective was the possession of Tripoli, and he bluntly said that public opinion would not support a war over the supposed Succession Treaty.[139] When therefore Tornielli asked what measures Salisbury was prepared to take, he expressed doubts as to the authenticity of the story and, more discouraging still, would give only his 'impression' as to what action the Mediterranean powers would take if that story proved to be true. They would, he said;

> ... probably address a friendly communication to France herself, or would address the Sultan of Turkey with respect to a succession over which he still claimed rights.

His scepticism increased when the existence of a treaty or designs of annexation were denied 'in the most categoric manner'

[136] SP/67/Dufferin to Salisbury/17 July 1890; Crispi, op. cit., pp. 440.
[137] G.P. 8/1872.
[138] SP/59/Salisbury to Lytton/23 Sep 1890; Cecil, op. cit., pp. 374-6.
[139] G.P. 8/1874.1875.1877.

by Ribot.[140] Still hopeful, however, Crispi sent an agitated personal letter and memorandum to Salisbury (without the knowledge of his distrusted ambassador Tornielli), in which his aim was now made clear. He would stop France, if need be, by a declaration of war, which would bring his allies Germany and Austria to his aid, and then occupy parts of Tripoli, which would 'act as a counter-weight to a French Tunisia'.[141] Italy could then depend on Salisbury 'to aid her and disarm the opposition of Turkey and France', because occupying Tripoli was necessary to forestall a French domination of the north of the Mediterranean. Crispi did realise after all that complete sovereignty for France in Tunis was only a matter of time.[142] An exuberant report from Crispi's agent Catalani, gave Salisbury's opinion as being that a change in the Mediterranean *status quo* would render 'Italy's occupation of Tripoli a necessity', but Salisbury's written reply on 4 August was a model of how to both please and restrain Crispi. It agreed that Tunis was bound to become French, but at a distant date, and that Tripoli could not be allowed 'to share the fate of Tunis'. To occupy Tripoli prematurely, however, would be dangerous as the Sultan would accept the support of Russia to preserve his independence.[143] That all this was effective may be judged by the fact that Crispi, in replying, seemed relieved and there was no more talk of action, beyond a suggestion that Paris should be told that the Tunisian protectorate was not to become 'a full sovereignty'.[144]

Salisbury was still discouraging Crispi, but he had been cordial in so doing, and had given a hint—though no promise— of gain for the future. Presumably he was beginning to take into account the fears the Germans had been expressing. Hatzfeldt alleged that, on 1 August, Salisbury had told him confidentially that he had discussed with Waddington the idea, previously

[140] FO 45/648/Tel 45/Salisbury to Dufferin/23 July 1890; D.D.F. 1/8/127; FO 45/645/185a/Salisbury to Dufferin/26 July 1890. The Germans got the same answer; G.P. 8/1883.
[141] SP/68/Crispi to Salisbury/23 July and memo. Berlin got the same information; Peteani, op. cit., p. 88.
[142] Ibid.; Crispi, op. cit., pp. 449-450; Cecil, op. cit., p. 372-3.
[143] SP/68/Salisbury to Crispi/4 Aug 1890; Crispi, op. cit., pp. 451-5; Cecil, op. cit., p. 373. Catalani was a former Councillor at the London Embassy.
[144] Crispi, op. cit., pp. 457-8; SP/68/Tornielli to Salisbury/16 Aug 1890.

mooted at the Congress of Berlin, of Tripoli going to Italy, and
that the ambassador, in welcoming it, left the impression that
France would claim the region between Barca and Tunis. It was
felt in Berlin that such a partition would lead to a Turkish
alliance with Russia. As the Triple Alliance was hardly in a
position to restrain Italy for fear of her leaving that alliance,
what was thought politic was a guarantee by Italy's partners,
especially England, that no other power should acquire Tripoli.[145]
Italy's Austrian ally, on the other hand, was as little interested
as ever in Tunis and as concerned to see the end of yet another
Italian storm in connection with it. When Kalnoky had gladly
passed on the French assurances to Crispi, the latter 'absolutely
declined' to believe them[146] and pretended to see in frontier
disturbances the possibility of 'a further edition of the affair of
the Kroumirs'. In fact, the Austrians were determined to give
Crispi no more than diplomatic support and Kalnoky said
frankly that it was impossible to discuss:

> . . . what had not occurred and what, in his estimation, was not
> likely to occur; the interests of Austria-Hungary, moreover,
> were so very remotely concerned . . . that he could only con-
> sider the Imperial Government as placed in the third line.[147]

Salisbury's views were nearer those of Austria than those of
Germany. He did not think that, unless generously 'compensated', Crispi would get tired of the Triple Alliance, and he
believed the Italian to be bluffing in order to get a written
guarantee that Tripoli would one day be his. This Salisbury was
determined not to give and his note of 4 August therefore fell
short of the German hopes and suggestions. Nevertheless, it
was to 'dissipate Crispi's suspicions' that Salisbury now
exchanged notes with Waddington, the effect of which, as has
been seen, was 'to prevent the agreement (of 5 August 1890)
from being interpreted to affect the Hinterland of Tripoli'.[148]
Further importunity from an 'agitated' Hatzfeldt led him to

[145] G.P. 8/1887.1888.1890.1891.1892. Caprivi opposed any immediate
acquisition of Tripoli.
[146] FO 403/150/127/Salisbury to Paget/26 July 1890; FO 45/648/Tel 43/
Dufferin to Salisbury/3 Aug 1890.
[147] FO 403/150/220 Conf/Paget to Salisbury/6 Aug 1890.
[148] SP/68/Salisbury to Dufferin/12 Aug 1890; Cecil, op cit., pp. 373-5.
See note 130.

send a private letter to Dufferin in Rome. The ambassador was told that, if Crispi were really 'hovering on the brink of a new alliance', he might go as far as:

> . . . to give him to understand, *verbally*, that while we were faithful to the rights of the Sultan, we fully recognized that Italy had a special interest in the integrity of the Turkish Empire as regards Tripoli; and that in case any catastrophe were to overwhelm the Ottoman dominion, that position . . . would have its natural bearing upon the distribution of the inheritance.[149]

It is not clear whether this assurance was actually given, as sometimes assumed.[150] Salisbury's private instructions to Dufferin concluded with the admonition that, if he did speak, which Salisbury 'deprecated unless his judgement lead to it', then his words 'should be plain enough to quieten Crispi without being plain enough' to furnish 'a weapon that could be used against us by the gossips of the Rome chancellery.'[151] After all, the intention seems to have been as much or more to reassure the Germans than the Italians. In fact, before Salisbury's letter was sent, Crispi had shown himself quite happy with the declarations made by the British minister, when a French annexation of Tunis was supposed to be on the cards.[152] On the other hand, Crispi on 25 August replied to a German suggestion to include Tripoli in the Anglo-Italian Agreement of 1887, by saying that it was 'no longer necessary', as Salisbury had recognised 'verbally and in writing that sooner or later Tripoli would have to pass to Italy'.[153] However, this language rather reflects the optimistic impressions of Catalani than the meticulously circumspect instructions to Dufferin, with their minimum of legal commitment.

Indeed, Catalani's telegram of 31 July had implied that, in the event of a French annexation of Tunis, Italy would have the support of England (on top of the presumed support of Germany) in favour of compensation in Tripoli, and it seemed now

---

[149] SP/68/Salisbury to Dufferin/12 Aug 1890; G.P. 8/1892.
[150] For example, Langer, *European Alliances*, p. 12; *Franco-Russian Alliance*, p. 126.
[151] As note 148; G.P. 8/1893.
[152] FO 403/150/Crispi to Tornielli/5 Aug 1890. By 11 Aug, Solms gathered he was 'secure of British support . . . for the future'; G.P. 8/1895.
[153] G.P. 8/1896.

obviously to Italy's interest to bring about that annexation by agreement with France. It is surely no coincidence that Menabrea, in Paris should immediately be instructed, on 1 August, to state that:

> If France wishes to give proof of her willingness to facilitate our peaceful acquisition of this territory as a compensation for Tunis, she should exert her powerful influence both at St. Petersburg and at Constantinople, where opposition is naturally to be expected.[154]

Crispi was as determined as ever to make his alliances pay, and that even without the knowledge of his partners. Ribot and Freycinet, who had been so recently forced through Italian drum-beating over the 'Succession Treaty', to declare that they had no intention of annexing Tunis, saw through Crispi's informal advances the desire for a pretext to lay hands on Tripoli, and would not move. The Italians were told that they would have to give up not only the capitulations but also the Triple Alliance, and, after Crispi had considered this academically, the discussions came to nothing.[155]

Concern had been caused in Paris, however, by hints that there was English approval for an occupation of Tripoli by Italy, as compensation for 'the march which France had stolen upon her in Tunis'. Ribot was also alerted by information suggesting preparations for an eventual *coup de main*. According to Ressman, he had been told that the annexation of Tunis would mean war and that he would be 'much mistaken if he imagined that Italy's allies would allow her to be crushed by France.' Asked if he supported the possible occupation of Tripoli, Salisbury, who had so recently deterred Italy from such a course, felt able to say 'with good conscience' that according to his information 'there was no truth that Crispi contemplated any such step'. British policy was still to uphold the Turkish Empire as long as possible and the occupation of Tripoli would be:

> . . . to drive the Sultan into the arms of Russia, and to bring the Eastern Question upon us suddenly, in its most formidable shape.

[154] Crispi, op. cit., p. 465. Menabrea had already reminded the French of Italian wishes for compensation.
[155] Ibid., pp. 462-473; D.D.F. 1/8/163.

He could not resist 'preaching' to Ribot, as he had often done to Waddington, 'that if they wanted a quiet life they must not attempt to alter the status of Tunis at present'.[156]

The summer of 1890 had, therefore, faced Salisbury with negotiations of special difficulty in which his room for manœuvre had been limited. In his determination not to relinquish Egypt, Tunis was a card of value and he had shown himself ready to play that card in order to obtain the cessation of French obstructionist tactics in Egyptian affairs. No French government, however, could have surrendered Egypt to England and survived, so that a limited agreement between the two powers was possible, but no reconciliation, and England had to rely in Egypt, as elsewhere, on the uncovenanted cordiality of the Germans (and their friends). As the Germans in turn feared defection from the Triple Alliance by Italy, which would have weakened them militarily in Europe, it would have been difficult to prevent a Crispi from attempting to exploit the situation with hopes of Tripoli in mind. His success, however, though he seemed not to realise it, was limited as far as England, the power most able to gratify his dreams, was concerned. Salisbury, as in the earlier incidents, had begun by being discouraging. German fears and importunity then persuaded him to be more cordial, while still discouraging Crispi, and finally to agree to the possibility of a cautious and veiled hint at the possibility of eventual gain to Italy. Even Salisbury's private correspondence contained nothing vaguely approaching a promise to secure the title deed of the desired property.

[156] SP/59/Salisbury to Lytton/23 Sep 1890; SP/58/Lytton to Salisbury/ 27 Sep 1890; FO 45/648/Salisbury to Dufferin/24 Sep 1890; Cecil, op. cit., pp. 375-6.

4

BRITISH STRATEGY AND TUNIS, 1888–1894

THE FRONTIER QUESTION

'France', wrote General Dal Verme despondently, four months after the Anglo-French Agreement of 5 August 1890:

arbitrarily moved the frontier of the Tunisian Regency farther eastwards for the purpose of drawing nearer to the capital (of Tripoli) . . . this work of gradual destruction was begun by the French as soon as they set foot in Tunisia, and it is still going on.

The anxious Italian then went on to forecast that France, as 'mistress of the coast from Morocco to Egypt', would upset the Mediterranean balance of power and eventually reach Wadai, Darfur and the Nile Valley.[1] What the French were doing in the south, however, was a question in which Salisbury, at this time evinced no great interest. In July he had told Münster scornfully that 'the real Hinterland to Algeria was the Sahara Desert', which could well be left to the French, and he seems to have considered the area as giving them a road simply to Timbuctoo and the Upper Niger.[2] This was no new policy. In this matter, as in others, he had been ignoring an opportunity to embarrass the French in Tunis.

Since the days of the occupation when large numbers of Tunisian tribesmen had fled into Tripoli before the expeditionary forces of Logerot, Philibert and Jamais—most to return later—the ill-defined frontier region had been more than usually uneasy and the raiding and counter raiding of the tribesmen more than usually disturbing. Moreover, not only the French and the Turks, but the Italians also were interested in an area from which, being far from the trade routes, reliable information was hard to get and subject to long delay. Crispi,

---

[1] Crispi, *Memoirs*, vol. 3, p. 43.   [2] G.P. 8/1703.

being convinced that Tunis would eventually become entirely French, was determined to obtain as compensation Tripoli, which in proprietorial anticipation, he was resolved should not become emasculated or the prey of France. A delimitation of the frontier was obviously to be desired, but negotiations to this end could not even be commenced by the Porte as long as it refused to recognise the French protectorate in Tunis.[3]

Salisbury displayed his disinterest clearly at the end of 1887. The French Geographical Society, on the strength of a newspaper report, had published a map showing the frontier on the river Mokta, well to the east of El Biban, the frontier claimed by the Turks. When Salisbury received an Italian request to persist in enquiries at Paris, he declined, saying that:

> . . . Her Majesty's Government were not directly interested in the matter, and persistent interposition on their part would create suspicion.[4]

At the same time he rejected an Italian proposal that the British and Italian consuls in Tripoli should proceed to the frontier 'to enquire on the spot' into the alleged encroachments and said that it was not expedient:

> . . . as it would be certain to be generally looked upon as a preliminary to some aggressive action.[5]

Moreover, Flourens himself claimed that France had faithfully observed the understanding she had with Turkey 'to respect the *status quo* pending settlement of the disputed frontier between Tunis and Tripoli'.[6] In point of fact, British diplomats were unaware that the French had made no official claim to a frontier on the Mokta and all they knew was that military posts were, at considerable expense, being established, the most southerly of which, at Douirat, was considerably to the north

[3] FO 102/167/19, 20, 23/Sandwith to Rosebery/21, 26 April, 5 May 1886; Crispi, op. cit., vol. 3, pp. 20-25.
[4] Ibid.; FO 45/573/345/Salisbury to Savile/16 Dec 1887; FO 27/2858/548/Egerton to Salisbury/20 Dec 1887. Flourens had referred to the 'Moulaya'—presumably the Mokta. Unknown to Britain and Italy, the French had already, on rather flimsy grounds, claimed the Mokta frontier in talks with the Turkish ambassador in 1886. French army maps had shown the frontier at Biban until 1883. In 1887 it was marked at Mokta; Martel, *Les Confins saharo-tripolitains de la Tunisie*, vol. 1, pp. 373-4, 377.
[5] FO 45/573/343 Conf/Salisbury to Savile/13 Dec 1887.
[6] FO 27/2904/27/Lytton to Salisbury/9 Jan 1888.

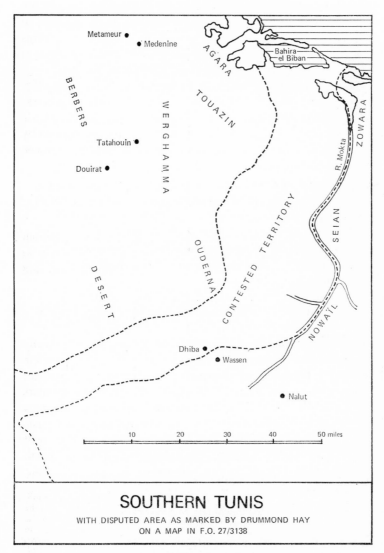

SOUTHERN TUNIS

WITH DISPUTED AREA AS MARKED BY DRUMMOND HAY
ON A MAP IN F.O. 27/3138

Fɪɢ ɪ

of the Mokta.[7] What military action there was consisted of troop movements to repress pillaging tribesmen, driven to despair by the general failure of crops. These movements none the less caused anxiety in Rome.[8]

Early in 1890, Tornielli was again complaining in London of a 'tendency on the part of the French to extend their authority in the direction of Tripoli', but enquiries only served to show that what had seemed an acquisition of 'eighteen villages in Gebel Nalout' was really mutual restoration of stolen cattle across the frontier, sponsored by the army.[9] It is impossible not to sympathise a little with the Italian fears during the Anglo-French negotiations on Tunis in the summer. For it should be remembered that the tribes on the Tunisian frontier were under the authority of General Allegro, now Governor of Gabès, the man who was 'generally acknowledged to have been the chief instigator of the notorious Kroumir insurrections in 1881'. Late in July too, news arrived of fighting, apparently the result of unauthorised seizure by the local French commander of sheep belonging to the returning tribesmen.[10] It is not really surprising that Crispi (as has been observed) was making overtures to the French in the autumn for a deal over Tunis and Tripoli, or that Lytton, after a conversation with one of the Italian representatives, should have concluded that 'Crispi was in a reckless fit'.[11] News that caused hardly a ripple of interest in the Foreign Office produced dire foreboding in the Quirinal. Spahis were moving in numbers to the frontier; works at the forts of Medenin and Tatahouin were rushed ahead, and the south was shrouded in military secrecy.[12] What Salisbury now thought of Crispi, his

[7] FO 27/2924/1/Sandwith to Salisbury/16 Jan 1888; FO 102/169/6, 18/ Sandwith to Salisbury/25 Aug, 28 Dec 1887. The other posts were at Zarzis, Bir el Ahmar, Tataouin, Kessur and Metameur.

[8] FO 27/2924/Tel, 9 Conf, Tel, 10/Sandwith to Salisbury/3, 4, 10, 10 July 1888; FO 45/600/137/Salisbury to Kennedy/5 July 1888.

[9] FO 45/645/23/Salisbury to Dufferin/31 Jan 1890; FO 27/2924/28/ Ricketts to Salisbury/1 Dec 1890; ibid/3014/3/Salisbury to Drummond Hay/ 28 Feb 1890; ibid/23/Drummond Hay to Salisbury/20 Mar 1890.

[10] SP/68/Tornielli to Salisbury/28 July 1890; FO 27/3014/54/Salisbury to Drummond Hay/7 Aug 1890; ibid/Tels/1, 1, 2, 6, 27 Aug 90; ibid/59, 68, 70/2 Sep, 25, 31 Oct; FO 403/150/Salisbury to Tornielli/7 Aug 1890; FO 27/ 3052/3/Drummond Hay to Salisbury/23 Jan 1891.

[11] SP/58/to Salisbury/27 Sep 1890.

[12] FO 27/3014/68, 70, 74, 75, 76, 78/Drummond Hay to Salisbury/25, 31 Oct, 7, 9, 10, 18, 29 Nov 1890.

dubious unofficial agents and 'information' was shown when he was told that 'there was reason to believe' that a strategic narrow gauge railway was contemplated, to run from Gabès to the important military and commercial centre of Ghadames and to Ghat. He sarcastically replied that:

> ... even if it were confirmed, I should not see in it any disadvantage to Italy in any future contingency ...

and did not even institute the normal enquiries.[13]

Crispi, indeed as ever, was miscalculating badly. The manner of his sanguine overtures to Paris 'behind Germany's back' alarmed the French so much that they had informed Salisbury, who wondered 'what intrigue Crispi was at now'.[14] Nor was that all. Fearing an Italian *coup*, they induced the Sultan to make a substantial increase in the Tripolitan garrison and to secure assurances from Italy.[15] Much of Crispi's 'reckless fit' stems from the Anglo-French agreement in August and the subsequent exchange of notes. Before its conclusion Tornielli had tried to intervene and impress on Salisbury:

> ... the inconveniences of admitting that the line of the Algerian Hinterland should be traced so as to interfere with the Tripolitan Hinterland.[16]

All Crispi's fears were expressed in the important memorandum drafted in December by General Dal Verme, how the eastern limit of the French sphere was not defined, how dubious were the safe-guards to the Sultan's rights, and how in practice the way to the east seemed open to France.[17] An Italian request for definition of the eastern limits of the French sphere, led to a heated discussion between Ribot and Menabrea, in which the former denied designs on Tripoli and claimed to be only attempting to divert part of the Sudan trade towards Tunisia.[18]

---

[13] FO 45/645/232a/Salisbury to Dufferin/29 Oct 1890. For the use of secret agents see note 11.

[14] SP/59/Salisbury to Lytton/23 Sep 1890; Cecil, op. cit., pp. 375-6.

[15] Turkish suspicion of Italy was considerable. D.D.F. 1/8/182; FO 27/3014/79, 86/Drummond Hay to Salisbury/19 Nov, 11 Dec 1890; Crispi, op. cit., pp. 46-50; FO 403/150/Malet to Salisbury/26 Dec 1890.

[16] SP/68/Very Conf/to Salisbury/28 July 1890; Crispi, op. cit., vol. 3, pp. 44-5.

[17] Crispi, op. cit., pp. 31-44; Peteani, op. cit., pp. 103-4.

[18] Peteani, op. cit., p. 105; Crispi, op. cit., pp. 55-59.

At the same time, an Italian press campaign and the exaspera-
tion it caused in France reached a pitch which Ribot characterised as dangerous. Italy was:

> . . . stretching the cord so tight that unless the present tension
> were relaxed it might ere long snap.[19]

Crispi had therefore failed dismally to come to an arrangement with France and had received abundant evidence of
Salisbury's disinterest. He now endeavoured somewhat
desperately to use to maximum advantage the friendship of the
Germans, who had been so worried lest he should tire of the
Triple Alliance. Marschall still felt it impossible to keep on ignoring what he called Crispi's 'perfectly groundless fears', without risk of 'weakening the present political grouping'. As a result
he was prepared to take up with the Sultan on Crispi's behalf
an alleged intention of the French discovered in an insignificant
press notice. This was to arrange with the Porte a delimitation
of the Tunis frontier which would secure for them the Tripolitan
Hinterland. What is more, he was ready to urge Britain to
support opposition at Constantinople to any territorial concession to France, emphasising the 'acute alarm' of Crispi over
Tripoli and Biserta and arguing that even a matter of such small
importance might 'lead to consequences out of proportion to
its intrinsic merit'.[20] To reinforce all this, Crispi had a few days
previously observed to Britain's ambassador that:

> . . . he had lately become conscious of a certain coolness being
> exhibited towards him by Her Majesty's Government and that
> there had not been adequate recognition of the constant and
> unswerving friendliness of his own attitude.[21]

After Massowah, the Tunis Schools and Kassala, Salisbury
could have justified coolness but, in what Hatzfeldt spoke of as

---

[19] FO 27/3001/Tel 63 Most Conf/Lytton to Salisbury/23 Dec 1890; ibid/
3000/426 Sec/24 Dec 1890. He requested England's good offices and declared
that France had 'no territorial ambition' in Tripoli.

[20] FO/403/150/Malet to Salisbury/26 Dec 1890; G.P. 8/1890. Cooperation was urged in the name of good Anglo-German relations, to strengthen
Crispi's confidence in Britain and to forestall an Italian proposition later to
acquire Tripoli.

[21] FO 45/647/222 Conf/Dufferin to Salisbury/22 Dec 1890. Salisbury
blamed Tornielli's reports as being flavoured 'with some of his own vinegar';
SP/68/Salisbury to Dufferin/7 Jan 1891.

his 'sceptical, but not always either well timed or well conceived attitude' to Crispi, he laughingly referred to 'lovers' tiffs'. A more tactful despatch to Rome, however, reminded Crispi especially of Britain's:

> . . . avoidance of action with respect to Tunis which could be injurious to Italian interests or could give any encouragement to an antagonistic policy on the part of the government of France.[22]

Yet he found he could not refuse the request to support the German action, though he did not hurry himself. First he suspiciously ascertained at Constantinople that White's Italian and German colleagues were not attempting to dissuade the Porte from agreement with France for the 'rectification' of the frontier. White had said this was disliked, especially by the Italians. The Grand Vizier in fact had been told that:

> . . . the group of friendly powers interested in the preservation of the territorial *status quo* of the Ottoman Empire could not view with indifference any cession of territory, however small and insignificant, on the side of Tripoli, even in the form of a so-called rectification.

After another anxious German request, Salisbury gave his support though he 'didn't understand why it was so urgent'[23] and Crispi's associates proceeded to tilt at another Italian windmill. Marschall even warned the French directly that 'general complications' would arise if France tried to expand further along the Mediterranean coast and that Tripoli was a 'European question'. The consequence was that the Porte was emboldened to inform the French that it would not entertain 'any representation or interference' in the frontier area 'inasmuch as the temporary occupation of Tunis still remained an open and unsettled question'.[24] In addition, even before Salisbury acted,

---

[22] FO 45/664/4 Conf/Salisbury to Dufferin/2 Jan 1891; G.P. 8/1900.

[23] FO 403/151/4 Tel/Salisbury to White/5 Jan 1891; ibid/4 Tel, 18 Conf/ White to Salisbury/6, 12 Jan 1891.

[24] D.D.F. 1/8/236. German instructions to Constantinople went on 27 Dec; Salisbury's concurrence was requested on 5 Jan and his instructions sent on 23 Jan. The Italians made no move presumably because of Turkish suspicion of Italy. FO 403/151/38, 8 Tel/White to Salisbury/30 Jan, 5 Feb 1891; ibid/7 Tel, 10 Tel/Salisbury to White/23 Jan 1891; Crispi, op. cit., pp. 62-3. Salisbury was now more concerned with French activities in Morocco; G.P. 8/1915.

Ribot had felt constrained on 22 January to publicly charac-
terise as 'the most gross inventions' reports of French troops
moving from Tunis to cut the links between Tripoli and the
Sudan. The Turks were given assurances that France had no
intention of violating Turkish possessions and that French
personnel had strict instructions to avoid an incident.[25]

In the meantime reports from Italian and British sources
spoke of French patrols penetrating 'five days march' into
Tripoli, to Wessen, Nalut and El Huamet and informing the
inhabitants that they were within Tunis. The Porte however,
according to the English ambassador, White, minimised the
incident and the ambassador's opinion was that, if the tribes
recognised French sovereignty:

> . . . the territory of Tunis would be increased and the French
> might thus obtain the road which they so warmly desired in that
> direction.[26]

Menabrea was so alarmed in fact that he suggested to Crispi
that the strategic caravan centres of Ghat and especially
Ghadames should be garrisoned by Turkish troops or that
Tripoli should be occupied by Italy.[27] Suddenly, however, the
venom was extracted from the Tunis-Tripoli question by the
unexpected fall of Crispi. Ironically enough it was over a minor
financial matter; for his monetary difficulties would have been
eased by access to the French money market, a privilege which
had been refused to him unless he would loosen his ties with
Britain and Germany.[28] Salisbury was, of course, delighted, in
spite of the foreboding of Kalnoky and Caprivi, and instructed
Dufferin to urge the new government tactfully to consider 'what
profit the African expenditure had brought or was likely to
bring to Italy.[29] It was therefore no doubt gratifying to hear that

[25] *Journal Officiel*, 23 Jan 1891; FO 27/3038/32/Lytton to Salisbury/
23 Jan 1891; D.D.F. 1/8/239.228.229.231.233.235.236; Peteani, op. cit.,
p. 108.
[26] FO 27/3052/4, 9/Drummond Hay to Salisbury/23 Jan, 25 Feb 1891;
FO 45/664/39/Salisbury to Dufferin/12 Feb 1890; FO 403/151/11/Salisbury
to White/13 Feb 1891; ibid/9 Tel/White to Salisbury/14 Feb 1891. In the
south also the Touareg were threatening, a later report said because of locusts;
FO 27/3052/23/Drummond Hay to Salisbury/15 June 1891.
[27] Crispi, op. cit., pp. 59-62.
[28] D.D.F. 1/8/181.183.185.194.244; FO 45/665/18/Dufferin to Salisbury/
4 Feb 1891.
[29] FO 45/667/3/8 Feb 1891; D.D.F. 1/8/251; Crispi, op. cit., p. 378
Albertini, op. cit., p. 70.

a ministerial declaration of policy almost paraphrased this advice and Anglo-Italian agreement was soon reached on the still outstanding question of Kassala and East Africa. This was not achieved, however, without substantial concessions by Salisbury.[30]

Crispi's successor, di Rudini, of 'the party of the right', reaffirmed the fidelity of Italy to the Triple Alliance, but felt that these obligations in no way precluded an understanding with France—which he immediately set out to achieve.[31] His views on the boundary question were far from those of Crispi and one of his first actions was to say publicly that:

> ... the events which had taken place there were of little import-
> ance and he was confident of the honourable intentions of the
> French Government.[32]

When further incursions were reported in March, it was now Austria which took the lead in recommending to the Porte special vigilance against French incursions. For that country was anxious to demonstrate solidarity at a time when a decision on the renewal of the Triple Alliance was imminent.[33] Neverthe-less, another Austrian proposal that a commission should settle the question was rejected by the Sultan on the grounds that it 'would imply a recognition of French rights in Tunis'. This led the Italians to take up a suggestion of Radowitz that further encroachments could be prevented by Ottoman troops occupy-ing the Tripolitan frontier villages, a suggestion Salisbury was induced to support.[34] The information di Rudini had, however, of conditions on the frontier was now contradicted by informa-tion given to the British Consul-General at Tripoli, Moore, by the Governor General and Commandant there. This was to the effect that all was 'perfectly quiet and normal' and that even the

[30] FO 45/667/9 Tel/Dufferin to Salisbury/14 Feb 1891; Langer, *Diplomacy of Imperialism*, pp. 110-112.

[31] FO 45/665/20, 29/Dufferin to Salisbury/10, 18 Feb 1891. For the unsuccessful negotiations over East Africa see Yehia, Galal, *La Grande Bretagne, la France et l'expansion italien avant Adoua*, pp. 961-996 (unpub-lished thesis; University of Paris). Ribot, however, as the price of friendly relations, wished to know the terms of the Triple Alliance and was refused; G.P. 7/1402.

[32] FO 45/665/37/Dufferin to Salisbury/5 March 1891.

[33] G.P. 8/1901.1902; Peteani, op. cit., pp. 108-9.

[34] FO 45/664/78 Conf/Salisbury to Dufferin/16 April 1891; FO 403/151/25 Tel/Salisbury to White/16 April 1891.

previous reports of French military incursions were unfounded. Presumably as a consequence, the Grand Vizier, who had promised the Italian representative that he would send frontier guards, now began to temporise and the conflict of evidence was only settled by a Special Commission sent by the Porte to investigate. Moore reported that not only was the Vali accused of conniving at the encroachments but that it was certain that French troops were on Tripolitan territory and had compelled tribesmen to pay taxes. It seemed to him that the Vali, under instructions, was ready to concede the strip of territory rather than quarrel with France, but 'in some round-about way' to save Turkish prestige.[35] An *Iradé* from the Sultan now authorised occupation of the area by Ottoman troops, while the Grand Vizier agreed that French objectives were to extend Tunisian territory, cut off Tripoli from its hinterland and open up the way into Africa.[36]

The storms which had been raised by Crispi, backed by an anxious Caprivi and tolerated by a disgruntled Salisbury, were now subsiding, though the frontier question had not been settled and for several years the powers concerned moved with circumspection. Trouble along the border area was endemic in the plains between Wad Fessi and the Mokta, if only because the nomad tribes held arable land by custom not title deed. Drummond Hay, the British Consul General at Tunis, after consulting old maps, the French editions especially, concluded that the disputed area belonged to Tripoli, but that since the occupation of the Regency, Tunisian tribes supported by the authorities had succeeded in monopolising all the arable and pasture land.[37] Certainly by 1891, he wrote, 'the Tripolitan frontiers were . . . clearly defined according to French views' in a map issued by the Military Geographical Service. As for the 'independent and turbulent tribes of the Werghamma districts' who were responsible for much trouble in the autumn, the French were in the near future to have some success in subduing them.[38]

[35] FO 403/151/135, 143 Conf, 158 Conf/White to Salisbury/6, 10, 22 April 1891 (encls.). Noel Temple Moore, C.M.G., had been Consul General since September 1890.
[36] FO 403/151/162 Conf/White to Salisbury/24 April 1891.
[37] FO 27/3138/12 Conf/Drummond Hay to Rosebery/15 March 1893.
[38] FO 27/3052/46/Drummond Hay to Salisbury/30 Oct 1891; ibid/Pr/ Drummond Hay to Currie/Oct 1891.

A rather more serious crisis arose in the summer of 1892. While reports on what occurred are conflicting, it seems that, in a typical dispute over land, Tunisian forces occupied Wassen, an oasis township of considerable strategic importance lying in Tripoli even according to the French map. It would appear that they withdrew after the 'pacific intervention' of the Turkish garrison at Nalut.[39] French interest in Ghadames, 'that coveted oasis', was obvious. A military interpreter disguised as an Arab was arrested on his way there and a market was established at Tatahouin, with the ostensible object of attracting traders and trade from Ghadames. Simultaneously a Swiss named Cornes was penetrating far into the desert.[40] Even the di Rudini government now showed signs of alarm and secured the support of the new British minister for foreign affairs, Rosebery, for representations at the Porte urging that yet more troops should be sent to the frontier area.[41] Delimitation was more desirable than ever and, by the end of 1892 there were preparations for a commission for this purpose. According to the frontier expert who took part in the commission on behalf of the Beylical government, Major Rebillet, no official correspondence had taken place in Tripoli in view of the Turkish refusal to recognise the Tunisian protectorate, but the Vali, who was 'well known for his French sympathies', had habitually discussed the question with M. Destrées. The result had been a proposition from the Porte for a delimitation commission composed exclusively of Turkish and Beylical officials. When this met, the French based their claim, a little dubiously, on the evidence of the German traveller Barth, but the Turkish members produced a 'Beylical decree of some antiquity' which designated Bahira el Biban on the coast as the frontier. Apparently the document turned out to be so obvious a forgery that they had to admit it. Thereupon the Turkish Commissioner, Riffad Bey, was

[39] FO 27/3093/53, 54, 56, Tel, Tel, Tel, 60 Conf/Drummond Hay to Rosebery/27, 30 Aug, 1, 5, 6, 9 Sep, 7 Oct 1892.

[40] FO 27/3093/11, 17/Drummond Hay to Salisbury/15 Feb, 1 Mar 1892; See also note 37. Two French officers were said to have been expelled from the Ghadames area in 1897; FO 27/3138/Drummond Hay to Salisbury/12 Nov 1893.

[41] FO 45/681/156, 161/Rosebery to Vivian/26 Oct, 11 Nov 1892; ibid/684/ 246/Vivian to Rosebery/22 Nov 1892. Cambon now compared Constantinople with Tunis 'at the time of the battles of Maccio and Roustan'; *Correspondance*, vol. 1, p. 357.

summoned to Constantinople and Rebillet was convinced that the French boundaries would be 'in future tacitly admitted by the Porte'.[42]

In May, the French were reported to be 'taking rather a menacing line at Constantinople' to get their views on the frontier accepted,[43] but how far the Sultan would surrender his position in the Tripolitan Hinterland to avoid a clash with France was only to be known in the future. What was known then was that, after the failure of the Commission, French posts were advanced into the disputed territory at Dhiba and in the neighbourhood of the Mokta.[44] The French had therefore successfully advanced the Tunisian frontier, in fact if not by right, but their efforts to establish direct relations with the people of Ghadames and to win over the Touareg tribes by establishing markets at frontier posts had achieved little.[45]

BISERTA

. . . the harbour of Biserta is now declared to be the point of concentration of all the French maritime forces in the great, unavoidable and decisive struggle for supremacy in the Mediterranean . . . and the fate of Europe may be decided in the Bay of Carthage.[46]

These words reflect a very real fear felt in many parts of Europe, from the time of the occupation of the Regency. Biserta, it was thought with its magnificent natural anchorage capable of harbouring in safety all the fleets of Europe and its commanding position athwart the great commercial highway between East and West, might make the Mediterranean a 'French lake'. Yet when those words were written, the British Government had come to the conclusion that a base at Biserta would make no significant change in the relative strength of naval forces in the Mediterranean.

[42] FO 27/3138/21 Conf/Drummond Hay to Rosebery/27 June 1893; FO 45/696/99 Conf/Rosebery to Vivian/31 May 1893; FO 27/3093/71/ Drummond Hay to Rosebery/19 Dec 1892; FO 27/3138/5 Conf, 8, Tel 16/ 27 Feb, 7, 11 Mar, 10 June 1893. There is a suspicion that the Tripolitan officials were bribed; ibid; FO 45/698/89/Vivian to Rosebery/17 Mar 1893.
[43] Ibid.
[44] FO 27/3138/37 Conf/Drummond Hay to Rosebery/10 Oct 1893.
[45] FO 27/3138/43/Drummond Hay to Rosebery/12 Nov 1893.
[46] The Times, 4 Sep 1892.

It may be recollected that in 1881 Saint-Hilaire had assured
Granville that the French had 'no more desire to annex Biserta
than any other part of Tunis' and that, while not excluding
eventual commercial development, they had no intention of
expending the enormous sums necessary to create a military
port—'at present'. Granville, of course, had contented himself
with the observation that, if the channel from the lake to the sea
were deepened to give access to large vessels, British ships
would have the right to use it, under the 1875 treaty, on the
same terms as French or Tunisian ships.[47] When, furthermore,
a Beylical decree (in 1883) had designated Biserta, along with
some sixteen other places, as a military stronghold, no remonstrance had been addressed to the French Government.[48] It was
not until October, 1886, however, that French engineers began
marking out a canal between the sea and the Lake of Biserta[49]
and the French Admiral Aube, a member of the influential
school of naval opinion known as the *Jeune École*,[50] was said to
be 'very anxious' to have a naval station there. It is not surprising that the British Admiralty should now ask the Foreign
Office whether there was any other understanding over Biserta
than those in Granville's published despatches. The answer
was in the negative.[51] No more surprising was the news early
in 1887 of torpedo boat activity and suggestive preparations at
Biserta. Aube openly told Menabrea himself that 'solely for
want of money, the Tunisian coast was not provided with
torpedoes'.[52] Nevertheless the French proceeded at a very moderate pace to deepen the channel and construct a mole as a
breakwater. In fact, for three months in 1887, they stopped

---

[47] FO 27/2493/474, 480/Lyons to Granville/14, 16 May 1881 (encls.);
A.P. vol. xcix, Tunis No. 6 (1881), *Correspondence respecting the Affairs of
Tunis*, Nos. 42.45.54.
[48] Gorrini, *Tunisi e Biserta*, p. 162.
[49] FO 102/167/30, Tel, 33/Sandwith to Iddesleigh/30 Aug, 19, 20 Nov
1886. The Italian account says the ubiquitous General Allegro made a
detailed survey and that Freycinet said that only commercial works at
Tunisian expense were intended; Gorrini, op. cit., pp. 163-4.
[50] Marder, op. cit., pp. 86-7. The *Jeune École* believed the torpedo boat
could overthrow the superior battleship strength and raid the commerce of
wealthier Britain. Others were Admiral Bourgeois and Gabriel Charmes.
Most French officers opposed raiding.
[51] FO 102/168/M2971 Conf/Admiralty to FO/10 Dec 1886; ibid/Conf/FO
to Admiralty/29 Dec 1886; FO 403/112/Memo/from Admiralty/10 Jan 1889.
[52] FO 102/169/1, 2, 3/Sandwith to Salisbury/18 Jan, 4, 21 Feb 1887;
Gorrini, op. cit., p. 164; FO 27/2855/Lytton to Salisbury/9 May 1887.

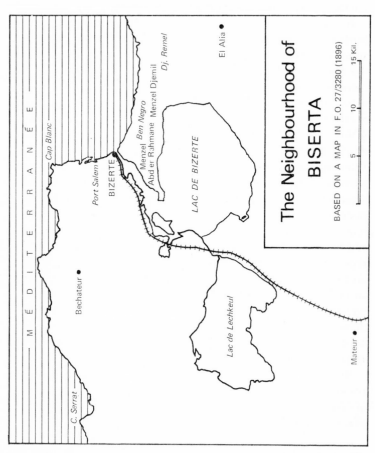

The Neighbourhood of
BISERTA

BASED ON A MAP IN F.O. 27/3280 (1896)

FIG 2

and seemed to have given up the whole idea.[53] By September, 1888, the canal was only three or four metres deep and the new breakwater still in a bad state, though in the following month, a transport arrived with 'coal, iron, torpedoes and machinery for the manufacture of torpedoes'.[54]

It was not, however, as might be reasonably anticipated, the fearful and excitable Crispi who brought Biserta back into the arena of Great Power politics but the Germans, and that at the height of the Schools crisis. In October, Waldersee, the German Chief of Staff, told Colonel Swaine that the French were 'seriously contemplating converting Biserta into a naval fortified port', and that Italy was alarmed and irritated.[55] On 8 November the German general staff compiled a memorandum on the importance of Biserta which was passed to the Italians. When the latter had not apparently responded adequately, they were again warned 'spontaneously' in the new year of the 'new disposition at Paris' to push on with the works at Biserta. At the same time Münster was told to advise Goblet not to 'snap his fingers' at Crispi—now intransigent in the schools question— and Salisbury was invited to join 'as on previous occasions' the representations at Paris.[56] In view of the fact that Bismarck was on the verge of proposing an alliance with England, it may be surmised that he was trying to create a bond of unity between Salisbury and the unloved Crispi, keep alive Franco-Italian disagreement over Tunis and have English support in the Mediterranean enhance the value of the Triple Alliance for Italy.

Bismarck might reasonably have anticipated a favourable response. In discussing the rumours of a French annexation of Tunis the previous August, Salisbury had told Wadding-ton:

[53] FO 102/169/4, 5, 11/Sandwith to Salisbury/16 May, 27 June, 6 Oct 1887. A new ship channel from sea to lake was also mooted.
[54] FO 403/112/15/Ricketts to Salisbury/11 Sep 1888; ibid/Memo/from Admiralty/10 Jan 1889; FO 27/2924/20/Ricketts to Salisbury/29 Oct 1888. There were orders at Toulon for coal stocks and a floating dock for Biserta.
[55] Holstein disclaimed any special information; FO 403/112/337 Conf/ Beauclerk to Salisbury/27 Oct 1888; ibid/Swaine to Beauclerk/24 Oct 1890. Peteani suggests that Crispi had neglected the Mediterranean for E. Africa; op. cit., p. 83.
[56] Gorrini, op. cit., pp. 164-5; FO 403/112/Memo/communicated by Leyden/5 Jan 1889.

. . . we should object to it very strongly and especially in view
of the control it would give over the port and arsenal of Biserta.[57]

Ricketts was now writing from Tunis that it would be easy to
intercept Mediterranean traffic from a naval arsenal at Biserta
and attack Malta or the Italian ports, so that annexation would
be a 'constant danger to Italy, England and Turkey'.[58] An
Admiralty memorandum also argued that slight expenditure
would create a perfectly secure, land locked harbour at Biserta
which, in words to be quoted by the Italians *ad nauseam* in the
years to come, would be 'the most important strategical position
in the Mediterranean'.[59] Salisbury, however, whatever his
views on Biserta, was in no mind to encourage a Crispi who was
'trailing his coat' in the schools incident and apparently on the
verge of hostilities with France. In addition, while appreciating
Bismarck's difficulties, he 'mistrusted the line that Germany
was taking'.[60] Before answering the request for combined action
in Paris therefore, he took the precaution of giving to Waddington a reminder of his 'very serious objection' to the fortification
of Biserta and the Frenchman replied that it would be impossible without a public vote beforehand in the Assembly.[61]
Salisbury then told the Germans that a concerted approach
might 'easily be misconstrued as a menace' and that he would
make a 'friendly representation' at a suitable opportunity.[62]
It was clear that the concern that had been shown by the Germans over Biserta had been artificial. Their expert, the military

[57] FO 45/600/172 Conf/Salisbury to Kennedy/17 Aug 1888.
[58] FO 27/2924/24/Ricketts to Salisbury (Memo)/12 Nov 1888. He said
that the entrance, now 12 feet, could easily be deepened and, in company
with ports at Tunis and Goletta, would be 'inaccessible when defended by
torpedoes'. Important reports from Tunis were now subject to considerable
delay, even though Salisbury had a warship sent to collect them; FO 403/
112 Conf/FO to Ady/14 Jan, 11 Mar 1889; ibid/Conf/Ady to FO/25 Jan
1889.
[59] FO 403/112/Memo/from Ady/10 Jan 1889; Gorrini, p. 165; Crispi,
op. cit., vol. 3, p. 89; FO 403/151/Memo/communicated by Tornielli/28 May
1891. The Admiralty memo would appear to be the one referred to by
Marder as an FO memo; op. cit., p. 149.
[60] FO 27/2952/2 Conf/Lytton to Salisbury/16 Jan 1889, min.
[61] FO 27/2950/Salisbury to Lytton/11 Jan 1889. Lytton wrote privately
that it was impossible to find the amount actually spent, on which point he
suspected 'the French Government itself was quite in the dark', but he
trusted Waddington's assurances; SP/58/18 Jan 1889.
[62] FO 27/2950/21 Conf/Salisbury to Lytton/14 Jan 1889; G.P. 8/1863.

attaché at Paris, declared himself 'positive' that nothing was being done or contemplated beyond clearing the canal and stationing a few torpedo boats there. Lytton too was sure that a French Government 'almost verging on bankruptcy' could not carry out the 'very long and expensive undertaking'.[63] The whole episode terminated after the incredible 'information' had been conveyed to Paris by a now sanguine Quirinal that:

> . . . the English Government being seriously alarmed . . . had invited the Italian and, he believed, the German Government to join in protesting against these proceedings. . . . The English and German protest would doubtless follow in due course.[64]

Lytton did take the opportunity to mention to the French minister the 'serious provocation' that a military port at Biserta would give, but added that Salisbury had been 'fully satisfied' by the assurances received. Goblet had in fact willingly renewed the declaration of Saint-Hilaire, saying that his government also had 'at present' no intention of enlarging and arming the port of Biserta. Crispi, far from satisfied, could do no more than enjoin watchfulness in London lest the balance of power in the Mediterranean should be upset.[65]

There can be no doubt that Salisbury was well aware at this time of the weakened position of Britain in the Mediterranean.[66] Not only had there been complacent neglect of a complacent navy for at least twenty years, at a time when naval power was beginning to face the new challenge of 'galloping obsolescence', but the strength upon the sea of a possibly chauvinist France, which by now possessed one of the most formidable armies in Europe, was making rapid progress. If the torpedo enthusiasts were to be believed, Britain could be forced to her knees by

[63] FO 27/2952/29 Conf/Lytton to Salisbury/18 Jan 1889. Gorrini, op. cit., p. 166. Salisbury apparently agreed on 'maximum vigilance', but said the works were of little importance.

[64] FO 27/2952/35/Conf/Lytton to Salisbury/25 Jan 1889; ibid/2950/46 Sec/Salisbury to Lytton/2 Feb 1889. This information came from Goblet.

[65] Ibid; FO 45/622/22 Conf/Salisbury to Dufferin/30 Jan 1889.

[66] The question is discussed at length in Marder, op. cit., pp. 84-7, 119-148; Tunstall, 'Imperial Defence, 1870-1897', *Cambridge History of the British Empire*, vol. 3, pp. 241-4; Cecil, op. cit., vol. 4, pp. 183-93; Ensor, *England, 1870-1914*, pp. 121-4, 286-9; also *Letters of Queen Victoria*, series iii, vol. 1, pp. 371, 399, 409-416, 456; FO 27/2956/566 Conf/Lytton to Salisbury/24 Dec 1889.

blockade. The feeling of general uneasiness engendered was heightened by the resignation of the junior Lord of the Admiralty, Lord Charles Beresford, and the deliberate indiscretions of the Adjutant-General, Lord Wolseley. Salisbury, by no means prone to alarm, was prepared to accept expert opinion that a French invasion was technically possible and also its corollary, the building programme of the Naval Defence Act of March 1889. By May, 1888, when fighting strength had rarely been more unequal to the task, it was realised that any realistic plan had to take into account the possibility of simultaneous hostilities with both France and Russia and, after that year, France concentrated most of her best warships at Toulon. It is obvious that the third naval power, Italy, would have welcomed an alliance with Britain, but it was clear in London that the Italian navy was already in decline and that the burden of defending Crispi's long coast line was not one lightly to be undertaken. When frenzied appeals for help against an imaginary threat came from Rome in July, 1889, it will be remembered that Salisbury was prepared to admit no obligation involving material action. Until the navy had been modernised and expanded, common prudence dictated a policy of extreme caution. Salisbury's disposition also to offend France as little as possible, while doing nothing to drive Italy into the arms of that power, made sense in military and naval terms. For, in the event of hostilities, all the Admiralty had was the dubious plan of concentrating the Channel and Mediterranean Fleets off Gibraltar, leaving a small 'reserve' to defend the home waters.[67]

After Crispi's abortive intervention over Biserta, the French went quietly ahead with their projects. In 1889 the harbour works made considerable progress; a floating dock was constructed; the channel was deepened further and, in May, the first torpedo boat entered.[68] A detailed Italian memorandum communicated to Salisbury in April argued that 'with but little difficulty' and expense a first class naval base could be established, which would command the sea routes, be a constant menace to Sicily, Sardinia and the south of the Peninsula and

[67] Marder, op. cit., pp. 84–7, 119–148, Tunstall, op. cit., pp. 241–4.
[68] FO 27/2971/12, 39/Ricketts to Salisbury/25 Feb, 20 May 1889; ibid/ 2953/166/Lytton to Salisbury/30 Mar 1889; ibid/3014/1 Conf/Drummond Hay to Salisbury/8 Jan 1890; FO 403/112/Memo/28 Nov 1889.

radically change the conditions of war in the Mediterranean to the advantage of France.[69] A succession of reports bore witness to the increasing interest in London. A naval captain asserted there were 'no extensive operations' there; in July a conflicting military intelligence memorandum predicted the construction of a base 'at an early date' and another report in November described the actual progress made.[70] Indeed, in the new year, there were so many visits to Biserta by 'naval or military officers . . . on independent or secret missions' that Drummond Hay complained that his friendly relations with the Beylical Government might be jeopardised, a view which met with scant sympathy from the first Lord, Lord George Hamilton.[71] Shortly after the Consul-General had visited Biserta, Prince Louis of Battenberg arrived and, independently, but nevertheless hard on his heels, the redoubtable Colonel Talbot, military attaché at Paris, with an engineer officer.[72] The Colonel felt that it would be 'difficult to overrate' the value of the ports of Tunis and Biserta when completed. In war Malta might be menaced and Britain's line of communications constantly threatened. 'The magnitude of the advantages' to French naval power in the Mediterranean bore no relation to the cost of construction, which, in any case, was to be met by the Tunisians and without recourse to the French Chamber.[73]

Throughout the summer the powers had a general idea of what was planned for Biserta, but information from the British Consular Agent there was 'wanting in accuracy and detail'. This is not surprising as he was also agent for a French shipping company. By the autumn, however, it was confirmed that an unpublished Beylical decree in the previous February had awarded a contract on very favourable terms for the construction and operation of a port to a group of French contractors of repute, who had formed the 'Port of Bizerta Company' with a capital of four million francs. In addition, the Tunisian budget

[69] FO 45/623/91 Conf/Dufferin to Salisbury/15 April 1889.
[70] FO 403/112/Ady to FO/29 April 1889; ibid/Conf/WO to FO/9 July 1889; ibid/Memo/28 Nov 1889.
[71] FO 27/3014/12 Conf/Drummond Hay to Salisbury/20 Feb 1890; ibid/Pr/to Drummond Hay/13 Mar 1890.
[72] FO 3014/14/Drummond Hay to Salisbury/23 Feb 1890.
[73] FO 27/2998/156, 247/Lytton to Salisubry/18 April, 29 June 1890. Talbot compared it favourably with Gibraltar, Malta or Aden.

set aside £100,000 for construction that year.[74] Drummond Hay obtained a plan of the new port 'from a reliable source' and made an extensive tour along the coast. He noted that the prospects of trade hardly warranted a commercial port at Biserta and pointedly observed:

> It is surprising . . . that the French Government should countenance a commercial undertaking of such magnitude which if successful must be the ruin of the capital, where they are now spending large sums of money in the construction of a canal and other costly improvements.

Moreover, new barracks for a considerable garrison were under construction, while the entrance was protected by torpedoes and surveys suggested preparations for early fortification of the surrounding hills.[75]

Crispi, of course, would have dearly liked his partners to bring pressure to bear in the spring at Paris, but he had little chance of success. In a general exchange of views, Tornielli and Salisbury agreed that France aimed at creating a base for torpedo boats, but the English minister said he could not understand why Italy should feel more menaced from Biserta than from Toulon or Corsica.[76] Crispi therefore endeavoured to revive enthusiasm in Berlin for Bismarck's idea of joint Anglo-German action in Paris. Caprivi, however, was no Bismarck. Not really interested in who controlled the Western Mediterranean, the new German government was convinced that a naval base at Biserta would prove particularly intolerable to Britain. They rejoiced therefore in the French development of the port, since it would 'bind Italy to the Triple Alliance' for as long as the English connection survived. When Salisbury

[74] FO 27/3014/22 Conf, 25 Conf, 29 Conf, 31, 32, 33, 64/Drummond Hay to Salisbury/18 Mar, 2, 22 April, 6, 8, 8 May, 14 Oct 1890; ibid/14/Salisbury to Drummond Hay/8 Oct 1890; Gorrini, op. cit., pp. 166-70; Crispi, op. cit., vol. 3, pp. 91-2; FO 403/150/126 Conf/Paget to Salisbury/13 May 1890. The concessionaires were the competent M. Couvreux (Suez Canal contractor; large fortune from Panama Canal contract; important European undertakings); and Messrs. Lesueur and Hersent (constructed port of Phillippeville). Even in Oct. only some of the terms were made public, but they included the valuable monopoly of fishing rights for 75 years and the expropriation of land was also made possible. See also note 75.

[75] FO 27/3014/69 Sec/Drummond Hay to Salisbury/28 Oct 1890; ibid/49, 62, 63/4 July, 23 Sep, 10 Oct 1890.

[76] Gorrini, op. cit., p. 168. The English record of the Italian proposal and its fate would seem to have been mislaid in the FO.

was informed of the Italian proposal, however, he gave the opinion that a fortified Biserta would not alter the power position in the Mediterranean. Explaining his apparent coolness and 'indifference' to the surprised Germans as based on a desire to curb Crispi's 'ardour', he expressed a fear that pressure might induce France to propose compensation for Italy in Tripoli and thus further dismember Turkey.[77] Salisbury's was the decisive voice. For the disinterested Kalnoky told the Italians that he would associate himself with their initiative only if they reached agreement with the other powers, 'above all with England'. A similar attitude was taken up in Berlin. When Crispi, therefore, in a telegram in June, pointed out that a military port at Biserta would 'close the Mediterranean', Salisbury decried the French 'fortlets' there and asserted that a 'united Anglo-Italian fleet would always preserve absolute superiority over that of France'.[78] During the Anglo-French negotiations, when there were the rumours of a secret French treaty with the heirs of the Bey, and the Italians were hinting at 'compensation', Crispi reverted once more to the 'menace' of Biserta, which he was sure was 'equally distasteful to England'.[79] In September, however, when news of the French company's concessions made him try London yet again, Currie, the Under-Secretary, gave him the unpalatable opinion that 'the declarations of 1881 did not constitute an absolute pledge' not to fortify the Tunisian coast. Any remonstration therefore lacked foundation.[80]

It was at this moment, of course, that Crispi was dropping hints to France that he would like a clandestine deal over Tunis and Tripoli. Now on 8 October, without the backing of England, he foolishly made his first attempt to tackle the French directly on the Biserta question. He met with as little success. Ribot, while denying any intention 'at present' to create a military port, seized the opportunity to assert that:

[77] G.P. 8/1862.1863.1864. The fortification of Tunis was proceeding openly, but Salisbury made no protest; FO 27/3014/13/Drummond Hay to Salisbury/21 Feb 1890.

[78] Gorrini, op. cit., pp. 168-9; Crispi, op. cit., vol. 3, p. 90. Caprivi did promise some action in Paris in Aug.

[79] FO 45/648/Tel 41 Very Conf/Dufferin to Salisbury/18 July 1890; SP/67/Dufferin to Salisbury/17 July 1890.

[80] Gorrini, op. cit., 170-1.

BDT L

The declaration formerly given did not constitute an international engagement and had the weight only of mere political declarations, the application (portée) of which could be modified by circumstances.

He went on to say that when they contemplated fortification they would act openly and that 'the Bey' had the sovereign right to proceed with the current plans, which were a menace to no-one and would, in any case, take 'a very long time' to execute.[81] As Crispi was already in what Lytton called a 'reckless fit', the result was a frenzy of activity, exacerbated by the fact that the Italian elections were near and that he had no wish to appear checkmated, in spite of his powerful friends, in every single North African question. He decided to concentrate his efforts on the Biserta issue, in which he still thought Britain was 'interested', feeling that this was his best chance of rallying those friends to his support,[82] and his first move was to request a joint Austro-German denunciation in London of 'the strange theories of Ribot'. Marschall condemned them with a satisfying severity, but Salisbury, 'between resignation and impatience' according to Tornielli, said that France would annex Tunis in the end, so that there was no remedy for the evils lamented by Italy. He agreed, however, to approach the French again, though 'the reply would be the same', and he told the Austrian representative that there was really no ground for action over port works allegedly commercial.[83] Action at Paris indeed had less chance than ever of success, since the French ambassador at Rome had somehow acquired a fairly accurate knowledge of Crispi's overtures together with Salisbury's unfavourable reaction. Ribot too was able to get early confirmation of this from Münster, who informed him that Berlin had not paid much attention to Crispi either.[84] Salisbury, in fact, did nothing more than to urge the French government, through Waddington, 'to refrain from any military construction at Biserta'.[85]

[81] D.D.F. 1/8/189; Gorrini, op. cit., p. 171; G.P. 8/1897; FO/403/150/123 Malet to Salisbury/26 Dec 1890.

[82] Gorrini, op. cit., pp. 175-6; SP/58/Lytton to Salisbury/27 Sep 1890.

[83] Hatzfeldt was told it would be 'unwise to demand explanations' until France revealed her hand. Gorrini, op. cit., pp. 172-3; FO 403/150/174/ Salisbury to Paget/13 Nov 1890; Crispi, op. cit., vol. 3, pp. 87-8.

[84] D.D.F. 1/8/200.219.223.

[85] FO 403/151/Tel 8/Salisbury to White/28 Jan 1891; Marder, op. cit., p. 150.

By December 1890 the Italians were convinced of the military character of the Biserta works and their alarm was acute. Biserta and Toulon, to Ressman, were 'two loaded pistols permanently held at the head of Italy by France', and the Italian press launched an anti-French campaign.[86] One especially forceful memorandum went from Rome to Vienna, Berlin and London, which was obviously intended to refute the view that the works 'did not as yet appear to be for military purposes'. It claimed that a fortified Biserta would enable France to pour up to sixty thousand men into Sicily before Italy could intervene from the relatively distant Madalena. Not only would Italy have to weaken her Alpine frontier to defend the south, but the junction of the Anglo-Italian fleets in the Southern Mediterranean would be prevented and British commerce under perpetual menace.[87] Crispi therefore formally requested his allies to remonstrate at Paris in association with England. Marschall, however, considered collective action an extreme step which might lead to war or the emasculation of the Triple Alliance and preferred to follow the English example and await 'more decisive and concrete facts'.[88] As for Salisbury, his irritation at this fresh Italian representation was hardly concealed, especially as complaints had also been made of a 'certain coolness' exhibited by Britain.[89] After he had refused to remonstrate with the French, Hatzfeldt deemed it inadvisable to ask him for more than an assurance to the Italians that he was 'paying attention' to events at Biserta and would consider steps if militarisation became obvious.[90] Even Tornielli, never over friendly towards Salisbury, blamed any coolness on the way Crispi was always sending him to bother the English minister about Biserta and Tripoli.[91]

[86] FO 27/3000/411 Conf/426 Sec/Lytton to Salisbury/8, 24 Dec 1890; ibid/3001/Tel 63 Most Conf/23 Dec 1890; SP 58/5 Dec 1890; FO 27/3038/54/18 Feb 1891.

[87] FO 403/150/Memo: *Bizerte, Porte Militaire*/cmd. 26 Dec 1890. Translation in Crispi, op. cit., vol. 3, pp. 89-97.

[88] Gorrini, op. cit., p. 173; G.P. 8/1898.

[89] FO 45/647/222 Conf/Dufferin to Salisbury/22 Dec 1890; 'Coolness' of course was denied officially; ibid/664/4 Conf/Salisbury to Dufferin/2 Jan 1890. Salisbury said there was no difference escept Kassala, which was Crispi's fault; SP/68/to Dufferin/7 Jan 1891.

[90] G.P. 8/1900.

[91] SP/67/Dufferin to Salisbury/8 Jan 1890. Crispi 'didn't understand the calmness of English statesmen'.

The letter Salisbury wrote for communication to Rosebery on the change of government eighteen months later has long been public. In it he explained that:

> The key to the present situation in Europe is our position towards Italy, and through Italy to the Triple Alliance.[92]

He was now, in private, ready to unburden himself in less flattering terms on the commanding position occupied by Rome and accurately assessed the cause of much of the trouble. 'They imagine their alliance is a pearl of great price', he complained to Dufferin, and, rejecting any obligation to pay 'for value received', added:

> To my mind the Italian alliance is an unprofitable, and even slightly onerous corollary on the German alliance. Germany and Austria are very useful friends as regards Turkey, Russia, Egypt and even France. They value the Italian alliance because it means many battalions to them; and for their sake we value it too. But by itself, it makes our relations with France more difficult, and it is of no use anywhere else.[93]

That 'anywhere else' included Biserta, about which opinion in British governmental circles was changing substantially. Salisbury, indeed, acknowledged a common interest with the Italians to limit French power on the south coast of the Mediterranean, but did not attach the same importance to Biserta as they did. He considered, in fact, that 'a great fortress like Biserta would be in the air'; cut off from supplies it would be useless unless complete command of the sea had been achieved. Nor, if the port were fortified, did he much value the right to remonstrate, which to him meant:

> ... nothing more than writing despatches which look well in the Blue Book, and have a satisfactory ring of vigour in their language.

This he would do, if necessary, but his whole nature rebelled

[92] Cecil, op. cit., vol. 4, p. 404. Salisbury told Malet that what he was afraid of was a 'too hurried *rapprochement* with France involving the abandonment of the Triple Alliance by Italy, a reconstruction of the Dreikaiser Bund and Russia on the Bosphorus'; FO 343/3/Pr/16 Aug 1892.
[93] SP/68/Salisbury to Dufferin/16 Jan 1891.

against what he scathingly called 'an exchange of apprehensions'.[94]

Salisbury had, of course, tried, with only partial success, to conceal his attitude from Tornielli and Hatzfeldt, an attitude which was soon to have the support of detailed naval argument. Indeed, only a few days before, the Director of Military Intelligence, Lt.-General Brackenbury, had in a memorandum reviewed the evidence pointing towards a militarised Biserta, with the traditional assumptions—which one 'need not be a sailor to see'—regarding its influence on naval warfare in the Mediterranean.[95] Four weeks later, in another memorandum on the importance of Biserta, which the youthful Naval Intelligence Department slyly remarked had been 'greatly overestimated in certain quarters', an extremely well reasoned attack was made on the traditional assumptions in general and the Italian December memorandum in particular. It was advanced that first class naval bases away from the mother country were 'unknown' and that Gibraltar, Malta and even Bombay, headquarters of a separate navy, had not been so developed. In a statement said to 'virtually exhaust the subject', it was argued:

> If they do not use the place, it is needless to discuss the question. If they use it with the whole of their fleet, they will not only have given up a base of very advantageous character at Toulon, which is seven or eight hours nearer to Gibraltar and the point of junction with the Brest fleet, but they will have burdened themselves with the maintenance of an additional line of communication. If they use Bizerta with only part of their fleet, they will divide their force. In other words, they will voluntarily do for us just the very thing which it is the object of our strategy to bring about.[96]

In similar vein, the likelihood of a descent on the Italian coast from Biserta was dismissed in detail on the grounds that Toulon would be much more convenient, entail one voyage instead of two and have all the shipping of Marseilles on which to call. It was conceded that the port might be used for small craft to raid

[94] SP/68/Salisbury to Dufferin/7 Jan 1891; Cecil, op. cit., p. 377-8.
[95] FO 403/151/DMI to FO/2 Jan 1891. This referred to Hay's information; see note 75.
[96] FO 403/151/DNI Sec Memo/cmd. 29 Jan 1891; Marder, op. cit., pp. 150-152.

shipping, though 'one (port) more or less' was immaterial. It was conceded that the port might conceivably become a 'formidable rival' to Malta commercially; but even the nearness of Biserta to Malta would, it was thought, simply make it more convenient for the despatch of ships from the latter to smash or blockade the former. Undoubtedly the most revolutionary conclusion, however, was that it was a positive advantage to have Biserta militarised, on the grounds that the more the French spent on the port, the less they would spend on ships. Admiralty advice to the government was, therefore, to 'encourage the French to persevere in their misdirected efforts' and to secure that desirable end:

> . . . by abstaining from putting so much pressure on them as to make them abandon their design, and by expressing just that judicial amount of apprehension which will make them obstinately persist in carrying it out in the belief that they are doing something damaging to the naval position of their probable future enemies.[97]

Though Salisbury did not go as far as this, it is easy to discern the origin of the views on Biserta expressed to Dufferin on 7 January.

Salisbury had been under considerable pressure from Hatzfeldt, who lectured him on his 'want of sympathy about Biserta', from Tornielli, who 'scolded him like an injured wife' and from Crispi, who 'reproached him like a neglected lover'.[98] It is not without significance therefore that, the day after he received the D.N.I. memorandum, Salisbury sent for Crispi's edification a despatch answering the appeal for concerted pressure on France, in which his point of view was cleverly and persuasively argued. First he once again reviewed the English anxieties after the occupation which had led to the assurances of Saint-Hilaire. Then he mentioned the recent declaration obtained by him from Waddington that the French had 'no intention of spending their

[97] FO 403/151/Sec/memo respecting Biserta as a French Naval Port/DNI to FO/29 Jan 1891.
[98] See notes 93 and 94. The German and Austrian ambassadors had mentioned Italian disquiet over his 'apathy'; see note 99. On 20 Jan, Crispi asked Tornielli if the Biserta works did not involve England's Mediterranean pledges to Italy. Tornielli prevented this approach because the English cabinet were against embarrassments, the public disinterested and parliament would condemn action on a secret agreement; Gorrini, op. cit., p. 176.

Lord Salisbury

Francesco Crispi

Gabriel Hanotaux

Théophile Delcassé

money upon fortifications at Bizerta', but stressed again that they had never given any guarantee as to the future. In the absence of any legal ground for remonstrance, Britain could, from what he called the 'larger prescriptions of the right of self defence', object to anything violently altering the balance of Mediterranean naval power. He pointed out, however, that this was a step of 'great gravity', to be justified only in exceptional circumstances. Salisbury made passing reference to the Admiralty opinion on the relative uselessness of a fortified Biserta with an understandable brevity. Then, examining in detail the 'grounds of suspicion' which might justify a demand for an explanation at Paris, he concluded that the evidence of military preparations was slight. His 'peroration' was brilliantly calculated to exercise the maximum of effect in Rome:

> Such shadowy and ambiguous indications . . . do not, in our judgement, justify us in demanding an explanation from the French Government. . . . It would not be met by a satisfactory, hardly perhaps by a respectful answer. It might irritate the French Government into action which otherwise they might not care to take. It would diminish the force of any representation which we might be justified in making later on; and it would . . . betray a susceptibility . . . which would lead the French people, at all events, to believe that the fortification of Bizerta was a policy by which great embarrassment could be caused. . . . Such a conviction might lend to the policy an attraction in their eyes which it does not possess at present.[99]

This powerful broadside was intended to quieten Crispi at a moment, for him, of desperation; for, on the next day and before it could be answered, Salisbury was gratified to hear the surprising news that the Italian ministry had fallen. Not that Crispi would, in all probability, have achieved much, since the Germans, in spite of their call to London for action, were evasively blaming their own 'caution and deliberation' on their infantry change-over to small bore rifles. Kalnoky's reaction meanwhile to the Italian appeal had been simply to draw the attention of the French Government to how a military port

[99] FO 45/664/26 Conf/Salisbury to Dufferin/30 Jan 1891. The Crispi *Memoirs* state erroneously that Salisbury showed 'passive courtesy' to the Italian appeals, without 'venturing to question the Italian minister's stringent logic'; vol. 3, pp. 97-8.

would disturb the Mediterranean balance of power—with the sole motive of 'tranquillizing' Crispi.[100]

It has been said that the Biserta question now 'fell out of sight for several years',[101] but this is not quite so. It is true that there was an end to the artificial storms conjured up by the egoist who had said, 'I am Italian policy and Italian policy is myself', and who felt the impoverished Italy could not renounce her 'civilizing mission in Africa'.[102] It is true that his successor, di Rudini, set out to lessen the tension with a France that seemed prepared to be more conciliatory.[103] Nevertheless, no Italian government could let Biserta fall out of sight for long and the new minister shared the national fear of a naval base there.[104] A less hostile France continued to deny to Austria and Germany that the port works had a military character and Billot, French ambassador in Rome, was as reassuring as Waddington in London. Because of this and Britain's 'change' towards Biserta, the new occupants of the Quirinal felt it impossible to take any vigorous action and so confined themselves to a study of the Anglo-Italian strategical differences.[105] The result was the receipt in London, Vienna and Berlin of yet another Italian memorandum, which sought to controvert the new British naval opinion. It asserted the 'strategic principle' that additional points of support gave additional mobility, that they increased the strength of a fleet and made escape possible if it were hard pressed. Concluding that the 'Foreign Office was ceasing to take an interest' in Biserta, it went on to argue that a fortified Biserta would seriously weaken Italy militarily, since the possibility of successful invasion from the south would cause her to break up the concentration of her forces in the valley of the Po. All of this, it argued, proved the great interest of her allies and 'probable ally', Britain, in opposing the creation of

[100] FO 45/664/26 Conf/Salisbury to Dufferin/30 Jan 1891; FO 403/151/22 Conf/Paget to Salisbury/31 Jan 1891; FO 45/665/18/Dufferin to Salisbury/4 Feb 1891.

[101] Marder, op. cit., p. 152.

[102] FO 45/603/239 Conf, 323/Kennedy to Salisbury/15 Sep, 12 Dec 1888.

[103] For example, his negotiations over E. Africa; Galal Yehia, *La Grande Bretagne, la France et l'expansion italienne avant Adua*, vol. 3, chap. 2 (thesis: University of Paris).

[104] FO 45/665/31/Dufferin to Salisbury/18 Feb 1891. Di Rudini seemed to Dufferin to have not given much attention to the subject, when the latter showed him Salisbury's despatch.   [105] Gorrini, op. cit., p. 180.

such a military base. The nagging suspicion was also voiced that Britain, already feeling herself threatened in the Mediterranean from Toulon, might ignore the creation of another though nearer danger in return for compensation elsewhere.[106] The reaction of Italy's friends could have been forecast. Vienna was reserved, Berlin supported the Italian thesis and, in London, Salisbury, professing incompetence, asked the opinion of the Admiralty on the memorandum. The reply, with scathing brevity stated that:

> . . . the arguments therein contained do not in any way alter their Lordships' opinion . . .[107]

The Anglo-Italian exchanges in the spring of 1891 served to crystallize attitudes towards Biserta for some years to come and the question was allowed to remain in abeyance except for an occasional rumble of discontent from Rome. In July, 1892, for example. the then foreign minister, Brin, in signifying Italian support for England in Morocco, observed that:

> . . . where Italy's interests were intimately concerned, such as in the case of Tunis, and lately of Biserta, England was rather ready to let things slide.[108]

Four months later, moreover, Vivian reported that the uneasy Italian government 'shared the regret of their predecessors' at the Admiralty opinion mentioned in Salisbury's despatch of 30 January 1891, and that their objections were still those set forth in the controverting Italian memorandum of May. As they recognised that their hands were tied by the British refusal to move, they looked for a British initiative 'at the proper moment' in asking France for explanations regarding fortifications.[109] General Dal Verme was perhaps right in blaming di Rudini 'for having allowed the question to sleep',[110] but, given the English attitude and the refusal of an assurance by France, it is difficult

---

[106] FO 403/151/Memo/11 Mar 1891/cmd. 28 May 1891.
[107] Gorrini, op. cit., p. 180; FO 403/151/Ady to FO/11 July 1891.
[108] FO 45/683/155 Conf/Vivian to Salisbury/29 July 1892.
[109] FO 45/684/237 Very Conf/Vivian to Rosebery/10 Nov 1892.
[110] Vivian to Rosebery: FO 45/684/2 Dec 1892; ibid/685/Tel 1870/2 Dec 1892; ibid/697/49/8 Feb 1893. The question seems to have been dealt with by the FO staff without Rosebery. Ribot had boasted of the Biserta works also; ibid/697/29 Conf/27 Jan 1893.

to see what practical steps the embarrassed ministry could have taken.

As for the progress of the works at Biserta, this was not remarkable in 1891 and 1892, but they were—to use Drummond Hay's words—being 'steadily carried on' and 'thoroughly executed'. The canal was only opened to the sea in March, 1892, and the first two torpedo boats entered the lake in the following October.[111] Though French officers had surveyed sites for two forts to command the entrance to the new harbour in 1891, though they had made the first approaches to the substantial British resident who owned the land, and though they had watched visiting foreigners with 'extraordinary vigilance', the arrangements were only completed and work begun by the spring of 1894.[112] Currie was right in saying that 'there was a long way from this to the creation of a military port and arsenal,' and the 'considerable progress' reported from Tunis by the autumn of 1893 referred mainly to the construction of jetties. Informed opinion had sensed the now reserved attitude in London over Biserta and the restraint which this imposed on Italian action, so that the French could go ahead with their plans. This they had by this time shown signs of being ready to do, but with the utmost circumspection.[113]

[111] FO 27/3093/23, 33/Drummond Hay to Salisbury/29 Mar, 25 May 1892; ibid/59/to Rosebery/3 Oct 1892.

[112] FO 27/3052/6/Drummond Hay to Salisbury/1 Feb 1891; ibid/3190/11, 12/Drummond Hay to FO/25 Feb, 15 Mar 1894; ibid/14, 15/to Kimberley/20, 26 Mar 1894.

[113] FO 27/3138/27, 33 Sec/Drummond Hay to Rosebery/21 Aug, 20 Sep 1893; *Dépêche Tunisienne*, 12 Jan 1892. The 1892 Tunisian budget estimated the port would cost £480,000 (half that sum being represented by concessions). The concessionaries were to have received £160,000 by the end of the year. The port of Tunis was to cost £555,000, with £480,000 being paid in 1892; FO 3093/4/Drummond Hay to Salisbury/15 Jan 1892.

5

BRITAIN AND THE "TUNIS BASE", 1894-1899

THE SPRING-BOARD INTO AFRICA

In one of the most gloomy of a number of pessimistic surveys, an Italian memorandum of January 1894 says that France,

> ... profiting by her experience of the faults which she had committed in Algeria, has taken neither Algiers nor Cairo for the basis of operations of her projected African Empire, but Tunis ...

The writer went on to depict a 'body of African agents', preparing protectorates for France, travelling with caravans, and, successfully associated with the Panislamism of the Arab, going 'from Syria to Obock, and from Morocco and Tripoli to the Soudan, laying the foundations of an empire no longer Levantine but Mussulman'.[1] This is an exaggerated picture, but, as the excitable Crispi and the impetuous Blanc had just been returned to power, it was to be expected that every Italian effort would be made to keep the question of French action in the south of Tunis and the associated problem of Tripoli and its hinterland in the forefront of Mediterranean politics. Moreover the Italians intended actively to involve Britain, not only because they felt that close association with that country was the solution to their problems from Morocco to the Red Sea, but also because of the fear that England might be edging towards a general settlement of African problems (including Tunis) with France, to the detriment of Italy. They considered that their country, through the apathy of the previous administration, had continued to miss its just dues, as it had done formerly in Tunis

[1] FO 45/716/28 Conf/Clare Ford to Rosebery/31 Jan 1894. Crispi's general attitude to the border question and his earlier policy is set out in Palamenghi-Crispi, *Memoirs of Francesco Crispi*, vol. 3, pp. 18-37.

and Egypt.[2] Tornielli indeed, was now consistently playing on this fear, and his opinion was endorsed by his far from Anglophobe colleague, Nigra.[3] Nor in fact were the French to disregard the possibilities of Tunis as a base for operations in North Africa.

Their interest and activity in the south of the Regency have already been noted, though in fact, when the Italian memorandum was written, that interest and activity was not as great as it was to become. It is true that Colonel de Labonne, French Military Attaché at Tunis, generally regarded as an authority on questions relating to the extension of French influence in North Africa, had told Drummond Hay in June 1893, with that surprising 'frankness' often shown by French empire builders, that the diversion of the Ghadames trade was not considered important as it was 'not of sufficient value'. What Frenchmen were concentrating on, according to him, was Tuat, which they hoped would become a great caravan junction and rail head between the Sudan and North Africa.[4] This was probably a blind, since it is certain that, after the failure to delimit the Tunis-Tripoli frontier, military posts had been set up in the disputed area; that a special body of troops ('Les Troupes Sahariennes') was being formed; and that travellers were assiduously discouraged in the south. Moreover that picturesque adventurer, Colonel Allegro, who had done so much to prepare for the military occupation of Tunis, was at this juncture busy—

[2] FO 45/716/26 Conf, 32 Conf, 33 Conf/Clare Ford to Rosebery/all 31 Jan 1894; ibid/719/Tel 36/Clare Ford to Kimberley/12 June 1894; ibid/Tel 58 Very Conf/Edwardes to FO/21 Sep 1894; ibid/718/197 Very Conf/ Edwardes to Kimberley/23 Sep 1894; G.P. 9/2053.2126. Peteani, *La Questione Libica nella Diplomazia Europea*, p. 139. In June also, Tornielli was enquiring whether English negotiations with France over Tunis were taking place.

[3] G.P. 8/1766.1767.1770.1911; FO 45/719/Tel 36/Clare Ford to Kimberley/12 June 1894; ibid/718/244 Conf/Clare Ford to Kimberley/23 Nov 1894. Tornielli, it should be remembered, was the friend of di Rudini, Crispi's political opponent, and both he and Nigra detested Blanc; ibid/702/Memo Barrington/18 Dec 1893. Italy's finances were also in a bad state, bank scandals touched the highest in the land and relations with France (affected by commercial war) were very bad; FO 45/699/258 Conf/Vivian to Rosebery/ 23 Sep 1893; ibid/700/261.271 Conf/Vivian to Rosebery/5, 12 Oct 1893; ibid/700/312 Conf/Edwardes to Rosebery/6 Dec 1893; ibid/719/Tel 4, Tel 7/ Clare Ford to Rosebery/6, 12 Jan 1894; ibid/719/46 Conf/Clare Ford to Kimberley/25 June; Ibid/718/257, 259/Clare Ford to Kimberley/13, 17, 18 Dec 1894.

[4] FO 27/3138/15 Conf/Drummond Hay to Rosebery/8 June 1893.

though now half blind—endeavouring to organise an important caravan to Ghadames, in his capacity as Governor of Gabès. The wooing of the Touareg at the Tunisian government markets of Kebilli and Tatahouin began to give hopes of unmolested trade with Ghadames and the exploration of routes from Tunis continued, so that one military interpreter actually visited the Niger and Hausa states.[5]

The alarm bells were sounded, of course, by the Italians, who had already informed London that the re-establishing of Anglo-Italian confidence was considered necessary to foil the threat from Tunis and to prevent Tripoli, and Morocco also, becoming 'mere coast stations without communications to the interior'.[6] They insisted that a largely barren Tripoli deprived of its caravan trade with Sokoto, Bornu, Baghirmi and Wadai, would be 'an empty jewel-case', which would soon fall into the hands of France, and urged Britain to endeavour to 'guard the rights of Turkey to the Hinterland'.[7] Kimberley was no more anxious at this time to take up the question of the southern frontier of Tunis than he was to assure the insistent Italians that Britain would maintain the most favoured nation clause of her Tunis treaty unaltered in any future agreement. All that Tornielli got, therefore, was a promise that the Turkish ambassador would be asked 'whether the attention of the Porte had been directed to the matter'. For, though Kimberley thought it 'not improbable' that the French would expand their influence to the south with a view to effecting a junction between their spheres of influence on the West and South of Lake Tchad, he felt it inopportune to raise the question with France as England had 'so many points of difference with the French' in other parts of Africa.[8]

French activity, however, was soon sufficient to cause an increase of vigilance in London. By August, Drummond Hay had reported that the obvious objective was to control the trade

[5] FO 27/3138/37 Conf/Drummond Hay to Rosebery/10 Oct 1893; FO 27/3190/4, 10, 13, 28/5, 23 Feb, 19 Mar, 23 May 1894; FO 27/3198/Conf/ DMI to FO/19 May 1894; FO 27/3190/32 Conf/Drummond Hay to Kimberley/30 May 1894; Memoirs of Crispi, vol. 3, p. 67, n.1.
[6] FO 45/716/32 Conf/Clare Ford to Rosebery/31 Jan 1894.
[7] FO 45/715/116 Conf/Kimberley to Clare Ford/4 June 1894; Crispi, op. cit., vol. 3, p. 70; Woolf, Empire and Commerce in Africa, pp. 132-3.
[8] Ibid.

routes so as to divert trade from Tripoli. If Turkey acquiesced, he added, local opposition was unlikely and could only be effective anyway with British support. The worried intelligence officer at Malta, in addition, drew attention to claims in the French semi-official press that Ghadames and Ghat were in the French sphere of influence and, on observing that Britain required Tripoli as 'a buffer state between Egypt and Tunis', extracted the comment from Kimberley that the question needed 'most careful watching'.[9] When, therefore, in September, Tornielli returned to the charge with further reports of French attempts to create a movement for the inclusion of Ghadames in Tunis and hinted that his government would be glad if England would bring the matter confidentially to the notice of the Porte, Kimberly agreed.[10] A German enquiry at Constantinople, however, apparently got a reply that France and Turkey were virtually in agreement over the frontier. The English ambassador also was told that the Turks were well aware of French encroachments which (like the Italians) they blamed on 'the Anglo-French delimitation of 5 August 1890'. Repeated Italian requests then induced England to suggest that the Turk should resume negotiations for frontier delimitation with France.[11]

The unwillingness of the Rosebery government to take a firm line towards France is not difficult to comprehend. The understanding between Paris and St. Petersburg, together with the visit to French waters of the Russian fleet, had made British government and naval circles painfully aware of their inability to cope with both the Toulon fleet and a Russian squadron in the Mediterranean.[12] In addition, a rather less self-assured Germany was out to 'exert pressure on England and make her more amenable'[13] by being uncooperative in the colonial field.

[9] FO 27/3190/41 Conf/Drummond Hay to Kimberley/11 Aug 1894; FO 27/3199/Acting DMI to FO/21 Aug 1894, encl. and minute.

[10] FO 45/715/207 Conf/Kimberley to Edwardes/10 Sep 1894.

[11] FO 45/718/219 Conf/Edwardes to Kimberley/25 Oct 1894. Clare Ford had also been told on 12 June that Turkey appeared entirely indifferent to what took place in the south of Tripoli; FO 45/719/Tel 36/to Kimberley.

[12] Marder, British Naval Policy, pp. 219-222.

[13] G.P. 8/2039. German opposition to Britain's Congo treaty with Belgium of 12 May; the threat to support France over Egypt in June; German sympathies in the Transvaal question at the end of 1894 increased the earlier coolness over Siam and several smaller issues such as Zanzibar or Morocco; FO 343/3/Pr/Kimberley to Malet/13 June 1894; ibid/Sec/Rosebery to Malet/16 Jan 1894, ibid/Pr/Kimberley to Malet/21 Mar 1894.

Rosebery and Kimberley had long been conscious that there had been 'signs of coolness or indeed something more' in Germany. They ruled out, however, as unpractical politically either entering the Triple Alliance or making a secret treaty with Italy, but confessed in June 1894 that they still could not 'pretend to read the riddle' of German unfriendliness. Clearly, if it continued, the consequence would be a breach with Germany and her allies.[14] With a British 'humiliation', as Lugard called it,[15] over her Congo treaty with Belgium in the offing, it is not surprising that the two British ministers should not wish another thorny question like that of the Tunis frontier added to their 'points of difference' with France. This is not surprising, as it was indirectly linked to the same problem as the Congo question—French access to the Upper Nile and the consolidation of France's North African empire. It was no time to quarrel with France and Russia, and any enthusiastic support for Italy in Tunis would, almost certainly, have no other result. For the hatred of the Italians towards the French at this moment, which was reciprocated could not but be inflamed by the success of French efforts to injure their commerce; by the Papal gift to the Republic of the rights of nomination to the Bishopric of Tunis, and by the return of the notoriously Gallophobe Crispi to power. Indeed Dufferin only a few months previously had expressed his belief that the Italians saw everything to gain by bringing on a European war. He had gone on to utter a solemn warning to the government to beware of France, now backed by Russia, both of which countries were now likely to be 'more exacting and peremptory'. For a revived France was seen as strongly hostile, had amassed enormous armaments and was likely to find British interests countering some of her most cherished ambitions on 'innumerable occasions'.[16] As in East Africa[17] therefore, the Italians were to find that any British

[14] Ibid; FO 343/3/Rosebery to Malet/3 Jan 1894; ibid/Kimberley to Malet/ 27 June 1894.
[15] JP/Pr/Lugard to Johnston/12 Jan 1896.
[16] FO 27/3121/450 Conf/Dufferin to Rosebery/3 Nov 1893; B.D. 2/351.
[17] For example, *Tribuna*, on 23 Aug 1894, observed bitterly, 'Germany probably thinks that it is not worth while to oppose French progress in Africa, seeing that England, who would have so great an interest in restraining it, has shown herself so very weak in this respect'; copy in FO 45/717/175/ Clare Ford to Kimberley/23 Aug 1894.

cooperation which involved a challenge to France and Russia would be hesitant, grudging and ineffectual.[18]

In the south of Tunis, the French did indeed become more 'exacting and peremptory', which was no more than was to be expected when the career diplomat, Hanotaux, with his intimate knowledge of African affairs, became foreign minister in May.[19] What certainly heralded a more active policy was the appointment of his rough, engaging, fiery, intelligent and very determined friend, the masterful Millet, as Resident-General.[20] The latter, in fact, shared something of the views of the Italians on the value of Tunis as a base of operations in Africa. As he said later, acquiring the sterile land of Tripoli had a double strategic value for him, in both facilitating 'the rapid penetration into the heart of the black Continent' to control the trade toutes and protecting from menace the frontiers of the Regency (where the right flank of Algeria and Tunis could be turned by a determined power, such as an Italy backed by the Triple Alliance).[21] Millet was not the man to make any secret of his ambitions and bluntly told a military officer, who had been reprimanded by his predecessor for too much activity against Tripolitan tribes,

> The further you push the more I shall respect you. You can tell that to everybody.[22]

Millet's forcefulness, of course, was simply an attempt to give effect to hopes that had been entertained from the first days of the occupation. The attempts from Algeria to establish political and commercial relations with the Saharan hinterland were to have been greatly facilitated by the near contact between sea and desert in Tunis.[23] Unfortunately, however, for those hopes, a series of expeditions gathering data for a railway,

[18] Giglio, La Politica Africana del'Inghilterra, pp. 475-6; Salvatorelli, La Triplice Alleanza, p. 197; Albertini, The Origins of the War of 1914, vol. 1, p. 80; FO 78/4784/Salisbury to Ferrero/2 Jan 1896; G.P. 11/2751. Tornielli had warned against an Anglo-French entente since 1892; G.P. 8/1735; Peteani, op. cit., p. 138; Serra, L'Intesa Mediterranea del 1902, p. 5.
[19] FO 27/3172/217a Conf/Dufferin to Kimberley/31 May 1894; FO 27/3173/299 Conf/Phipps to Kimberley/28 July 1894.
[20] FO 27/3190/47 Drummond Hay to Kimberley/23 Sep 1894; FO 27/3237/17 Conf/Haggard to Kimberley/20 Mar 1895.
[21] Millet, Notre Politique Extérieure, pp. 93-6.
[22] FO 27/3237/18 Conf/Haggard to Kimberley/20 Mar 1895.
[23] Bernard et Lacroix, La Pénétration Saharienne, p. 91.

notably that of Flatters in 1881, fell victim to the Touareg, whose savage disposition and precarious livelihood had not been improved by the decline in the caravan trade following upon the suppression of slavery. Even the determined Cardinal Lavigerie had given up attempts to use the routes across the Sahara when, in the same year, three of his White Fathers had been murdered in an attempt to reach Ghadames. Beyond their established military posts, therefore, the Sahara had more and more been closed to the French, and sporadic attempts to open it up had only claimed further victims.[24] After 1890, however, more vigorous efforts were made, and, from Tunis, a disguised French agent admitted he had travelled (in 1891) from a still imperfectly known south of the Regency, to Ghadames, Bornu, Wadao and Lake Tchad. Simultaneously, a M. Cornetz, described in French literature as a 'young French engineer', and in a despatch of the English Consul-General as an eccentric and eventually completely mad former professor of mathematics, began three years life in the desert which resulted in the production of excellent and most vauable maps and information.[25] Others followed.

The active and intelligent Millet, anxious to get a personal acquaintance with the south, soon decided to tour the outlying districts accompanied by his Director of Agriculture, his Director General of Public Works, his naval and military attachés and a Secretary of Legation. The most surprising inclusion in his party, however, was the new English Consul-General, Haggard; for the Resident-General, having some English blood himself, was very friendly and seemed to take it as a compliment to France that a diplomatic officer of the rank of minister should have been appointed by Britain.[26] Moreover, he displayed the reckless indiscretion which characterised him by frankly discussing the objectives his government had in mind. The man

[24] Ibid, pp. 93-103; Blet, *Histoire de la Colonisation Française, France d'Outre-Mer*, pp. 125-130; Priestley, *France Overseas*, pp. 148-9. As a Tunisian paper remarked, with about one million in an infertile area as large as France, 'the Touareg are literally always hungry'; *Dépêche Tunisienne*, 29 June 1896. They were divided into four sections, and the two in the north were generally rivals.

[25] Bernard et Lacroix, op. cit., pp. 123-4; FO 27/3237/18 Conf/Haggard to Kimberley/20 Mar 1895.

[26] FO 27/3237/4, 13/Haggard to Kimberley/8, 4 Feb 1895.

who could be heard saying, 'When we have the Soudan', pointed out the frontier of Tunis on the Mokta and then drew his finger due south from Tozeur remarking:

> We prefer to leave that vague. We don't want to allow the Turks to erect (opposer) a barrier between us and the Soudan.[27]

Official circles in Tunis, and indeed the semi-official press, were actively canvassing the idea that the 'inevitable' railway crossing North Africa should originate from the Regency, possibly to link up with one from Senegal to Lake Tchad[28] and the great French objective, in fact, was to direct the trade of Tripoli with the interior into southern Tunis. The experienced military attaché, Commandant Rebillet, who had a voice in policy making, estimated the caravan trade of Tripoli to be worth nearly eleven million francs, though this was probably a serious exaggeration.[29] It is clear that the policy was to revive old routes, overcome Touareg aversion to Europeans and do everything to nourish the trade coming to Tunis with concessions.[30]

These hopes were, however, soon to meet with a severe reverse. A consequence of the English decision to advance to Dongola was, on the one hand, that French empire-builders were aroused to a fever of patriotic activity and, on the other, that the feeling of hostile rivalry towards Britain was strengthened. In June 1896 for example, the explorer and 'accepted

[27] FO 27/18 Conf/Haggard to Kimberley/20 Mar 1895.

[28] FO 27/18 Conf/Haggard to Kimberley/20 Mar 1895; FO 27/3237/26, 27 Conf/Haggard to Kimberley/1, 7 May 1895. Haggard thought that, as the French opened up the interior, Manchester goods could use Tunis as a pipeline to 'pour their produce into the French sphere of influence and thus thourgh the whole of North and Central Africa.'

[29] The English Consul-General in 1891 thought it worth 8,500,000 francs; FO 27/3238/97 Conf/Haggard to Salisbury/2 Dec 1895. Largeau thought the figure at least twelve millions in 1875, but Pervinquière in 1911, noting the grim poverty of Tripoli, thought it more like one million; Pervinquière, *La Tripolitaine interdite*, pp. 183-5, quoted Woolf, op. cit., p. 137.

[30] FO 27/3238/97 Conf/Haggard to Salisbury/2 Dec 1895, encl. Rebillet felt that Tunis was best place.1 to attempt this by way of Ghadames, Ghat, Air and Kano. See also, for conciliation of the Touareg, efforts to divert trade and exploitation of minor successes; FO 27/3237/41 Conf, 83 Conf, 100 Conf/ 17 June, 30 Oct, 19 Dec 1895. An amusing by product was the report of a military explorer that he had seen survivors of the Flatters mission, which, as Flatters' presumed widow had married an influential general, only led to his dismissal; FO 27/3238/64 Conf/Haggard to Salisbury/11 Aug 1895. The French also showed an interest in Bon Grara, possibly a 'second Biserta' and a better terminus than Gabès; ibid/65 Conf/12 Aug 1895.

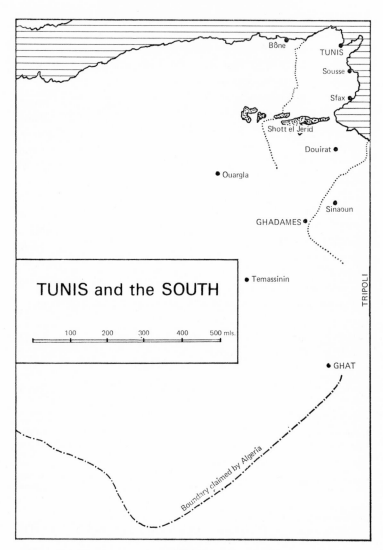

FIG 3

authority on African affairs', Béhagle, told a Tunis meeting that a counterpoise had to be found in Africa for the decline of French influence in Europe and prolonged cheering greeted his assertion that acquisitive England had provoked a spirit of combination against her and would speedily decay.[31] Preparations for expeditions were hurried forward; the departure of Allegro's much delayed caravan was announced for the autumn, and Béhagle himself purposed proceeding to Lake Tchad and Biskra, with the ostensible object of demonstrating the greater economy to be made by merchandise for Europe from Lake Tchad travelling to the Mediterranean rather than the Atlantic coast.[32] Far more important in its consequences, however, was the activity of 'a renegade Italian', the Marquis de Mores. A violent Anglophobe, he induced an excited meeting, which included ministers, heads of departments and the General Commanding, to pass a resolution expressing sympathy with the dervishes, whom he proposed to help against England. In a country where 'he couldn't have hired a camel without the permission of the authorities', he received clandestine support from the government and the Chamber of Commerce and Agriculture at Sousse, and, rashly putting his trust in Touareg and Chaamba tribesmen, was murdered a hundred miles south of Douirat, in the neighbourhood of Ghadames.[33]

As he had made a final speech that he intended to rouse up the native peoples against English influence, and as he had taken the 'precaution' of writing a letter to a Tripoli firm of Maltese traders, whom he fondly imagined to be English secret agents, threatening vengeance if he should be murdered, the result—in the circumstances—can easily be imagined. As in other similar cases, notably that of Oliver Pain twelve years previously,[34] the

[31] FO 27/3280/20 Conf/Haggard to Salisbury/2 June 1896. FO 27/3281/46 Conf/17 July 1896.
[32] Ibid.; FO 27/3280/18 Conf/Haggard to Salisbury/29 May 1896. The respective costs were estimated to be 300 and 1,000 francs a ton.
[33] FO 27/3280/15 Conf, 18 Conf/19, 29 May 1896. Bernard et Lacroix, op. cit., p. 143. A detailed account of the background and aims of the Marquis is to be found in Martel, op. cit., vol. 1, pp. 680-99. Millet's government was clearly inconsistent, discouraging de Mores' dangerous venture for the most part (as had the Algerian authorities), but then facilitating the acquisition of camels and reliable drivers.
[34] Pain went to join the dervishes, was rejected and died of fever, as Slatin Pasha, who took him prisoner and interpreted when he was before the

French press showed a determined eagerness to attribute the disaster to English intrigue. Angry looks encountered the English representative when he ventured abroad and papers like *Le Figaro*, *Éclaire*, *Matin*, *Libre Parole* and *Politique Coloniale* avidly sought to lay the murder at the door of emissaries of England and, even more incredibly, of her 'faithful ally', the Sheikh of Senoussi.[35] The career of this slightly deranged hero is rather more important than would appear at a cursory glance. In the first place, the attempt to make Tunis a 'base of operations' for France's projected North African empire received a decisive check. Maybe this was the final disappointment after a period when so much effort had yielded so meagre results; but after this, the modest Saharan trade, which had been so exaggerated, seems to have made no progress and the torch of French colonial expansion blazed elsewhere.[36] Having failed, the Marquis was disavowed by authority, and, though he continued to be a press martyr, the Residency asserted that it had tried to stop him, and an unusually subdued Millet, apparently rather ashamed of the fiasco, characterised as 'imbéciles' those who had earlier supported the Anglophobe resolution.[37]

The second significant result of the de Mores episode was to bring more into the open the views the French now held regarding the Tunisian hinterland. On Millet's return from Paris in October 1895, reference had been made in the semi-official press to the Treaty of Ghadames of 1862 concluded with the

---

Mahdi, bore witness to Cromer; SnP/268/2/Cromer to Sanderson/6 April 1902. The 'melodramatic story' is in the memoirs of Rochefort, who 'consoled himself with Mme. Pain'.

[35] FO 27/3280/28/Haggard to Salisbury/18 June 1896; ibid/3265/187/ Howerd to Salisbury/22 June 1896; ibid/3292/Wild & Wild to Curzon/30 June 1896; ibid/3266/210/Howerd to Salisbury/12 July 1896. Béhagle, in a letter to the press, accused 'Consul' Arbib (one of the Maltese) of murdering de Mores in the way Oliver Pain had been murdered; FO 27/3281/46 Conf/ Haggard to Salisbury/17 July 1896.

[36] Bernard et Lacroix, op. cit., p. 145. Rebillet had argued that Touareg hostility was due to proximity to Algeria and would be diminished by the more benevolent Tunisian policy. Allegro had triumphantly carried off an elephant's tusk, the one valuable item in a Ghadames caravan, to Paris; FO 27/3238/83 & 97 Conf/Haggard to Salisbury/30 Oct, 2 Dec 1895. A hundred caravans in six months from the Soudan was claimed, but the trade was still obviously very small; FO 27/3280/35 Conf/Haggard to Salisbury/ 30 June 1896. For Rebillet's arguments see, *Relations commerciales de la Tunisie avec le Soudan*, 1896.

[37] FO 27/3281/10 Conf/Haggard to Salisbury/1 July 1896. Millet's 'adjoint', Révoil, had hitherto strenuously denied the resolution's existence.

Amenokal of the Imouchar, a treaty of mutual friendship under which the Touareg had promised to facilitate and protect the trade of Frenchmen and Algerians.[38] When now the French press cried out for vengeance and reparation from the Porte, the Tunisian administration denied that the murder had taken place in Turkish territory. It was asserted that, by the convention concluded between Salisbury and Waddington on 5 August 1890, the hinterland south of Algiers and Tunis (from Tunis to Lake Tchad) had been placed in the French sphere of influence so that towns like Sinaouin, Ghadames and Ghat might be Turkish, but the surrounding territory came under French influence. Assurances from Paris as to the integrity of Tripoli therefore obviously had their limitations, and an incredulous Haggard wrote home that, according to the French theory, 'a very large part of what had been considered Tripoli would cease to be so'.[39] Motta, the Italian representative in Tripoli, also drew his government's attention to the French map of Tunis produced that year by the General Staff, which showed Touareg territory as *res nullius*, and said that this convenient theory could place even Ghadames and Ghat in the Tunisian hinterlands.[40] Millet indeed did himself consider those towns 'provisionally occupied by the Turkish garrisons' and to be in the Tunisian hinterland.[41] As two years previously, moreover, little opposition to French designs was to be anticipated from the Porte, whose Governor General in Tripoli was only too ready to quote the 1890 agreement and to disclaim responsibility for a murder committed 'in Touareg territory'.[42] Now, however, talk of a punitive expedition to avenge de Mores was discouraged, Hanotaux told the Italian ambassador that there was no such intention, and confident talk of occupying Ghadames,

[38] FO 27/3238/83 Conf/Haggard to Salisbury/30 Oct 1895; ibid/3345/13/ 17 Mar 1897.
[39] FO 27/3280/31 Conf, 32 Conf/Haggard to Salisbury/23, 24 June 1896.
[40] D.D.I. 3/1/119.
[41] Millet, op. cit., p. 94. Articles to the same effect in the *Dépêche Tunisienne* were probably inspired; see extract in FO 27/3280/32 Conf/Haggard to Salisbury/24 June 1896. Ghadames had been garrisoned in 1840; Ghat as late as 1874.
[42] FO 27/3280/35 Conf/Haggard to Salisbury/30 June 1896; ibid/3281/ 44 Conf/14 July 1896. Mr Jago, Consul-General in Tripoli, thought that Turkish indifference could be partly explained by the possibility of merchants, if necessary, avoiding the route through Ghadames.

as well as French interest in Bon Grara, the 'second Biserta', the port to link sea and desert, died down.[43] Henceforth the French concentrated on strengthening and increasing their military outposts in the south of Tunis.[44]

While French action in the Tunis 'base' was, therefore, building up to climax and anticlimax, Salisbury showed no more inclination to be involved in hostility with France on the issue than his predecessors, and for cogent reasons. In addition to the increasing difficulties, already noted, that he had to face in his relations with Germany, Russia and the United States, his policy in the Mediterranean had to be adjusted to new conditions. The fact that English opinion had changed towards the Turk,[45] that the English fleet could no longer dominate the Straits,[46] that the Austrian was becoming more and more disgruntled because Britain would not undertake their defence,[47] that Russian influence had become supreme with the Porte[48] and that England's prime concern in the Eastern Mediterranean had perforce shifted to the defence of her interests in the Nile Valley,[49] all this meant that Salisbury was far from willing to seriously challenge France in any matter of less than vital interest to his country. He had no wish, however, to lose the friendship of the Italians, any more than that of the Austrians, and was 'unwilling to refuse any request which in his view could be properly acceded to';[50] but the Zeila episode, which

[43] FO 27/3281/40 Conf, 43/Haggard to Salisbury/7, 11 July 1896; ibid/ 3266/210/Howerd to Salisbury/12 July 1896; D.D.I. 3/1/119; FO 27/3281/49 Conf, 53 Conf/Haggard to Salisbury/6 Aug, 5 Sep 1896. There is some evidence that there had been preparations for an advance column to Ghadames.

[44] FO 27/3281/77/Haggard to Salisbury/20 Oct 1896.

[45] FO 7/1240/24 Dec/Salisbury to Monson/4, 26 Feb 1896; A.A.E./Angl/ 911/7/de Courcel to Berthelot/7 Jan 1896; Garvin, *Life of Joseph Chamberlain*, vol. 3, p. 69.

[46] PRO 30/40/14/Ardagh Memo No. 5 Sec/Oct 1896; Penson, 'New Course in British Foreign Policy', op. cit., p. 126; Cecil, *Biographical Studies*, p. 35; Marder, op. cit., pp. 245-251.

[47] Walters, 'Lord Salisbury's Refusal to Revise and Renew the Mediterranean Agreements', *The Slavonic and East European Review*, vol. 29, pp. 271-283; FO 7/1241/59 Sec, 60 Sec, 63 Sec, 90 Most Conf/Monson to Salisbury/18, 18, 21 Feb, 18 Mar 1896.

[48] See Note 46.

[49] *Letters of Queen Victoria*, series 3 vol. 3, pp. 72-3; FO 45/747/65 Conf/ Salisbury to Clare Ford/20 May 1896; Cecil, op. cit., pp. 56-7.

[50] FO 45/747/65 Conf/Salisbury to Clare Ford/20 May 1896. He fought in the Cabinet against 'any policy that would cut Austria adrift'; SP/84/to the Queen/19 Feb 1896.

thwarted the Italian desire to face France with Anglo-Italian
solidarity in the Red Sea, had made even an Anglophile Italian
minister feel that he could no longer count on the friendship of
England.[51] It is not surprising that the activity in the south of
Tunis occasioned considerable alarm in Rome.

Whether or not Salisbury, in August, 1895, was really simply
speculating on possibilities or seriously considering appeasing
the Italians (in the expected event of an early Ottoman collapse)
by supporting their claim, among others, to Tripoli,[52] it is
certain that when Ferrero elaborated the idea four months later,
Salisbury just listened and remarked:

> I merely pointed out that they (the possibilities) were con-
> tingent on the occurrence of an event we should all deplore and
> which, as far as we could at present see, was anything but a
> certainty.[53]

In the following April, the Italians again began ringing the
alarm bells when their agent in Tunis reported an incursion by
Spahis well into Tripolitan territory 'ravaging the country and
destroying crops' and were not quietened by the explanation of
Révoil that the Spahis had been collecting tax from a Tripolitan
tribe which had sown crops in Tunisian territory. 'The lamb is
troubling the wolf's drinking water', said Haggard, who had
reported the south sealed off to travellers, and in June, when a
concentration of troops at Medenine was noted, Machiavelli
claimed confirmation of 'another and more serious conflict'
provoked by Tunisian irregular cavalry (Spahis) which was
again denied.[54] The French explanation of the activity of
Tunisian forces was the same in Tunis and Paris, that the recent events in the Sudan and Abyssinia involved danger from
awakened Moslem fanaticism from the Atlantic to the Red Sea,[55]
which in no way soothed Italian anxieties when their press was
filled with 'authoritative assertions' that France was determined

[51] Serra, *L'intesa mediterranea del 1902*, pp. 7, 9; G.P. 8/2005; *History
of the Times*, vol. 3, p. 255.
[52] G.P. 10/2370-2380. Italian historians seem convinced of the offer;
e.g. Serra, op. cit., p. 8; Peteani, op. cit., pp. 142-3; Salvemini, *La politica
estera dell'Italia*, p. 103.
[53] FO 45/732/181/Sec Salisbury to Clare Ford/5 Dec 1895.
[54] FO 27/3280/11, 12, 13 Conf, 23 Conf/Haggard to Salisbury/19, 20, 22
April, 8 June 1896.
[55] Ibid.; D.D.I. 3/1/31.39.

to seek compensation for Egyptian disappointments in Tripoli. For the Italians had not forgotten the circumstances under which the French had occupied Tunis and any such developments in Tripoli, said the English ambassador, would create 'a regular explosion'.[56] Though given comforting opinions as to French intentions from Vienna, Berlin and London[57] and given assurances from France as to the preservation of the *status quo* in Tripoli, the tide of Italian suspicion came again to full flood when Berthelot resigned, the French ambassador again referred to 'the danger of fanatical excitement', and Italy was being shown the big stick in the negotiations over her Tunis treaty.[58] It is not surprising that the Quirinal should have made yet another attempt to call on London for support.

It was, however, less than ever the moment to ask England for help against France. For it has already been observed that at this juncture Salisbury was being forced into an uncongenial dependence on the Germans and the Triple Alliance and had been trying to deal softly with an increasingly awkward France which was soon to advance new claims in the Niger negotiations, annex Madagascar and send Marchand on his way from Paris. In his negotiations on the Tunis treaty also, Salisbury had begun to 'stonewall', and, in the circumstances, the answer he gave to the Italians contained no hint of promised support against to unilateral French action:

> . . . I have informed General Ferrero that Her Majesty's Government were strongly opposed to any French advance on Tripoli, but that on this as on other questions connected with the *status quo* in the Mediterranean, the course which Her Majesty's Government would think it right to take in any contingency could not be decided until the contingency arose.[59]

This declaration demonstrated to the Italian government, as clearly as the Zeila episode had to its predecessor, that it would be dangerous to rely on English help in any question

[56] FO 45/748/70, 93/Clare Ford to Salisbury/1, 18 April 1896; ibid/751/Tel 33/1 April 1896.
[57] D.D.I. 3/1/42.46.47.50.62; FO 45/751/Tel 35/Salisbury to Clare Ford/7 April 1896; ibid/748/79 Conf/Clare Ford to Salisbury/10 April 1896.
[58] D.D.I. 3/1/54.57; D.D.F. 1/12/368. Bourgeois, the President of the Council, stressed the importance of the integrity of the Turkish Empire on 2 April; FO 45/747/46 Conf/Salisbury to Clare Ford/16 April 1896.
[59] FO 45/747/Salisbury to Clare Ford/16 April 1896.

involving the possibility of a conflict with France. Serra remarks that, if there had been any doubts as to the English interpretation of the 1887 agreements in relation to the question, they had disappeared by the spring of 1896. 'The various approaches', he says, 'to the London government were met with a formally negative position'.[60] The English minister's declaration had, of course, only mentioned Tripoli. As for the Tunisian hinterland, the chances of English opposition to the French here, especially with Salisbury at the Foreign Office, had been in fact particularly hopeless from the first. For the 'rights of the Sultan' in the 1890 arrangements had been deliberately left vague, on the insistence of the French, who, even then, had countered the reluctance of Salisbury to admit that a protectorate could have a hinterland, by saying that it didn't matter, 'as Algeria circled Tunisia and extended as far as Ghadames'.[61] Later on, when the Italians were in a frenzy of anxiety, after the conclusion of the Anglo-French agreement of March 1899, and asked for a public assurance that Salisbury had refrained in the agreement from any opinion as to the 'extent and nature of the Turkish claims', he was to show his disinterested attitude even more clearly. He asserted that he had never accepted the doctrine of the hinterland, and, even assuming the Libyan desert to be in the Tripolitan hinterland, he could not put on record what he thought should be done with it in the event of a Turkish collapse.[62]

The Second Toulon

'Biserta seizes the Mediterranean by the throat.'[63] If this opinion of Hanotaux is to be taken as genuine, and there is no reason to doubt his sincerity, it would explain much of his attitude towards North Africa and not only his extreme sensitivity at times over Tunis, but his tendency to overstate the

[60] Serra, op. cit., p. 22. This is the best account of what Salisbury's policy meant to the Italians. See also pp. 18-27.

[61] D.D.F. 1/8/141/ Peteani, op. cit., pp. 103-4; *Memoirs of Crispi*, vol. 3, pp. 42-44. 'The effect of these notes is to prevent the agreement from being interpreted to affect the hinterland of Tripoli. The importance of this is not great', wrote Salisbury; SP/68/to Dufferin/12 Aug 1890.

[62] FO 45/797/Memo by Sanderson/4 April 1899, min. by Salisbury; ibid/65/Salisbury to Currie/25 April 1899.

[63] Hanotaux, *La Paix latine*, p. 276. The military paper was by Lt.-Col. Espitalier.

significance to France of the question in his dealings with London. So important was the port in his eyes that he asserted that it was to get Biserta that France had occupied Tunis in the first place and, a few years after his fall from power, quoted with approval a military study which said:

> If one combines the sphere of action from Biserta with those from Mers-el-Kebir, Algiers, Ajaccio and the metropolitan ports, it is easy to see that the entire western basin of the Mediterranean is under our tactical control and that Biserta is the key to our action on the eastern side.[64]

In 1897, as the Cretan imbroglio slowly resolved itself, the time had seemed to him ripe for a conclusive settlement of the Tunis question and 'the liberation of Biserta', so that, from his point of view, one positive advantage had emerged from the commercial negotiations, 'that formidable conflict of opinions and interests'. This was that French naval power in the Mediterranean was enhanced by the possession of a 'second Toulon'.[65]

Though not all Frenchmen by any means held views as extreme as those of Hanotaux, yet, in official and unofficial circles, the seductive attractions of a military port at Biserta continued to constitute a persistent force in the 1890's. With only Toulon in the Mediterranean, the French navy was said to be like 'a bird tied with a string to one cage'.[66] A militarised Biserta would be a 'counter balance to Gibralta and Malta, and the defence of Algeria, which possessed only artificial ports'.[67] It would be a North African Kiel on a coast with few

---

[64] Ibid., pp. 276-9. Most of Hanotaux' observations on Biserta are reproduced in *Memoirs of Crispi*, vol. 3, pp. 105-8. The English translation is, however, an unhappy one and sometimes inexact. M. Pelletan, Minister of Marine, is also quoted as declaring, in 1902, that Biserta was a guarantee of French supremacy in the Mediterranean; ibid., p. 105. Some contemporary French writers express the same view. For example, Pellegrin thinks the First World War 'fully confirmed all hopes'; *Histoire de la Tunisie*, p. 192. It may be noted that at the end of 1896, when it seemed possible that Russia might seize the Bosphorus, Hanotaux was insistent on naval preparedness and the stationing of torpedo boats at Biserta; D.D.F. 1/13/50.

[65] Hanotaux, op. cit., p. 281.

[66] Article in *La Dépêche de Toulouse*, 12 Feb 1894, reproduced in *La Dépêche Tunisienne*, 18 Feb 1894; FO 27/3190/9 Drummond Hay to Rosebery/21 Feb 1894.

[67] *Report of the Tunisian Chamber of Agriculture* (in favour of a naval port at Biserta), quoted, FO 27/3190/38 Drummond Hay to Kimberley/23 July 1894.

anchorages[68] and, with its wonderful strategic position, would give France 'a harbour out of reach of all danger.' Nevertheless, the French proceeded with their plans for the port with the utmost caution. The Minister of Marine, Admiral Besnard, admitted in February 1898 in reply to the criticisms of a predecessor, that the naval authorities had 'as everyone knew' long studied the militarisation of Biserta, but the realisation of their plan had been postponed 'for reasons that were not at all within the domain of the Admiralty'.[69] Perhaps, as Hanotaux put it, the other European nations had been too 'vigilant'.[70] However, the necessity for remaining mistress of the western Mediterranean and maintaining communications with Algeria and Tunis was recognised by the admiral as a fundamental duty.[71]

Naval opinion in London as to the value of Biserta had not changed substantially. Presumably the French were to be encouraged, by appropriate exhibitions of concern, to 'persevere in their misdirected efforts'[72] and to waste their substance on fixed installations there in preference to fighting units. Even developments as important as the Russian naval visit to Toulon in October 1893 and the subsequent Franco-Russian alliance, the apparently unpleasant implications of which caused so great an upheaval in English naval and governmental circles,[73] did not lead London to endorse views such as those of Hanotaux on the subject of Biserta. This was so even though British naval strength at this time barely exceeded that of France and Russia together, though the naval building estimates of the new allies were substantially greater than Britain's, and though the Mediterranean Squadron alone was no match for the forces based on Toulon.[74] Information had also been received of Russian intentions to keep a permanent force in the Mediterranean. Nevertheless, at this stage, even the Italians, who

---

[68] FO 27/3237/57, 59/Haggard to Salisbury/20, 29 July 1895.
[69] FO 27/3393/67/Monson to Salisbury/10 Feb 1898.
[70] Op. cit., p. 281.   [71] See Note 69.
[72] FO 403/151/DNI Memo/29 Jan 1891.
[73] This is fully dealt with in Marder, op. cit., chap. 10; Langer, *Diplomacy of Imperialism*, pp. 45-50, 422; *Franco-Russian Alliance*, pp. 360-362. See also Dufferin's assessment in FO 27/3121/450 Conf/to Rosebery/3 Nov 1893 and similar Italian misgivings in FO 45/699/226 Conf/Vivian to Rosebery/13 Sep 1893.
[74] Langer, *Diplomacy of Imperialism*, p. 46.

believed fully in the dangers to them of a militarised Biserta, discounted the reports that a French port might be ceded to Russia as a naval station.[75] The quiet visit of the British fleet to Italian ports was certainly no answer to the Franco-Russian alignment, in view of the questionable value of support from the Italian navy.[76]

When failure to face the problem had led to the fall of Gladstone and failure to solve it had assisted the fall of Rosebery, finding an answer to it became the responsibility of Salisbury, a development not without its irony. For, with his lack of Admiralty experience, the new minister could hardly be said to excel in naval matters and it was not difficult for him to miscalculate.[77] The characteristic imperturbability of Salisbury tended to take on the guise of over-confidence in the field of sea power. Certainly even Rosebery had not, after Toulon, the unwisdom to contemplate the risk of sending the fleet up the Straits to Constantinople, as Salisbury did at the height of the Armenian crisis, nor to ask petulantly whether the fleet were 'made of porcelain' when he lacked the assurance to override Admiralty opinions evolved over more than four years.[78] The man who told Hatzfeldt in June 1896, 'with great self confidence and unusual decision', that he was quite sure Britain could deal successfully with both France and Russia in the Mediterranean, was not likely to take fright and cast aside the accepted British naval opinion as to the worth of Biserta, which, as has been seen,

[75] FO 45/699/218 Conf/Edwardes to Rosebery/31 Aug 1893; ibid/226, 254 Conf/Vivian to Rosebery/13, 27 Sep 1893.
[76] The Italians were anxious for the visit and Rosebery not to disappoint them. Though Italy had been shaken by the Bank Scandals and economies made in naval expenditure, Brin dubiously claimed its efficiency to be 'greatly improved'; Vivian to Rosebery/FO 45/698/101, 106, 145, 154/20, 30 Mar, 11, 20 May 1893; FO 45/699/254 Conf/27 Sep 1893; FO 45/701/Tels 67 & 68, 70/29, 30, 30 Sep; Ibid/Pr. Tel/Currie to Vivian/1 Oct 1893; Ibid/31 Tel/to Vivian/9 Oct 1893; FO 45/702/Admiralty to FO/26 July 1893.
[77] Cecil, *Biographical Studies*, p. 35. Marder calls him a 'thorn in the side of the Admiralty' and says, 'Salisbury's strong point was not naval strategy'; op. cit., p. 77. In 1896 he was predicting that naval warfare in future would be 'conducted by vessels which did not love the open ocean and which could not get far from the coast or from supplies'; *The Times*, 17 Aug 1896.
[78] G.P. 12/1/2918.2934; Cecil, op. cit., p. 35; PRO 30/40/14/Ardagh Memo No. 5 Sec/Oct 1896; Penson, 'New Course in British Foreign Policy', op. cit., p. 134. The more technical arguments of the Admiralty are noted in Marder, op. cit., pp. 245-251.

he had embraced during his earlier period of office. He still felt that Biserta might be a source of weakness to France by splitting her fleet and that a fleet taking refuge there would be 'entirely in the air', since there was nothing but the harbour, while England still had Malta and Gibraltar.[79] Ferrero was told exactly the same two years later[80] and it was, indeed, the view which Tornielli had, three years previously, stigmatised as 'an excuse and' a 'childish assertion'.[81]

Any chance, however, that Salisbury might modify his attitude towards Biserta out of consideration for Italian arguments and fears soon disappeared. In spite of periodic tributes to the traditional friendship, there was an increasing lack of real cordiality from 1894 onwards, which showed itself even before the comparatively Anglophile Crispi was replaced by the Francophile di Rudini.[82] On England's side, not only was there mounting pessimism over the value of support from Italy in the Mediterranean in view of that country's political and economic instability, but expert naval opinion, concerned as it was with the possibility of Russian naval cooperation with France in that sea, was less and less impressed by the advantage of Italy as an ally in war and more and more by the naval burden that might be entailed in her defence[83]—especially after her demoralising and weakening loss of men, money and prestige in Abyssinia.[84] In yet another issue, therefore, Britain could not be expected to give support to Italy at the price of antagonising France, though

[79] G.P. 12/1/2917.
[80] D.D.I. 3/2/337. Tornielli too, after eight years, was still bitterly animadverting against the British view; FO 27/3393/4 Conf/Gosselin to Salisbury/ 6 Jan 1898; ibid/14 Conf/Monson to Salisbury/12 Jan 1898.
[81] G.P. 8/1745. See also Crispi, op. cit., vol. 3, p. 98.
[82] FO 78/4784/20 Conf/Clare Ford to Salisbury/6 Feb 1896; Glanville, Italy's Relations with England, p. 28; G.P. 11/2767. There was divergence over Italy's African policy and Italian disappointment with Salisbury's Mediterranenan policy; FO 78/4784/22/Salisbury to Clare Ford/26 Feb 1896; Peteani, op. cit., p. 145; Serra, op. cit., p. 22; FO 45/757/Salisbury to Ferrero/6 April 1896.
[83] PRO 30/40/14/Ardagh Memo No. 7/28 Oct 1896; Brassey, Naval Annual, 1897, p. 33; Tunstall, 'Imperial Defence, 1870–1897', Cambridge History of the British Empire, vol. 3, p. 245; Marder, op. cit., pp. 271, 576-580.
[84] PRO 30/40/14/Ardagh Memoranda 5 & 7/Oct 1896; FO 45/748/94/ Clare Ford to Salisbury/18 April 1896; ibid/749/116/Clare Ford to Salisbury 17 May 1896; B.D. 6/Appendix IV. Salisbury said that the Italians 'were always sturdy beggars', but it is not known when; Newton, Lord Lansdowne, p. 485.

her policy involved nevertheless keeping a close watching brief over French activities in Biserta.

There French plans were slowly maturing. No longer did French ministers deny any intention of creating a military port 'at present' but frankly asserted their right to do so. When, in March 1894, *Figaro* commended the 'patriotic resolve' to begin military works, Casimir-Périer told the Italians that the object was to protect the channel entrance, cynically adding that this was due to the unusual concentration of Italian troops in Sicily—which had been sent there, in fact, to restore order.[85] When Kimberley was informed, he simply told Tornielli that he had 'not heard anything of the fortifications referred to'.[86] A few weeks later, however, as a result of a 'casual observation' to the French ambassador, he learned that no fortifications were intended at that time 'though of course France had a right if she pleased to erect them'.[87]

The government in London was well informed of developments in Biserta itself by its efficient Consul General, Drummond Hay, who was appreciably assisted by the fact that his Consular Agent was not only by far the largest landowner and merchant in Biserta and on good terms with all classes,[88] but actually possessed much of the very land on which the French fortifications were planned. For three years therefore, since engineer officers had first selected the sites of the future installations, information had been received on the acquisition of land by the Tunisian Government and also on the import, to various parts of the Regency, of field guns, large quantities of ammunition and cables for subterranean torpedoes.[89] In mid 1893 the French were a very long way from the creation of a military port and arsenal, but it was clear in London that the benefits from fortifications would not be commercial in character.[90] The

[85] Crispi, op. cit., vol. 3, pp. 102-104; FO 45/715/62 Conf/Kimberley to Clare Ford/12 Mar 1894; ibid/719/'Tels. 3, 6, 19/Clare Ford to FO/6, 7 Jan, 4 Mar 1894.

[86] Ibid. Kimberley felt anyway that 'the safe road to India was round the Cape'; SnP/268/1/Sec/to Sanderson/20 Oct 1894.

[87] FO 27/3169/155/Kimberley to Dufferin/18 April 1894.

[88] FO 27/3280/6a Conf/Haggard to Salisbury/27 Mar 1896.

[89] FO 27/3093/33 Drummond Hay to Salisbury/25 May 1892; ibid/11 Sec/Salisbury to Drummond Hay/29 June 1892; ibid/52 Sec/Drummond Hay to FO/15 Aug 1892.

[90] FO 27/3138/27 Drummond Hay to Rosebery/21 Aug 1893 and min.

possibilities were slim of Biserta competing against Tunis, with over twenty times its population and trade, with far superior communications to a hinterland of far superior wealth. It might be feasible for the harbour, if the Port Company were adequately supported by the French Government, to rival Malta as a coaling station and port of call for the innumerable vessels passing Cape Blanc, but the conclusion was surely valid that everything pointed towards the formation of an important naval station having, as Drummond Hay put it, 'no more pretensions to compete commercially with Tunis than Toulon with Marseilles'.[91] The year 1894, therefore, saw the construction of the port and its strategic railway to Tunis pushed vigorously ahead and a series of detailed reports and maps from the English Consulate General marked progress. They showed the establishment of the forts of Dar-el-Coudia (or 'Spanish Fort') and Djebel Roumadia defending the entrance, from the time the land was expropriated or purchased (as in Bourke's case) until they were equipped with artillery.[92] The French hoped that the arsenal and its railway link could be established within twelve months.[93]

A lot had been accomplished, but no second Toulon was yet even in sight. Two British artillery officers 'who had missed their steamer to Malta' were not impressed and thought that the defences could only prevent a sudden raid. Lord Meath, who had been several years in the diplomatic service and had been 'primed' by military and naval experts before his visit, was more sensible to the possibilities. He felt that the British naval view that a beaten and pursued fleet could not take refuge in Biserta had been negatived by the large artificial harbour completed outside the entrance and 'perfectly defended by fire from the Shore'. Though of the opinion that the Biserta defences

[91] FO 27/3190/17, 38 Drummond Hay to Kimberley/5 April, 23 July 1894.
[92] FO 27/3190/11, 12 Drummond Hay to Rosebery/25 Feb 1894; ibid/ to Kimberley/15, 19, 26, 34, 36, 48, 51/26 Mar, 24 April, 18 May, 7 July, 23 June, 22 Oct, 15 Nov 1894. The 'Spanish Fort' appeared finished in May 1895 and a third fort, Monte Negre, already had 8 guns visible even to the short-sighted and militarily ignorant new Consul-General, Haggard; FO 27/3237/28/to Kimberley/9 May 1895.
[93] FO 27/3190/16 Drummond Hay to Kimberley/31 Mar 1894; ibid/3237/ 8a Haggard to Kimberley/22 Mar 1895.

could easily be taken from the rear by a landing force, he felt that the port could be made practically impregnable.[94]

In 1895, however, the French ran into so many difficulties that it almost seemed as if their hopes were doomed to ignominious failure. Not only did the current in the channel prove dangerous but an awkward rock was discovered in the canal, in which a no doubt complacent British Admiralty took some interest.[95] Even before this, few large ships used Biserta and French opinion was humiliated when the Captain of the 'Touraine' refused to enter and pointed to the fact that the fleet had still failed to make an appearance.[96] Indeed, more than one estimate found that the trade of Biserta was decreasing after the opening of the port that year and one reason for the French interest in Bon Grara at this time, apart from its possible usefulness as a base for expansion southwards or for raids on Malta or the Nile, may have been the fear of Biserta proving useless. For Machiavelli said that an eminent Italian engineer had been consulted and had asserted that enormous expenditure would be necessary to overcome the difficulties.[97] The question whether Biserta could be used as a naval port was, in fact, not finally settled until the French Mediterranean Fleet under Admiral Gervais passed through the canal in May 1896.[98]

By now the French were less than ever ready to welcome British interest in Biserta. Early in 1896, Captain Lord Charles Beresford, who had requested permission to visit Toulon and Biserta, received a ticket of admission for Toulon only.[99] Nevertheless, H.M.S. 'Fearless', taking Haggard on a tour claimed, in March, the distinction of being the first British warship to enter the small artificial harbour and outer lake.

[94] FO 27/3280/1 Conf/Haggard to Kimberley/4 Jan 95; ibid/3237/5 Conf/Haggard to Kimberley/15 Feb 1895.
[95] FO 27/3237/Conf 28.31.47/Haggard to Kimberley/9.22 May, 24 June 1895; ibid/5 Conf/FO to Haggard/30 July 1895; ibid/3250/M5672/Ady to FO/27 July 1895.
[96] FO 27/3237/38 Conf/Haggard to Kimberley/14 June 1895.
[97] Ibid/25/Haggard to Kimberley/26 April 1895; FO 27/3238/62.65.74. Conf/Haggard to Salisbury/11, 12 Aug, 7 Oct 1895. The lack of commercial success led to so much friction between the Port Company and the French Government by May 1897, that Millet was hooted by the French colony; FO 27/3345/17/Haggard to Salisbury/2 May 1897.
[98] FO 27/3280/14 Haggard to Salisbury/16 May 1896.
[99] FO 27/3219/573/Salisbury to Dufferin/20 Dec 1895; ibid/3264/1/ Dufferin to Salisbury/1 Jan 1896.

When the Commander in Chief, Mediterranean, advanced the possibility of a visit in the summer, Bourke said he was 'convinced they (the French) would not allow the English fleet to enter the inner lake'.[100] The state of French opinion, as Anglo-French relations deteriorated, was to be gauged by a report that the English fleet had 'practised the operation of blockading Biserta'. Especially in Tunis, the French press exploded with indignation at the 'impertinence', and even the semi-official organ, forced to recant twice through the intervention of Haggard, kept reverting to the question.[101] Asked for a report, Admiral Culme Seymour informed the Admiralty that he had proceeded on the direct course from Malta to Gibraltar, with his nearest ship at least twenty miles from Biserta and had been simply engaged in some firing practice at a towed target.[102] It was, moreover, at this juncture that the de Mores murder was stirring up somewhat waning French enthusiasm in the possibilities of creating another Biserta at Bon Grara, the cost of which would again be borne by the native inhabitants of Tunis. For the confident hope existed in French circles in the Regency that, with the fortress of Biserta in the north and that of Bon Grara in the south, 'Malta would be in a bad way'. All this, of course, would be seen as 'financial folly' in the British Admiralty, although Haggard warned that:

> Bon Grara at a few hours distance is uncomfortably close as a base for a torpedo boat raid—the one form of attack from which Malta is supposed not to be quite secure.[103]

Nevertheless, France continued still at a moderate pace only towards the creation of a naval station at Biserta. So moderate indeed was the pace in 1897 that when Tornielli, disturbed over reports that the French were making a strong naval station for the use of the Russians at Biserta, endeavoured to cause alarm in the British Embassy in Paris, even his own foreign

[100] FO 27/3280/6a Conf, 21/Haggard to Salisbury/27 Mar, 21 May, 2 June 1896.
[101] FO 27/3281/Conf 46, 83/Haggard to Salisbury/17 July, 14 Nov 1896. Similar rumours that 'soundings had been made' near Biserta were heard in 1901 and a similar answer given; FO 27/3558/Most Conf/Ady to FO/1 Oct 1901.
[102] FO 27/3293/FO to Ady/30 Aug 1896; ibid/MO418/Ady to FO/21 Dec 1896.
[103] FO 27/3281/49 Conf/Haggard to Salisbury/6 Aug 1896.

minister, Visconti Venosta, thought the reports improbable and merely instituted enquiries. Salisbury was plainly incredulous.[104] It is true that Hanotaux in February 1898, on his own initiative denied any negotiations to cede Biserta and the Russian Government maintained absolute reserve.[105] There was, however, something in Tornielli's claim of a change in the attitude of Admiral Besnard, hitherto inclined like England to question the value of Biserta until the French naval forces should be substantially larger.[106] For, though the French had indeed been 'hastening slowly' owing to lack of funds and spending on Biserta in 1897 a small fraction of the English expenditure on Gibraltar, the D.N.I. in London was aware that more than double the rate of expenditure was planned for the next four years.[107] Before anything was done, however, the question of Biserta was submerged in the mountainous emotional seas of the Fashoda crisis, which caused both the protagonists to hurriedly review their position in Tunis from a military rather than a legal angle.

Biserta was, therefore, in no condition in 1898 to show that she could 'seize the Mediterranean by the throat'. That Hanotaux and others believed it possible had not altered the plodding caution with which the French had advanced towards the creation of a naval port. Nor had any great concern over Biserta as yet showed itself in London, in spite of the chances of Russian naval action in the Mediterranean, in spite of Italian belief in the potentialities of the strategic port and in spite of signs that the development of the base was to be hastened.

[104] FO 27/3393/4 Conf/Gosselin to Salisbury/6 Jan 1898; ibid/14 Conf/ Monson to Salisbury/12 Jan 1898; D.D.I. 3/2/320.322.328.337. The Franco-Italian rapprochement, however, did receive a temporary setback. By August, the commercial negotiations ceased for a period, Crispi supporters campaigned against the fortification of Biserta in *Tribuna* and Pope Leo xiii, disquieted by the di Rudini government's moves towards France, caused Cardinal Rampolla to warn the French that Italy would never leave the Triple Alliance; Dethan, 'Le Rapprochement franco-italien après la chute de Crispi jusqu'aux accords Visconti Venosta sur le Maroc et la Tripolitaine (1896-1904) d'après les Archives du Quai d'Orsay', *Revue d'Histoire Diplomatique*, vol. lxx, p. 330.
[105] D.D.I. 3/2/349.353.370. Hanotaux incidentally had been insisting, in Dec 1896, on naval preparedness at Biserta; D.D.F. 1/13/50 note.
[106] FO 27/3393/69/Monson to Salisbury/10 Feb 1898. See also notes 104 and 105.
[107] *Questions Diplomatiques et Coloniales*, 15 April 1898, (Article—'Bizerte, point d'appui de la Flotte)'; and observations of DNI in FO 27/3394/188/ Monson to Salisbury/18 April 1898; D.D.I. 3/2/232.301.

TUNIS AND THE FASHODA CRISIS

According to the moral standards we see in use, only those
nations are respected which compel respect.

These sardonic words of Lebon[108] are perhaps more than usually
applicable to the relations of the Mediterranean powers at the
time of the Fashoda crisis. For, though the seeds of conflict
might have been sown in the Nile valley, the very chance of
hostilities breaking out made the possible combatants consider
their opportunities for defence and offence at all points. This
was especially true of Tunis, the significance of which in general
strategy had been investigated for some years not only from a
naval but also from a military angle.

In the view of the Intelligence Division in London, France
had, as early as 1894 and by an unparalleled effort, 'raised
herself from the dust to her old position among the nations'.[109]
At that time it was known that the French staff held the opinion
that 'the next war would be decided on the Rhine' and influential military voices urged that a militant colonial policy might
not only embroil their country with England, Italy and China,
but compromise national defence and end all hopes of recover-
ing Alsace-Lorraine. The professional mind in England also,
aware of the difficulties facing the country,[110] had noted

. . . the state of tension which existed between the nations of
Europe, leagued in opposing camps and ever ready to anticipate
a hostile movement . . .

a state of tension which could result in war.[111] Certainly Britain
could regard that hypothesis with no equanimity until her
naval construction programme had succeeded.

The French troops in Tunis formed part of the army corps
which had its headquarters near the railways in Algeria and,
four years before Marchand reached Fashoda, London was well

---

[108] *La Politique de la France en Afrique*, p. viii.

[109] France, now at the zenith of her power, had spent £720 million
(sterling) in twenty three-years, and her army now totalled 4.5 million, but
her population was stationary and Germany was outpacing her; FO 27/3198/
WO Memo Conf/Jan 1894.

[110] See Notes 12-16.

[111] FO 27/3198/Conf/DMI to FO/13 Jan 1894; ibid/Sec/18 June 1894.
There were several alarms on the Franco-Italian frontier and Morocco.

informed, even of their plan for mobilisation. In spite of the obsession with Alsace-Lorraine, all units in Africa stood at a higher peace-time establishment than any other French troops, except certain corps on the continental frontiers and, in an emergency, action was to follow a pattern copied from German practice. First, the garrison would receive warning of a 'period of political tension' and, in the second stage, it was ordered to pass to the 'preparatory period of mobilisation'. Troops that could be spared from Algeria, though not Tunis, were then to be despatched to the metropolitan country and the total force was kept at sixty to seventy thousand men.[112] When the crisis of 1898 developed, therefore, the D.M.I., Sir John Ardagh, was on the alert for signs anywhere that the 'period of political tension' had arrived officially, and was able to indicate how unfavourable a time it was for French military operations, when the artillery was being rearmed and mobilisation especially difficult. Nevertheless, he warned the Foreign Office that, without weakening the French hold on Tunis or Algiers, an expeditionary force of twenty to twenty-five thousand men could be raised from the garrison troops to attack Mediterranean targets such as Egypt, Cyprus, Malta or Gibraltar. As a consequence, instructions were given to all British representatives to report periodically the gross steam tonnage available in all the French North African ports.[113]

The main sequence of events before and during the Fashoda crisis is now well known[114] and it has been noted how, earlier in the year, Salisbury had, in anticipation, kept his hands free from complications with the Russians over Port Arthur, and come finally to agreement with Hanotaux on the Niger question. As for Tunis, the British Consul-General throughout the whole crisis was none other than that fervent protagonist of the French cause at the time of the occupation, Sir Harry Johnston. His

[112] Ibid; FO 27/3249/Sec/DMI to FO/25 April 1895; ibid/Pr/Barker to Sanderson/8 May 1895; FO 27/3238/85.95/Haggard to Salisbury/12 Nov, 19 Dec 1895.
[113] FO 27/3430/DMI to FO/24, 28 Oct 1898; ibid/3419/Tels. Conf/FO to Johnston & Consul General, Algiers/29, 29 Oct 1898. In Nov there were only four reliable steamers of 800 tons each in Tunisian ports; FO 27/3419/ Johnston to Salisbury/5 Nov 1898.
[114] A good account is in G. N. Sanderson, *England, Europe and the Upper Nile*. See also, Shibeika, *British Policy in the Sudan;* Riker, 'A Survey of British Policy in the Fashoda Crisis', *Political Science Quarterly*, vol. 44.

relations now could hardly have been more cordial and intimate with Millet who, as late as August 1898, when both were on leave, wrote:

> . . . I assure you that when I have to return to my post, one of the most agreeable prospects will be to meet you again, and to take up the thread of our conversations on Africa and colonies. I can tell you frankly that, in about fifteen years of diplomatic posts, I have often had good English colleagues, but I have never met one of so vast an intellect (esprit), so energetic, so full of precise information—and of a nature so congenial as you. I hope that our occupational hazards keep us together as long as possible. . . .[115]

In his turn Johnston felt that Millet's removal at this time would be 'hurtful to British interests',[116] that he was 'one of the most likeable French officials with whom an Englishman could deal' and that they 'could not possibly be enemies'.[117]

Johnston, however, like Millet, did not allow personal friendships to deflect him from his duty to his country, but he found that one of his greatest difficulties was the transmission of the valuable information he was collecting to the Foreign Office. For the French postal authorities were now tampering with his mail and even altering the figures in cypher telegrams,[118] while experience showed that the captains of Italian steamers were to be no more trusted.[119] Whenever possible, despatches were therefore sent to Malta and important ones by hand, even the relatively important hand of his principal Vice-Consul, Lascelles, when 'dangerous information' on Biserta had been obtained.[120] The reports and advice of the English representative, who was known personally to Salisbury,[121] were certainly not ignored in London. It was learned that, on 31 October, secret orders had

[115] JP/Millet to Johnston/24 Aug 1898. See also Oliver, *Sir Harry Johnston*, pp. 282-284.

[116] FO 27/3419/Johnston to Salisbury/26 Aug 1898.

[117] *The Story of My Life*, p. 343.

[118] One example is probably the cypher telegram to Salisbury on 1 Nov (FO 27/3419) where the strength of the Biserta garrison is said to be 25,000 not the more accurate 3,200 in notes drawn up on 3 Nov (ibid/Conf/4 Nov 1898).   [119] Ibid.

[120] FO 27/3419/Sec & Nil/FO to Johnston/3 Nov, 16 Dec 1893; ibid/Sec & Conf/Johnston to Salisbury/3, 4 Dec 1898; FO 27/3478/Chief Secretary, Malta to FO/2 Mar 1899.

[121] He had visited and was well known at Hatfield House; JP/to Johnston/22 Dec 1893.

been transmitted to all French forces in Tunisia to prepare for
a general mobilisation on a war footing;[122] that work was going
on night and day on fortifications near Carthage and that the
Biserta garrison, already strengthened after unfounded rumours
in May of a possible sudden descent by a strong British fleet,
was again being reinforced.[123] Secret notes were sent by way of
Malta, which described French defence preparations, the new
watch being kept along the coast from Biserta to Cap Nègre and
the reliance to be placed by Tunis, in case of attack, on troops
being sent from Algiers on the single-track railway. Johnston
also gave his views as to how an assault on Tunis should be
handled. The way, he urged, was to subdue the 'wretched
fortifications' of Sfax with a large force, after which:

> . . . one might roll up a wave of insurrection against the French
> which would repel advancing forces from Algeria and ultimately
> lock up the French troops in fortresses.[124]

His belief that a south, deeply hostile to France, would rise
against its rulers when a British force landed, was undoubtedly
strengthened by a nocturnal visit from Sheiks and 'Senusi'
emissaries, who assured him, according to his secretary-
brother, that they would then 'drive the French into the sea'.[125]
In the event of hostilities he planned to leave for Malta to
'await events' and thence to accompany any British and Italian
descent on Tunisia.[126] What he did not tell London was that in
the event of war, which would have been 'provoked solely by
the hotheads of the French Colonial Office', he and Millet had
a mutual understanding. This was to safeguard each other's
property in Tunis, and he persuaded himself that he and the
French Resident 'saw the question in the same light' and that the
latter was convinced of the impossibility of defending the
country'[127]

[122] FO 27/3419/Tel/Johnston to Salisbury/2 Nov 1898.
[123] Ibid/Sec & Tel/Johnston to Salisbury/21 May, 1 Nov 1898; D.D.I.
3/2/433.
[124] FO 27/3419/Conf/Johnston to Salisbury/4 Nov 1898 (and attached
Secret notes).
[125] Alex Johnston, *The Life and Letters of Sir Harry Johnston*, p. 171.
[126] See Note 124. He urged the precaution of despatching the archives to
Malta and the replacement by Italy of the aged Machiavelli.
[127] A. Johnston, op. cit., p. 174; H. Johnston, op. cit., p. 358. The contrast
in Millet's tone may partly perhaps be explained by political exigencies;
op. cit., pp. 8-9.

Johnston soon found himself working in conjunction with the military and civil authorities at Malta. He quickly discovered lack of cooperation between those authorities and an Admiralty, now so supremely confident that, when war seemed imminent late in October, had abandoned the pre-arranged strategic plan, that entailed a 'cut and run' to Gibraltar by the Mediterranean fleet, in favour of a concentration at Malta—which was to be balanced by a similar concentration of the Channel fleet at Gibraltar.[128] For the Senior Intelligence Officer had let it be known that 'he could get nothing out of the navy' in answer to anxious enquiries over the small islands lying between Tunis and Sicily, Lampedusa, Linosa and Pantellaria. The more energetic and certainly more influential Johnston not only got the matter taken up by the Foreign Office, but was sacrilegious enough to challenge pontifical naval assurances that the islands were 'all perfectly well known', that there were no protected anchorages of real use and that no account need be taken of them while under Italian control. This simply led to the observation that:

> . . . French vessels had recently made an examination of the islands as if with a view to using them for an attack on Malta or on the commerce of the straits.

In relation to developments in naval warfare, full knowledge of the possible usefulness of the islands had 'seemed to him to be lacking'.[129] With the Maltese government his relations were closer and, after notes and a map 'of very great importance' on Biserta fortifications had been sent, Sir Arthur Freemantle, the Governor, invited him to the island in December to discuss the defences of Tunis.[130]

In the months immediately after Marchand's recall, when England and France were both furiously attending to their defences and thereby keeping the flames of mutual suspicion ablaze, Johnston reported an appreciable build up of military forces and artillery in Tunis and asserted in January 1899 that

[128] Marder, op. cit., pp. 323-328.

[129] Johnston to Salisbury/FO 27/3419/Conf/4 Dec 1898; ibid/3430/Sec/ FO to Ady & CO/27 Dec 1898; ibid/3478/M.0794.98-03/Ady to FO/5 Jan 1899; ibid/3467/Tel/Johnston to Salisbury/1 Feb 1899.

[130] Ibid; FO 27/3419/Tel/Johnston to Salisbury/8 Dec 1898. Alex Johnston says that consequently Sir Harry was to have accompanied Malta's expedition against Tunis; op. cit., p. 174.

the French authorities were acting 'as if war was imminent'.[131] However confident the British Admiralty might be at this moment and however much French naval authorities might be disposed to deem such confidence justified, it is fairly clear that the government in London had taken seriously the D.M.I.'s warnings of the possibility of Tunis being used as a base for a military attack in the Mediterranean. This is evident both from an enquiry in February as to whether Johnston had seen any indications of 'an expedition against Egypt through Tripoli' and the presence in Tunis, in this period of tension, of Sir John Ardagh himself.[132] A simultaneous study of the question by the Intelligence Department in London, which Sanderson thought 'interesting and satisfactory', was forwarded to the Foreign Office so that 'Lord Salisbury might see the groundlessness of any apprehensions on this score'. The 'delivery 'of ten thousand men to Egypt was adjudged impossible on practical grounds because of absence of water, the immense distance and the difficulty of transport; on political grounds because of Tripolitan hatred of the 'Frank' which would persist even if objections of a jealous Porte could be overcome.[133] In a much more detailed report, which received the Foreign Office accolade of being 'worth reading', Johnston came to the same conclusion. Far from preparing an offensive, France had denuded the south of the Regency of troops to reinforce the defences of the capital and at that moment 'could not spare a man from her garrisons in Tunis and Algeria', which were no more than strictly necessary to keep down a native rising. He conceded that '50,000 picked men commanded by another Napoleon' might reach Egypt in six weeks if Turkey and Italy were neutral, but such a force could not be accommodated in North Africa prior to hostilities since the recent and smaller reinforcements had caused so much difficulty. His argument was clinched as follows:

After the outbreak of war either France would have lost command of the sea, and therefore would be unable to send any

---

[131] By mid February, 8,950 had arrived and 4000 more were reported due and arriving in small detachments; FO 27/3467/Pol, Pol, Sec, Tel, Sec/ Johnston to Salisbury/26 Jan, 1, 11, 23, 25 Feb 1899; ibid/Tel.Sec/FO to Johnston/10 Feb. For naval preparations see Marder, op. cit., pp. 330-331.
[132] Ibid; FO 27/3467/Tel.Sec/Johnston to Salisbury/11 Feb 1899.
[133] FO 27/3478/Sec/DMI to FO/1 Feb 1899.

more troops at all to Tunis or else she would have become for a time mistress of the Mediterranean, and then would be able to send a naval expedition to Egypt.

The south of Tunis was in fact at the mercy of ten thousand men landed between Sfax and Gabès and the only offensive force was a 'cadre' of Franco-Tunisian cavalry, ready at a moment's notice, to 'dash across the desert' in order to vindicate the French determination that no other European power should possess Ghadames and Ghat. These conclusions were supported by a report of considerable precision on the location of the 24,250 French troops in Tunisia.[134] Ardagh's own appreciation of French intentions did not reach London until April, when a calmer atmosphere prevailed. Equally sure that defensive motives predominated, he found the canal from Goletta to Tunis 'practically undefended' and Biserta itself but weakly defended by batteries, so that:

> . . . it would be unwise and dangerous to expose battleships and cruisers to the risk of being corked up by closing the only entrance.

Further enquiries at Alexandria had confirmed the belief in the impossibility of the desert approach, but Ardagh clung to his idea that the Tunisian ports were favourably situated for a raid upon Malta and argued prophetically that the French could now endeavour to make the defence of the Regency secure against a 'recurrence of alarm'.[135] Further evidence, if it were needed, of the extreme concern of the Foreign Office over Tunisia during the period of crisis, is found in the fact that the only other intelligence report retained separately in its archives for 1899 was that of another military officer who travelled through North Africa from Morocco to Tunis, a report which was 'too secret to print'. This confirmed that French hopes were centred on the possibility of a Trans-Sahara railway, which the current Lamy-Foureau expedition had been designed to further, and, after calculating the possibilities of an outside invasion, opined that:

[134] FO 27/3467/Sec/Johnston to Salisbury/25 Feb 1899.
[135] FO 27/3478/Sec/DMI to FO/18 April 1899.

... had war broken out in the Spring, a very slight encouragement would have caused a rebellion embracing the whole of Algeria and Tunis.[136]

The unanimity of these reports must have been reassuring in London and, as for Biserta, military and civilian opinion reinforced naval opinion as to its comparative uselessness to the French. For Johnston, visiting the 'much over-rated harbour' with his brother, was not unnaturally struck with the resemblance to Santiago, where the Spanish fleet had been trapped the year before and, like Ardagh:

... sincerely hoped the French Mediterranean fleet would be so fatuous as to shut itself up in this bottle with an easily obstructed mouth.[137]

Though the ex-minister Hanotaux denied the validity of a comparison with Santiago and knew 'no sight more imposing' than the defences of the port, that was after the passage of four years and after much hard work.[138] At the time of Fashoda the opinion of Edouard Lockroy, former minister of marine, is surely valid. France had no port of refuge in the Mediterranean, he protested, except Toulon, and Biserta had:

... neither docks, nor stores nor the necessary appliances for executing any naval repairs.[139]

Even after the agreement of 21 March 1899 had appeared to settle the main issue between England and France, relations were far from normal and the fortification of Biserta was rushed ahead. The British Vice-Consul there reported in November the extensive undertakings and plans to make the port at an early date impregnable for the French fleet. He added that, for the first time, France and not Tunis was footing the bill.[140]

The same despatch contained a warning that English officers visiting Biserta should be careful in view of the 'very strong feeling' towards Britain. Indeed, in a matter of days, London was being informed of an 'outbreak of spy mania' and of the

[136] FO 27/3479/Sec/DMI to FO/3 Aug 1899.
[137] H. Johnston, op. cit., p. 358; A. Johnston, op. cit., pp. 274-275.
[138] Hanotaux, La Paix Latine, pp. 281-282.
[139] FO 27/3393/69/Monson to Salisbury/10 Feb 1898.
[140] FO 27/3467/35 Conf/Berkeley to Salisbury/24 Nov 1899.

arrest and release of a colonel who had gone 'poking about
Biserta with a pair of field glasses', to the great indignation of
French papers like the *Petit Marseillais*.[141] Even someone as
Francophile as Johnston found he could make little headway
against the tide of ill feeling that followed Fashoda. In spite of
the fact that his personal relations with French officials were
quite friendly, French susceptibilities were 'so morbidly excited'
that he avoided official communications as much as he could,
since virtually all the despatches he sent to the French Residency
went unanswered. In fact Johnston was prepared, in order
to preserve his relations with Millet, to make no official complaint in the face of pinpricks and manifest injustice to British
residents—such as arrangements abruptly cancelled and the
dismissal from employment of Maltese who refused French
citizenship. When he saw Maltese and Gibraltar Jews preparing
to leave the country, however, to avoid a repetition of 'what had
taken place in Algeria'. he was moved to declaim, in words that
would have been strange on his lips only a few months before,
against:

> . . . the growing disposition of the French to consider their pos-
> sessions in North Africa as only intended for the occupation,
> profit and enjoyment of French citizens.[142]

His only action indeed was to pin up a Government of Malta
proclamation for army recruitment, and so many dispossessed
fishermen, discharged railway employees and others came forward that he thought 'two regiments might be furnished from
Tunis'.[143] Chamberlain, never friendly to Johnston in any case,
was clearly dissatisfied and wanted to put pressure on the
Residency to answer the Maltese complaints; but the more
conciliatory Salisbury was prepared to allow the French 'a little
more time' and action was left to Johnston's discretion.[144]

During the Fashoda crisis, therefore, the problem of Tunis,

[141] FO 27/3506/3 Conf/Berkeley to Salisbury/6 Jan 1900; ibid/3528/Memo/
Berkeley to Crowe/1 Feb 1900.
[142] FO 27/3467/14/Johnston to Salisbury/8 April 1899.
[143] Ibid.; ibid/Tel. 4/FO to Johnston/13, 29 April 1899; ibid/Tel/Johnston
to Salisbury/13 April 1899.
[144] FO 27/3478/Conf/CO to FO/5 May 1899. Chamberlain had also been
critical of Salisbury during the crisis; Garvin, *Life of Chamberlain*, vol. 3,
pp. 231-232.

in British eyes, was part of the larger North African problem
and interest in Tunis was focussed on its possibilities as a base
from which hostile attack might come to the strategically vital
area around the Nile Valley. Salisbury's terse comment to
Queen Victoria on the agreement of 11 March 1899 was:

> It keeps the French entirely out of the valley of the Nile and
> restores to Egypt the province of Darfour.[145]

In Italian eyes, however, Tunis was the base of operations to
come and the unhappy Italian ambassador in London told
Sanderson that he was being 'denounced as a traitor' for not
having discovered and warned his government of the Anglo-
French arrangement, seen in Rome as a threat to Tripoli and its
hinterland.[146] Admiral Canevaro, now foreign minister, indignantly described Britain's action as perfidious and dishonest, but
unfortunately for him had already stated explicitly that the
matter would not interest Italy so long as the agreement affected
only the region south of 15° latitude,[147] which was just what
Salisbury claimed that it did. He said he had simply wished 'to
prevent the extension of France eastward of the designated line'
and rejected Italian pleas for 'an exchange of notes or an assurance of which Admiral Canevaro could make public use'.[148]
Indeed, the minute which Salisbury wrote on the record of the
Italian request and which Sanderson read to the ambassador,
de Renzis, reflects clearly the English minister's Mediterranean
policy:

> I do not see how any disavowal or protest on our part is pos-
> sible. There is no precedent in international history for this
> vivisection of Turkey. We have had our object in view to prevent
> the extension of France eastward of the designated line. We
> have never accepted the doctrine of the Hinterland; and even
> if we admitted the Libyan desert to be the Hinterland of

---

[145] SP/84/p. 159/Salisbury to Queen/21 Mar 1899.
[146] FO 45/797/Memo Sanderson/4 April 1899.
[147] Peteani, op. cit., pp. 151-2. Italian susceptibilities are seen clearly in
the enclosure to FO 45/784/214/Currie to Salisbury/4 Nov 1898, and were
fanned by a report that Cromer thought France might obtain compensation
for Fashoda east of Lake Tchad. FO 45/785/Tel. 52 Conf/Currie to Salisbury/
3 Nov 1898.
[148] Ibid; ibid/Memo Sanderson/10 April 1899; ibid/65/Salisbury to
Currie/25 April 1899; B.D. 1/236.247-249.251.252.359.

Tripoli, we certainly could not put on record what we think ought to be done with it in case Turkey were to go to pieces. It is the oddest interpretation of the engagements we entered into in the Treaty of Paris.[149]

Once again, therefore, Salisbury had shown, in a question in which Italian susceptibilities were most easily to be wounded, his unwillingness to pledge himself in advance to Italy, especially when opposition to France might be involved; nor would he even permit public affirmation of a 'desire to act in accord with Italy for the maintenance of the *status quo* in the Mediterranean'. When the vital link with India and the Far East through Suez and the Red Sea had been safeguarded on the banks of the Nile, he seemed in no hurry to prevent the Gallic cock scratching in unwanted sand, however precious that sand to the Italians. Still no 'glutton for territory', his major preoccupation, as the new French ambassador, Cambon, (like his predecessor) remarked time and again, was the conflict between French protectionism and British commercial interests.[150]

All this was to have considerable significance. For, in worried Italian eyes, a new international alignment was coming into being. All through the crisis of October and November 1898 the Italians, who told London that in the event of war they 'could only remain neutral or side with England', made naval preparations to defend their neutrality against the much feared possibility of a French attack.[151] At the same time, however, the long desultory negotiations for a commercial agreement with France came successfully to a reassuring conclusion. For Méline had fallen from power and with him Hanotaux, who had placed so much store on the ability of Marchand and the Abyssinians to 'throttle Egypt should England continue to ignore French remonstrances',[152] and who had turned a deaf ear to pleas for an early agreement with Italy.[153] It seems fairly clear

[149] FO 45/797/Sanderson Memoranda/4, 10 April 1899, ibid/65/Salisbury to Currie/25 April 1899; B.D. 1/251.
[150] Cambon, *Correspondance*, vol. 2, pp. 13, 14, 15, 18, 20.
[151] FO 45/785/Tel 38 Sec, 42 Sec, Tel 55 Sec, Tel 56 Sec/Currie to Salisbury/26, 28 Oct, 7, 10 Nov 1899; ibid/Tel 152 Sec/Salisbury to Currie/27 Oct 1898. Urgent French enquiries if there was an Anglo-Italian understanding were also reported to London.
[152] Steed, *Through Thirty Years*, vol. 1, p. 106, quoted Kennedy, *Salisbury*, pp. 389-390.   [153] Dethan, op. cit., p. 331.

that Canevaro was playing a double game, no doubt inspired by the weakness of his country. The Franco-Italian agreement had taken Monson, in Paris, completely by surprise, due to the 'mendacity' of Delcassé and Tornielli in denying that negotiations were taking place and to the 'unnecessary dissimulation' of the Italian government in 'talking big' of their determination to mobilise if France should threaten their interests in the question of Raheita.[154] Italy was apparently to emerge from the fire scatheless by being neutral and extending sympathy to each protagonist. Even the able Camille Barrère, new French ambassador at Rome, to whom the commercial peace owed so much, reported that it had caused a 'veritable clap of thunder', so that Italian participation in a maritime war was now impossible,[155] Canevaro followed this up in the new year with much soothing talk on how Britain had nothing to gain from even a victorious war with France and—what aroused attention in Paris—that England could not seriously consider a landing in France, Algeria or Tunisia as 'we sailors knew the difficulties'.[156] Yet simultaneously he was telling Currie that 'getting advantage' from the new French attitude involved no change towards the Triple Alliance or England.[157]

Italy had therefore retained a foot in each camp until the Anglo-French agreement on March 1899 and the refusal by Salisbury of assurances, which caused at the Consulta an 'agonising reappraisal' of Italian policies. The emotion and anxiety caused by the 'blank cheque' which seemed to have been given to France was heightened by the fact that the Italian allies, Germany and Austria, were prepared to offer sympathy rather than support, and, as irritation in the chamber propelled the Italian government towards resignation, Salisbury argued that an unfettered Britain was more of a guarantee of the *status quo* in the Mediterranean than one pledged not to interfere in the disputed area.[158] Visconti Venosta, foreign minister again in May, had long kept a watchful eye on the state of English

[154] FO 27/3398/634 Most Conf/Monson to Salisbury/21 Nov 1898.
[155] Dethan, op. cit., p. 332.
[156] A.A.E./GB/RF/18991–900/7, 2 Conf/to Delcassé/20, 21 Jan. Canevaro also urged no French acceptance of disarmament proposals, which would mean 'perpetual servitude' to Britain.   [157] B.D. 1/347.
[158] Peteani, op. cit., pp. 155-156; Dethan, op. cit., p. 333; B.D. 1/252.

relations with France and with Germany, though not simply to be able to 'keep in line'. As the percipient Barrère observed, the Italian minister's policy was 'not German, nor English; he pursued an Italian policy'.[159] After the March agreement he became quite convinced not only that Britain had chosen to cultivate the friendship of France in preference to that of Germany, but that Italy was regarded as a *quantité négligeable*. If his hypothesis were correct, the logic of the situation would then surely demand that, to obviate the possibility of her Mediterranean interests being sacrificed to the all powerful friendship, an accommodation would have to be sought with France. It would also mean that, if the way to cooperation with England had once lain through Berlin and Vienna, it now lay through Paris. The Italians, said Barrère:

> . . . are really becoming interested in peace because they need us.[160]

On his side, Delcassé was quite prepared to consider a deal which involved taking advantage of the Anglo-Italian coolness and dealing a blow, in fact if not in theory, to the Triple Alliance; but he showed nothing of the urgency to dispel those acute fears of a French advance into Tripoli that was felt in Rome. Indeed, appalled by the intensity of the reaction to the Anglo-French agreement, Cambon and Barrère both urged him to make a declaration of disinterest in the territory. Delcassé, however, was calculating advantage to a nicety. His first reward was in the fall of the to him 'unreliable' Canevaro and the second when, to the initial disgust of Barrère, he demanded, and in the end successfully, a declaration of Italian disinterest in Morocco in exchange for the French declaration of disinterest in Tripoli.[161] The road led straight to what one historian called the 'funeral oration of the Triple Alliance'.[162] The Anglo-French agreement of March, 1899 had, however, set in train two new lines of development in the relations of the powers. That Italy had been excluded and that no assurances had been

[159] A.A.E./GB/RF/1897–1898/Barrère to Delcassé/20 May 1898.
[160] Dethan, op. cit., p. 332; B.D. 1/355.
[161] Ibid, pp. 334-337; Anderson, *The First Moroccan Crisis*, pp. 4, 22.
[162] Stuart's description of Bülow's speech of 8 Jan 1902 after a further Franco-Italian exchange of secret letters pledging neutrality; *French Foreign Policy*, p. 86.

forthcoming from Britain which would relieve fears of a French advance into Tripoli from Tunis, meant that—as in the case of her Tunis treaty—Italy faced France alone. This not only made it possible for Delcassé to begin the process of 'dealing one by one' with those powers with interests in Morocco (a technique which had been so successful in depriving the European countries of their position in Tunis), but led to a bitter coldness in the Italian attitude towards Britain, all of which was to be of considerable significance in the future. As Visconti Venosta said to his successor in February 1902:

> . . . as far as England is concerned there are no difficulties but you may say there are also no relations.[163]

[163] LP/227/16/Pr/Rodd to Barrington/29 July 1902.

6

COMMERCIAL AND STRATEGIC CONSIDERATIONS IN BRITISH POLICY

COMMERCIAL CONSIDERATIONS IN THE FORMULATION OF POLICY

One would expect that the foreign relations of a nation of shopkeepers would seek to further the interests of the shopkeepers. What is surprising in the 'Salisbury era' is not that trade and industry had influence, but how restricted that influence in fact often was. High policy naturally sought to protect British commercial rights and investments, especially in the fields where such commerce and investment were most concentrated. Yet the experience of those engaged in the Tunis trade shows that there was sometimes little systematic consultation between their representatives and the government even when decisions affecting them directly were being considered. It was only when the important cotton industry became worried and there might have been repercussions in the constituencies that the Foreign Office and its commercial department hastened to consultation.[1] Tunis was, of course, not of major importance to the British export trade; but along with Algeria, Egypt and the area of the lower Niger, it did comprise the only part of North Africa in which trade and finance had some real significance. This did have a certain influence on British policy.

The Tunis question also reflected some of the main preoccupations arising from Britain's changing economic position in the world, a position changing not only because the relative strength of certain other countries was increasing, but because a country increasingly dependent on imported foodstuffs was automatically dependent on the trade that helped to pay for those foodstuffs. Whereas the doctrine of free trade exerted

[1] Marsden, *Britain and the End of the Tunis Treaties*, chaps. 1 and 3.

considerable influence on the international scene in the 1860's that situation—so beneficial to Britain—soon altered. By the 1880's, Germany, the U.S.A. and, in particular, France and her colonies became more and more protectionist in outlook. Wherever the French extended their influence and territory, British commerce was sure to be hampered if not virtually excluded, as happened in Algeria. There were long years of depression when Britain's share of world trade fell and when it was in smaller markets (and in the Far East) that she managed best to hold her own. Business men were not, in the circumstances, likely to countenance the unrequited loss of even one outlet for their goods with equanimity.

In the period before 1878, when Britain was endeavouring to bolster up the independence of Tunis in the face of possible menace from France or Italy and when the crumbling Regency was falling ever more heavily in debt, it was to Frenchmen that the Beylical government became indebted—and this in spite of the fact that the London money market was still second to none. For if, as has been said, 'the movement of British capital to other lands was one of the shaping forces of Great Britain's economic structure and political destiny',[2] it is an inescapable fact that, from the middle of the century onwards, British capital refused to flow in quantity to Tunis. Investors, less concerned now with a Europe where loans from Paris and Berlin were increasingly available, less concerned temporarily with an United States plagued with domestic troubles, poured their money into the development of India, Canada, South America, Egypt and, until the collapse of 1876, Turkey.[3] Inevitably the relative disinterest shown in Tunis had its effect on British policy. Having resisted a Tunisian declaration of insolvency in 1867, which could have resulted in a French occupation of the country, the British representative, eight years later, brought to a successful conclusion a commercial treaty that, in practice, removed almost every impediment in the way of British enterprise in the Regency—all to little avail.

The signing of the agreement virtually coincided with a general financial crisis leading to a three year depression in trade and industry. As this bore especially heavily on Britain,

[2] Feis, *Europe the World's Banker*, p.5.   [3] Ibid, pp. 17-20.

not a few of the enterprises she had in fact established in Tunis failed and many of these fell into the hands of Frenchmen. If this trend of events is taken into account, it is not particularly surprising that, in 1878, when Salisbury was pondering some form of compensation for France, his thoughts should turn to Tunis. There seems, however, to be no evidence that commercial interests were consulted during the period that Britain's traditional policy towards Tunis was being so drastically modified. Nor does there seem to have been anything said of the future position of the British business man when the 'civilising influences of France' were to have extended themselves over the country. 'England', wrote Salisbury, 'has no special interests in the region which could possibly lead her to view with apprehension and distrust the legitimate and expanding influence of France',[4] and this toleration, in practice, was extended to mean non-interference in the dubious and far from 'legitimate' activities of French subjects like Sancy.

It was indeed only on the eve of the occupation of Tunis that the Liberal government of Gladstone and Granville expressed determination to maintain Britain's 'commercial and maritime rights' in Tunis; but then they were highly irritated over both the Cyprus convention and the compensation promised to France. It may be inferred that, in this case, British commercial interests represented first and foremost to the Liberals almost the only right it was, in fact, possible to defend. This was better than nothing to a government which would have liked to oppose the French advance root and branch and which did, indeed, risk war to venture into the tangled legal maze of the Enfida question. As subsequent cases showed, the concern of the Liberals was simply to maintain existing rights, both national and individual. Salisbury's attitude was very different. To him, at least until 1890, commercial privilege in Tunis was no more than a pawn, to be played at will and possibly sacrificed on the chess board of high policy. For the sake of an accommodation in Egypt, he had thought to dispose secretly of Britain's Tunis treaty before members of parliament representing the cotton industry got wind of what was afoot. What brought him up sharply was the vigour of protests from the various chambers of

[4] FO 27/2300/493/Salisbury to Lyons/7 Aug 1878.

commerce and the embarrassing revelation that government statistics relating to trade with Tunis were hopelessly inaccurate. Clearly it was 'much more important than he had thought' and the bargain proposed to France was hurriedly revised to safe-guard the interests of 'king cotton'. In the remaining negotia-tions between Britain and France in 1890, the Tunis card remained unplayed in Salisbury's hand, retained 'on account of Egypt' and, of course, on account of Italy. What was now certain was that it could never be played without reference to Man-chester.

After 1894, the Italians were naturally hoping that Britain would not surrender her rights in Tunis—and the French were hoping that that was just what Britain would do. What is significant is that it was not until the following year that the Foreign Office began to get a realistic picture of the extent of British trade with Tunis, since the trade returns of the French-controlled administration were unreliable. The Board of Trade's own figures were based on these and were known in Manchester to be incorrect. There the chamber of commerce was on the alert, in view of the denunciation of Italy's treaty with Tunis, and had to be reassured that Britain was preserving intact her rights to most-favoured-nation treatment. It was clearly under-stood now by the board that the loss of those rights would provoke an outcry—especially in the cotton industry, which was most dependent of all on the export trade and which was bearing the brunt of the exceptionally difficult conditions prevailing on the international market. Though Salisbury was disposed to be conciliatory towards France, it was, therefore, palpably obvious that there were limits on his freedom of action regarding Tunis, and the almost unanimous reaction of the cotton manufacturers could only serve to reinforce his deter-mination not to surrender Britain's treaty rights without equivalent concessions from Paris. French hopes for an early customs union with Tunis were consequently wrecked, based as they had been initially on the erroneous impression that it would be possible to denounce the English treaty at will.

At this time it was the necessity for finding new markets among the 'half civilised and uncivilised nations' that loomed large in the minds of some of the ministers in London. Dilating on this theme in May 1895, Salisbury said that Britain might, if necessary, have to shoulder 'new responsibilities of Empire and government' to secure that end.[5] Yet it was the tariff barriers of other countries and the monopolising of trade in their new colonial territories that was responsible. Granville, for example, did not object at all to the French making colonies of 'barbarous districts'. What irritated Britain was their habit of granting differential privileges to their own subjects, and he tried to find ways of getting this across to them.[6] As Salisbury told the French frankly in January 1897, 'If you were not such rabid (acharnés) protectionists, we should not be such gluttons for territory'. Almost exactly a year later he was making the same point in the Anglo-French squabble over Nigeria. 'Our object', he said, 'is, as we have more than once declared, not territory but facility for trade'.[7] It is interesting to note that Cambon himself came to hold much the same views as Salisbury on this question. Commenting on a Times article in December 1899, which asserted that French colonies would never prosper without free trade, especially when Frenchmen could not be induced to establish themselves in them, Cambon fully supported the writer's opinion. His country's possessions, he argued in a communication to Paris, could only gain from the development of trade, even if that trade were in the hands of foreigners. This provoked a wry ministerial comment at the Quai d'Orsay in the margin of his despatch, '. . . only too evident, and too impractical also with the ideas dominant in Parliament'.[8]

Salisbury's endeavours to come to terms with France faced numerous obstacles. His proposal, years before, for the lowering and equalising of the tariffs of Tunisia and Algeria had not been welcomed. Now he faced, not merely the hostility of Chamberlain and Curzon to attempts to purchase good relations with France by concessions outside Europe, but the determination of the cotton industry that trade with Tunisia should not be one of the concessions. Their spokesman objected in June 1896 to

[5] Benians, 'Finance, Trade and Communications, 1870-1895', *Cambridge History of the British Empire*, vol. 3, p. 227.

[6] PRO 30/29/203/to Lyons/2 May 1883.

[7] AAE/GB/RF/1897-98/19/de Courcel to Hanotaux/18 Jan 1897; FO 27/3416/Tel. 4 Af/Salisbury to Monson/28 Jan 1898; Marsden, op. cit., p. 55.

[8] AAE/GB/RF/1899-1900/323/Cambon to Delcassé/12 Dec 1899.

even a small differential duty in favour of France, though, some months later, a chamber of commerce expert from Manchester conceded unofficially that this would not damage their dominant position in the sale of cotton goods to Tunis. In the end, their interests were safeguarded, almost in their entirety, by the convention signed on 15 October 1897. Two points of significance may be observed. In the first place, the interests of other exporters to Tunis, less important and with less influence, had been ignored and there were loud complaints from the dealers in Indian jute, cotton seed and the whole range of Maltese produce. The second point of significance is that, by an error of drafting, the relatively small item of cotton yarns had been left out of the special terms negotiated in the treaty. As a consequence, the new and strongly protectionist tariff in Tunis, which the treaty made possible, soon gave a body blow to the British export of yarns—an excellent example of the fundamental problem facing Britain all over the world. That Salisbury, left to himself, would have made greater concessions to France on grounds of high policy, is quite clear. The new arrangement over Tunis, in fact, represented a turning point in his conduct of foreign affairs. For the harder line it symbolised had emerged from a major clash of opinions in London involving Salisbury's wish not to exacerbate a dangerous situation, the insistence of Chamberlain and Curzon on a stronger line towards France generally, and the determination of the cotton industry that it should not be excluded by French tariffs from Tunisia as it had been elsewhere.

STRATEGIC CONSIDERATIONS
IN THE FORMULATION OF POLICY

Strategy obviously played its part in the formulation of British policy and Tunis had its strategic importance. It was, of course, one of the many 'buffer states', the independence of which from European control safeguarded British trade routes and British territories overseas. From the 1830's onward the Foreign Office had an uneasy feeling that French power in the Mediterranean would be increased by possession of the Tunisian coast and anchorages, to say nothing of how such an extension of

French territory might lead to an increased disposition in Europe to carve up the Ottoman empire. In a far from reassuring report on Biserta in 1864, based on a visit nineteen years earlier, Admiral Spratt asserted that it was possible to construct a really formidable naval base there.[9] It was this concern over what seemed to be the strategic possibilities of Tunisia, in the hands of a strong power, that made sense of the steadfast determination of successive British governments to prevent the Regency falling into the hands of a potentially hostile great power. In the reigns of Louis Philippe and Napoleon III the French, as Granville put it, were 'constantly biting at Tunis, and as often stopped by the decided language of successive Foreign Secretaries'.[10] Warnings in 1836, 1843 and 1864 to a France which had seized Algeria in 1830 and revived dreams of the Mediterranean becoming a 'French lake' were paralleled by similar deterrents to Italian ambitions. In 1874 Granville re-stated Britain's traditional policy, saying that he had always opposed so called 'rectification' of the frontier between Algeria and Tunis because it would give the French 'a commanding position in the Mediterranean'.

British policy in Tunis was, therefore, to a considerable extent motivated by a concern to protect the vulnerable Mediterranean 'corridor' at one of the points where hostile local naval superiority might break the chain of communications. As in the cases of Egypt and Morocco, statesmen in London at this time entertained no serious belief in the necessity for England to consider occupying the Regency itself. Indeed, British policy regarded with relative equanimity the development of French influence there. If Wood could stimulate the development of British commercial interests, as was being done in Egypt, so much the better, and he had a free hand to do so; but no further action was contemplated. The lords of the Admiralty had, in reality, a healthy respect for the fleet based at Toulon and were far from confident that they could maintain naval supremacy in the Mediterranean at all times. Indeed, for reasons of economy, the old standard enabling Britain to take

[9] FO 102/74/Salisbury to Paget/28 July 1864. See Ganiage, *Les Origines du Protectorat Français en Tunisie*, p. 37.
[10] Fitzmaurice, *Life of Granville*, vol. 2, p. 234.

on the navies of two or three other powers had been discarded for one giving only marginal superiority over France. Since, however, Britain's prime interest was the defence of the political *status quo* and this would almost always gain the support of some of the powers interested in the Mediterranean, the relative complacency shown in London may, perhaps, be justified on strategic grounds.[11] It is, therefore, very understandable that attempts should be made to 'place the Regency beyond the reach of foreign attack and aggression' by the time honoured method of maintaining the Bey's legal dependence on the Sultan. The Mediterranean *status quo* was in fact indivisible.

Nothing could have better illustrated the truth of this than the collapse of Turkey in 1876. For it ended the hopes nourished so assiduously since the 1830's, that the land forces of a revitalised, stable and reformed Turkey would complement the British navy in containing any Russian advance in the Eastern Mediterranean calculated to threaten the safety of the direct route to India. It has been seen how Britain was ready to face up to possible war with Russia rather than allow the disastrous terms imposed by that country on Turkey in 1878 to stand and how the island of Cyprus was selected by the Beaconsfield government as a base from which to forestall any attack on the threatened area. Whether the strategic implications of the subsequent 'promises' giving France hopes of compensation in Tunis were fully considered, is difficult to say. The confidential correspondence between Salisbury and Lyons, the ambassador at Paris, provides almost the only indication of the motives behind the decision and there is a significant absence of any reference to naval or military opinion on the subject. When Salisbury first enquired in May 1878 whether the French were set on acquiring

[11] Graham, *The Politics of Naval Supremacy*, pp. 67-68, 78-80; Robinson and Gallagher, op. cit., pp. 76-78. Britain still had the largest navy in the world. However, it must be remembered that sea power tended to be held in disrepute after the failure of the superior French navy to blockade the Germans in the Baltic in 1870. In 1871, the prime minister said he thought the navy was comparatively valueless except for defence of the home shores; Marder, op. cit., pp. 45, 67, 120. Moreover, British ships were widely dispersed. For example, in 1874 the numbers at each station were: China..20; E. Indies..9; Australia..9; Pacific..9; S. E. Coast of America..5; Cape of Good Hope..5; W. African Coast..11; N. America and W. Indies..16; Mediterranean..16; Home Waters..7; Bartlett, 'The Mid Victorian Reappraisal of Naval Policy', in Bourne and Watt, *Studies in International History*, pp. 207-8.

Tunis, and 'especially Cape Bona', he said that if they did so it would not cause him the 'slightest jealousy or fear'. As for the ambassador, Lyons actually thought that Britain's principal interest in the Regency was as a source of provisions for Malta. Décazes, he added, had talked of Malta being gripped in a vice between Sicily and Tunis, if the Italians got hold of the Regency, a danger he himself discounted.[12]

Salisbury himself, of course, had never served at the Admiralty and naval affairs constituted a field where it was possible for him to miscalculate. His mind was fixed at this time on the strategic problems involved in protecting Turkey for as long as he could, particularly since the French—who should have helped—were unable or unwilling to do so. In Europe the assistance of 'Austria, Greece the Rhodope mountaineers and others' would suffice. In Asia, he felt Britain had no alternative but to 'mount guard' herself from a suitable base. Cyprus was indeed far from being the most suitable base, if in fact it could be considered suitable at all, but it was chosen because others, such as Alexandretta, or Syria, might have roused suspicions of British intentions—especially on the part of France. He was quite confident that the powerful fleet assembled at Portsmouth and Britain's 'first rate ironclads' in the Mediterranean could meet any appeal to force decided on in Paris.[13] Beaconsfield himself wrote, 'I feel confident, when the hour arrives, that I will be able to show that the establishment of the Balkan frontier, and all its accessories, has materially strengthened the Ottoman Domain, and was surely no mean diplomatic triumph'.[14]

Why then, it may be asked, did Salisbury apparently suggest as compensation for Britain's acquisition of impoverished Cyprus the richer prize of Tunis, especially when the Cyprus base was only necessary because of France's own default in her obligations to help defend Turkey. In the first place, he was certainly prepared to go a long way to avoid a breach with France and it is equally clear that he wished to preserve the guarded but useful Anglo-French cooperation at Cairo, one of

[12] SP/A 26/Salisbury to Lyons/11 May 1878; SP 7/Lyons to Salisbury/ 15 May 1878; Newton, *Lord Lyons*, vol. 2, p. 139.
[13] SP 26/Salisbury to Lyons/22 May, 5 June 1878; Newton op. cit., vol. 2, p. 150. See also note 11.
[14] FO 363/1/to Tenterden/2 July 1878.

the consequences of the Russian advance in the Near East. In the second place, it does seem as if, in characteristic fashion, he was actually conceding no more than France—judging by the trend of events in Tunis—might reasonably hope to acquire some day in the future, a day still possibly to be relegated to the indefinite future by Italian and Turkish opposition. The nation-wide demands in France for a 'surprise' seizure of a Mediterranean island and what Salisbury called 'lurid touches about war' in official communications from Paris[15] showed at least how desirable it was to conciliate France. There is one general conclusion, however, which is inescapable. Britain had ceased to give her traditional support to one of the three North African states whose independence from European control had hitherto been deemed essential for the security of the route through the Mediterranean. Presumably Tunis was regarded as of less vital concern than Morocco or Egypt.

Even if not calculated on a close estimate of Britain's relative power and even if based on the dubious assumptions that the navy could effectively measure up to any emergency, Salisbury's strategy with regard to France was not illogical. The new French navy was now increasing in strength, and, after years of complacent neglect, the British navy was entering a period when it could not unaided face with confidence a war with both France and Russia simultaneously. For while Britain's sea-power would have to be responsible for defending her far flung imperial routes and territories, hostile forces could, it was said, concentrate on harrying Britain's shipping, Britain's possessions or even the British homeland itself. By 1882, indeed, the navies which the continental powers had begun to build in the 1870's presented a formidable problem. Whereas Britain had twenty first class ships, France now had sixteen and Germany nine. In addition Italy, Austria and Russia each had a modern navy in the early stages of development.[16] Yet there was still another difficulty of which the policy makers were more

[15] SP 26/Salisbury to Lyons/20 July 78.
[16] The transition from the wooden ship to the iron clad and the rapid technical development in arms, armour and new weapons such as the torpedo, made much of Britain's numerically superior fleet obsolete; Brassey, *The British Navy*, (1882) vol. 2 (ii), p. 226, quoted Langer, *European Alliances and Alignments*, p. 302; Marder, op. cit., p. 120.

conscious at this stage, and this was the fact that the internal weaknesses of Muslim buffer states along the Mediterranean 'corridor' were undermining Britain's established defensive strategy over a wide area. Before leaving office in 1880, Salisbury had come to believe that the Turkish bastion in the Near East could not be much longer maintained. Thinking, as always, of his main objectives, he observed, 'It would be of no little advantage to delay the fall of Turkey till our railway has been made to Candahar. It would be a great success to defer it till the revolution in Russia has taken place'.[17] At the Porte itself, Britain's influence was clearly on the wane and the accession of the Turkophobe Gladstone to power not surprisingly led to a distinct deterioration in Anglo-Turkish relations. Other powers, especially the Russians, were only too willing to step into Britain's empty shoes at Constantinople, so that Britain's traditional defensive strategy in the eastern Mediterranean became much more difficult to execute.

In the linked problem of the central Mediterranean, the occupation of Tunis provided yet another challenge. Having previously criticised Salisbury's policies, the Liberals now found themselves virtually obliged to follow them, however half heartedly. They unwillingly retained the Cyprus base, though the purpose for which it had been acquired was being emasculated, and equally unwillingly paid the 'compensation' they felt Salisbury had promised France. Granville, impressed by the arguments of Admiral Spratt, distinguished as a survey officer, considered that the acquisition of Biserta by the French would give them overwhelming predominance in the Mediterranean; and, though the First Lord of the Admiralty, Northbrook, was not prepared to accept the view that Malta was in danger, he conceded that French possession of Biserta was 'the most dangerous thing to British interests in the Mediterranean'.[18] The prime minister felt Salisbury had committed them and, in any case, objected to the cooperation with the Italians that would be inevitable if the French were to be halted. Divided and confused, the Gladstone government decided to do nothing and to do it in such a way as not unnecessarily to exacerbate Anglo-

[17] Medlicott, *Bismarck, Gladstone and the Concert of Europe*, p. 72.
[18] Ibid., p. 310.

French relations. Though convinced, therefore, that Britain's strategic interests were suffering, they felt they had to make do with the not very satisfactory 'assurance' of the French that there was no plan for a military port at Biserta 'at the present time'.

The 'helpless flounderings' of Gladstone and Granville in the following year leading to the occupation of Egypt were only too clearly not the consequence of calculations based on the needs of imperial defence. For some years in fact Egypt was regarded as no more than a burden to be shaken off if at all possible. It would be invidious to recapitulate how three more years of muddled and shortsighted Gladstonian policies in Africa, the Pacific, the Balkans, and Central Asia left Britain with hardly a friend among the nations and more than a few potential enemies. Nothing could have better illustrated how Britain's freedom of action was now circumscribed than the crisis of 1885. This was when Russia, already threatening interference in Bulgaria, took by force the disputed area of Penjdeh on the borders of Afghanistan, so that British troops had perforce to be hurriedly withdrawn from the Sudan. Otherwise, as Granville pointed out, the English would, in a war with Russia, have had to 'endure what any Power might choose to lay upon them and be compelled to forgo all voice or share in the destinies of the world'.[19] For the long forward progress of the Russians through Central Asia had finally brought them to the often ill defined boundaries of the 'buffer' states of Afghanistan and Persia, behind which India hoped to be secure. Henceforth, fears however unrealistic, of invasion, coupled with possible revolution in India itself, were endemic.[20]

The answer Salisbury, on his return to power, devised to the problem of strengthening Britain's position, is well known. The Mediterranean agreements of 1887 established through Italy a link with the central powers for general cooperation to preserve the *status quo* in the Mediterranean, the Black Sea and the Straits. To this prudent measure of reinsurance with its

[19] Q.V.L., 2nd ser., vol. 3, pp. 640ff, quoted *Cambridge History of the British Empire*, vol. 3, p. 126. Germany's quarrelsome attitude and co-operation with France against Britain may be noted; see Medlicott, op. cit., pp. 153-7. In France, of course, Boulangism, as anti British as anti German, was on the increase.

[20] Greaves, op. cit., p. 3. Kimberley anticipated Russian pressure in Central Asia to further designs with regard to Turkey.

minimum of actual commitment and its worthwhile effect on French chauvinism and Russian ambitions, was added an examination of the state of British defences. This was in fact a consequence of widespread uneasiness in the country. For any realistic strategy would now have to allow for the possibility of hostilities simultaneously with France and Russia, at a time when the condition of the navy had rarely been less equal to the task. No alarmist, Salisbury felt obliged to accept expert opinion that a French invasion was technically possible. In the Mediterranean, where France was henceforward concentrating the best of the warships assiduously constructed since 1878, Britain was no longer top dog. Indeed, a naval war with France alone could now be considered hazardous, and the main challenge to Britain in a naval war would clearly come in the Mediterranean. Nor could this situation be remedied by alliance with the third sea power, Italy, since that country's navy was in decline and any advantage of an alliance would be far more than outweighed by the burden of helping to defend the long Italian coastline. If general hostilities broke out, the only war plan the Admiralty felt possible was to concentrate the Channel and Mediterranean fleets off Gibraltar, leaving a small 'reserve' to defend home waters.[21] Until the navy could be expanded and brought up to date, common prudence dictated the policy that Salisbury in fact followed—to offend the French as little as possible, while doing nothing to drive Italy into the arms of that power. Developments in Central Asia could also do nothing except reinforce this caution on Salisbury's part, since the dangers there of Russian activity were so acutely felt that he repeated the earlier warnings of the Liberals. An advance beyond Penjdeh to Herat would mean war. Yet, at the same time, the War Office felt it impossible to strike at Russia

[21] France had six first class and four second class battleships together with four armoured cruisers in the Mediterranean. Britain had six first class battleships and an armoured ram. Britain had 22 battleships altogether in July 1888, plus the 8 (and ram) in the Mediterranean, where France had 15. Between 1888 and 1891 the Toulon fleet increased from 15 armourclads and 6 unarmoured cruisers to 19 armourclads and 14 cruisers; Marder, op. cit., pp. 129, 131, 146. War with France would have meant despatching 9 battleships to the Mediterranean leaving the Channel and foreign stations inadequately defended. The constant necessity for relieving ships on distant stations and technical difficulties also kept the number immediately available at a reduced level.

without allies, if only because of lack of manpower, and an attack through the Black Sea in collaboration with the Turks seemed an increasingly impractical proposition. Unlike its predecessor, therefore, the War Plan of 1890 was essentially defensive in character.[22]

Thus it is easy to understand Salisbury's attitude towards the many attempts of Crispi to stir up trouble with France in the hope of gain for Italy—with, of course, the help of his British and German partners. Had he wished, Salisbury could have easily found opportunities to support Crispi against France, in the storm over the Tunis schools for example. Yet he did not do so. All invitations from Rome to 'joint action' or 'concerted measures' were met with temporisation. Salisbury would go no further than to say that he believed England would be inclined to help Italy if 'gratuitously' attacked by France. When Crispi, as has been seen, claimed in a moment of unjustifiable panic in 1889 that the Mediterranean agreement entitled him to expect military help, the result was a brutally frank rejoinder from Salisbury. There was, he reminded Crispi, no such pledge of material aid. The fact of the matter was that, to Salisbury, the association with Italy was rather burdensome and to be endured only for the sake of the assistance given by the Triple Alliance in areas of strategic importance. It was the Germans and Austrians he considered 'useful friends' in his dealings with Turkey, Russia, Egypt and France. Yet in 'leaning' to the central powers, Salisbury did not intend to build a wall of hostility between London and Paris. What he wanted from the Germans was cordiality, which he got because they felt that Britain alone could keep Italy firmly in the Triple Alliance in the face of French pressure. When they went to the length of offering Britain an outright alliance (in 1889), Salisbury deftly side stepped the proposal, but he was only too glad to be able to end a source of Anglo-German friction with the Zanzibar-Heligoland agreement. Indefinite postponement of a settlement, he saw clearly, would have quickly cooled off the German cordiality he wished to preserve and forced him to look for new friends among the countries of Europe.

[22] Greaves, op. cit., pp. 75-76, 117. See also Penson, *Foreign Affairs under Salisbury*, p. 14.

It may be reasonably inferred, however, that it was to the 'two power standard', a navy equal to defeating any two European navies combined, that Salisbury looked to give security to Britain in the future. In the meantime he was careful not to provide fuel for the fires of Boulangism, or its aftermath, in France. In the questions of Massowah and the Tunis schools, far from whole heartedly siding with Italy, he declined to commit himself. When France exploded with indignation over the 'moral damage' she had suffered in Zanzibar and there was bellicose talk of annexing Tunis, Salisbury made substantial concessions in the colonial bargaining that followed. So great were these that even the French ministers themselves conceded that 'Madagascar and the Empire of the Sudan were well worth the trivial position they occupied at Zanzibar'. What Salisbury could not do, however, was to make concessions over Tunis, as this would have estranged Italy and probably the other Triple Alliance powers. Britain then would have returned to the exposed position she had occupied in 1885. By now the decision had been made, for essentially strategic reasons, against an early evacuation of Egypt, which effectively ruled out any reconciliation with France. The 'Tunis card' had still to be retained in England's hand on that account. Not, of course, that Salisbury had any objections to the 'Gallic cock' scratching in the sand south of Tunis, provided it did not cause complications by showing an interest in Tripoli, which the Italians had mentally marked down for their own and which, in any case, was too close to Egypt for Britain to be disinterested.

By 1891, the professional strategists had a few shocks in store for Salisbury. For the critical eye of the youthful naval intelligence department had been turned on the Mediterranean and the first change of policy it suggested concerned Tunis. Only two years before a memorandum from the Admiralty itself had described Biserta as 'the most important strategic position in the Mediterranean'. Subsequent French activities there had caused acute alarm to the Italians, who had visions of having to withdraw men from their Alpine frontier (to the detriment of their Germans allies) in order to guard against the possible invasion of Sicily. Salisbury had attempted to counter these fears by saying that Anglo-Italian forces would always outnumber those of France. Now, however, in January 1891, the director of naval intelligence produced a cogent memorandum which confidently asserted that a naval base at Biserta would prove more of a burden to France than an advantage and that one additional hostile port on the North African coast would not alter the position of the powers in the Mediterranean. Let the French, they argued, be encouraged to 'persevere in their misdirected efforts' and waste their substance on fixed installations rather than on what really counted—ships of war. This had an immediate effect on policy in so far as it made Salisbury even less inclined to support Italian protests about Biserta at Paris and gave the Italians yet another reason to feel disgruntled over the policies of the London government.

However, the real shock for Salisbury was yet to come. It arrived in the form of a joint memorandum from the directors of military and naval intelligence[23] suggesting nothing less than that British policies in the eastern Mediterranean were now based on an assumed capacity to act that did not exist. For, instead of the Naval Defence act restoring to Britain her former unquestioned supremacy on the sea, it had simply acted as a spur to greater naval construction in Russia and France. The crux of the memorandum lay in the uncompromising assertion that the defence of Constantinople, a fundamental characteristic of foreign policy for so long, could no more be undertaken. The existence of a possibly unfriendly and numerically superior fleet at Toulon was said to neutralise British action in the eastern Mediterranean. As furthermore the Sultan had significantly fortified the Dardanelles but not the Bosphorus, he might conceivably allow the Russian Black Sea fleet to pass through the Straits. It was possible to envisage the defeat of the Mediterranean fleet rashly operating in the Straits and subsequently the defeat of the then outnumbered Channel fleet. At the same time the commander-in-chief in India discarded his war contingency plans for severing Russian communications with troops advancing from the Black Sea. In its place he drew up a new plan for defence of the Indian frontiers themselves.

[23] Marder, op. cit., chap. 9 passim; Greaves, op. cit., pp. 215-7; Lowe, op. cit., p. 86; Tunstall, op. cit., p. 245; Grenville, Lord *Salisbury and Foreign Policy*, p. 393. The memorandum crystallised ideas developed over three years.

BDT P

The impact on policy of these new ideas on strategy was not immediate, though they were clearly incompatible with the traditional lines on which the Foreign Office had been proceeding. The reason was twofold, that the new doctrine failed to fully convince the sceptical Salisbury and that the question of the Straits did not present itself to the Liberal government of 1892-1895 in an acute form requiring possible action.

The problems of the new administration have been discussed—how Rosebery sought to continue the policies of Salisbury and how that was difficult in view of the changed Franco-Russian relationship and the now uncooperative attitude of Germany. If the Russians were to get naval assistance from the French, Britain would 'need the help of the Triple Alliance', according to Rosebery and the War Office.[24] In view, therefore, of increasing Teutonic unfriendliness, the visit of the Black Sea fleet to Toulon seemed ominous. Not only were the naval authorities in London convinced that they were already unable to cope with France and Russia in the Mediterranean, but the combined estimates of the two powers exceeded Britain's by a ratio of five to three.[25] In 1894, the director of military intelligence, Sir John Ardagh, concluded that Russia could then 'seize Constantinople by a *coup de main* whenever she pleased' and England could do nothing about it singlehanded.[26] The Liberals' answer to the problem, like that of the Conservatives in 1889, was a sharp increase in naval expenditure

[24] Quoted Penson, 'New Course in British Foreign Policy', cit., p. 130. Russia now had a modern Black Sea fleet consisting of 5 powerful battleships (two launched in 1890 and 1891) plus cruisers and torpedo boats; Marder, op. cit., pp. 146, 153.

[25] Tunstall, op. cit., p. 245; Marder, op. cit., pp. 162-3. Russia's new Mediterranean squadron was small, with only one second class battleship and 3 cruisers; but there was no guarantee that the Straits Convention of 1841 would prevent the modern Black Sea Fleet, with its 4 new battleships (3 first class) and 2 first class under construction, giving support. (The Russian Baltic fleet had one first class, 3 second class and 6 third class battleships, with 7 building.) Britain's Mediterranean fleet was inferior to the French, which had 17 battleships (8 first class), 10 cruisers and 81 large, new torpedo boats; while Britain had only 11 battleships (9 first class), 7 cruisers and 12 small torpedo boats. The French navy also had its modern base at Toulon, while Gibraltar was hardly a naval base at all. With Russian support, therefore, the French would have a marked superiority. Britain's first class battleships altogether totalled 15 (with 7 building), France's 9 (6 building and 3 projected) and Russia's 3 (6 building and 1 projected); Marder, op. cit., pp. 182-3, 204.

[26] PRO 30/40/14/Ardagh Memo No. 5 Sec/Oct 1896.

(at the price of Gladstone's resignation); but, in the period before such measures could take effect, the unwillingness of the Rosebery administration to take a firm hand with a more confident and more 'awkward' France is not difficult to comprehend. There was, for example, less willingness than ever to support the Italians in their squabbles with France, whether in the question of the Tunis-Tripoli frontier or in East Africa. There was no 'proof of friendship', as urgently requested by the Quirinal, in the form of a pledge not to surrender British rights in Tunis. Indeed, the rather haphazard Grey declaration on the Upper Nile[27] was the one real challenge made to French ambitions. Even co-operation in the Turkish question with France's ally in the summer of 1895 was welcomed for as long as it proved possible.

In the period of mounting difficulty for Britain following the return of the Conservatives to power, what had a most pronounced effect on Salisbury was the discovery that his cabinet colleagues were at one with the Admiralty in vetoing his desire to send the fleet up the Straits during the Armenian crisis. The consequences of such a course, as seen by the service departments, were dramatically described by Ardagh some months later:

> . . . And in what a false and dangerous position we would have placed ourselves! In front the Bosphorus defences and the Russian Black Sea Fleet—in rear, the but half crippled works of the Dardanelles and the whole naval power of France.[28]

Though a little ungraciously, especially as he anticipated an early collapse of the Turkish empire, Salisbury accepted the decision with its wide implications for future policy. He was, however, realist enough to acknowledge that Russia was in a position to seize Constantinople at will and that British policy in that region was now essentially one of bluff.[29] He was rebuffed in his attempts to come to an understanding with Russia, but at least the attempts are understandable. For he also fully appreciated the importance, strategically, of a Bulgaria no longer hostile to Russia.[30] The logic of the situation clearly indicated that

---

[27] On this see Sanderson, *England, Europe and the Upper Nile*, pp. 213-15.
[28] As note 26.   [29] Grenville, op. cit., pp. 81-83.
[30] FO 7/1240/24 Sec/Salisbury to Monson/26 Feb 1896.

British interests in the Mediterranean henceforth involved control of the Nile valley rather than influence with the Turk. Equally clearly there would be little disposition to add a quarrel with Russia to the confrontation with that country's French ally that the new emphasis in British strategy would inevitably occasion. As for France, now at the peak of her military strength, the director of military intelligence noted, in a comforting memorandum in December 1895, the failure of the long French preparations to transport 15,000 men to Madagascar.[31] This was good news for those who feared that France might seize a favourable opportunity to accomplish the difficult technical feat of invading England. It was, in the circumstances, manifestly sensible to establish the *dètente* with France leading to agreement on Siam and negotiations on the Niger and Tunis, even though the discussions arranged soon showed French expectations of wholesale British concessions that had little chance of being realised.

The ostensible German threat of intervention in South Africa Salisbury was able to meet quite easily by the flying squadron that Chamberlain organised. At the same time, it was obvious that Salisbury did not wish to incur the enmity of Austria and Italy, if it could be avoided, nor, despite the German attitude, to see the Triple Alliance disintegrate. That he could not pay Austria's price for continued friendship by undertaking the defence of the Straits and pledging Britain to military action in advance, did not mean that he wished the entente of 1887 to collapse either. His attitude towards Italy is instructive. If he broke with Italy, it would be an indication that any 'leaning' towards the Triple Alliance was finally and irrevocably at an end, and a break with Italy was, in March 1896, very possible. After so much apparent deference to French interests by Britain regarding Tunisia and Zeila, indifference to the Italian plight after Adua would have been too much for Anglo-Italian understanding. The Dongola expedition provided the necessary gesture of support; but it must not be forgotten that it also served to strengthen Britain's hand in an area of vital strategic concern. Salisbury himself frankly recognised that sooner or later he would have had to act to drive back the

[31] Marsden, op. cit., p. 12.

dervishes, and that was why the expedition moved down the Nile rather than from, say, Suakin.[32] Of course, what made the whole thing tactically possible was that prevailing German hostility had necessarily been converted to active support of a measure to help its Triple Alliance partner. The inevitable bitter reaction of France could therefore be disregarded and French unpleasantness in Tunis, West Africa, Madagascar and the question of the Egyptian finances met by as much temporisation as possible in each case. De Courcel came to the conclusion that it was British policy to oscillate advantageously between the two European alliances and that the expedition was designed to prevent the collapse of one of them.[33] This was partly true; but he might have added that Britain's strategic position and the alignment of the powers gave the London cabinet little freedom of manœuvre.

With the Eastern Question threatening again to explode in the autumn, it did seem desirable to examine Britain's defences and this is what Salisbury proceeded to do. Perhaps his almost legendary disinclination to take the advice of military experts without a pinch of salt had a certain justification. Nothing could have been more full of impending doom than the War Office analysis of the situation. Britain was too weak, argued Sir John Ardagh, to meet all possible contingencies. Without a friend among the European powers except an Italy enfeebled by the Adua catastrophe, Britain was supposed to be facing a hostile Dual Alliance, an unfriendly Germany and an increasingly unfriendly Austria, a quarrelsome United States, a South African republic arming and legislating against her, menace in the Upper Nile from the Congo State and France, and menace from a French and Russian dominated Abyssinia. In the event of war, Gibraltar and Malta would depend on military reinforcements which could not be guaranteed them. The Black Sea fleet was to be expected in the eastern Mediterranean, so that the holding of Egypt was essential, while at the other end of the Mediterranean it was more than desirable to preserve the *status quo* in Morocco. France and Russia were seen as irrevocably

---

[32] FO 45/747/65 Conf/Salisbury to Clare Ford/20 May 1896; Robinson and Gallagher, op. cit., pp. 348-9.
[33] D.D.F. 1/12/320.384; AAE/Angl/913/to Berthelot/13 Mar 1896.

hostile all over the world and any casual incident as maybe leading to war. Ardagh's conclusion, one that the War Office had been arguing since 1890, was dramatic, 'Better all the risks of the triple alliance than such a calamity'.[34] Admiralty advice was very similar. War with France and Russia together meant that 'supremacy would have to be fought for everywhere'. Asia Minor, wrote the director of naval intelligence, Admiral Beaumont, would become a Russian base and Britain would need three fleets and three bases in the Mediterranean, at Gibraltar, Malta and Alexandria. Russian development as a first-class naval power in the Mediterranean was 'certain'. Once more the importance of keeping hold on Egypt was stressed— '. . . it may be said that if there was no Suez Canal, it would not be long before there was no India'.[35]

Though Salisbury made no attempt to change the main lines of his policy and join or move closer to the Triple Alliance, there is little doubt that, on this occasion, the scarifying military and naval memoranda were taken very seriously. As late as June 1896 he seems to have told Hatzfeldt 'with great self confidence' that he was quite sure that Britain could deal successfully with both France and Russia in the Mediterranean.[36] Now he made every effort to avoid a clash with Russia or, of course, with Russia's ally. In the Tunis negotiations a conciliatory solution was necessary 'on general political grounds'[37] and equally comprehensible was Salisbury's feverish anxiety in the spring of 1897 for conciliation on all outstanding disagreements. It seemed after all not impossible that France and Germany might co-operate in the Transvaal question which, like the squabble in West Africa, was becoming more dangerous.

Yet the worrying memoranda of the War Office and Admiralty soon seemed to have lost a lot of their effect upon policy. Chamberlain and Curzon intervened in the Tunis negotiations to forestall concessions to France by Salisbury[38] and henceforward British policy took a harder line, with Chamberlain free to pursue policies involving possible war with France in West Africa. Luckily perhaps there was less danger in this than there

[34] As note 26; Marder, op. cit., pp. 268-70, 569-77.
[35] Marder, op. cit., pp. 270-3, 578-80.   [36] G.P. 12.i.2917.
[37] Marsden, op. cit., p. 58.   [38] Ibid., p. 70.

would have been a few months earlier, if only because Russia's 'eyes of desire' were fixed now, not on the Straits, but on future gain in the Far East. The display of naval power at the Spithead review also led to a slightly more sanguine frame of mind at the Admiralty[39] and less inclination on the part of impressed rivals to challenge that power—until they too were stronger on the sea.

There was soon to be apparent need of all the strength Britain possessed. By the spring of 1898 she and France were on a collision course and it seemed a question of chance whether it should occur over the Niger or the Nile valley. The Russian occupation of Port Arthur came as an unwelcome additional problem. After all, it challenged Britain's 'open door' policy and the integrity of China, which a parliamentary resolution had just declared 'a matter of vital importance to British commerce and influence'. It was at this juncture that Salisbury, while most of his cabinet colleagues demanded a confrontation with Russia, showed superior tactical skill in the use of British power and successfully counselled against any action. '. . . I don't think we carry guns enough to fight them and the French together', he said, for he was thinking of the coming clash with France.[40] This was again the policy of 'limiting the amount of heather ablaze' at one time; but it also made fairly certain that Russia would not intervene in an Anglo-French conflict. In any case, a war in the Far East followed by another in Africa would have been the worst possible strategy. It would have been almost impossible to have avoided a damaging withdrawal of forces from the China seas under most unfavourable circumstances. The volatile and changeable Chamberlain, who would have thrown down the gauntlet to Russia, regarded Britain's 'humiliation' as a sign of intolerable weakness. His answer, of course, was to seek an ally— and in the next few years virtually every possible candidate received his support at some time.

There would be little point in saying more about the Fashoda incident than to make the obvious comment that seapower made

---

[39] Marder, op. cit., pp. 280-1.

[40] Kennedy, *Salisbury*, p. 276; Sanderson, op. cit., p. 326; Grenville, op. cit., pp. 146-7. The number of battleships and cruisers possessed by each country (with numbers under construction in brackets) were: Britain 52 (12), 18 (8): France 27 (8), 9 (10); Russia 12 (10), 10 (1); Germany 17 (5), 3 (2); Italy 15 (2), 3 (2); U.S.A. 5 (8), 2; Japan 3 (3), 1 (6); Marder, op. cit., p. 314.

possible Salisbury's policy and diplomatic victory. Naval construction since 1894 was now telling. The British navy had a pronounced superiority over the French alone, so much so that a supremely confident Admiralty abandoned the former strategic plan entailing a 'cut and run' to Gibraltar by the Mediterranean fleet, in favour of a concentration at Malta. The Channel fleet was to balance this by a similar concentration at Gibraltar.[41] Perhaps, however, it should not be forgotten that Britain was throwing down the glove to an adversary who never intended to fight on such an issue anyway.[42] Not that it can be said that there were no misgivings in London. It was overland from Tunis that the perennially pessimistic director of military intelligence thought that France might strike at Egypt. In the months after Marchand's recall, therefore, while suspicion still blazed on both sides of the channel, he joined in person in the exhaustive enquiries on the spot. These not only showed how unlikely it was that even another Napoleon would attempt the feat, but that the French would have their work cut out to hold on to Algeria and Tunis—especially in view of the inevitable revolt on the part of the indigenous population. Biserta itself was seen to be poorly defended and certainly in no position as yet to 'seize the Mediterranean by the throat'. There were, of course, still the Italian fears of a French advance from Tunis into Tripoli, fears heightened enormously by the Anglo-French agreement of March 1899 and the subsequent refusal of Salisbury to give any assurances to Rome.

This was all very much in accord with the recommendations of the service ministries three years before. Britain had been ready to stake all to assure herself of control of the Nile valley; the *status quo* was being supported in Morocco; the position in the Mediterranean had been strengthened; interest in Turkey had waned, and Italy was being shown little consideration. Soon, however, British strategists were to face seemingly new and serious causes for worry. In the planning and development of Russian railways the military voice had been especially loud and the strategically important Trans Caspian and Trans Siberian lines were now nearing completion. In South Africa an ill-considered war served both to show up the weaknesses of the

[41] Marder, op. cit., pp. 323-8.   [42] Sanderson, op. cit., p. 361.

army and to tie down available forces. As it was not until the Russian conflict with Japan, five years in the future, that the even greater weaknesses of the Russian military and naval machine were to be revealed, the nightmare of Russian attacks to come continued to disturb the sleep of politicians in London. The loss of India, thought the most vulnerable point of the empire, was considered almost the most devastating blow that could be suffered, and this, it was assumed, was the target Russia had set herself. In 1900 Salisbury still thought that Russia would advance on India in order to force Britain to acquiesce in a new Russian empire carved out of China. Balfour agreed. 'The weakest spot in the Empire is probably the Indian frontier', he said. 'A quarrel with Russia anywhere, about anything, means the invasion of India.'[43]

The long-established habit of considering Russia as one of the principal potential enemies continued to dominate British military thinking for yet a few years. On paper it appeared as if the two-power standard on the sea was only just being maintained, while Russia, Germany, Japan and the United States were busy on ambitious construction programmes. As for the efficiency of the fleet, Admiral Beresford stated that its 'want of preparation was in many ways worse than the Army before South Africa exposed necessities that were wanting'. The serious deficiencies of the French fleet and the notorious inefficiency of the Russian were ignored.[44] On the land, the 'limitless' hordes of 'invulnerable' Russia were contrasted with the numerical limitations of British and Indian forces. It was assumed that the Franco-Russian combination would be willing and able to take advantage of the disintegration of such states as Persia, China or Morocco and that the way out of such difficulties was to abandon the traditional 'isolation'.

It is not surprising that the Admiralty—as will be seen—should wish to concentrate its power as far as possible in home waters and the Mediterranean. This was one of the objectives behind the Hay-Pauncefote treaty with the Americans as well as the alliance with the Japanese.

[43] Greaves, op. cit., p. 16; Grenville, op. cit., pp. 294-6; Monger, op. cit. pp. 8-13, 94; Nish, *The Anglo-Japanese Alliance*, p. 205.
[44] Marder, *From Dreadnought to Scapa Flow*, vol. 1, p. 10.

The strategic purpose behind that alliance was also that the naval forces of the new ally would assure for the time being the defence of Britain's commercial interests in the Far East, and removed the possibility of Japan joining the Russians.[45] The Mediterranean agreement with Italy, similarly served to strengthen Britain's position in an important area, where possible French or Russian retaliation for the Japanese alliance would have been embarrassing. It would have been doubly embarrassing if the *rapprochement* between France and Italy had led to Italian participation in moves against British interests. It was, at this time, just beginning to be realised that the new German navy was designed for operation in the North Sea only and against Britain, but, in 1903, Balfour and the Committee of Imperial Defence still thought the most serious problem to be the defence of India, and still trembled helplessly at the thought of attempting to cope with the Russian hordes. Two years more would elapse before a Japanese David would humble the Muscovite Goliath and the Russian 'bogey' be finally laid. What was new was that a largely Germanophobe Foreign Office was asserting that the most dangerous threat to British interests was now that emanating from Berlin.[46] The outcome of this peculiar situation has already been noted. Flying in the face of his military advisers (because of fears of war in the Far East), Lansdowne concluded the agreement of 1904 with France, in the full knowledge that there would be trouble to come from Germany because of the clauses concerned with Morocco. That trouble duly came; but at least Anglo-French disagreement over North Africa and so many other dependent territories could now be allowed to fade into oblivion.

[45] Nish, op. cit., pp. 174, 373. See also chapter 7.
[46] Monger, op. cit., pp. 94-100.

7

THE TUNIS QUESTION
AND THE GREAT POWERS

Repercussions on International Relations

There would appear to be two things necessary to complete this study of the Tunis question in British Mediterranean policy. In the first place it would seem desirable to make a brief survey of its effects on the relations of the great powers. In the second place, in order to appreciate the consequences of thirty years of diplomacy over Tunis and allied problems, it would seem advisable to examine in more detail the circumstances under which Lansdowne's departure from Salisbury's policies took place. What made Tunisia of importance in international relations was above all its geographical position, a base from which it seemed possible that a strong power could both dominate the central Mediterranean and expand overland to the south or east. British policy towards Tunis from the 1830's onwards was, therefore, part of the wider policy of safe-guarding the route to India by doing everything possible to sustain a Turkey strong enough to withstand Russia and to preserve the independence of the lesser Muslim states of Egypt, Tunis and Morocco. The threat to the integrity of the Regency came from France and Italy, with the result that Britain found herself involved in periodic diplomatic confrontations with those powers. In the 1870's the success of this British policy was placed in jeopardy not only by financial instability in Tunis (as in Egypt and Turkey) leading to the domination of her financial affairs by French, British and Italian interests, but also by the new pattern in relations between the European powers in the aftermath of the Franco-Prussian war.

In the nature of the case, Tunis exerted an almost continuous influence on relations between Britain and France. The French had become much more friendly and, concerned like Britain to keep the Russians out of Constantinople, made efforts to limit internecine rivalry in territories bordering the route to India, more important than ever to Britain now that the Suez canal was in operation. There was one exception—Tunis. The appointment of Roustan as Chargé d'Affaires in 1874 heralded an intensification of the forty-year-old struggle for influence in the Regency. For it was felt in London that even a 'rectification' of the Tunis-Algeria frontier might give France an undesirable mastery of the central Mediterranean. While fear of Germany deflected French eyes away from Europe, the Germans, Austrians and Russians—with gains to themselves in Turkey in mind—all made suggestions that Egypt should become British and Tunis French or Italian. French suspicion, Italian fear and British support for the *status quo* (if only because of the unpredictable consequences of destroying it), scotched these proposals.

Tunis next came to the fore when Salisbury was considering 'compensation', however undeserved he felt it to be, for the wound to French self-esteem caused by the Cyprus convention. The evidence now available suggests that the intense, and rather hypocritical, indignation in France induced Salisbury to be far more specific in his promise to Waddington than he had intended to be at the Congress of Berlin. To keep on good terms with the French, whose co-operation against the advance of Slav power in Europe and Asia he needed and duly got, he agreed to stand aside from the struggle to decide the future of the Regency. This and the sudden retirement of Richard Wood, the agent so detested by the French, was the limit to which Salisbury was prepared to go to buy French collaboration. To keep on good terms with the Italians, on the other hand, he told them nothing about his assurances to the French. It was surely unfortunate, from Salisbury's point of view, that the Quirinal, totally ignorant of the fact that British assistance was unlikely to be forthcoming, should have decided to initiate a serious challenge to the French in Tunis and thus provoke them to resort to extreme measures. To please the French in Tunis was to displease the Italians, who never forgot that theirs was the largest European 'colony' there or that the strategic position of the Regency could make it a menace to Italian security.

The occupation of Tunis that followed had a pronounced effect on the relations of the great powers. The Liberal ministers in London found themselves, much to their disgust, risking war with France, first of all in the dubious Enfida dispute and then during the actual invasion itself. One legacy, certainly, was a great deal of resentment in Britain. On the French side too there had been, even before the occupation, a growing reserve towards British Mediterranean policies (for example in Morocco), and during the crisis itself, the Ferry government resented the fact that it did not get a more sympathetic attitude from London. With so appreciable a decline in Anglo-French cordiality, a frame of mind had been created on both sides of the Channel in which the British occupation of Egypt could have no other effect than to destroy what was left of the 'liberal alliance'. Inevitably relations between Britain and Italy also took a turn for the worse. At a moment for Italy of humiliation and despair, when the stability of the monarchy itself seemed in question, London rejected offers of co-operation from Rome and St. Petersburg and stood idly by advising 'moderation'. It is hardly necessary to reiterate how the Italian sense of outrage, which had to be limited to what Bismarck called 'a fire of straw', led Italy into an alliance with Germany and even the traditional enemy, Austria. Painfully aware of its helpless isolation and domestic difficulties, the government in Rome had, the year before, even refused to co-operate with Britain in the occupation of Egypt. Moreover, the British policy of siding more with France in Tunis than with Italy continued. For, with Bismarck exerting pressure in the colonial field and the Russians ostensibly challenging the integrity of Afghanistan, Granville was ready to be relatively conciliatory to France by yielding up consular jurisdiction in 1884 as well as rights in the Financial Commission—to the disgust of Italians. The crisis in Tunis, therefore, followed so soon by that over Egypt, resulted in Anglo-French discord, impelled Britain towards collaboration with the new Triple Alliance, which the crisis had helped to create, and transformed France into a possible candidate for Russian friendship. It did more. It was the first step towards creating an international climate in which a general 'scramble' for colonies could take place.

Despite the French occupation, the Tunis question continued to influence the relations of the powers. For the Italy of Crispi, which regarded the Regency as an 'Italian colony occupied by France', was determined to use to its own advantage its new partnerships with Germany and (through the Mediterranean Agreements of 1887) Britain. Of the many incidents conjured up by Crispi, those over the Tunis-Tripoli boundary, the Tunis schools decrees, the Tunisian regulations on real property, municipal taxes and Biserta were the most serious and there was a real possibility of war. The reaction of Salisbury, who saw any help he gave to the Italians simply as an 'onerous corollary' to his desire to keep on good terms with the Germans, was to hold Italy at arm's length. He emphasised that Britain had made no pledge of military support and he gave more comfort and support to the French in the crisis than he need have done. Indeed, when matters with the French came nearly to breaking point over the Zanzibar and Heligoland agreement of 1890 and the Quai d'Orsay threatened to annex Tunis, Salisbury made generous concessions to France in North Africa. No real reconciliation was possible, however. For the French were determined to continue their obstructionist tactics in Egypt, and, as long as they did, Salisbury was determined as a counterweight to hold on to British treaty rights in Tunis, in spite of repeated French pleas for their surrender.

In the mid 1890's, Italy's international position was decidedly affected by French determination to get rid of the treaty rights of foreigners in Tunis. Italy in fact found herself isolated. For her ally Germany refused to become embroiled in the Mediterranean after the conclusion of the Dual Alliance; Austria willingly sold her rights in Tunis to France; and Britain, desiring better relations with Paris, declined any conflict on Italy's behalf. When, in 1896, Italy was obliged to give way to France, it proved to be the first step towards a full reconciliation with that country, and also the first step away from dependence on the Triple Alliance. More, it ushered in a period of almost unprecedented coolness in relations with Britain. For French statesmen, however, the first objective was to weaken Britain's resistance by securing the abandonment of rights by all other powers. For some years therefore the Tunis question was a variable element in the relations of the two countries. Salisbury's promise to negotiate for a new treaty formed a part, welcome to France, of the *détente* of January 1896 that was so abruptly destroyed by news of the Dongola expedition. During a moment of fear, at the end of the year, that the Russians might start a conflict by seizing the Bosphorus, Hanotaux pressed Salisbury urgently to settle all questions causing discord, especially Tunis and Madagascar. But this mood soon passed. Hardly any issue stirred French emotions more than that of Tunis, and there were indications, during the difficult and prolonged negotiations, that it might have led to a bitter commercial war by France against British trade with the Regency. When the new treaty altering Britain's legal position in Tunis was signed on 15 October 1897, however, it led to little discernible improvement in relations. The hard bargain insisted on by Salisbury's colleagues had seen to that. But at least a major source of ill will between the two countries had at last come to an end. Taken in conjunction with the Siamese and Niger conventions it helped to ensure that only a 'limited amount of heather' was alight at the time of Fashoda, and it may be said that these agreements were a necessary pre-requisite to the future entente. Yet one problem still remained, the Tunis-Tripoli frontier and the fears of Italy in particular that the French would expand across it. It was in dealing with this question that Lansdowne, as will be seen, made his most serious departure from the policies hitherto pursued in the Mediterranean.

A matter of hardly more than secondary importance in itself, the Tunis question had, therefore, for more than a generation, assumed a position of some significance in international affairs; it had provided a particularly delicate field of battle and dissension at a time when the alliances and alignments of the great powers were in a process of radical change. Under the control of a France that more and more regained the confidence in its destiny shaken by the Prussian war, Tunis, from its very strategic position opposite Sicily, had aroused fears of practical domination of the Mediterranean at the hands of the growing French fleet. Although the British Admiralty at the time had not shared those fears, the fact that a man like Hanotaux, in office and afterwards, believed that 'Biserta had the Mediterranean by the throat', and the worried Italian felt he might be right, had been a factor of some moment. For a generation the Tunisian question had soured the relations of France and Italy as effectively as the Egyptian question had soured the relations of France and Britain. For a generation the Tunis question had acted as one of the lesser irritants that added perennially to the exacerbation of Anglo-French relations. As a base of operations in the scramble for North Africa, Tunis had raised the hope of the French and caused dismay to the Italians, while, in the end, it played no insignificant part in the train of events leading to a major re-alignment of the great powers.

LANSDOWNE'S POLICY AND THE 1902 AGREEMENT WITH ITALY

The change in Britain's international position between 1899 and 1906 is well known. As the reins of power slipped slowly from Salisbury's hands, his policy of not committing Britain to action in circumstances that could not be foreseen was superseded. The new alignments that emerged owed much to a Mediterranean situation which the developments described in the preceding chapters had helped to create. Less robust souls than Salisbury were filled with alarm at Britain's ostensibly dangerous isolation in a hostile world. As far as the Mediterranean was concerned, the state of relations with France and Italy in particular—both countries with powerful allies and bordering Britain's life-line to the east—left much to be desired at the turn of the century. In Paris, Delcassé professed to be following a 'policy of entente',[1] the thorny problems of Tunis and West Africa had been settled and even the 'parti colonial' (though not Delcassé himself as yet) had finally written off Egypt.[2] War had been avoided. But relations between Britain and France had rarely been so bad. To the perennially irritating squabbling over such questions as Madagascar and Newfound-

---

[1] AAE/GB/RF/1899–1900/T80/Delcassé to Cambon/13 Aug 1899; B.D. 1/238; D.D.F. 1/14/577; ibid., 15/76; Guillen, 'Les Accords coloniaux franco-anglais de 1904 et la naissance de l'entente cordiale', *Revue d'Histoire diplomatique*, vol. 82 (1968) p. 316.

[2] Andrew, *Théophile Delcassé and the Making of the Entente Cordiale*, pp. 103-10.

land, Delcassé added a gratuitous confrontation with a claim
to a coaling station near British-dominated Muscat,[3] planned
a final settlement of the increasingly dangerous question of
Morocco without reference to London, and volunteered a large
loan to build a railroad from Orenburg to Tashkent in the hope
of increasing the Russian threat to India.[4]

Reporting from the other side of the Channel the 'ever
increasing malevolence' of the press there, Cambon feared that
a speedy end to the Boer war would simply give Britain a welcome opportunity to pick a quarrel with France. His Russian
colleague observed that, to judge only from the press, the two
countries were 'on the verge of a rupture'.[5] In the same mood,
the French foreign minister kept urging the council of ministers
to look to the defences of Biserta, Diego Suarez and Indo-China
adding that, if war could not be avoided, it 'should not be for
their part purely defensive' and they should examine the
possibilities of invading England, Egypt or Burma, while
inducing their Russian ally to attack India.[6] But for German
reticence he might even have supported some form of collective
intervention in South Africa, and the consequence of a personal
visit to St. Petersburg in August 1899 was that the alliance with
Russia (which country had been of little real comfort during the
trials of Fashoda and had shown a disconcerting interest in
disarmament) was strengthened to provide for mutual military
assistance against Britain as well as against Germany.[7] All
through 1901 also this dualism in French policy continued.
While Cambon dropped hints to Lansdowne as to the desira-
bility of an amicable agreement in Morocco and Newfoundland,
Delcassé resumed earlier soundings at Berlin for a colonial

[3] Dilks, *Curzon in India*, vol. i, pp. 118-36.
[4] Monger, *The End of Isolation*, p. 4; Andrew, op. cit., pp. 124-5, 137.
[5] AAE/GB/1899–1900/290/Cambon to Delcassé/11 Nov 1899; ibid/538
Very Conf/Delcassé to de Vauvineux/21 Nov 1899; ibid/copy of Despatch
No. 78/de Staal to Russian M.F.G./24 Nov 1899. Cambon wrote bitterly,
'It is only because Russia is not very vulnerable and we offer on all parts of
the globe rich prey for British greed, that we are blamed with the greatest
acrimony'.
[6] Ibid/Note by Delcassé/28 Feb 1900. A council of ministers was formed
to go into these questions.
[7] D.D.F. 1/16/208; ibid/2/3/pp. 601-5; Renouvin, 'L'Orientation de
l'alliance franco-russe en 1900–1901', *Revue d'Histoire diplomatique*, vol. 80
(1966), pp. 193-5; Guillen, op. cit., p. 316. It was due to Delcassé also that
Russia turned down a loan of gold to Britain.

agreement dealing especially with Morocco.[8] Even his policy
towards Italy was, at this time, directed more towards ending
her co-operation with Britain than detaching her from the
Triple Alliance,[9] and the opportunity to do just that seemed at
hand.

For the 'traditional friendship' between London and Rome
had also cooled to a degree without precedent. A chill had
entered into the relations of the two countries even in the time
of the Crispi ministry, and had thereafter become even more
pronounced when it became clear to the Consulta that it could
not rely on British support in any question involving the possibility of conflict with France.[10] But what was the last straw to
the Italians was what they read into the North African convention of 21 March 1899, which, as has been seen, they
interpreted—despite all Salisbury's denials—as a direct threat
to the integrity of Tripoli or its hinterland. France seemed to
them to have been given *carte blanche* in the area.[11] Shortly
before, Canevaro had frankly declared that the occupation of
the hinterland by another power would be 'so extremely fatal to
our interests that no government in Italy would tolerate it'. His
successor, Visconti Venosta, in like vein, asserted that 'after
Tunisia Italy could not tolerate the French occupying Tripoli'.[12]
To the dismayed Italians the trend of events seemed to be
dictating fundamental changes in policy. They had faced France
alone in 1896 over the Tunis negotiations, and the agreement of
that year, as Salvemini has observed, went a long way towards
wiping out one of the motives which had led Italy into the Triple

---

[8] Guillen, *L'Allemagne et le Maroc de 1870 à 1905*, pp. 572-77; Monger,
op. cit., pp. 38-44.
[9] Andrew, op. cit., p. 140.
[10] Marsden, 'Salisbury and the Italians in 1896', *Journal of Modern
History*, vol. 40 (1968), passim.
[11] See chapter 5. Admiral Canevaro and his successors chose not to
remember that the pro-memoria handed to Salisbury on 4 Nov 1898 which
said that, 'If compensation for France [for Fashoda] is looked for to the east
of Lake Tchad in the region south of latitude 15°, touching the extreme north
of the lake then it is a matter which would be perfectly indifferent to Italy';
FO 45/784/214/Currie to Salisbury; B.D. 1/236. Under the 1899 agreement
Britain and France engaged not to acquire territory or influence north of
15°, which barred French designs in the Nile valley and left France free to
do as she wished in a considerable area to the north and north-east of Lake
Tchad.
[12] Ibid.; D.D.I. 3/3/212; Serra, *L'intesa mediterranea del 1902*, pp.
25-7.

Alliance in 1882.[13] Franco-Italian friction had been further
reduced by the end of the commercial war two years later.

Now again in 1899, convinced that France was aiming at
occupying Tripoli or at least diverting her inland trade to Tunis
or Algeria,[14] they came to feel that they could only preserve
Italian interests in Tripoli by direct agreement with France.
For when, to forestall the assumed danger, the Italians asked
both France and Britain for formal engagements not to acquire
territory or political influence 'north of the parallel of latitude
which touches the southern extremity of Fezzan'. Delcassé
naturally refused. He wished 'to avoid damaging the principle
of maintaining the integrity of the Ottoman Empire'. [sic][14]
Salisbury declined at the same time to discuss the future
destination of Tripoli, giving as reasons that its ownership was
not in doubt and that he could not fetter Britain with a promise
of inaction in circumstances impossible to foresee. Italian
pleading for an assurance that Britain 'continued to be in accord
with Italy in desiring to maintain the *status quo* in regard to
countries on the Mediterranean coast' received the stonewall
reply that the Anglo-French agreement had nothing to do with
rights or claims in the region over which Italy was showing
concern.[15] Italian *amour-propre* was further injured by a British
decision to end the use of Italian in Maltese courts of law and
by British policy in China. When Canevaro demanded a naval
base at San-Mun, Salisbury offered diplomatic support but
objected strongly to the use of force, which alone could have
made success possible. The result was a humiliating rebuff to
the Italians from the Tsongli Yamen and a further exacerbation
of their discontent with British policy.[16]

How Britain would attempt to cope with the hostile French
and disgruntled Italians was for the most part decided by

[13] Salvemini, *La politica estera d'Italia dal 1871 al 1915*, p. 112.
[14] B.D. 1/249; Dethan, 'Le Rapprochement franco-italien après la chute
de Crispi jusqu'aux accords Barrère-Visconti Venosta sur le Maroc et la
Tripolitaine (1896–1900)', *Revue d'Histoire diplomatique*, vol. lxx, p. 334.
[15] FO 45/797/Memoranda by Sanderson/4, 10 April 1899; ibid/852/18
Conf/Lansdowne to Currie/3 Feb 1902; B.D. 1/246.252; D.D.I. 3/3/225.226.
247.254.
[16] B.D. 1/60.247; D.D.I. 3/3/156.162.170.178.186.187.192.200; Glanville,
Italy's Relations with England, pp. 88–91. Salisbury wished to conciliate
Italy but feared a counter move by the Japanese; Nish, *The Anglo-Japanese
Alliance*, p. 70.

Salisbury's successor at the Foreign Office. Compared with Salisbury, Lansdowne was at best a very pedestrian minister and had come straight from the War Office, where even he admitted he had not been an unqualified success.[17] His experience as war minister and as Viceroy of India left him convinced that Britain could not, with her own strength alone, meet the danger of action by France's ally, Russia, in India, China and Persia. This led him progressively to replace Salisbury's policies with some of his own, which lacked much of his predecessor's consistency and logic. Thus Salisbury's sense of realism told him that want of mutual interest, apart from increasing mutual antipathy, made an alliance between Britain and Germany impossible. 'Germany', he said, 'is in mortal danger on account of that long undefined frontier of hers on the Russian side. She will never stand by us against Russia; but is always inclined to curry favour with Russia by throwing us over'.[18] Lansdowne, on the other hand, pursued the will-o'-the-wisp of an understanding with Germany to the end of 1901, despite the fact that even the rather vague and harmless Anglo-German agreement on China of 16 October 1900 was being interpreted by Germany in an unexpectedly restrictive way.[19] Equally unrealistic was his sanguine attempt to get the Russians to co-operate to limit the expansion of their own influence, particularly in Persia and China, although both he and Lamsdorff knew that Britain had not the power to compel a halt to that expansion.[20] More

[17] Newton, *Lord Lansdowne*, p. 190. Salisbury's comment on the army Lansdowne and his colleagues sent to South Africa was, 'If we had had an army of Red Indians we should have been in many respects better off'; Salisbury to Curzon, 23 Sep 1901, quoted Dilks, *Curzon in India*, vol. 1, p. 202.
[18] Salisbury to Curzon, 17 Oct 1900, quoted Dilks, op. cit., vol. 1, p. 136. See also B.D. 2/86. Germany's attitude was, to Salisbury, the best of reasons for not quarrelling with France.
[19] B.D. 2/17.77.81.92.93.94; Grenville, *Lord Salisbury and Foreign Policy*, pp. 337, 346-7, 358-62, Balfour, incidentally, would have preferred to join the Triple Alliance rather than conclude an alliance with Japan; Nish, op. cit., p. 305.
[20] Nish, op. cit., pp. 179-80; Grenville, op. cit., p. 402. Marder (in *The Anatomy of British Sea Power*, p. 429) gives comparative naval strengths in the Far East in April 1901 as follows:—

	England	Russia	France	Japan
Battleships	4	5	1	5
Armoured cruisers	2	6	1	4
Cruisers (1st and 2nd class)	11	2	6	10
Destroyers	7	6	1	13

successful, however, was the limitation of Britain's naval commitments in the New World as a result of the Hay-Paunce-fote treaty on Central America in November 1901, which did make war with the Americans almost inconceivable.

The simultaneous negotiation of the alliance with Japan, signed on 30 January 1902, seems also to have had its 'wishful thinkful' element. Having ostensibly convinced himself that British and Japanese policies in the far east were identical, Lansdowne seemed sure that the agreement would help to preserve peace and put out of his mind any argument to the contrary.[21] Superficially the alliance seemed advantageous. It would make an unlikely settlement of Russo-Japanese difficulties, to the assumed detriment of Britain, less likely still. It would make the Russians think twice before advancing further in the Far East (or Central Asia) and, if they clashed with the Japanese, it would reduce Britain's chances of being involved. France, knowing of Britain's commitment, would be far less ready to intervene. The Japanese navy would help protect the interests in China of Britain, whose naval burden would there-fore be reduced—a hope not in fact realised. But what Lans-downe chose to ignore in his haste to sign (only Salisbury prevented him by-passing the cabinet!) was that the Japanese also had rights under the treaty and could now face the pos-sibility of conflict with Russia over Korea with greater equani-mity.[22] If such a war took place, British interests would there-after depend heavily on the goodwill of the victor. Moreover, the chances of Britain being involved in war in unforeseen circum-stances did now exist; her position in Europe and central Asia derived little or no benefit and the dangers of a hostile coalition against her in the Mediterranean were increased.

A not-altogether accurate assessment of Britain's strategic problems lay behind Lansdowne's policies.[23] Behind the pres-sure for an alliance with Germany or Japan and acquiescence in control of the Caribbean by the Americans, lay the conviction that the forces available were inadequate to defend the empire without assistance. The Admiralty was becoming convinced of

---

[21] B.D. 2/102.105.124; Grenville, op. cit., p. 423, chap. 16, passim.
[22] Monger, op. cit., p. 58; Marder, op. cit., pp. 429-30.
[23] See chapter 6.

the necessity for reducing its far eastern and American commitments to concentrate resources where the decisive battles of the future were expected—in home waters and the Mediterranean. Selborne, the First Lord, said that the Dual Alliance, if supported by Germany, would be too strong for the navy. Indeed in 1900 there was much press talk of possible invasion, a contingency discounted by expert opinion. Admiral Fisher declared naval forces inadequate to carry out the new war plan, which involved the concentration of the Channel and Mediterranean fleets at Gibraltar, with a detachment at Malta to check the Russian Black Sea fleet if necessary. Beresford, his second in command in the Mediterranean, even thought the fleet barely sufficient to cope with the Russians alone. The result was a 'Mediterranean scare' in the press that reached its peak in the spring and summer of 1901 with demands for the navy to be placed on a 'war footing'. In August, a War Office assessment of the military needs of the empire, circulated to the cabinet, concluded that offensive action in war could be taken far more effectively against France than Russia and should be aimed mainly at the seizure of naval bases, especially Biserta:

> Biserta the most important of those defended ports, is the French naval base on the southern littoral of the Mediterranean. So long as it remains in French hands, its strategic situation constitutes it a standing menace to our line of communications with India and even to Malta itself. Biserta is the key to the French possessions in North Africa. With Biserta in our hands, the occupation of Tunis would be an easy matter, and in possession of these two places, we could directly menace the overthrowal of French authority throughout both Tunisia and Algeria.[24]

The new war plan of 1 July 1901 also singled out the French fleet as the main target in any possible war, even if the Russian

[24] Cab 38/1/6/Military Needs of the Empire in a war with France and Russia/12 Aug 1901; Marder, op. cit., pp. 396-8; Grenville, op. cit., pp. 403-4; Dilks, op. cit., vol. 1, p. 154. The other ports were Dakar, Martinique, Diego Suarez, Saigon and Noumea. A later survey concluded that a French invasion could have been attempted in March 1900; Cab 38/2/9/Liability of the U.K. to French invasion during the South African war/3 March 1903. In 1901 Britain had 45 battleships in commission or reserve, while the Dual Alliance powers had 43, Germany 14, the U.S.A. 7 and Japan 5. Lansdowne himself said in March 1901 that no policy involving war was possible without the support of another power as long as hostilities in South Africa continued; Monger, op. cit., p. 12.

fleet should be active. In December, the Intelligence Department, in a survey of France's military resources, noted the strategic value of the North African coast and described Biserta as now 'so fortified, armed and equipped as to constitute, next to Toulon, the most secure French naval arsenal in the Mediterranean'. It was thought that the invasion of Britain might seem 'both attractive and feasible' to the French chiefs of staff and Field-Marshal Roberts agreed on 10 January 1902 that this was far from impossible.[25] The Dual Alliance would soon be, on paper, twice as powerful as Britain in the China seas and despondency was further increased by the realisation that the growth of a first-class German navy would, as the First Lord put it in November 1901, 'place Germany in a commanding position if ever we find ourselves at war with France and Russia'.[26] Certainly any possibility of joint action by the navies of the Dual and Triple Alliances, one of Fisher's nightmares, would be a matter of the gravest concern in London. Even the loss of Italian support in the Mediterranean and its transference to the putative enemy, France, might turn that sea into a 'Latin lake'. Yet, at the turn of the year, this was what seemed distinctly possible.[27]

The ebullient, ambitious and excitable new Italian foreign minister, Prinetti, had little of Visconti Venosta's cautious approach to state affairs and could not resist publicising the improvement which had taken place in relations with France. In April 1901 the Italian fleet paid a formal visit to Toulon and,

[25] Cab 38/1/8 Sec/The Military resources of France and probable method of their employment in a war between France and England/27 Dec 1901; ibid/9 Sec/Memo/10 Jan 1902; Marder, op. cit., p. 398 n. 9. Lord Roberts became later the leader of the 'Bolt from the Blue' school which emerged about 1905 in opposition to the 'Blue Water' school which thought the fleet capable of preventing invasion; Marder, *From Dreadnought to Scapa Flow*, vol. 1, p. 345. The Admiralty, not unnaturally, claimed it could prevent a large French army landing; Grenville, op. cit., p. 422.

[26] Cab 37/58/81/Memo by Selborne/4 Sep 1901; Marder, *From Dreadnought to Scapa Flow*, vol. 1, p. 107. There was, however, no war plan as yet directed against the Triple Alliance. Admiralty policy was, in fact to maintain parity with France and Russia combined and rely on the unlikelihood of hostilities with Germany, Japan and the U.S.A.; Monger, op. cit., p. 12.

[27] At the beginning of 1901, Britain had 10 first class battleships and one second class in the Mediterranean (with 10 cruisers and 16 destroyers). The French had 11 battleships and the Russians one, plus the Black Sea Fleet; but the French also had 93 torpedo boats and 2 destroyers, many very fast, while the Russians had two torpedo boats and a further 22 in the Black Sea; Marder, *The Anatomy of British Sea Power*, pp. 399-400, 418. Britain's battleships were increased to 13 in 1902; Glanville, op. cit., p. 108.

in December, Prinetti disclosed to the Italian parliament the existence of a guarantee from the French concerning Tripoli. They would not extend their influence past the line laid down in the Anglo-French convention of 1899 nor interfere with the caravan trade. He went on to say that, 'The friendly relations between the two countries have become such as to make explanations possible between the two governments, as frank as they are satisfactory, on their respective interests in the Mediterranean. . . . And these explanations have led them to declare the perfect concord of their views'.[28] This French guarantee, unknown to the Foreign Office and indeed to Italy's allies, had been given as part of a secret bargain, formalized in an exchange of letters dated 14 and 16 December 1900, by which Italy also engaged not to develop her influence in Tripoli unless France should modify the 'political or territorial condition' of Morocco.[29] Delcassé had exacted a stiff price for his assurance that there would be no expansion eastwards across the Tunisian frontier. He even denied the Italians access to essential French finance until they agreed to re-orientate their foreign policy. During 1901, therefore, Prinetti took an anti-British and anti-German line in Moroccan affairs. In fact, anxious not to miss the assumed opportunity for action in Tripoli while Britain was preoccupied in South Africa, he impatiently pressed the French to 'regulate the Moroccan question'.[30] Inhibited, however, by French 'timidity' in Morocco, he decided to use the increased freedom of action conferred on Italy by the *rapprochement* with France, by the consequently diminished dependence on British goodwill in the Mediterranean and by Britain's own difficulties, to embark on a policy of limited confrontation with the London government. What he intended to do, with the support of the new king, Victor Emmanuel, was to inflate minor incidents into

[28] D.D.F. 2/1/201.549; *La Tribuna* and *Il Popolo romano*, 15 Dec 1901, quoted Serra, op. cit., pp. 33-34, 69-70; Peteani, *La questione libica nella diplomazia europea*, p. 178; Seton-Watson, *Italy from Liberalism to Fascism*, p. 325.

[29] FO 101/94/37 Conf/Currie to Lansdowne/15 March 1902, encls.; D.D.F. 2/1/1.6.17.81.376; Dethan, op. cit., pp. 334-7. Only a veiled public reference to the agreement was made when Visconti Venosta said, on 19 Dec 1900, that Italy supported 'existing conditions' in Tripoli and considered her interests 'to be assured by declarations, quite recently confirmed, and by sufficient guarantees'; B.D. 8/6.

[30] Ibid; D.D.F. 2/1/152; Guillen, *L'Allemagne et le Maroc*, pp. 653-5.

major issues in the hope of profiting from the new international situation and compelling a revision of British policy in a way beneficial to Italy.

This policy, so reminiscent of Crispi's, soon found its opportunities. An unfortunately worded note from the British ambassador at Rome, Lord Currie—on the way an English sea captain had been treated by Italian law officers and the courts— led Prinetti to demand through unofficial channels that he be recalled. The ambassador escaped this fate for the time being only by publicly eating humble pie, withdrawing his note and apologising to the king in person. A second dispute, over reports on the behaviour of the Italian legation in Pekin from *The Times* correspondent, gave Prinetti his pretext to impugn the objectivity of the paper's Rome correspondent also—successfully. For an indignant Wickham Steed was despatched forthwith to Vienna. Yet this procedure, 'enough to make chickens laugh' as the President of the council of ministers remarked, had the desired effect.[31] What Prinetti's accusations had done was to place the British government and press somewhat on the defensive and anxious to show that they were not unsympathetic towards Italy. This gave him an excellent opening to take up the whole question of Italy's relations with Britain, sure that Currie, if not eating out of his hand, would be at least much more pliable. It is worth noting that detailed investigation by an Italian historian has led him to the conclusion that the ambition to occupy Tripoli cannot be considered simply as a desire for colonial expansion. It was designed, he says, to adjust Italy's position among the European powers and to re-establish the 'Mediterranean equilibrium' upset by the occupation of Egypt and Tunis, by the desuetude of the *entente à trois* of 1887 and by France's new forward policy in Morocco.[32]

Up to this moment Lansdowne had followed the lines laid down by Salisbury in his attitude towards Italy and North Africa. When, at the end of 1900, Currie had attempted to get Salisbury to state whether he wished Italian co-operation or

[31] Serra, op. cit., pp. 86-112.

[32] Serra, *L'intesa mediterranea*, pp. 112, 120-21; 'New Sources on Anglo-Italian Relations, 1896-1902', *Occidente*, vol. xi (1955), p. 276. The first work is the most exhaustive on relations between Britain and Italy in this period and has gone deeply into the archives of both countries.

neutrality in any war with France, the prime minister as ever declined to commit himself in advance.[33] The ambassador had then gone on to tackle Lansdowne, listing for his benefit the reasons for Italian 'coolness'. But the new minister also declined any pledge to defend Italy and advised Currie to persevere in showing 'all possible civility and goodwill towards the Italian government.'[34] Prinetti's disclosure of France's guarantee regarding Tripoli, followed by cryptic but thought-provoking remarks to the press from Delcassé, led Lansdowne to suspect that Italian support for France in Morocco was what the French had required in exchange.[35] But there was as yet no apparent change in his general attitude towards Italy. Prinetti, however, now had the bit between his teeth. Convinced that Britain was seriously disturbed over the loss of preponderance in the Mediterranean, which had depended, according to him, on Franco-Italian discord,[36] he subjected Currie to a bitter tirade against the Salisbury government's 'habitual neglect' of Italy. What he particularly objected to was its omission to make any communication respecting the Anglo-French agreement of 1899 and the 'abolition' [sic] of the Italian language in Malta.[37] He did not even bother to dissimulate his objective, an occupation of Tripoli 'on the same terms as England held Egypt or Cyprus', and made it clear that he wished Britain to give assurances regarding the province similar to those made by the French.[38]

[33] LP 227/16/Currie to Barrington/27 Nov 1900; B.D. 1/350.

[34] Ibid.; LP 227/16/Lansdowne to Currie/12 Dec 1900; Newton, op. cit., pp. 212-14. During the negotiations with Germany in May 1901, unwillingness to shoulder the burden of Italian defence was one of the reasons Lansdowne gave why Britain could not enter the Triple Alliance. As late as December, he was proposing an Anglo-German agreement guaranteeing the *status quo* on the shores of the Mediterranean, Adriatic, Aegean and Black Seas—which would have ended Italian hopes of Tripoli or Albania; B.D. 2/82.93; Glanville, op. cit., pp. 99-100.

[35] B.D. 8/6.8. On 1 January 1902, Barrère, the active French ambassador at Rome, also stated publicly, 'The period of Franco-Italian misunderstanding in the field where their vital interests are involved belongs henceforth to the past and there exists a perfect harmony of views between the two governments. There are therefore no Mediterranean questions any more between France and Italy . . .'; D.D.F. 2/2/5.

[36] D.D.F. 2/1/587; Peteani, op. cit., pp. 206, 209-10. Barrère and others shared this opinion; D.D.F. 2/2/57.

[37] Victor Emmanuel spoke to the same effect; FO 45/853/1 and 8 Conf/ Currie to Lansdowne/1, 5 Jan 1902; B.D. 1/355.356.

[38] FO 101/94/2 Conf/Currie to Lansdowne/1 Jan 1902; FO 800/857/Tel 1 Conf/Currie to Lansdowne/2 Jan 1902; B.D. 8/4. Prinetti concealed his intention to obtain Turkish acquiescence by threats; Serra, op. cit., pp. 130-31.

Currie was moved to comment on the prevailing optimism in Rome, which he contrasted with the despondency of a few months previously.[39]

Prinetti's ostensibly reckless histrionics, of which Crispi would no doubt have approved, had at first little effect. Lansdowne, of course, could guess at the nature of the Franco-Italian agreement of 1900 from guarded references made to it at the time by Visconti Venosta.[40] After all, Britain too had been asked for, and refused, a similar assurance. But he could not know whether Prinetti's recent announcement of France's guarantee left unsaid that there were now other far-reaching secret understandings with that country. Yet he seemed at first genuinely puzzled why the French assurances should have caused so much general excitement.[41] The estimate of the situation he passed to Salisbury, fairly accurate though he could not be sure of that, was clearly influenced by information supplied by the Austrians:

> It looks indeed as if the Italians were parading a somewhat mythical assurance alleged to have been received from France in the hope of obtaining a substantial assurance to the same effect from England.[42]

For Prinetti had just sketched out the terms of the declaration he desired, which stipulated that Britain would not 'in any eventuality' expand beyond the limits laid down in the Anglo-French convention of 1899, especially towards the Vilayet of Tripoli. This, of course, was just the declaration of disinterest refused by Salisbury to Canevaro and it was again resisted. Lansdowne would by now have willingly re-assured Prinetti, but he and Salisbury agreed that they could go no further than make a statement that the 1899 convention did not touch Tripoli or affect the interests 'present or prospective' of other powers.[43]

[39] FO 800/132/Currie to Lansdowne/24 Dec 1901.
[40] See note 29.
[41] FO 403/322/13/7/Lansdowne to Plunkett/7 Jan 1902; B.D. 8/8. Bertie and Currie were also not concerned; FO 800/173/Memo by Bertie/22 Dec 1901; LP 227/16/132/Currie to Lansdowne/24 Dec 1901. Salisbury himself was unmoved by German allegations that Britain was now 'even more isolated' in the Mediterranean; Peteani, op. cit., pp. 207-8.
[42] FO 101/94/9 Sec/Lansdowne to Plunkett/14 Jan 1902; ibid/Lansdowne to Salisbury/15 Jan 1902.
[43] FO 45/857/Tel 3/Currie to Lansdowne/13 Jan 1902; FO 101/94/Lansdowne to Salisbury/15 Jan 1902; ibid/Tel 3/Lansdowne to Currie/20 Jan 1902; FO 45/852/18 Conf/Lansdowne to Currie/3 Feb 1902; B.D. 1/359.

The prime minister was particularly anxious to avoid any public statement which could be held to affect the poorly demarcated Egypt-Tripoli frontier, since it would, as he put it, cause France to 'blaze up'.[44] When Prinetti attempted to get Britain's proffered statement amended so as to secure for Italy 'the reversion of Tripoli', Lansdowne objected that this contradicted treaty obligations to Turkey. He cast doubt, and with some justice, on Prinetti's assertion that Austria, Germany and France had all given assurances that left the Italians 'free to select their own time for realizing their designs'. The declaration asked for, he said, was impossible.[45]

Yet there were signs that Lansdowne was reconsidering his Italian policy. Part of Salisbury's political credo had, of course, been to eschew pledges to great powers possibly involving war in unforeseen circumstances and to preserve the integrity, for as long as possible, of the shaky Muslim states along the Mediterranean high road to the far east. To those in the cabinet not wedded to the Salisbury tradition, the international situation already discussed and their assessment of defence problems seemed to indicate the sort of radical change of policy envisaged in the abortive alliance negotiations with Germany. It must be remembered that, in January 1902, the situation in Manchuria again looked serious and Lansdowne was pressing hard for the conclusion of the Japanese negotiations, so that the knowledge of Britain's far eastern alliance would act as a 'sobering warning' to Russia.[46] That there was now less talk of war with France did not mean that Anglo-French relations were good either, simply ultra-correct and handled gingerly on both sides. But the French were still seething. Monson, the ambassador at Paris, drew attention in January to the Anglophobia permeating the Chamber of Deputies. Even Delcassé himself was on edge until March under the belief that Britain (with German support) was preparing a protectorate over Morocco—the one development which he thought would force France to draw the

[44] Ibid.; FO 101/94/Tel 1/Lansdowne to Currie/9 Jan 1902; ibid/Tel 8/Cromer to Lansdowne/14 Jan 1902. Because of Egypt, Salisbury drew Cromer into the discussions.

[45] FO 45/847/Tel 6/Currie to Lansdowne/21 Jan 1902; ibid/Tel 5 Conf/Lansdowne to Currie/24 Jan 1902; ibid/852/18 Conf/Lansdowne to Currie/3 Feb 1902; B.D. 1/359/.

[46] Nish, op. cit., p. 215. The treaty was signed on 30 Jan 1902.

sword.[47] As for Germany, a bitter 'war of words', as Holstein called it, came into being in the aftermath of the alliance negotiations, with Chamberlain and Bülow indulging their rancour in public and opinion in both countries not slow to respond. As a consequence, the Admiralty began to question in the spring whether a navy capable of coping with the Dual Alliance alone was sufficient.[48] It is easy to see, therefore, that active Italian hostility would be unwelcome in the extreme to the British government at this juncture, especially if linked to French hostility, and Lansdowne would do much to avoid it. As the Director of Naval Intelligence, Prince Louis of Battenberg, said, a year later, 'no more formidable coalition could be brought against us in the Mediterranean' than France, Italy and Spain.[49]

It is difficult to find any precise statement from British records as to why policy changed,[50] but evidence of the change itself is clear. 'It would be undesirable', minuted Lansdowne on 15 January, 'to snub the Italian government just now.' A fortnight later, apparently as a direct result of the breach between Britain and Germany, Chamberlain, in a parliamentary speech fulsome with praise for the traditional friendship with Italy, withdrew the Maltese language decree which he had maintained for three stubborn years. 'I trust', said Lansdowne to the Italian ambassador, 'that we shall not be less successful in dealing with any other causes of difficulty'.[51] On the question of Tripoli, he

[47] FO 425/254/14 (31 Conf)/Monson to Lansdowne/24 Jan 1902; Andrew, op. cit., p. 187; Monger, op. cit., pp. 74-75; Guillen, 'Les Accords franco-anglais', op. cit., pp. 324-5.

[48] FO 800/115/Strictly Conf/Holstein to Chirol/3 Jan 1902; B.D. 2/96; Rich, *Friedrich von Holstein*, vol. 2, pp. 665-69; Monger, op. cit., pp. 67-69. Though the Anglo-Japanese alliance of 30 January was calculated, in Lansdowne's view, to prevent a violent disturbance of the *status quo* in the Far East, it could also—if successful in this—divert Russian ambitions, as the Germans feared, back to Europe, the Mediterranean and the Near East; Ibid; FO/45/852/26 Conf/Lansdowne to Currie/12 Feb 1902.

[49] Monger, op. cit., p. 131. Salvemini and Peteani are agreed that Britain had to assure herself of at least Italian friendship in the Mediterranean and prevent Italy falling under predominant French influence; Peteani, op. cit., p. 214.

[50] Lansdowne's private correspondence with Currie covering the period when the discussion was made had unfortunately been mislaid.

[51] FO 45/852/12/Lansdowne to Currie/29 Jan 1902; ibid/857/Tel 6/Currie to Lansdowne/21 Jan 1902; Amery, *Life of Chamberlain*, vol. 4, pp. 176-8; Wickham Steed, *Through Thirty Years*, vol. 1, pp. 159-64; Peteani, op. cit., p. 209; Glanville, op. cit., pp. 88-9, 112-13. Britain was also attempting to meet Italian wishes in Africa and showing consideration for Italian susceptibilities in several other instances; Serra, op. cit., pp. 147-8, 162.

now began to give ground and declared himself ready to give an assurance that Britain, though still supporting the *status quo*, would endeavour to see that any unavoidable change should not be 'to the detriment of Italian interests'.[52] When Prinetti replied that the phrase 'in conformity with Italian interests' was preferable, Lansdowne and Salisbury conferred, gave their assent and, to obviate a possible breach of treaties with Tripoli's Turkish overlord, stipulated that any support of Italian interests should only be 'so far as was compatible with conventional obligations'.[53] A major step had been taken and the two statesmen knew very well what they were doing. Lansdowne frankly acknowledged that the 'Italian interests' concerned were of a 'land grabbing' character, while Salisbury saw only too clearly that his correctitude as to Britain's legal obligations towards the Porte could only serve to 'save their face'.[54] Obviously, if any alteration in the *status quo* was to be 'in conformity with Italian interests', the time would surely come when Italy would be unable to resist the temptation to ensure that such an alteration became necessary. All this is very far indeed from Salisbury's 1899 policy when, discussing the Libyan desert, he had said sternly, '. . . we certainly could not put on record what we think ought to be done with it in case Turkey goes to pieces. It is the oddest interpretation of the engagements we entered into in the Treaty of Paris.'[55] But then it was Lansdowne who, though deferring to Salisbury on points of detail, was really deciding the main lines of policy now and the aged and ailing prime minister was on the verge of retirement.

[52] FO 45/852/18 Conf/Lansdowne to Currie/3 Feb 1902; B.D. 1/359. Lansdowne's actual words were, 'I am therefore ready to give a positive assurance that His Majesty's Government have no aggressive or ambitious designs in regard to the Vilayet of Tripoli, that they continue to be sincerely desirous of maintaining the *status quo* there as in other parts of the coast of the Mediterranean, and that, if at any time an alteration of the *status quo* should become inevitable, it would be their object that such alteration should not be of a nature to operate to the detriment of Italian interests'.
[53] FO 45/857/11 Conf/Currie to Lansdowne/9 Feb 1902; FO 101/94/ Lansdowne to Salisbury/10 Feb 1902; FO 403/322/74 (Tel 8)/Lansdowne to Currie/12 Feb 1902.
[54] Ibid.
[55] FO 45/797/Sanderson Memoranda/4, 10 April 1899; ibid/65/Salisbury to Currie/25 April 1899; B.D. 1/251. It must be said, also, that Salisbury's reasons for refusing a declaration to Italy had been largely negatived by France's pledge to non intervention; FO 101/94/4 Conf/Currie to Lansdowne/ 2 Jan 1902; B.D. 8/5.

For an unstable character already ill with the disease that was to paralyse him in a few months,[56] Prinetti had not played his cards badly. He had revealed what mattered in the French guarantee. Yet he repeatedly refused requests to show Lansdowne the text or say when it had been signed, even while suggesting a similar guarantee from Britain.[57] Lansdowne had, therefore, no means of guessing accurately the extent of Italy's reciprocal commitments to France and this uncertainty can be seen in his attempts to glean any available bits of information from Deym, the Austrian ambassador.[58] Prinetti scooped up one further dividend from this favourable situation when he succeeded in watering down Salisbury's proviso as to 'conventional obligations' by substituting the less precise phrase, 'obligations resulting from the treaties which at present form part of the public law of Europe'.[59] What, of course, was painfully absent from the declaration as it now stood was any *quid pro quo* for Britain, any assurance that Italy would not pocket her gains and turn her back on Britain in the Mediterranean in favour of her new French friend. Even as Lansdowne was ascertaining that the armed forces and Lord Cromer could see no objection to the proposed declaration, there came the rather hurtful and ostensibly ungrateful final refusal by Prinetti to divulge the text of the French declaration. A tantalizing extract was read to Currie, which, as it were, rubbed salt in the wound. Lansdowne therefore decided to make Britain's assent to the new declaration dependent on the addition of a new vital clause which read:

> This assurance is given on the understanding and in full confidence that Italy on her part has not entered and will not enter into arrangements with other powers in regard to this or other

[56] Serra, 'New Sources on Anglo-Italian Relations', op. cit., p. 275.

[57] FO 101/94/Tel. 3, 36/Lansdowne to Currie/20 Jan, 7 Mar 1902; FO 45/857/Tel. 9/Lansdowne to Currie/19 Feb 1902; ibid/Tel. 15/Currie to Lansdowne/21 Feb 1902; B.D. 1/360. The information that Italy's draft declaration of 13 January was 'identical' left Lansdowne unmoved, and he suspected he was being asked for a wider guarantee than the French had given; FO 45/857/Tel. 9/Lansdowne to Currie/19 Feb 1902.

[58] FO 403/322/13 (7)/Lansdowne to Plunkett/7 Jan 1902; FO 101/94/9 Sec/Lansdowne to Plunkett/14 Jan 1902; ibid/17 Conf/29 Jan 1902; FO 45/587/19/19 Feb 1902.

[59] FO 45/857/Tels. 12 Conf, 13, 15/Currie to Lansdowne/15, 18, 21 Feb 1902. There were also a few modifications of geographical terms in the interests of accuracy.

portions of the coast of the Mediterranean of a nature inimical to British interests.[60]

Few more powerful inducements could have been found to ensure that Italian policy would not clash with that of Britain in the future, for as long at least as Tripoli remained Turkish. Few more satisfactory assurances could have been devised, in the circumstances, that the existing Franco-Italian under-standing contained nothing harmful to Britain. When, a few days after Currie handed the completed declaration to Prinetti on 11 March,[61] the Italian minister finally allowed Lansdowne to look into the mouth of the horse he had just purchased, he was to find the animal a little long in the tooth. Reading at last the text of the French guarantee and realising it had been given as far back as December 1900, Lansdowne exclaimed, 'It was the old Visconti Venosta affair after all!'[62] He made the dubious claim later that he had really known all along.[63] But the fact is that Prinetti had effectively exploited the international situation to get the *rapprochement* with Britain he wanted and that his playing on Foreign Office fears of non-existent Italian pledges to France had an element of the confidence trickster about it.

The understanding arrived at was of far greater significance than would appear at first sight. Superficially all that had happened was that Britain had made a spontaneous and uni-lateral declaration to reassure the Italians rather than a carefully negotiated agreement. But the judgement of Salvemini, endorsed by Peteani and Serra, is that the understanding was such as to bear comparison with the now defunct Mediterranean Agree-ment of 1887.[64] The first noticeable consequence was an immedi-ate and appreciable improvement in Anglo-Italian relations.

[60] FO 101/94/Sec/FO to Admiralty/26 Feb 1902; ibid/Lansdowne to Salisbury/4 Mar 1902; FO 403/322/126 (36)/Lansdowne to Currie/7 Mar 1902; B.D. 1/360. The failure to communicate the Franco-Italian agreement on Morocco, which was generally assumed to exist, was regarded by Lansdowne as 'fishy'; Monger, op. cit., p. 74.

[61] FO 170/595/Currie to Prinetti/11 Mar 1902; FO 101/94/37 Conf/Currie to Lansdowne/15 Mar 1902. The full text is printed in B.D. 1/360.

[62] Ibid. Prinetti also said that, as regards Morocco, he had only given France a simple assurance of disinterest; B.D. 1/361.

[63] LP/227/16/cancelled draft/Lansdowne to Rodd/5 June 1902. 'I have always believed', wrote Lansdowne, 'that the Italian government did not really get much more out of the French government than they had already obtained, although it suited her convenience to make a splash about it.'

[64] Serra, *L'intesa mediterranea*, p. 185; Peteani, op. cit., p. 218.

Speaking for the government in the House of Lords, Lansdowne said that there was 'no country that they wished to be or were on more friendly terms with than Italy'. 'The word alliance', responded the semi official *Tribuna* in Rome, 'is not too strong notwithstanding the absence of any formal and written agreements', a view Lansdowne's parliamentary under-secretary, Lord Cranborne, thought very sound. Prinetti himself added to the chorus with a reply to a question in the chamber to the effect that Anglo-Italian relations 'could never have been more cordial and intimate' than at that moment.[65] The net result was that, for the immediate future, Britain's position in the Mediterranean was improved, particularly as the fleet was being simultaneously strengthened. In addition, Lansdowne's fears of increased Franco-Russian hostility, as a consequence of his treaty with Japan, were relieved. The retort of the two powers was only a feeble declaration (on 16 March), from which it was clear the French were refusing to back further Russian adventures in the far east,[66] and it is at least logical to presume that the Russians in turn would not fall over themselves to support French interests in the Mediterranean. Even Delcassé's reaction to the news that Prinetti had received some form of guarantee from Britain concerning Tripoli was muted. This, despite his sensitivity and suspicion towards any improvement in Anglo-Italian relations, was because he thought erroneously that Lansdowne had conceded far less than in fact he had.[67]

More important, however, were the signs that new alignments between the European powers were taking shape, involving Britain, and centred on the Mediterranean. The catalyst was Italy, and, as Britain drew closer to that country in the Mediterranean, so did France. Of course, Italy still remained a member of the Triple Alliance, since no government in Rome could have risked a complete break with the central powers. But the alliance was renewed without change on 28 June even though Prinetti had made urgent pleas for modifications.[68] Full of

---

[65] FO 45/855/*Tribuna* extract, with minutes/23 June 1902; D.D.F. 2/2/153; Glanville, op. cit., p. 122.

[66] See note 27; Nish, op. cit., p. 238.

[67] D.D.F. 2/1/534.572.533; ibid/2/2/152; Andrew, op. cit., pp. 187-9.

[68] Albertini, *The Origins of the War of 1914*, vol. I, pp. 120-4; Peteani, op. cit., chap. 12. Prinetti asked for a public declaration, for France's benefit, of the defensive character of the alliance and for *carte blanche* in Tripoli, in

resentment, the Italian minister impetuously decided to take his understanding with France a stage further, something again fortuitously facilitated by the improvement in his relations with Britain. For Delcassé was by now absolutely determined to strengthen his links with Rome, convinced that Lansdowne was trying to erode French influence with Italy, as well as with Morocco and Spain. He was therefore prepared for a far-reaching agreement, without stubbornly insisting, as on previous occasions, on a formal withdrawal by Italy from the Triple Alliance.

On his side, Prinetti, with the same touch of chicanery he had shown in his negotiations with Lansdowne, promised an end to military arrangements made with the central powers against France—without mentioning that they had already provisionally lapsed. The result was the exchange, on 30 June 1902, of the so-called 'Prinetti-Barrère' notes, by which the two powers gave each other a free hand in Tripoli and Morocco respectively. Each pledged herself also to neutrality, if the other should be attacked or 'should find herself compelled, in defence of her honour or her security, to take the initiative of a declaration of war.[69] Only a 'veritable act of madness' by the French, as Prinetti put it, could now take Italy into war against them, and it is clear that he had, on a legal pretence, evaded obligations to Germany which hitherto might be said to have existed in the spirit, if not the letter, of the Triple Alliance. The agreement also altered the military balance between France and Germany. Taking all into account, Barrère certainly had a point when he said that the Anglo-Italian agreement was linked by invisible threads with that between France and Italy.

It can be argued with some force that similar invisible threads linked the new Franco-Italian agreement and the entente between Britain and France two years later. In Paris it was as clear as it was to the Foreign Office that the Italians would take any opportunity that came along to cash their various 'promis-

addition to guarantees on Italian interests in the Balkans and a satisfactory commercial treaty. Two days after the renewal of the alliance, the Austrians did give a declaration of disinterest in Tripoli and Cyrenaica.

[69] D.D.F. 2/2/168.194.329. annex pp. 692-9; Serra, *Camille Barrère*, chap. 5, *L'intesa mediterranea*, pp. 190-9; Andrew, op. cit., pp. 186-9; Albertini, op. cit., pp. 125-32.

sory notes' regarding Tripoli. Indeed, a bare month after Britain's declaration, Prinetti was attempting to obtain Turkish agreement for the flow of Italian emigrants to be directed to Tripoli and for special privileges to be granted enabling them to form a sort of 'self governing' colony.[70] It is not surprising therefore that there should be, in July, discussions in the Quai d'Orsay on policy to follow in the event of an Italian move in Tripoli and the consequent almost irresistible pressure for a French move to obtain 'compensation' in Morocco. Under a plan that was drawn up, the aim was to get Spanish support for the *status quo*, for agreed zones of influence in case Morocco should disintegrate and for subsequent diplomatic co-operation to face claims, especially from Germany and Britain. To soothe the latter, Tangier could be neutralised, commercial freedom guaranteed and further 'elements complementary to an entente' found, probably in Africa. A week later, Cambon, on his own initiative, tested Lansdowne's reaction to a proposal along these lines, and found the British minister 'perfectly ready to discuss the subject' in the 'frankest possible manner'. Delcassé's approval was obtained and negotiations began. 'It will be long,' wrote Cambon, 'it will give rise to much bargaining, but at last we are talking and that's a lot.'[71]

He was, of course, right and any idea of a comprehensive settlement of outstanding disputes in the immediate future was still something of a pipe dream. But in a little over a year and a half the discussions thus begun were to produce that very result. In part this was owing to the hard bargaining anticipated by Cambon. In part it was owing to changed circumstances— Spanish reluctance to collaborate through fear of British reactions, increasing British antipathy towards Germany and especially the realisation in Paris and London that discord between them was more and more dangerous at a time when their respective allies were on a collision course in the far east. It is difficult not to agree substantially with Dethan when he

[70] FO 101/94/172 Conf/O'Conor to Lansdowne/10 April 1902; ibid/73/ Currie to Lansdowne/21 April 1902; ibid/168/Lansdowne to Currie/14 May 1902; FO 403/322/220 (187)/Lansdowne to O'Conor/28 May 1902. Lansdowne had informed the Turks that he still supported the *status quo* and respect for conventional obligations.
[71] B.D. 2/321.322; D.D.F. 2/2/333.369; Cambon, *Correspondance*, vol. 2, pp. 75-6; Newton, op. cit., p. 267; Guillen, op. cit., pp. 670-1.

expresses the view that the Anglo-French agreement of 1899 gave a marked impetus to the Italian movement towards France and that the 'new ties uniting us [the French] in the Mediterranean with our latin sister precipitated the conclusion of the Entente Cordiale'.[72]

What Lansdowne had done in 1902, therefore, was to commence building an alien structure on the foundations laid by Salisbury. For if there was any one consistent thread in Salisbury's policies after his return to power in 1895, it was the progressive settlement of the numerous questions in dispute with France. Milestones on this road to a better understanding were the agreements concerning Siam, Tunis, the Niger and the Upper Nile, in spite of the fact that the second and third were the outcome of hard-fought and sometimes acrimonious negotiations and the fourth involved a major diplomatic humiliation for the French. That this trend was to reach its logical conclusion in a comprehensive bargain, while Lansdowne was in office, was not the result of any statesmanlike assessment of Britain's needs and opportunities. The digressions of the abortive negotiations for a German alliance and the approach to Russia are evidence enough to the contrary. In fact the expediency of the moment and a disposition to heed the gloomy prognostications of military and naval experts in a way that would have been quite foreign to Salisbury seemed to dominate Lansdowne's judgement. Yet the 1902 agreement with Italy, coming as it did so soon after the settlement with the Americans and the alliance with the Japanese, was not in its way an illogical sequel to earlier developments. For Salisbury's agreements with France were largely instrumental in propelling the Italians, willy-nilly, into the agreements they made with France—from that over Tunis in 1896 to the Tripoli-Morocco arrangement of 1900. It was, therefore, a little ironic that the Franco-Italian *rapprochement* itself should have been used so effectively by Prinetti to extract from Lansdowne his declaration on Tripoli and so restore close relations with Britain. The chain reaction was still not complete. Better Anglo-Italian relations in turn played their part in producing the Prinetti-Barrère notes on Tripoli and Morocco, involving in addition no less than the

[72] Dethan, op. cit., p. 333.

emasculation of the Triple Alliance itself. A major diplomatic
upheaval was under way and the stage was set for the final
resolution of colonial differences between Britain and France
that was in the end to mean so much. It is, however, a little
alarming to reflect that Salisbury's policies—of bolstering up
backward but strategically important states and keeping aloof
from military alliances—should have been discarded by a man
whose ideas often seemed so dominated by military expediency
that he seemed unaware of the possible long-term consequences
of his innovations. He could have done worse than remember
the dictum of his predecessor:

> If you believe the doctors, nothing is wholesome; if you
> believe the theologians, nothing is innocent; or if you believe
> the soldiers, nothing is safe. They all require to have their strong
> wine diluted by a large admixture of common sense.[73]

[73] Ryan, 'The Marquis of Salisbury', *History Today*, 1951, p. 36.

APPENDIX

Tunis and Salisbury's Conduct of Foreign Policy

There is no such thing as a fixed policy, because policy like all organic entities is always in the making . . . Politics is a matter of business; our allies should be those most likely to help and not hinder the interests of which we, as a Government, are the trustees.[1]

Salisbury's words are those of a man who, for over a quarter of a century, showed himself a superb craftsman in the art of policy making. He was above all things a realist and he went out into the 'market place' of international politics determined to get the best bargain possible. He expected to make no gains without paying for them, but he did insist that the price should be a fair one. His basically religious outlook was tempered by the assiduity of a keen lawyer protecting the interests of his clients. 'Egypt', he once remarked characteristically, 'is argumentatively a tough nut to crack . . . It is part of the great problem of modern diplomacy—how to exclude the Turk from any kind of power in provinces of the Turkish Empire, while strenuously maintaining its independence and integrity.'[2] A despatch from Salisbury's pen was usually a model of precision, but let anyone beware who thought he could assume any obligation not stated in as many words. The Siamese agreement of January 1896 is a good example of this. In spite of it being widely hailed as a great concession to France, British interests in Siam had not been sacrificed. The simultaneous promise to discuss a revision of the Anglo-Tunisian treaty of 1875, assumed by many in France to herald a surrender of British rights, was no more than Salisbury was already bound to do under the terms of the treaty itself. Discussion clearly meant discussion and not an obligation to agree to any change in existing conditions.[3] If

[1] B.D. 6, p. 780.   [2] SnP 268/11/to Sanderson/23 April 1897.
[3] In the same way the 'promises' of 1878 were that Britain would not oppose the legitimate extension of French influence, not that Britain would help France to acquire Tunisia.

this raising of false hopes smacks of sharp practice, it should in fairness to Salisbury be remembered that he was scrupulous in not promising what he had no right to promise. He objected strongly to Waddington talking in 1878 as if he were making him 'a liberal wedding present' of Tunis and he would likewise never give the Italians hope of support for the acquisition of Tripoli. All the pressure of the Triple Alliance in 1890 would only induce him to give a cautious and veiled hint that there might be no British objection to possible Italian gain, if some catastrophe were to overwhelm the Ottoman empire.

Salisbury's methods, however, were by no means perfect. There is no doubt now that fears once held of large-scale deficiencies in the record of his diplomacy were without foundation; but Lady Gwendoline Cecil was still right in saying that he would not infrequently 'conduct the opening and most critical phase of a negotiation exclusively in personal interviews or private letters[4] . . .' This was partly owing to an innate tendency towards secretiveness, but equally no doubt to his belief that there were occasions when the taking of notes inhibited discussion. Cabinet meetings were a case in point and there were no minutes. What made this dislike of notetaking sometimes dangerous in his conduct of foreign affairs was that he would on occasion share with a foreign diplomat the delight he took in speculative discussions on the future trend of events. According to his daughter he was 'careless of giving considered expression to his opinions', though he would resent having casual opinions later quoted in evidence.[5] It is not to be wondered at that misunderstandings occurred. Conversations which Salisbury regarded as private or exploratory were taken seriously as official communications. At Berlin in 1878, he told Waddington that he would not block a French occupation of Tunis should the way otherwise be clear. What he was seeking to prove to the French was that he was not trying to disturb the balance of power in the Mediterranean. Waddington, however, returned to Paris believing he had Tunis 'in his pocket'. When it is remembered that, in a subsequent conversation, Salisbury failed

[4] Cecil, *Life of Salisbury*, vol. 3, p. 20.
[5] Quoted Penson, *Foreign Affairs under Salisbury*, p. 10. SP 26/Salisbury to Lyons/24 July 1878.

to make the experienced French ambassador, d'Harcourt, understand his point of view, the suspicion is inevitable that the lucidity and precision he displayed on paper were not so much in evidence when he negotiated verbally. Most notorious of all, it goes without saying, was the fanciful 'plan' for dividing up the Ottoman empire that Hatzfeldt reported in 1895, though in that case the German ambassador must take a large share of the blame. For it was grand strategy, the 'larger prescriptions of national interest', that exercised Salisbury's mind. All else was subordinate, unless public opinion, which he always took most seriously, were involved.

Thus, when the initial decision was made in 1878 to give France some encouragement in Tunis, the interests of the 'English colony', of the Maltese and of commerce generally, were hardly considered. In 1890 the Tunis 'card' was in his hand, ready to be played, until protests from the chambers of commerce brought him up sharply, and the settlement of 1897 took into account only those interests able to exert political pressure. Individuals were likewise pawns in the diplomatic game, as his treatment of Wood bears witness. To keep the British agent completely ignorant of the exchanges at Berlin and after regarding Tunis, while denying any 'offer' to France and telling him to reassure the Bey, may have been technically 'correct'. It may have been intended to indicate to the French that any 'promise' he had made applied to a contingency possibly remote; but it involved also summarily ending the long career of a public servant in circumstances bound to cause mental distress. At least there was generous compensation for Wood, and this compares favourably with the shabby treatment meted out by the Gladstone government to Wood's unfortunate successor, Reade, including the unsavoury negotiations behind the back of the consul-general.

Someone who was accorded hardly more deference by Salisbury than lesser diplomatic subordinates was the military 'expert'. For, in his prime, with each policy he put forward supported by long hours of 'homework' at Hatfield, Salisbury controlled policy in some detail. As his daughter remarked, his 'overmastering desire to bring every detail within the grasp of his own comprehension gave to him . . . the power that comes

APPENDIX

APPENDIX   255

with knowledge'.[6] It seemed to follow quite naturally that the
'strong wine' of the expert had to be diluted by a 'large ad-
mixture of common sense'. That common sense he appeared
confident he could provide and, by and large, he was right. In the
middle of the twentieth century he would, no doubt, have received the grammatically dubious accolade of being 'unflappable'.
In practice, he was apt to reject professional advice which
suggested that Britain's forces were incapable of meeting their
traditional responsibilities—perhaps a healthy corrective to that
tendency in the government to exaggerate the power of rivals
and especially of Russia. Thus he was not particularly concerned about Biserta in 1878, and accepted without protest the
revolutionary idea, for 1891, that a naval base there would be no
threat to the Mediterranean balance of power. Yet shortly after
he challenged with the utmost vigour the naval doctrine that
the fleet could no longer, if asked, invest the Straits, and only
accepted it, still protesting, four years later. On the other hand,
while Sir John Ardagh fretted in 1897 over the progress being
made by Marchand, Salisbury was quite calm. 'I suspect the
whole thing of being a bogy', he remarked coolly. 'The judgement of the War Office in this matter is slightly biased by a
desire for something brilliant.'[7] In the aftermath of Fashoda he
did not think of questioning the reports that an invasion of
Egypt from a base in Tunis was not very practicable.

With his colleagues in the cabinet he was less assertive, which
was unfortunate, for on the whole they were men of lesser
stature. His influence on the work of departments other than his
own was limited, even when prime minister, if only because he
felt it unwise to 'jog the elbow' of anyone engaged in carrying
out a task. This was serious enough when it involved no more
than a free hand for the colonial office to pursue a policy in
Africa with quite a different emphasis to his own. It was cata-
strophic for the ordinary evolution of policy when Chamberlain
began to interfere in foreign affairs, as he began to do in the

---

[6] Cecil, *Biographical Studies*, p. 50.
[7] SnP 268/11/Min. by Salisbury/18 Sep 1897. In April he had argued
against a bellicose policy in South Africa, saying, 'I am astounded at reading
the recommendations of Sir John Ardagh. I suppose he represents the dominant view of the Horse Guards. . . . I cannot conceive of a more unwise
policy'; LP 277/29/to Lansdowne/21 April 1897.

Tunis negotiations in 1897.[8] Indeed, some months earlier, when Salisbury had proposed sending Sir Harry Johnston as high commissioner to South Africa rather than as consul-general to Tunis, Chamberlain (probably at Rhodes' instigation) succeeded in getting the major post for Milner.[9] It is tempting to advance the opinion that if Salisbury had shown a little more determination on this single issue the Boer war might not have taken place.

The way in which policy developed under Salisbury strongly suggests that what mattered to him was the 'immediate interest of his country' and that this was worked out without over-elaborate calculations of what the future might hold. Curzon's bitter criticism of him is now well known. 'There are no settled principles of policy', he complained, 'in relation to any part of the world; and everyone from the exalted head down to the humblest clerk sits there anxiously waiting to see what will turn up next.'[10] What Curzon criticised was perhaps the very quality that made for success in Salisbury's conduct of affairs. For it is debatable whether any genius has ever been born who could enunciate 'principles' on which the complex issues affecting the foreign relations of a country can be decided. Without any doubt the hapless flounderings of Gladstone and Granville in their almost laughable attempts to decide questions like the Enfida case on principles of abstract justice were no commendation. Indeed there were so many divisions of opinion based on principle in the Liberal administrations of 1892–1895, that clearly only Rosebery's exclusive control over foreign affairs and his determination to follow in Salisbury's footsteps prevented even more chaotic policies than before.

Even so Salisbury certainly had what might be called working rules which were the results of empirical reasoning rather than abstract principle. The fact of democratic government meant to him that he could not pledge his country to go to war in circumstances which could not be foreseen; since the sovereign parliament might repudiate any such undertaking. This did not mean that he was isolationist in outlook, for he was always

---

[8] Marsden, *Britain and the End of the Tunis Treaties*, pp. 70-71.
[9] SP/Johnston to Salisbury/16 Feb 1897; A. Johnston, *Life and Letters of Sir Harry Johnston*, pp. 154-5; Oliver, *Sir Harry Johnston*, p. 115.
[10] Grenville, *Lord Salisbury and Foreign Policy*, p. 297.

ready to co-operate with other powers to further mutual interests. It was characteristic of him to remark somewhat irreverently, as he did on one occasion when there was a danger of offending Roman Catholics in the Mediterranean, that the Pope was 'to be looked upon in the light of a big gun, to be kept in good order and turned the right way'.[11] Thus between 1887 and 1892, he secured the practical support of Germany and Austria and was conscious of paying for it by maintaining an 'unprofitable and slightly onerous' partnership in the Mediterranean with the Italians. Incidents, like those over the Tunis schools decrees, showed that his determination to preserve the peace, if not absolute, was real. Relations with France were not to be allowed to deteriorate until hostilities were inevitable; Italy was not to be allowed to use the arms of her powerful friends to increase her territories in North Africa. Salisbury's simple rules ensured flexibility in his approach to the duties of his office and were reinforced by a realistic outlook. While, therefore, he desired in 1895 to continue his earlier policies, he permitted his respect for cold fact to make the decision in favour of a new course. Austrian requests to extend the *entente à trois* into a fixed commitment at Constantinople were doubly impossible in his eyes. They involved both a pledge which a future parliament might repudiate and an undertaking to do something which his colleagues had agreed was impossible.

Though there was something, therefore, in Sanderson's jesting remark to Hatzfeldt that the Foreign Office under Salisbury 'had not got a policy and worked from hand to mouth',[12] it would be wrong to take this comment too literally. For, during his last period of office, he was, in Tunis as in West Africa, according to his daughter, trying to sink 'political capital' in the hope of a return in the form of goodwill on the 'foreseen inevitable day' when relations with France reached breaking point.[13] Though this policy was frustrated by the egregious Chamberlain, it was Salisbury's assessment of the general situation in the last years of the century that was to be vindicated by events, and Cambon summed up the colonial secretary quite fairly as a 'man of the moment', following public

[11] SP 68/to Dufferin/15 Nov 1889.   [12] B.D. 2/98.
[13] Cecil, *Biographical Studies*, p. 57.

opinion while giving the impression of leading it.[14] As for
Salisbury, few would quarrel with the epitaph coined by his old
adversary. He was, said Hanotaux, the 'tête dominant' among
the statesmen of Europe.[15] It would be interesting to speculate
on the trend of foreign policy in the early years of the present
century if a man of the intellectual calibre of the youthful
Salisbury had been at the helm. Salisbury would no doubt have
approved of the exercise.

[14] AAE/GB/RF/1901–3/to Delcassé/22 Jan 1903.
[15] B.D. 2/310.

BIBLIOGRAPHY

(with abbreviations used)

(a) *Primary Sources (unpublished)*

FO 27   Foreign Office correspondence, France, in the Public Record Office (P.R.O.).

FO 102   Foreign Office correspondence, Tunis (P.R.O.).

FO 45   Foreign Office correspondence, Italy (P.R.O.).

FO 146   Correspondence of the Paris Embassy (P.R.O.).

FO 335   Correspondence of the Tunis Consulate-General (P.R.O.).

FO 170   Correspondence of the Rome Embassy (P.R.O.).

FO 403   Confidential Print, correspondence, Africa and the Slave Trade (P.R.O.).

FO 425   Confidential Print, correspondence, Western Europe (P.R.O.).

FO 101   Foreign Office correspondence, Tripoli (P.R.O.).

FO 363   The Tenterden Papers (P.R.O.).

FO 343   The Malet Papers (P.R.O.).

PRO/30/29   The Granville Papers (P.R.O.).

PRO/30/40   The Ardagh Papers (P.R.O.).

The Gladstone Papers, in the British Museum.

SP   The Salisbury Papers, at Christ Church, Oxford.

SnP   The Sanderson Papers (P.R.O., now in series FO 800).

LP   The Lansdowne Papers (P.R.O., now in series FO 800).

WP   The Wood Papers, at St. Anthony's College, Oxford.

JP   The Johnston Papers, microfilm copies in the Royal Commonwealth Society Library; originals in the Central African Archives, Salisbury, Rhodesia.

AAE/Tunis   Political correspondence, Tunis (1875–86), of the Ministère des Affaires étrangères, in the archives at the Quai d'Orsay, Paris.

AAE/Tunis/Ccl   Commercial correspondence, Tunis (1872–1901), of the Ministère des Affaires étrangères.

AAE/Angl   Correspondence, England (to 1896), of the Ministère des Affaires étrangères.

AAE/GB   Correspondence, Great Britain (1897–1900), of the Ministère des Affaires étrangères.

(b) *Primary Sources (published)*

B.D.   *British Documents on the Origins of the War*, edited by G. P. Gooch and H. Temperley.

259

A.P.   Accounts and Papers. State Papers (St.P.).
D.D.F.   *Documents diplomatiques français (1871–1914)*, series 1 and 2.
L.J.   *Documents diplomatiques. Révision des Traités Tunisiens, 1881–1897* (Paris, 1897).
L.J.   *Documents diplomatiques. Affaires de Tunisie, 1870–1881* (and *Supplément*, avril–mai 1881) (Paris, 1881).
D.D.I.   *I Documenti Diplomatici Italiani*, third series (1896–97), vols. 1-3.
   Trattati, convenzioni, accordi, protocolli ed altri documenti relativi all'Africa (Ministero degli affari esteri), vol. 2.
G.P.   *Die grosse Politik der europäischen Kabinette, 1871–1914* (Berlin, 1922–27).

(c) *Memoirs, Autobiographies, Biographies and Letters*

C. Andrew, *Théophile Delcassé and the Making of the Entente Cordiale* (London, 1968).
A. Billot, *La France et l'Italie. Histoire des années troubles, 1881–99* (Paris, 1905, 2 vols.).
G. E. Buckle, *The Life of Benjamin Disraeli, Earl of Beaconsfield*, vol. 6, 1876–81 (London, 1920).
G. E. Buckle (ed.), *The Letters of Queen Victoria* (Q.V.L.), second and third series (London, 1926–32).
P. Cambon, *Correspondance, 1870–1924*, with commentary and notes by H. Cambon, vols. 1-2 (Paris, 1940).
G. Cecil, *The Life of Robert, Marquis of Salisbury*, vols. 2-4 (London, 1921–32).
   Biographical Studies of the Life and Political Character of Robert Third Marquis of Salisbury (printed for private circulation).
T. Palamenghi-Crispi (ed.), *The Memoirs of Francesco Crispi*, translated by M. Pritchard-Agnetti (London, 1912–13, 3 vols.).
D. Dilks, *Curzon in India* (London, 1969, 2 vols.).
A. R. D. Elliot, *The Life of George Joachim Goschen, first viscount Goschen, 1831–1907* (London, 1911, 2 vols.).
E. Fitzmaurice, *The Life of Granville George Leveson Gower, second Earl Granville* (2nd ed., London, 1905, 2 vols.).
C. de Freycinet, *Souvenirs, 1878–1893* (Paris, 1914).
G. Gorrini, *Tunisi e Biserta, memorie storiche di Giacomo Gorrini*, with preface by F. Salata (Milan, 1940).
J. L. Garvin and J. Amery, *The Life of Joseph Chamberlain* (London, 1932–34, 1951, 4 vols.).
S. Gwynn and G. M. Tuckwell, *The Life of the Rt. Hon. Sir Charles W. Dilke* (London, 1917, 2 vols.).
S. Gwynn (ed.), *The Letters and Friendships of Sir Cecil Spring Rice* (London, 1929).
A. Johnston, *The Life and Letters of Sir Harry Johnston* (London, 1929).

H. H. Johnston, *The Story of My Life* (London, 1923).

C. A. Julien, 'Jules Ferry', in *Les Politiques d'expansion impérialiste* (Paris, 1949).

A. L. Kennedy, *Salisbury*, 1830–1903 (London, 1953).

P. Knaplund, 'Letters from the Berlin Embassy', being the *Annual Report of the American Historical Association for 1942*, vol. 2 (Washington, 1944).

A. Lang, *The Life of Sir Stafford Northcote, first Earl of Iddesleigh* (Edinburgh, 1890, 2 vols.).

J. Morley, *The Life of William Ewart Gladstone* (2nd ed., London, 1913, 2 vols.).

Lord Newton, *Lord Lyons, a record of British diplomacy* (London, 1905–7, 2 vols.).

Lord Lansdowne, a Biography (London, 1929).

R. Oliver, *Sir Harry Johnston and the Scramble for Africa* (London, 1957).

A. Ramm (ed.), *The Political Correspondence of Mr. Gladstone and Lord Granville*, 1868–76, Royal Historical Society, Camden series, vols. lxxxi, lxxxii (1952).

The Political Correspondence of Mr. Gladstone and Lord Granville, 1876–86 (Oxford, 1961, 2 vols.).

N. Rich, *Friedrich von Holstein* (Cambridge, 1965, 2 vols.).

Lord Ronaldshay, *Life of Lord Curzon* (London, 1928, 3 vols.).

W. Taffs, *Ambassador to Bismarck. Lord Odo Russell, first Baron Ampthill* (London, 1938).

(d) Secondary Sources

L. Albertini, *The Origins of the War of 1914*, trans. by I. M. Massey, vol. 1 (London, 1952–56, 3 vols.).

E. W. Anderson, *The First Moroccan Crisis, 1904–6* (Chicago, 1930).

M. S. Anderson, *The Eastern Question, 1774–1923* (London, 1966).

W. C. Askew, *Europe and Italy's Acquisition of Libya*, 1911–12 (Durham, North Carolina, 1942).

J. Bardoux, *Quand Bismarck dominait l'Europe* (Paris, 1953).

La Défaite de Bismarck (Paris, 1953).

C. J. Bartlett, 'Great Britain and the Spanish Change of Policy towards Morocco in June 1878', *Bulletin of the Institute of Historical Research*, vol. xxxi (1958).

E. A. Benians, J. Butler and C. E. Carrington (eds.), *The Cambridge History of the British Empire*, vol. 3 (Cambridge, 1959).

A. Bernard and N. Lacroix, *La Pénétration saharienne, 1830–1906* (Algiers, 1906).

R. F. Betts, 'L'Influence des méthodes hollandaises et anglaises sur la doctrine coloniale française à la fin du XIXe siècle', *Cahiers d'Histoire*, vol. 3 (Grenoble, 1958).

H. Blet, *France d'outre-mer*, vol. 3 (Paris, 1950).

C. Bloch, *Les Relations entre la France et la Grande-Bretagne, 1871–78* (Paris, 1955).

G. Bourgin, 'Francesco Crispi', *Les Politiques d'expansion impérialiste* (intro. by P. Renouvin: Paris, 1949).

E. Brandenburg, *From Bismarck to the World War*, trans. by E. A. Adams (London, 1927).

A. M. Broadley, *The Last Punic War. Tunis, Past and Present* (London, 1882).

H. Brunschwig, *French Colonialism, 1871–1914* (London, 1966).

H. Cambon, *Histoire de la régence de Tunis* (Paris, 1948).

R. de Card, *Traités de protectorat conclus par la France en Afrique* (Paris, 1897).

E. M. Carroll, *French public opinion and foreign affairs*, 1870–1914 (New York, 1939).

F. Chabod, *Storia della politica estera italiana dal 1870 al 1896*, vol. 1, 'Le Premesse' (Bari, 1951).

L. Chiala, *Pagine di storia contemporanea*, vol. 2, Tunisi, 1878–81 (Turin–Rome, 1892).

S. Cilibrizzi, *Storia parlamentare, politica e diplomatica d'Italia*, vol. 2, 1870–96, vol. 3, 1896–1909 (Milan, 1929).

d'Estournelles de Constant, *La Politique française en Tunisie* (Paris, 1891).

(P.H.X.), 'La France en Tunisie', *Revue des Deux Mondes*, vol. 79.

E. F. Cruikshank, *Morocco at the Parting of the Ways* (Philadelphia, 1935).

A. B. Cunningham, *The Early Correspondence of Richard Wood, 1831–1841* (London, 1966).

J. Darcy, *France et Angleterre, cent années de rivalité coloniale. L'Afrique* (Paris, 1904).

P. Deschanel, *Histoire de la politique extérieure de la France* (Paris, 1936).

Y. Delbos (preface by), 'La Question italienne en Tunisie', 1868–1938, *Cahiers d'Information Françaises*, No. 3 (Paris, 1939).

G. Dethan, 'Le Rapprochement franco-italien après la chute de Crispi jusqu'aux accords Visconti Venosta sur le Maroc et la Tripolitaine (1896–1904) d'après les archives du Quai d'Orsay', *Revue d'Histoire Diplomatique*, vol. lxx (1956).

A. Dupuy, *La Tunisie dans les lettres d'Expression française* (Paris, 1956).

R. C. K. Ensor, *England* (Oxford, 1936).

Félix Faure, 'Le Ministère Léon Bourgeois et la politique étrangère de Marcellin Berthelot au Quai d'Orsay', introduction by F. Berge, *Revue d'Histoire Diplomatique*, vol. lxxi (1957).

F. R. Flournoy, *British Policy towards Morocco in the Age of Palmerston*, 1930–65 (London and Baltimore, 1935).

W. K. Fraser-Tytler, *Afghanistan* (Oxford, 1950).

J. Ganiage, *Les Origines du protectorat français en Tunisie, 1861–81* (Paris, 1959).

'Une Affaire tunisienne, l'affaire de l'Enfida', 1880–82, *Revue Africaine* (1955).

'Les Européens en Tunisie au milieu du XIXᵉ siècle (1840–1870)', *Cahiers de Tunisie*, vol. 3 (1955).

D. K. Ghose, *England and Afghanistan* (Calcutta, 1960).

A. Giaccardi, *La conquista di Tunisi. Storia diplomatica dal congresso di Berlino al trattato del Bardo* (Milan, 1940).

C. Giglio, *La politica africana dell'Inghilterra* (Padova, 1950).

W. T. Gidney, *The History of the London Society for Promoting Christianity amongst the Jews*, 1809–1908 (London, 1908).

G. Giolitti, *Memoirs of my Life*, trans. by E. Storer (London, 1923).

J. L. Glanville, *Italy's Relations with England, 1896–1905* (Baltimore, 1934).

E. H. Glenny, *Mission to the Kabyles and other Berber Races of North Africa*, occasional paper (London, 1884).

S. Gopal, *British Policy in India, 1858–1905* (Cambridge, 1965).

G. S. Graham, *The Politics of Naval Supremacy* (Cambridge, 1965).

R. L. Greaves, *Persia and the Defence of India, 1884–1892* (London, 1959).

J. A. S. Grenville, *Lord Salisbury and Foreign Policy* (London, 1964).

'Goluchowski, Salisbury and the Mediterranean Agreements, 1895–1897', *The Slavonic and East European Review*, vol. xxxvi (1958).

P. Guillen, *L'Allemagne et le Maroc de 1870 à 1905* (Paris, 1967).

'Les Accords coloniaux franco-anglais de 1904 et la naissance de l'entente cordiale', *Revue d'Histoire Diplomatique*, vol. lxxxii (1968).

Lord Hankey, *Diplomacy by Conference* (London, 1946).

G. Hanotaux, *Contemporary France*, trans. by E. Sparvel-Bayly of *Histoire de la France contemporaine*, vol. 4, 1877–82 (London, 1909).

Le Partage de l'Afrique, Fachoda (Paris, 1909).

La Paix latine (Paris, 1903).

E. Hertslet, *Map of Africa by Treaty* (London, 1894).

J. D. Hargreaves, 'Entente manquée. Anglo-French relations 1895–6', *Cambridge Historical Journal*, vol. xi (1953–55).

Prelude to the Partition of West Africa (London, 1963).

G. D. H. Howard, *Splendid Isolation* (London, 1967).

R. R. James, *Rosebery* (London, 1963).

M. M. Jefferson, 'Lord Salisbury and the Eastern Question, 1890–1898', *Slavonic and East European Review*, vol. xxxix (1960–61).

V. M. Khvostov, 'L'Alliance franco-russe et sa portée historique', in *Travaux des Historiens Soviétiques pour le Xᵉ Congrès International des Sciences Historiques à Rome* (Moscow, 1955).

P. Kluke, 'Bismarck und Salisbury', in *Historische Zeitschrift*, vol. 175.

P. Knaplund, *Gladstone's Foreign Policy* (New York and London, 1935).

W. L. Langer, *European Alliances and Alignments, 1871–1890* (2nd ed., New York, 1950).

W. L. Langer, *The Diplomacy of Imperialism, 1890-1902* (2nd ed., New York, 1951).
The Franco-Russian Alliance, 1890–94 (Cambridge, Mass., 1929).
'The European Powers and the French occupation of Tunis, 1878–1881', *American History Review*, vol. 31 (1925–36).
A. Lebon, *La Politique de la France en Afrique, 1896–98* (Paris, 1901).
D. E. Lee, *Great Britain and the Cyprus Convention Policy of 1878* (Cambridge, Mass., 1934).
E. de Leone, *La colonizzazione dell'Africa del Nord* (Padua, 1960, 2 vols.).
B. Lewis, *The Emergence of Modern Turkey* (Oxford, 1961).
C. J. Lowe, *Salisbury and the Mediterranean, 1886–1896* (London, 1965).
'Anglo-Italian Differences over East Africa 1892–1895 and the Effects upon the Mediterranean Entente', *English Historical Review*, vol. lxxxi (1966).
A. J. Marder, *The Anatomy of British Sea Power. A History of British Naval Policy, 1880–1905* (London, 1940).
'British Naval Policy in 1878', *The Journal of Modern History*, vol. 12 (1940).
From Dreadnought to Scapa Flow, vol. 1 (Oxford, 1966).
A. Marsden, 'Britain and the "Tunis Base", 1894–1899', *English Historical Review*, vol. lxxix (1964).
Britain and the End of the Tunis Treaties, 1894–97 (*English Historical Review*, Supplement No. 1, 1965).
'British Policy and the 1875 Convention with Tunisia, 1875–1885', *Atti del 1 Congresso Internazionale di Studi Nord-Africani* (Cagliari, 1965).
'Salisbury and the Italians in 1896', *Journal of Modern History*, vol. 40 (1968).
'Britain and her Conventional Rights in Tunis, 1888–1892', *IIe Congrès International d'Études Nord-Africaines: Actes du Congrès* (Aix-en-Provence, 1968).
A. Martel, *Les Confins saharo-tripolitains de la Tunisie 1881–1911* (Paris, 1965, 2 vols.).
W. N. Medlicott, *The Congress of Berlin and After* (London, 1938).
Bismarck, Gladstone and the Concert of Europe (London, 1956).
'The Gladstone Government and the Cyprus Convention, 1880–1885', *The Journal of Modern History*, vol. 12 (1940).
W. Miller, *The Ottoman Empire, 1801–1913* (Cambridge, 1913).
G. Michon, *L'Alliance franco-russe* (1927).
J. L. Miège, *Le Maroc et l'Europe, 1830–94* (Paris, 1961–63, 4 vols.).
R. Millet, *Notre politique extérieure de 1898 à 1905* (Paris, 1905).
La Colonisation française en Tunisie (Tunis, 1899).
R. Möller, 'Bismarck's Bündnisangebot an England vom Januar, 1889', *Historische Vierteljahr-Schrift*, vol. 31 (1938).

'Noch einmal Bismarcks Bündnisangebot an England vom Januar, 1889', *Historische Zeitschrift*, vol. 163 (1941).

G. W. Monger, *The End of Isolation, 1900–1907* (London, 1963).

P. T. Moon, *Imperialism and World Politics* (New York, 1926).

H. Nicolson, *Diplomacy* (London, 1939).

Lord Carnock (London, 1930).

I. N. Nish, *The Anglo-Japanese Alliance, 1894–1907* (London, 1966).

North Africa, the quarterly record of the Mission to the Kabyles and other Berber Races (London, 1886–1906).

F. V. Parsons, 'The "Morocco Question" in 1884: An early Crisis', *English Historical Review*, vol. lxxvii (1962).

'The North-West African Company and the British Government, 1875–95', *Historical Journal*, vol. 1 (1958).

A. Pellegrin, *Histoire de la Tunisie* (Paris, 1938).

L. M. Penson, 'The Principles and Methods of Lord Salisbury's Foreign Policy', *Cambridge Historical Journal* (1935).

'The New Course in British Foreign Policy, 1892–1902', *Transactions of the Royal Historical Society*, fourth series, vol. 25 (1943).

Foreign Affairs under the third Marquis of Salisbury (London, 1962).

L. Peteani, *La questione libica nella diplomazia europea* (Florence, 1939).

H. I. Priestley, *France Overseas* (New York, 1938).

A. Raymond, 'Les Tentatives anglaises de pénétration économique en Tunisie, 1856–77', *Revue Historique*, vol. 214 (1955).

'Salisbury and the Tunisian Question, 1878–1880', *Middle Eastern Affairs No. 2*, St. Anthony's Papers No. 11 (London, 1961).

'Les Libéraux anglais et la question tunisienne (1880–1881)', *Cahiers de Tunisie*, vol. 6 (Paris, 1955).

P. Renouvin, 'Le 19e Siècle de 1871 à 1914', *Histoire des Relations Internationales*, vol. 6 (Paris, 1955).

'L'Orientation de l'alliance franco-russe en 1900–1901', *Revue d'Histoire Diplomatique*, vol. lxxx (1966).

T. W. Riker, 'A Survey of British Policy in the Fashoda Crisis', *Political Science Quarterly*, vol. 44 (1929).

S. H. Roberts, *The History of French Colonial Policy, 1870–1925* (2 vols., London, 1929).

R. Robinson and G. Gallagher, *Africa and the Victorians* (London, 1961).

P. J. V. Rolo, *Entente cordiale* (London, 1969).

M. M. Safwat, *Tunis and the Great Powers, 1878–81* (Alexandria, 1943).

L. Salvatorelli, *La triplice alleanza, 1877–1912* (Milan, 1939).

G. Salvemini, *La politica estera di Francesco Crispi* (Rome, 1919).

La politica estera dell'Italia, 1871–1915 (Florence, 1944).

G. N. Sanderson, *England, Europe and the Upper Nile, 1882–1899* (Edinburgh, 1965).

E. Satow, *A Guide to Diplomatic Practice* (London, 1917, 2 vols.).

S. B. Saul, *British Overseas Trade, 1870–1914* (Liverpool, 1960).

W. Schüssler, 'Noch einmal Bismarck zwischen England und Russland, 1889', *Historische Zeitschrift*, vol. 163 (1941).

E. Serra, *Camille Barrère* (Milan, 1950).

L'intesa mediterranea del 1902 (Milan, 1957; abridged in *Nuova Antologia*, vols. 89–90, 1954–55).

'L'accordo italo-francese del 1896 sulla Tunisia', *Rivista Storica Italiana*, vol. 73(3) (1961).

'L'Italia e la "grande svolta" della politica inglese nel Mediterraneo (1895–1896)', *Rivista di Studi Politici Internazionali*, vol. xxxiii (1966).

'New Sources on Anglo-Italian Relations: 1896–1902', *Occidente*, vol. xi (1955).

C. Seton-Watson, *Italy from Liberalism to Fascism* (London, 1967).

H. Seton-Watson, *The Russian Empire, 1801–1917* (Oxford, 1967).

R. W. Seton-Watson, *Disraeli, Gladstone and the Eastern Question* (London, 1935).

M. Shibeika, *British Policy in the Sudan, 1882–1902* (Oxford, 1952).

H. W. Steed, *Through Thirty Years* (London, 1924).

J. Stern, *The French colonies, Past and Future* (New York, 1944).

G. H. Stuart, *French Foreign Policy, from Fashoda to Sarajevo, 1898–1914* (New York, 1921).

B. H. Sumner, *Russia and the Balkans, 1870–1880* (Oxford, 1937).

H. Temperley, 'British Secret Diplomacy', *Cambridge Historical Journal*, vol. 6.

The History of the Times, vol. 3, 1884–1912 (London, 1947).

A. J. P. Taylor, 'British Policy in Morocco, 1886–1902', *English Historical Review*, vol. xxxix (1960–61).

A. P. Thornton, 'Rivalries in the Mediterranean, the Middle East and Egypt', *The New Cambridge Modern History*, vol. 11 (Cambridge, 1962).

M. Toscano, 'Tunis', *Berliner Monatshefte*, vol. 17 (1939).

W. C. B. Tunstall, 'Imperial Defence, 1870–1897', *Cambridge History of the British Empire*, vol. 3 (1959).

M. Vidal, 'Le Duel franco-italien en Tunisie au XIXe siècle', *Bulletin de la Société d'Histoire Moderne* (October 1947).

H. Vivian, *Tunisia and the Modern Barbary Pirates* (London, 1899).

E. Walters, 'Lord Salisbury's refusal to revise and renew the Mediterranean Agreements', *The Slavonic and East European Review*, vol. 29 (1950).

L. Woolf, *Empire and Commerce in Africa* (London, 1920).

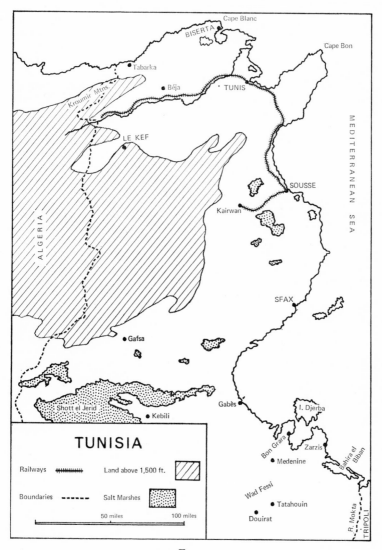

Cape Blanc

BISERTA

Cape Bon

Tabarka

Béja

TUNIS

Kroumir Mtns.

MEDITERRANEAN SEA

LE KEF

SOUSSE

Kairwan

ALGERIA

SFAX

Gafsa

Shott el Jerid

Kebili

Gabès

I. Djerba

Bon Grara

Zarzis

Bahira el Biban

TUNISIA

Medenine

Railways   Land above 1,500 ft.

Wad Fessi

Boundaries   Salt Marshes

Tatahouin

50 miles   100 miles

Douirat

R. Mokta

TRIPOLI

FIG 4

INDEX

Marsden, Arthur.
　　British diplomacy and Tunis, 1875–1902; a case study in Mediterranean policy.　New York, Africana Pub. Corp. ₁1972, c1971₁

　　x, 276 p.　illus.　23 cm.　$12.50

　　Bibliography : p. 259–266.

251151

　　1. Tunisia—Foreign relations—Gt. Brit.　2. Gt. Brit.—Foreign relations—Tunisia.　　I. Title.

DT257.5.G7M37　　　　327.42′061′1　　　　71–180671
ISBN 0–8419–0110–4　　　　　　　　　　　　　　MARC

Library of Congress　　　　　　72 ₁4₁